S0-ARG-729

WASHINGTON SAFE DEPOSIT
SAFE

PENN
AVE
1885

ear the end of the trolley era, an inbound Route 20 PCC gets its trolley
wered and plow attached at 36th and Prospect Streets N.W. Photo by
aul Dolkos.

100 YEARS OF CAPITAL TRACTION

100 YEARS OF CAPITAL TRACTION

THE STORY OF STREETCARS IN THE NATION'S CAPITAL

LeRoy O. King, Jr.

Taylor Publishing Company

Library of Congress Catalogue Card Number.

72-97549

Frontispiece:

The heyday of the street car in Washington has been captured in this delightful scene by noted railroad artist Howard Fogg. A Pennsylvania Avenue Capital Traction train at Peace Monument in the spring of 1910.

Page VIII: Track reconstruction at 14th and G Streets NW, 1941 Capital Transit Photo, author's collection.

Front end paper: Pennsylvania Avenue east from the Treasury in horse car days 1885. Author's collection.

Back end paper: Pennsylvania Avenue east from the Treasury about 1949. Photo by Robert A. Truax. Fred W. Schneider collection.

© 1972 By LeRoy O. King, Jr.

With affection to my Father,
whose work made this book possible.

CONTENTS

The rise and fall of the street railway industry was a phenomenon of the American scene that lasted barely a hundred years. The epoch of the Electric Trolley was even shorter. They were distressing headaches, these street cars, whose early abandonment was said to be a sure cure for much of our urban traffic dilemma.

In Washington, that verdict was rendered in 1956. Today, there is something pathetic about the street painted with yellow stripes to designate bus lanes reserved for the common good, as against the same street previously marked with rails intended for the same purpose; with the difference that the Electric Car was quieter, of far greater capacity, and much less polluting. Though needs there be – – which even a bus cannot fulfill; and in lessons which are, alas, too late, the capital city founders in the lacuna between the end of street cars and the advent of Metro.

To many readers, the history of "Electric Traction" makes a strong appeal. Perhaps it's just a nostalgic tug on the pleasant memories of a gentler less-frenzied way of things. Or could it be a kind of rational admission, half realizing that we had the right answer all along? The story of it is fascinating – – as much for the adventure, as for its record of achievements wrought by bold men and private ownership which, as regards city transport is, in itself, a unique experience today.

In a city so jealous of its fine arts and esthetic heritage, the mundane business of public transit did not come cheap; for there were many restrictions, such as the early veto of overhead wires so commonplace in other cities, or the entrenched aversion to one-man operations so generally acceptable elsewhere, which produced the costly trial and error, the frustrations, and the ingenuity required for solutions. But above all it produced a dogged determination that, despite these obstacles, Washington was, nevertheless, to have an efficient railway system.

Never before has this aspect of local history been told in its entirety. With this volume we are heirs to the writings, the photography, and the vast library of LeRoy O. King, Senior, whose lifelong pursuit of this subject was without equal. That his endeavors should one day find expression throught the efforts of LeRoy O. King, Junior, seems singularly appropriate; not alone for the vast wealth of that collection which documents much of his work, but that Roy, Junior should have inherited the same abiding interests, the same devotion to historical accuracy, the perception and dedication so necessary to the writing of this book.

John E. Merriken

22 March 1972

Impressive Washington Railway and Electric 586 ready for initial service on the Rockville line. Taken at P Street shops September 2, 1908. Photo by LeRoy O. King, Sr.

Not long ago, Washington had one of the nation's outstanding streetcar systems. Well kept, modern electric cars provided frequent service to all parts of the city. In early 1962, at Congressional insistence, the last of these gave way to buses. At that time, because I have always been interested in the subject, I felt its history should be recorded. I have tried to give the complete story from a traction fan's viewpoint. I hope it will appeal to others.

Fortunately, I could call on my Father and a number of our friends for help. The late LeRoy O. King, Sr., amassed an extensive collection of material on the history of Washington street railways. His knowledge of the subject was without equal and the foundation of this book rests on his generous help. Most of it is his work.

Robert A. Truax carefully searched microfilm records of early Washington newspapers for obscure data on the beginnings of the horsecar lines. He also, on occasions too numerous to recall, furnished data, checked questionable facts and lent material from his collection; he has also been a helpful advisor.

John E. Merriken spent endless hours suggesting changes in the original manuscript. He will surely recognize some of his wording. He has also given me the benefit of his wide knowledge of Washington's rolling stock. The title is his suggestion.

Edgar Gilchrist's voluminous comments on rolling stock have cleared up many troublesome points. Alfred E. Savage's painstaking searches of old company records contributed many details. John W. Dodge and John H. White both made helpful suggestions on the original manuscript. Gerald Cunningham has been most helpful in the reproduction of major maps. Charles E. Grossman made the excellent maps on pages 131 and 145, Tom Pickle those on pages 100 and 173 and the map on page 129 is the work of Charles Wagner. Andrew Maginnis made the fine car drawings. William D. Gray spent several weeks in the tedious search of government collections for a number of the interesting pictures. The delightful frontispiece was done by Howard Fogg, his first street railway subject. Charles Murphy has made many helpful suggestions but deserves special mention for publishing "Capital Traction Quarterly", "The Transfer Table" and "Headway Recorder" 1940-1968 which, in their day, encouraged the writing of much of the background material.

In the spring of 1972, the Universal Marion Corporation of Jacksonville, Florida, corporate sucessors to Capital Transit, donated fifty-six cartons of Capital Transit historical date to the Columbia Historical Society. This gift was made possible through the assistance of Mr. Oliver L. Maddux, President of Universal Marion, Charles E. Bennett, Congressman from Florida and Mr. Joseph M. Glickstein, Sr. These records, which I examined through the courtesy of Robert A. Truax, Librarian and Assistant Curator of the society, yielded in addition to a number of interesting photographs, answers to many puzzling questions on the company's rolling stock which otherwise would never have been known.

Kincaid Photo Service, Dallas, improved on a number

912 view of Union Station. Two-car train at right would soon be replaced when all of the Capital Traction Jewetts, one of which is at the far eft, arrived. Library of Congress.

of illustrations by capable photo processing. Joe Goodson, Taylor Publishing Company, has served as an able and pleasant technical advisor. James King has helped with some exacting photo work and my wife, in many instances, cleared up some awkward English. Both of them showed remarkable understanding and gave encouragement.

Others who have been helpful are Harold Buckley, Jr., Harold Cox, Paul J. Dolkos, John L. Hammerley, Edmond Henderer, J. Randolph Kean, Ara Mesrobian, the late Barney Neuberger, Miss Jeannette Patrick, Lee Rogers and Paul Stringham. My thanks go to typists Pauline Mott, Sarah Wood, Carol Naab and Lee Webb. Photographs have been acknowledged individually where possible. My sincere thanks to all who have helped. They have been more than generous.

Early scene at the foot of Capitol Hill in 1866 showing a first generation Washington and Georgetown horsecar. The steam train is on a connection from the Baltimore and Ohio to the Orange and Alexandria. This connection ran in 1st Street and Maryland Avenues to Long Bridge. The steam road, built for Civil War service, was torn up in 1872. "Harper's Weekly", Robert A. Truax collection.

INTRODUCTION

Washington is located in what was once Maryland on the North Bank of the Potomac River. Is is unusual in that it is a planned city. Its street pattern generally conforms to the design made by Major Pierre L'Enfant when the city was established as the seat of government.

Streets are laid out in four quadrants with the Capitol at the center. North Capitol, East Capitol, and South Capitol Streets along with the Mall form the four sections of the city which are: Northwest, Northeast, Southeast and Southwest. Numbered streets run north and south both east and west of the Capitol. Alphabetical streets run east and west, both north and south of the Capitol. Superimposed on the grid are diagonal avenues named for the various states. Characteristic of the plan are a number of circles and squares where several avenues and streets intersect.

Rolling, fairly rugged hills rise to the north and northwest from the river. Some prominent hills are the bluffs on the north side of the Potomac to the west, Mt. St. Albans at Wisconsin and Massachusetts Avenue, Tenleytown Hill at Wisconsin Avenue and River Road, Asylum Hill in Anacostia and, of course, Capitol Hill.

The government of the District of Columbia is unusual for a democracy. For most of the period with which this book will be concerned, Congress has, in effect, been Washington's city council and it has been involved in all but the most minute of the City's problems including those of public transportation.

Washington's climate is generally mild with occasional heavy snows and cold snaps in winter and hot humid spells in summer.

Washington's growth has paralleled, of course, that of our Federal Government. Usually the growth has been moderate but with short periods of rapid growth during the Civil War, World War I, the Depression and World War II.

As in other cities, the street railway, by providing quick, frequent and cheap transportation, began the movement to the suburbs. The movement was slight with horse cars but accelerated rapidly with the coming of the electric car. Real estate values were set by the closeness of the land to a car line. Indeed, a number of lines were built to develop real estate. Thus, major suburbs developed along the car lines and centers of shopping at their junctions.

Major projects such as the building of Union Station, the development of Government Offices in Potomac Park in World War I, the Federal Triangle in the Depression and the Government Offices in the Southwest Mall in World War II all had a major effect on street railway traffic patterns.

As the capital city, Washington is the scene of frequent parades which provided challenging operating problems for the street railways.

Washington's transit history contains interesting variations from that of the industry as a whole. As with a number of major railway systems, Washington's sprung from several horse car operations. Usually, in the 90's, the larger systems quickly converted to electric cars with an occasional short flirtation with the cable car. In contrast, because of Congressional prohibition against downtown overhead wires, Washington was the scene of many unsuccessful experiments.

Finally, after the idea was imported from Budapest by Theodore Noyes of the *Washington Star*, the city's Metropolitan Railroad constructed an underground conduit system. This system, which became standard for the city, was highly unusual and found in only one other American city, New York.

In its heyday, Washington's electric traction system featured two large companies operating both city and suburban services, several separate suburban lines, and three interurban lines.

This book is concerned with those lines which are logically predecessors of later day D C Transit. Space limitations dictate that reference be made to the Washington-Virginia, the Washington and Old Dominion and the Washington, Baltimore and Annapolis Railways only as their activities affect the city system.

CHAPTER ONE
THE HORSE CAR COMES TO
WASHINGTON

The Washington and Georgetown Railroad Company

Washington was a small, unimproved and relatively un-important city in 1860, the eve of the Civil War. Population was a mere 61,122. The notion of a strong central gov-ernment was a distant thing; shortly a number of states would forcibly contest the idea of a central government of any kind in Washington.

Following the original horsecar line in New York in 1832, a number of more progressive American cities—New Orleans, Brooklyn, Boston, Philadelphia, Baltimore, Pitts-burgh, Cincinnati and Chicago—all had horsecar systems by 1859. Yet in 1860, Washington's public transit consisted of one line of horsedrawn omnibuses. The omnibuses were nothing more than urban stagecoaches and, given the condi-tion of early Washington streets, were indeed primitive transit.

The ultimate operator of omnibuses was Gilbert Vander-werken,* and his line ran from Georgetown to the Navy Yard via M Street and Pennsylvania Avenue.

The first street railway proposal in Washington was one presented to Congress in 1854 by George Yerby and others. There was considerable public objection and little came of the project.

Gilbert Vanderwerken, Bayard Clark, Asa P. Robinson and their assigns had obtained approval from Congress to construct a double track line from the west gate of the Capitol to Georgetown via Pennsylvania Avenue and 15th Street. Although $20,000 worth of stock was sold by De-cember 1, 1859, no construction took place.[1]

The fact that Washingtonians followed McDowell's army to the First Battle of Bull Run as sightseers in July, 1861, tells something of the great changes that would occur when the Union Army returned defeated. Washington, in addition to congestion already caused by government activity, be-came an armed camp. By October, 1862, there were 252,-000 soldiers encamped around Washington.

In this day and age, it is perhaps difficult to see why a

*Gilbert Vanderwerken (1810-1894) was a pioneer omnibus and railroad car builder in Newark, New Jersey. In 1948-50 he moved to Washington to take personal control of his established omnibus line. He died at what is now Vanderwerken, Arlington County, Virginia. John Clagett Proctor, "Gilbert Vanderwerken," *The Sunday Star*, August 5, 1951, p. C2.

nation engaged in civil war would encourage construction of a rail line with consequent use of needed resources for little apparent advantage. There are several factors to con-sider, however. First of these is the fact that since Washing-ton streets were unpaved, a metal wheel on a metal rail was a considerable improvement over horse omnibuses. An-other is that the country's political leaders were then wiser in the ways of modern war than is generally suspected. They no doubt saw that efficient public transit in Washington would materially help the war effort.

The charter called for three lines as follows:

Georgetown-Navy Yard. This line began at Bridge and High Streets (now Wisconsin and M) in Georgetown ran east to Pennsylvania Avenue, then via Pennsylva-nia Avenue, 15th Street, and Pennsylvania Avenue to the foot of Capitol Hill. Then around the northwest quadrant of the existing Capitol grounds to New Jer-sey Avenue and B Streets North. Here a branch was to run in New Jersey Avenue to the Baltimore and Ohio Railroad depot at New Jersey Avenue and C Street. The main line was planned to continue on B Street, then south across the east face of the Capitol to A Street south, then east on A Street to its intersec-tion with Pennsylvania Avenue and then to the Navy Yard via the Avenue and Eighth Street East.

Seventh Street. This line was to run from Boundary (later Florida Avenue) to the Potomac River in Sev-enth Street West.

Fourteenth Street. This line was to run from Boundary south to 15th and New York Avenue and then to 14th and New York Avenue to a connection with the Georgetown-Navy Yard line.

In keeping with military significance associated with this venture, the charter also established the gauge "to corre-spond with that of the Baltimore and Ohio Railroad." It further provided that the corporation "shall, on demand of the President of the United States, Secretary of War, or Secretary of the Navy, cause to be transported over said railway any freight cars laden with freight for the use of the United States."

The company's charter called for a strict schedule of completion. Sixty working days after the company was or-ganized were allowed to complete the Georgetown-Capitol portion, sixty additional days for the Capitol-Navy Yard portion, and the balance of the road had to be completed by six months from the date of the act granting the charter. The act was dated and the charter granted May 17, 1862.

Little time was lost by the new venture. Directors and officers were elected June 10, 1862. They were John Carter Marbury of Georgetown, Henry D. Cooke, George Gideon and Harris C. Fahnestock of Washington, Edward W. Clark and J. Barlow Moorehead of Philadelphia and William A. Darling of New York. Mr. Cooke was elected president and Mr. Fahnestock secretary-treasurer of the new street railway.[2]

At this first meeting, the board authorized negotiations to purchase from Vanderwerken stables, barns and such other property as might be useful to the W & G. Negotiation continued until June 27 when it was agreed to purchase horses, omnibuses and personal property of the Vanderwerken line for $28,500. Real estate was to be leased for $2,500 a year (plus $500 for insurance). Transfer of properties and assumption of lease took place July 1, 1862.

As will be seen later, the omnibuses were used to augment the first horse car operation. As they became surplus the Board (on October 8, 1862) voted to donate twenty of them to the army for use as ambulances. The army accepted and later all were so donated.[3]

Vanderwerken became a director in the new company and his stables at 3222 M Street, later bought by the W & G, became the location of important shops throughout the entire railway era. Two days after the first board meeting, on June 12, 1862, ground was broken near the Capitol and construction began with a force of one hundred men under the supervision of Mr. William Wharton of Philadelphia.[4]

Cars were ordered, at first, from Murphy and Allison of Philadelphia. Later, because of the inability of one firm to build the cars in the time required, the job was split with John Stephenson and Kimball and Gorton.

The first cars arrived from Murphy and Allison July 11, 1862. One was a closed car and the other an open car. The closed car was described as follows:

> The regular car measures inside about seven by fifteen feet, and will seat comfortably about twenty persons. The seats on the sides are covered with fine silk velvet, and the windows, which are of stained and plain glass, combined, are furnished with cherry sash and poplar blinds, besides handmade damask curtains. . . . The car is handsomely painted, both inside and out, the prevailing color being white, the outside is cream color and white, with a fine painting in the center, and the words "Washington and Georgetown R. R." at the bottom. The wheels are of different colors, contrasting well with the body of the car and giving it a picturesque appearance.[5]

Work progressed steadily with service beginning from the Capitol to the State Department July 29, 1862. At the State Department, patrons transferred to Vanderwerken omnibuses for continuation to Georgetown. This first service utilized ten cars. The newspaper article describing the original service ended thus: "Farewell old bus, you're well nigh played out."[6]

Occasionally, extensions of service were held up by inability of the car builders to keep pace and by inability to ship cars due to wartime traffic on the railroads. But extensions were put in operation as follows:

Date	Route
8-12-62	Capitol to Washington Circle
8-20-62	Capitol to Georgetown
9-12-62	B&O Depot to Georgetown
10-3-62	Navy Yard to Capitol
10-23-62	7th St./Pa. Ave to N St.
11-15-62	7th St./Pa. Ave to River 14th St. Line

All data from *The Star*

On November 15, 1862, the entire road was formally opened by a trip with directors, city officials and members of the press over the Seventh Street Line to the steamboat wharves. This was followed by a trip to the Metropolitan Hotel where the party was entertained at a dinner provided by the Directors. The entire construction was finished five days prior to the time allotted by the charter.[7]

Vanderwerken Omnibus in use prior to the first horsecars circa 1860. Author's collection.

Original routings announced by the company were:

Georgetown-B&O Depot	35 cars
Navy Yard to 7th & N St. N.W.*	16 cars
B&O Depot to 14th & Mass. Ave, N.W.*	12 cars
B&O Depot to 7th St. wharves	12 cars

By July 1, 1863, the line was established as a financial success as evidenced by these figures.

*smaller cars operated from 7th & N N.W. to the Park (Boundary St.) and from 14th & Mass. Ave. N.W. to Boundary.[1]

A May 23, 1865, view looking east into Pennsylvania Avenue from the Treasury showing original horsecars of the Washington and Georgetown. The crowd is gathered for a review of returning veterans of the Sixth Corps of the Army of the Potomac. Handy Studios, author's collection.

Total receipts from passengers	$ 249,160.08
Net earnings	61,323.66
Dividend paid	45,000.00
To surplus July 1, 1863	13,323.66

Four thousand car miles per day were operated with 490 horses and seventy cars. Typical wages were $8 a week for drivers, $500 a year for timers and $600 a year for conductors. Fare was five cents with free transfer.

By July, 1863, the routes had been changed to:

Route	No. of Cars
Georgetown - Navy Yard	28
Georgetown - B&O Depot	21
7th Street - Boundary to River	16
14th Street - Boundary to 15th & NY Avenue	5
Total —	70

All lines operated on a five minute headway.[8]

At two of its several grades, Washington and Georgetown used "hill horses" northbound on 15th Street and eastbound on South B Street (Capitol Hill). An extra horse was harnessed to an eye at the right side of the platform to help the car up the hill. When the car reached the top of the hill, an employee returned the extra horse to the bottom for the next car up. An interesting, but not unexpected problem with the hill horses was that, to the annoyance of District officials, horses waiting assignment at the foot of Capitol Hill ate freely of the tree leaves in the area.

This, then, is the beginning of Washington's street railway era. The Pennsylvania Avenue line of the Washington and Georgetown would become one of the most famous in the United States. It passed the White House, Treasury and the Capitol as well as the Center Market, the main business district and the city's most fashionable hotels. And, of course, its rails would be on the route of parades from those of the victorious union armies to the inaugural of John F. Kennedy.

An act of Congress, dated June 30, 1864, granted permission to extend both the 7th Street and 14th Street lines as far north as the company was willing. The company never took advantage of the authorization in the case of the 7th Street line and the 14th Street line didn't venture north of Boundary (Florida Avenue) until cable days.

In March, 1875, an act provided for several changes in the Washington and Georgetown which would establish its routes for the balance of the horse car era and, in some cases, beyond.

The first of these arose from the enlargement of the Capitol grounds. In place of the old routing which ran across the east face of the Capitol, new tracks were constructed which routed main line cars from First and Pennsylvania N.W. south along First Street to B Street south then

Gold pin given on retirement March 15, 1863, of Washington and Georgetown starter, Charles A. Littlejohn. Littlejohn must have been originally a Vanderwerken employee. Robert A. Truax collection.

Eastbound Washington and Georgetown car crossing Rock Creek on M Street Bridge. Picture was taken between 1875 and 189 Author's collection.

Washington and Georgetown ticket from the '80's. Signature side is maroon on white while the reverse is burnt orange on white. Author's collection.

Washington and Georgetown 14th Street car on a co winter day in the '80's. Library of Congress.

east along B Street to Pennsylvania Avenue S. W. B & O station cars were routed north on First Street from First and Pennsylvania N.W. to Indiana Avenue and then to New Jersey Avenue where the B&O Depot was.[9] Work on this new route was completed shortly after authorization.

The 1875 act also authorized a change in the routing over Rock Creek into Georgetown. Probably fearful that the Washington aqueduct bridge (in line of Pennsylvania Avenue) couldn't stand ever increasing wagon traffic and horse cars, authorities ordered the route changed. By October 4, 1875, cars were operating over the new route which was north over 26th St. N.W. to the M Street bridge and then over it to Georgetown.[10] At first the new route was single track and only one car was allowed on the bridge at a time. This routing, incidentally, lasted until 1916 when the present bridge on Pennsylvania Avenue was constructed.

The final extention authorized by the 1875 act permitted extention from 7th and Water Street S.W., Water Street P Street and along P Street to the Arsenal gate (later Fort Leslie J. McNair). Joint use of Anacostia and Potomac tracks was provided for. First, in 1875, the company only extended the line to Sixth Street where the steamboat wharves were.[11] The balance of the route wasn't finished

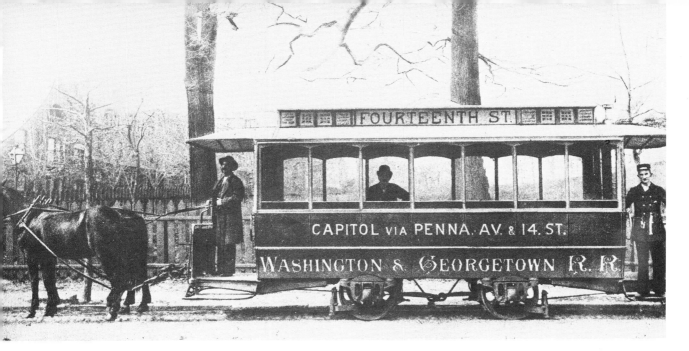

ephenson-built horsecar at carbarn on Florida Avenue near 14th Street in 1889. This car later became a cable trailer and an
:ctric trailer. Handy Studios, author's collection.

terior of a New York Stephenson-built horsecar which was typical
the era. Museum of the City of New York.

until 1880[12] when stables and a car shed were established
on P Street between Water and Four and a Half Street S.
W.

Metropolitan Railroad Company

The second horse car enterprise in the city was the
Metropolitan Railroad Company.

The original charter, dated July 1, 1864, authorized a
line running east from 17th and H Street along H to 14th,
south to F Street, east to 5th, south to D, east on D, Indiana
C and south on New Jersey to A Street. Westbound cars
operated north on New Jersey to D Street, thus creating a
one-way routing around the Indiana Avenue, C Street, New
Jersey and D Street area.

Ground was broken near the War Department November
17, 1864.[13] Construction progressed without incident and
by January 6, 1865, operation began between the Capitol
and the War Department.[14] The original cars were furnished
by Murphy and Allison of Philadelphia and,[15] as was the
case with the W & G RR, some difficulty was reported
getting them to Washington because of wartime traffic.[16]

On the western end the line ran south on 17th to New
York Avenue where there was a car barn. This barn was on
the site of the present Corcoran Art Gallery. On the east
end, the line turned east into A Street for a short distance.
Neither of these two extensions was ever authorized by
Congress. Astonishingly, this company was to make a relatively frequent practice of this, sometimes gaining Congressional authority after the fact. This original route became
the heart of the later Washington Railway and Electric in
much the same way that the original Washington and
Georgetown route became the heart of the Capital Traction
Company lines.

The Metropolitan remained as described until 1872. Two

Metropolitan Railroad horsecar at the Capitol in the early '70's. Cars were rerouted to avoid the Capitol ground in 1875. Francis B. Tosh collection.

Original Metropolitan horsecars in an 1866 view looking north on 17th Street below Pennsylvania Avenue. The building is the Navy Department. Robert A. Truax collection.

other railroads were to bear on the future of the Metropolitan: the Connecticut Avenue and Park Railway Company and the Union Railroad Company.

The Connecticut Avenue and Park was chartered July 13, 1868. This road was, in effect, an extension of the Metropolitan north on Connecticut Avenue from 17th and H Streets to Boundary Street (now Florida Avenue). Incidentally, it was at this time that routing of both tracks around the west side of Dupont Circle was established. Much later this would cause a traffic problem and all sorts of reasons would be given for the routing. The simple fact was that, in anticipation of a branch to Georgetown, this was the least expensive solution.

The road was completed and operations begun on or about April 5, 1873. Originally it was single track. Metropolitan horsecars were used, but operation was by the Connecticut Avenue and Park Railway until June 20, 1874. On this date, without Congressional authority, the Metropolitan Railroad Company absorbed this company pursuant to a resolution adopted on June 6, 1874, by a joint meeting of the board of directors of both companies.

The Union Railroad Company was chartered by an act of the Legislative Assembly of the District of Columbia, approved January 19, 1872. Construction started May 9, 1872.[17]

On the 29th of August, terms of consolidation with the

Metropolitan were agreed upon and on November 8, 1872, the two two roads combined—another action entirely without Congressional authority.

The Union ran west to Georgetown from Connecticut Avenue via P Street, West (P)* and 3rd (P) Streets. Return was south on Fayette (35th), east on 2nd (O) and Dumbarton, north on Montgomery (28th), and east on P Street to Connecticut Avenue.

The Metropolitan completed the road and operated it in conjunction with the Connecticut Avenue and Park and their own road. First cars to the western terminus of the road operated September 25, 1873.[18]

In the spring of 1872, the eastern end of the Metropolitan was extended. The extension ran along A Street to 1st Street, east to East Capitol Street, and east on that street to 9th Street East—a distance of about one mile—where there was a turntable.

In 1872, construction began on the Ninth Street Branch. Partial operation began May 22, 1872,[19] with complete operation the following summer. This line ran south on 9th from M Street north to B Street, then along B to Missouri

*Georgetown street names didn't conform to the City of Washington's pattern until 1880. Thus, I have used the original names and shown the later names in parentheses.

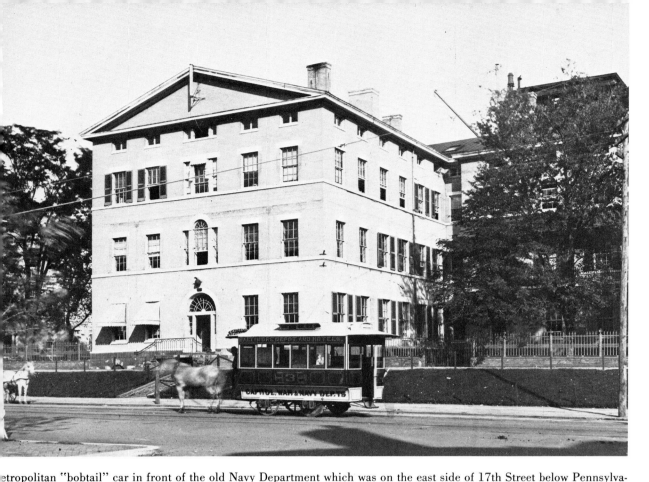

etropolitan "bobtail" car in front of the old Navy Department which was on the east side of 17th Street below Pennsylva-
a Avenue. Taken in the late '70's. Handy Studios, author's collection.

Avenue to 4 1/2 Street to O Street South near the U. S.
Arsenal. At Ninth and F Streets N.W. the F Street line
became single track to cross the then single track Ninth
Street line. At the crossing, there was a small turntable to
allow cars to be shifted from one line to the other for barn
moves.

On December 4, 1872, the Metropolitan acquired the
Boundary and Silver Spring Railroad Company. This company, chartered on January 19, 1872, had authority to
construct a road north along the Rockville Turnpike (later
Georgia Avenue) from Boundary Street to the District
Line — Metropolitan constructed this road to Rock Creek
Church Road or, as it was then known, Cammack's Corner. Since Metropolitan bought the B & SS which started
at Boundary and Rockville Pike, it must be assumed that
the Metropolitan constructed an extension from M Street
north to Boundary and east on Boundary to Rockville
Pike about 1873.

On January 31, 1873, the B & SS was conveyed formally
to the Metropolitan by deed.

The car barn for the B & SS was on the west side of the
line in the vicinity of Georgia Avenue and V Street N. W.
This location became a barn, stable and shop in 1875. Later
this property became a loop for the end of the 9th Street
line, and later still a convenient lay-over point for extra cars
to handle large crowds to special events at the ball park.

In the fall of 1874, the Metropolitan moved its main barn
from 17th and New York Avenue N.W. to ten acres of land
on West (P) Street just west of Rock Creek. The location
would serve as main shops for the Metropolitan and its
successors until abandoned by the Capital Transit Company
in 1934.[20]

The year 1875 also brought removal of Metropolitan
tracks from the Capitol grounds. Congress had given the
Officer in Charge of Public Buildings and Grounds authority to force removal of tracks on the Capitol grounds and
grant subsequent new routings. Instead of turning south on
New Jersey Avenue, thence to A Street and east on A to 1st,
the new route continued on C Street to Delaware Avenue,
south on Delaware to B Street North, east to 1st to the old
route. Thus, as far back as the 70's we see the establishment
of street car routes that would last the entire rail era.

Operations of the Metropolitan settled down to a routine
from the standpoint of routes, at least, for the next fifteen
years. In 1888, the Brightwood Railway was chartered and
eventually became the operator of the Metropolitan's Silver
Spring Branch. This, of course, was the old Boundary and
Silver Spring. As a horse car operation of the Metropolitan
it seems to have been less than successful and was thus
turned over to the Brightwood. This story is later discussed
under history of the Brightwood Railway.

Trimble-built Metropolitan horse-car en route downtown at Wisconsin Avenue and O Streets in Georgetown. Electrified Georgetown and Tennallytown tracks on Wisconsin Avenue date the picture in the early '90's. Handy Studios, author's collection.

Left, westbound Metropolitan car crossing P Street bridge over Rock Creek in the '80's. Handy Studios, author's collection.

Below, F Street looking west from 9th in the early '80's. Notice that the crossing is single track to accommodate a turntable to change cars between the two Metropolitan routes. Author's collection.

etropolitan open horsecar on East Capitol Street near 9th Street. A number of these Trimble-built cars
ter served as electric trailers. Taken about 1890. The conductor, whose name was Dick, was a favorite
th the kids. Handy Studios, Author's collection.

Columbia Railway Stephenson horse-car. Taken in 1891, probably near 15th and H Streets N.E. Handy Studios, author's collection.

Anacostia and Potomac Number 20, a Jones-built horsecar photographed in 1890 at the foot of Asylum Hill in Anacostia. Author's collection.

Belt Line "bobtail" car on Maryland Avenue S.W. on a winter day in the early '90's. Handy Studios, author's collection.

Columbia Railway Company

A third horsecar operator, the Columbia Railway Company, was chartered by an Act of Congress dated May 24, 1870. The original route was east on New York Avenue to K Street, past the south side of the old Northern Liberties Market, then down Massachusetts Avenue to H Street and on H Street to the eastern tollgate of the Columbia Turnpike Company, a distance of five and a half miles. The eastern gate of the turnpike was at what was later 15th and H Streets N.E.

The line was originally single track with turnouts; but in October, 1871, it was decided to construct double track which was completed in March, 1872. Cost of the road, as a double track line, together with nine cars, forty horses, land and stables was $99,971.19.

The original barn was located on 15th Street, just north of Gales Street, N.E. Cars went south on 15th Street to enter the barn. In later years, with the acquisition of adjoining property, the newer car house extended through the middle of the same block, affording a more accessible entrance from the main tracks on Bennings Road.

The Columbia was required to make a minimum of eight trips a day at least six days a week. The company was reported to have seven cars and fifty-six horses in 1885. In 1887, the fleet had grown to twenty-three cars and seventy-one horses.

This, then, was the extent of the Columbia line until electric days. Not a very complicated line, but none the less an important and profitable one.

The most exciting feature of a horsecar ride out the Columbia line was crossing the B & O at grade. The steam locomotive was always impressive, but one can imagine its being even more so when crossing the tracks of one in a slow horsecar. The crossing was protected by gates, and there were instances where the gates were lowered while a horsecar was in transit, no doubt causing considerable consternation among the passengers. No accidents of major proportions are known to have occurred though.

The Columbia, along with several other companies in Washington, operated the economical but unpopular "Bobtail" type horse car. This kind of car, pulled by one horse, was a one man car and, as such, had no rear platform. Hence the name Bobtail. Passengers entered a rear door and had to go to the front of the car to deposit their fare under the eye of the driver which was of course inconvenient for the passenger. In addition, the cars were small and crowded. Dislike of Bobtail cars grew to such proportions in the early 90's that a riders' strike was organized against the Columbia Railway. Passengers simply refused to put their fares in the box at the front of the car until the company agreed to larger two-horse cars and conductors. The strike lasted but a few days and the company capitulated. Shortly thereafter, on July 29, 1892, Congress prohibited one horse cars in Washington.

As a result of this, Columbia, in an attempt to recoup their financial advantage, built the only known spliced horse cars in their own shops.[21]

Anacostia and Potomac River Railroad Company

On March 19, 1872, Congress authorized the Anacostia and Potomac River Railroad Company to construct a horsecar route from the north end of the Navy Yard Bridge, across M Street to Water, to 11th Street S.W. to Ohio Avenue to 14th Street N.W., and thence to 14th and Pensylvania Avenue N.W. Thus began another of the city's major horsecar operations. The charter called for a five cent fare and also authorized crossing the river on the Navy Yard Bridge into Uniontown (later Anacostia). It's interesting to note that the earlier bridge at this point carried John Wilkes Booth on his flight to southern Maryland after his assassination of President Lincoln.

Although chartered in 1872, work wasn't started until October, 1875, because of difficulty in raising the required capital. The original line operated was from what is now Nichols Avenue and V Streets in Anacostia,* across the Navy Yard bridge and to Seventh and M Streets S.W. via 11th and M Streets. At first, the Engineer in charge of Public Buildings and Grounds refused permission to lay tracks on the bridge. The company appealed his decision to the Judge Advocate General of the Army who held in their favor. This matter solved, work began in April, 1876. A barn and stable were constructed at Nichols Avenue and V Street. The road was single track with turnouts.

Operation began with two cars on July 3, 1876.[22] A year later, on July 13, 1877,[23] the line was reported in operation to Seventh and Water Streets S.W. via M Street South where connection could be made with Washington and Georgetown cars. Additional cars were put on July 16, 1878,[24] allowing the headway to be reduced from twenty minutes to ten. Also in 1878, the Anacostia end of the line was extended to the foot of Asylum hill.

Up to this time, nothing had been done to construct the rest of the route authorized by the charter. When, in 1879, the company asked permission to build the route along Water, 11th, Ohio and 14th Streets to 14th and Pennsylvania Avenue N.W., they were refused permission because the time limit in the charter had expired.[25]

The Capitol, North O Street and South Washington Railway Company

An act of March 3, 1875, created the Capitol, North O Street and South Washington Railway Company. This road, later known simply as "The Belt Railway Company," was to become an integral part of the Anacostia and Potomac. The original authorized route circumscribed the then downtown area. Starting at the Capitol grounds, the road ran north on 1st Street West to G, west on G to 4th, north on 4th to O Street, across O to 11th Street West, south on 11th Street to E, west on E to 14th, south on 14th to Ohio, on

*At that time it was Johnson and Monroe Streets and Anacostia was called Uniontown.

Obio east to 12th, south on 12th to Virginia, east on Virginia to Maryland, and east on Maryland to 1st Street West where it began.

Operation began December 1, 1875. The road was double track throughout except for the portion on O Street North which was single track with turnouts. The car barn and stables, with a capacity of fifty horses and one hundred cars, was located at Third and B Street S.W.[26] In a few months, the road requested and got authority (under an Act dated May 23, 1876) to add a single track in P Street North. Where this was done, westbound cars used P Street, and eastbound cars used the original O Street trackage thus making the entire road double track.

On March 3, 1881, Congressional authority was granted for the following:

1. Removal of Capitol, North O Street and South Washington tracks on Ohio and 12th Street.
2. New tracks south on 14th to C to Virginia Avenue. (Actual construction was 14tb to C to 11th and north on 11th to existing track at 11th and Virginia.)
3. Extension north from 11th and P Street to 11th and Boundary.
4. Extension from 11th and Water S.W. to Water and M Street S.W.

The next extension authorized came by virtue of an Act dated March 1, 1883. This allowed extension from 11th and E Street N.W., along E to 9th, and south on 9th by joint operation on Metropolitan's 9th Street line to Louisiana Avenue, then southwesterly on Louisiana to Ohio and on to 12th and Ohio.

An Act of August 9, 1888, authorized operation east along B S.W. from 14th to 12th. This replaced the awkward 1881 routing via 14th, C, 11th and B to Virginia Avenue.

Now we return to the Anacostia and Potomac for it was in 1888 that Congress authorized the A & P routing north of the Navy Yard Bridge that was to last until the reroutings of the 1930's. An Act of August 1, 1888, authorized the company to lay tracks from 7th and M Street S.E., via 7th, G, 4th, E, Canal, B, 3rd, Missouri Avenue, 6th Street, B Street to a point near Center Market. This Act also provided for a line from 2nd and M Street S.W. to 2nd and Canal via 2nd Street S.W.; and a route from 7th and G Street to the E Street entrance to the Congressional Cemetery via G, 17th, and E Streets. Predictably, the cemetery line was known as the Ghost Line. It was said that cars operated at night without passengers or drivers.

The line from 7th and M Street S.W. to 7th and G was never built. An Act of March 24, 1890, authorized the change of this route from 11th and M Street S.W., up 11th to G Street, and across G to 7th and G, joining the original route there. Construction of the road, with the exception of tracks on 2nd Street, was carried on in 1890 and completed by January, 1891. The 2nd Street trackage was completed

later in 1891, making the entire length of the line operated by the A and P thirteen and one-half miles.

In 1892, the company owned 156 horses, sixteen summer (open) cars, and twenty-eight winter (closed) cars, all two-horse.

Meanwhile, over in Anacostia, the same act permitted an additional track on the bridge and an extension via Nichols Avenue to the Government Hospital and beyond that via Nichols Avenue and Livingstone Road to the District line. It's important here to note that the extension never was completed to the District Line: its maximum extent, even in the electric era, was what is later Upsal Street. Horsecars did operate to the Government Hospital.

Finally, the act authorized a single track in Harrison Street to the entrance of the German Orphan Asylum, but there is no evidence that this was ever constructed.

At the end of 1889, double tracks from 11th and G Street S.E. to the Center Market were completed. The cemetery extension was completed by May 30, 1891, while the 2nd Street line from M to Canal was completed August 1, 1891.

The next landmark in the history of the A & P was the extension from 9th and B Street N.W., up 9th to G over Metropolitan tracks, over G to 11th on Eckington and Soldiers' Home tracks, south on 11th to E Street, east on E Street to 9th on tracks of the Capitol, North O Street and South Washington Railway, then return to 9th and B via Metropolitan tracks. The Act called for installation of necessary switches and for the exchange of tickets with other roads where their tracks unite. All this was to take place as a result of an Act dated April 30, 1892.

At this point in its history, the company serviced its eight and one-half route miles with fifty-two cars and 230 horses. For the most part, the line was laid with eighty-pound grooved rails. These were placed on white oak ties placed three feet six inches apart. With a view to future conversion from horse to an as-yet-undetermined mechanical form of propulsion, the company had purchased square #330 at the head of 11th Street N.W. for a powerhouse location. This location later was to become the Eleventh Street Barn.

In July 29, 1892, an Act requiring two horses per car was the first of several which, in effect, caused the receivership of both the Anacostia and Potomac and the Capitol, North O Street and South Washington. One-horse cars were prohibited after January 1, 1893.

On February 18, 1893, the Capitol, North O Street and South Washington was authorized to change its name to "The Belt Railway Company."

The "Gay Nineties" were anything but gay for the affairs of the Belt and A and P. They were years of financial hardship which would end in consolidation of both roads. As the decade wore on, the argument turned from the idea of equipping each car with two horses to the idea of compressed air motors and finally to an underground electric system.

Both companies were financially unable to comply with the two-horse idea, let alone the more modern and more

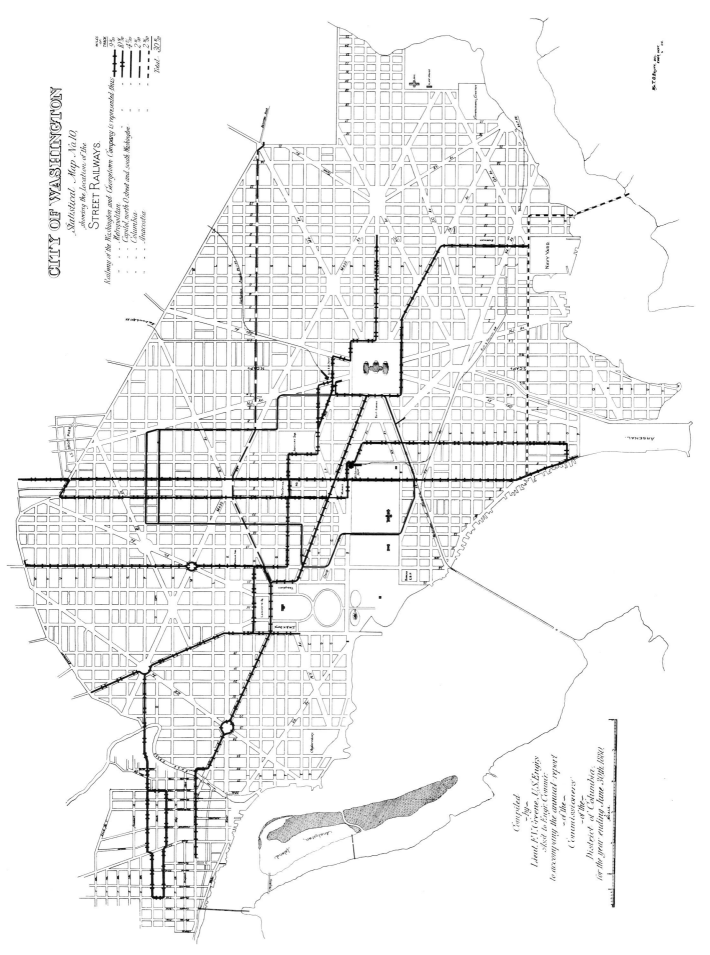

Capitol, North O Street and South Washington ticket. Red border with blue center on white background. Both sides identical. Robert A. Truax collection.

Metropolitan ticket. Black lettering on yellow stock. Robert A. Truax collection.

expensive solution. In June, 1896, the Belt was authorized to build the LeDroit Park extension, but it was not to be operated with horsepower. This extension was to run from 4th and O Street N.W. to 7th and Pomeroy (later W Street) via 4th, Florida, Harewood, Elm, Linden, and Pomeroy. This route was operated by horse, despite Congressional prohibition. The June, 1896 Act called for air motors in six months, but only if satisfactory. If unsatisfactory, the Belt was required to adopt the underground electric system within eighteen months of the date of the Act. The time for air motors operation was extended to July 1, 1897, by Act of February 3, 1897. No record exists to show actual Belt experiments with air motors. It's probable that Eckington and Soldiers Home experiments served to discourage use on both properties. An indication of the deterioration of Belt services was a statement in the Act calling for submission to the District authorities of a proposed schedule for a portion of the Belt line. Several adverse financial circumstances are recorded for the year 1896 in the affairs of the Belt.

In September, 1896, M. Ament Company obtained a judgment for $641.33 for materials furnished the Belt. Belt couldn't satisfy the judgment since the property was encumbered with mortgages. The Ament Company then sued the Belt Railway, Messrs. S. R. Bond, C. H. Cragin and the American Security and Trust Company. Bond, Cragin and American Security were trustees under the mortgages, and the suit's purpose was to appoint a receiver and force sale of the Road.

At this time, while there were to be other new horsecar operations, the end of the era was at hand. Numerous electric railway experiments took place in the United States and elsewhere, culminating in the first practical electric railway in Richmond, Virginia, in January, 1888. Naval Academy graduate Frank Sprague, aided, incidentally, by Lt. Oscar T. Crosby* and others, was responsible. Washington's first electric line came soon after Sprague's Richmond success.

*Oscar T. Crosby (1862-1947) West Point 1882. Later became general superintendent of the Sprague Electric Railway and Motor Company. Later he became the founder of both the Washington Traction and Electric Company and the Potomac Electric Power Co. *The Star,* January 2, 1947.

Pullman-built Belt Line two-horse car of the '90's. Handy Studios author's collection.

Belt Line "bobtail" car. Robert A. Truax collection.

CHAPTER TWO
THE EARLY ELECTRICS, THE CABLE CAR, AND EXPERIMENTS

The Eckington and Soldiers' Home Railway Company
of the District of Columbia[1]

Barely six months after Sprague's Richmond success, the Eckington and Soldiers' Home Railway of the District of Columbia was chartered. The Act of Congress granting the charter was dated June 19, 1888. The charter called for construction of a railway starting at 7th and New York Avenue, east of Mt. Vernon Square, running east along New York Avenue to Boundary Street (now Florida Avenue), Boundary to Eckington Place, north to R. Street, R to 3rd, 3rd to T and T to the car house at 4th Street N.E., a distance of two and a half miles.

The line was constructed by the Thomson-Houston Company to the finest standards of the day. It was double track with center pole overhead trolley construction from 7th Street to Boundary, then single track to the barn.

Operation began October 17, 1888. The president was Mr. George H. Truesdale. Original equipment consisted of three deck-roof, open platform, closed motors by Brill. These cars were numbered 1, 2, and 3. The road also had at least one ex-Washington and Georgetown horsecar numbered 146. It was used as a trailer.

An experimental trip on October 15, prior to the opening of the line, was described by the October 18, 1888, issue of the *Washington Star*. The following quotation describes the excitement of the first electric car operation in the city:

> The cars do not differ materially from those found on other lines—except no place to hitch horses. Platforms front and rear and the familiar brake—against the dash board is a small wooden cylinder about 5" in diameter. On top is a polished crank—the driver turns the crank and the car starts.
>
> Flying along New York Avenue, which is brilliantly lit at night by clusters of electric lights at the top of iron poles, the occupants of the car became conscious that they were creating something of a sensation. The interior of the car is fitted up with mahogany . . . seats with springs are upholstered in slate-colored plush, brilliantly lighted, the *Star* can be read in any part of the car."

This article also gives the cost of the car bodies as $1,150 each.

In June of 1889 the company began construction of an extension of its line from 4th and T Street N.E. along 4th Street to Bunker Hill Road. This extension was placed in operation during the winter of 1889-90. The new line was constructed of 60-pound rails. The directors also decided on additional equipment, and eleven additional cars were acquired from Brill. Four of these (Nos. 4-7) were closed motors with vestibules, and seven (Nos. 8-14) were double-deck trailers.

The road's charter was amended April 30, 1890. This amendment called for extension south on 5th from New York Avenue to G Street, west on G to 15th. It also granted extension of the Cemetery branch north on Lincoln Road to the entrance to Glenwood Cemetery. The route of the branch was west from 3rd and T Street N.E. to 2nd, north on 2nd to what is now V Street, then west to Lincoln Road, and north on Lincoln Road to the Cemetery gate. It further provided for a route north on North Capitol Street from New York Avenue to the Soldiers' Home. Those familiar with Washington street railways will begin to see the development of the later Brookland and Maryland lines.

Of great significance in the development of Washington electric operation was the provision that operation on 5th and G Streets, if electric, must have underground wires. In those days, the City of Washington was considered to be that portion of the District south of Boundary Street. Any operation with overhead wires in this area was prohibited by law after July 1, 1893. It was this idea, of course, that gave rise to experiments with storage battery cars, compressed air cars, surface contact systems, the late adoption of cable traction and the final adoption of underground conduit for the entire downtown system in Washington. Once exposed to the marvels of the electric car, neither the government nor the citizens would long tolerate the horse car.

The 90's were interesting, experimental and expensive times for most railway managements in Washington. Progress, in the form of the electric railway, was temporarily stifled because of proper Congressional concern about downtown Washington's appearance. Of course, the overhead wire problem didn't affect the suburban lines, several of which would be built before a solution was found to the problem of underground current collection at the end of the decade. Pioneer in the search for an acceptable motorized system was the Brightwood Railway.

Brightwood Railway Company
of the District of Columbia

On October 18, 1888, the Brightwood Railway Company of the District of Columbia was chartered by Congress with the authority to construct a road from Boundary Street to the District line on 7th Street Extended and Brightwood Avenue (later Georgia Avenue). M.M.Parker, A.A.Thomas, Cal Anderson, C.B.Pearson, and Joseph Paul of the District were the original incorporators. Congress gave authority to run horse, cable or electric cars, and authorized maximum capital stock of $60,000 if horsepower was used, or $102,000 if electric power was used. Maximum fare was fixed at five cents per passenger or six tickets for twenty-five cents.

Eckington and Soldiers' Home motor and double-deck trailer. Thought to be on North Capitol Street just north of Florida Avenue. Taken about 1891. Handy Studios, author's collection.

Eckington and Soldiers' Home motor and ex-Washington and Georgetown open horsecar as trailer. Note Washington and Georgetown Railroad lettering on end of benches. Believed to be on T Street west of 3rd N.E. Handy Studios, author's collection.

May 10, 1889, was the date of a contract for materials for construction from the end of the Metropolitan's Silver Spring Branch to the District line. On completion of the road by Brightwood, it was leased to the Metropolitan. The contract with the Metropolitan was dated November 11, 1889.

On the same date as the Metropolitan lease, a contract was signed with the Judson Pneumatic Street Railroad Company of New York. Judson agreed to construct, at their expense, a single track road from Boundary Street to Rock Creek Church Road. The track was apparently beside and in addition to the existing horse car tracks. It was single track with turnouts.

Judson's system "consisted of two parallel tubes six or eight inches in diameter which were installed in an underground conduit, and revolved against a set of staggered friction wheels attached to and depending from the car, and impelled the car on the principle of the screw. The rotary motion was imparted to the tubes by small engines about

pening day, October 17, 1888, of Washington's first electric line, e Eckington and Soldiers' Home. Photo was taken at the city end the road on New York Avenue just east of 7th Street N.W. Note -Washington and Georgetown open trailer. Smithsonian Institu- ●n.

five hundred feet apart, along the tubes. As the air escaped from the exhaust, it absorbed so much heat from the surrounding atmosphere that the ice so generated clogged the gearing of the engines by which the pipes were turned, and was an insuperable obstacle to efficient operation of the device."[1]

On June 11, 1890, Judson offered to sell the pneumatic operation to the Brightwood for $45,000. Brightwood accepted the offer probably based on fair weather performance. When the Judson failure was obvious, the company decided to electrify.

At the time the Judson experiment was purchased, Brightwood also decided to buy the Metropolitan's Silver Spring Branch.

Washington and Georgetown Cable Cars[2]

The Washington and Georgetown Railroad Company was the first of two Washington cable car operators. They converted their entire system—starting with the 7th Street line which opened May 12, 1890—a year and a half after Eckington and Soldiers' Home electric operation.

At this time Washington and Georgetown had three lines, 7th Street, Pennsylvania and 14th Street.

The 7th Street line was three and a half miles long and ran from the Arsenal (later Fort McNair) at Maine Avenue and P Street to 7th and Boundary Avenue (later Florida Avenue). The route was westerly on Water Street (Maine Avenue) to 7th, then north over 7th to Boundary. This portion of the route remained unchanged for the balance of rail operation in the District. Later, of course, it was part of the 7th-Georgia line.

The power station was in the barn at Water Street and P S.W. in the building that later became Southern Carhouse. A continuous cable was used for the entire route. A typical train would have an open grip car with one or two trailers. Trailers were open or closed, dependent on the season; but there were no closed grip cars. As was customary, cars were painted different colors to denote different routes. Seventh Street trains were painted yellow with cream trim. A three-minute headway was maintained from 5 a.m. to 1 a.m. requiring sixteen trains.

The Pennsylvania Avenue line cable operation commenced August 6, 1892. The route was the same as the horsecar route. By this time the horsecars avoided the Capitol grounds by using 1st Street West and B Street South.

This line was operated by two cables running out of the powerhouse at 14th and E Street N.W., later the site of the District Building. The "Georgetown" cable served the western end while the "Navy Yard" cable served the eastern end. The speed of the cable was 9.9 mph. This line was extended on its western end to a new terminal at 36th and M Streets with service opening July 12, 1895.

Trains were similar to 7th Street trains but were green with cream trim. A three-minute headway was maintained from 5:00 a.m. to 1:00 a.m., and this required twenty-eight trains.

Fourteenth Street cable operation started the same day

Above. 7th Street cable line under construction between F and G Streets N.W. Probably late 1889. Author's collection.

Right. Stephenson-built Washington and Georgetown grip car 1 for the 14th Street line. Museum of the City of New York.

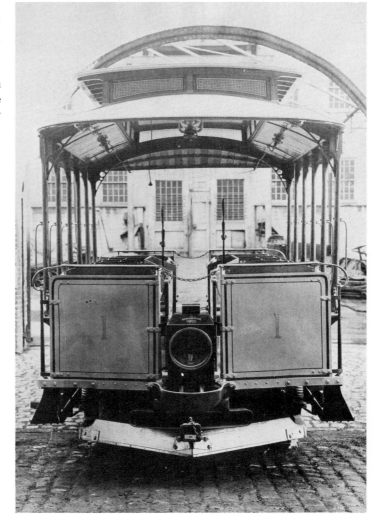

Top. 7th Street cable train. Open grip car and closed trailer were built by Laclede of St. Louis. Leet Brothers, author's collection.

Bottom. Pennsylvania Avenue from the Treasury about 1896, near the end of cable operation for Capital Traction. Note the absolute lack of traffic discipline and the unfinished Post Office. Handy Studios, author's collection.

Looking south on 7th Street from north of G Street N.W. Cable train bound for the ball park while an EDCO storage battery car on the Eckington and Soldiers' Home crosses at G Street. Author's collection.

Washington and Georgetown (later Capital Traction) cable powerhouse and office at 14th and E Streets N.W. Mt. Vernon train is at left. Handy Studios, author's collection.

On the night of September 29, 1897, fire destroyed Capital Traction's 14th Street cable powerhouse, hastening the end of the company's cable operation. Author's collection.

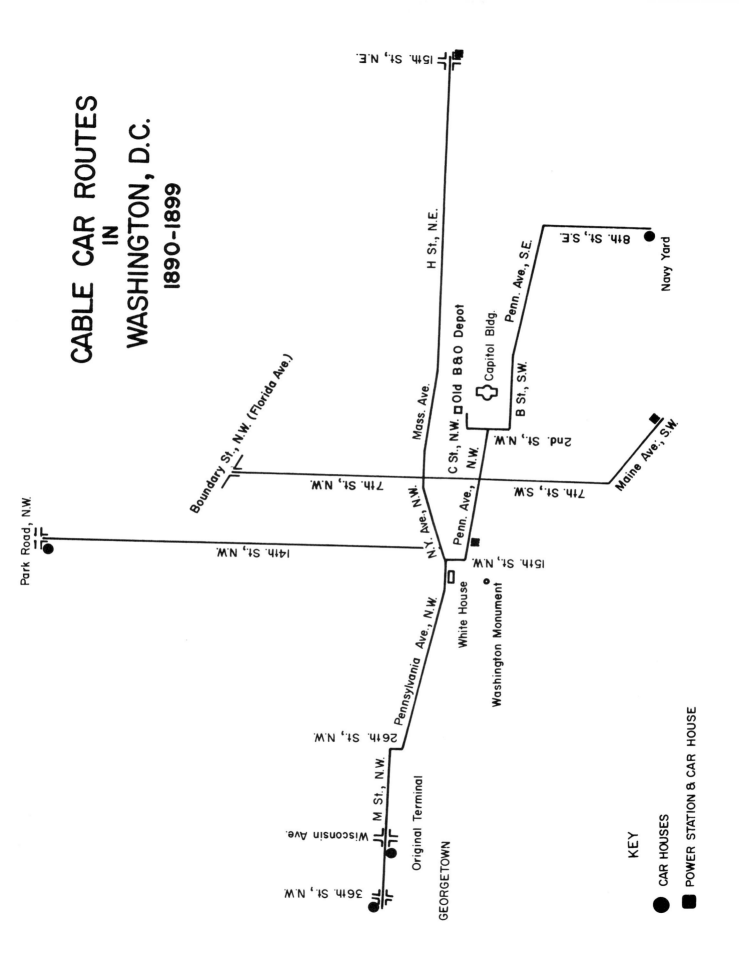

CABLE CAR ROUTES
IN
WASHINGTON, D.C.
1890-1899

15th St., N.E.

H St., N.E.

8th St., S.E.

Navy Yard

Penn. Ave., S.E.

Mass. Ave.

Old B&O Depot

Capitol Bldg.

B St., S.W.

C St., N.W.

2nd St., N.W.

Boundary St., N.W. (Florida Ave.)

7th St., N.W.

7th St., S.W.

Maine Ave., S.W.

Park Road, N.W.

14th St., N.W.

N.Y. Ave., N.W.

Penn. Ave., N.W.

15th St., N.W.

White House

Washington Monument

Pennsylvania Ave., N.W.

26th St., N.W.

M St., N.W.

Wisconsin Ave.

Original Terminal

36th St., N.W.

GEORGETOWN

KEY

● CAR HOUSES

■ POWER STATION & CAR HOUSE

23

After the fire. Looking north on 15th Street from Pennsylvania Avenue, with the Treasury in the background, horses haul Capital Traction cable trailers. Author's collection.

as Pennsylvania Avenue and for the 14th Street portion of its route used a third cable operated out of the powerhouse at 14th and E Street N.W. This line started at the old B & O Depot at New Jersey Avenue and C Street N.W. and ran via C and 1st Street West to Peace Monument. Here it joined the Pennsylvania Avenue line. At 15th and New York Avenue, the 14th Street line left the Pennsylvania Avenue line, went east on New York Avenue to 14th Street, then north to 14th and Park Road N.W. At 14th and Park Road there was a car barn, which was used until 1907 when it was replaced by the 14th and Decatur barn. In the 30's, this building was a market, but it has since been torn down.

Of course, 14th Street cable cars used the Pennsylvania Avenue cable from 15th and New York Avenue to Peace Monument. From Peace Monument to the B & O Depot at New Jersey Avenue and C Street, a supplementary cable powered by the Pennsylvania Avenue cable was used. Transmission machinery for this supplementary cable was in three underground vaults under Pennsylvania Avenue near Peace Monument. This cable travelled at six mph. The 14th Street portion was approximately three miles long.

As with Georgetown and 7th Street lines, trains were the rule. They were yellow and cream. The same headway was provided, which took twenty-two trains.

A 7th Street cable would normally last eighteen months, while a Pennsylvania and 14th Street cable, because of more curves, lasted only four to nine months.

The Washington and Georgetown was merged into the Rock Creek Railway on September 21, 1895; and the name changed to the Capital Traction Company. The Rock Creek Railway was an electric suburban line running from just east of 7th and U Street along U Street out Connecticut Avenue to Chevy Chase Lake.

The new Capital Traction Company then was a combination of two forms of traction and would not really be an integrated property until the whole system was electrified.

Following is a roster of cable equipment:

Open Grip Cars

Laclede Car Company	24
John Stephenson Company Ltd.	74
Total	98

Open Trailers

J. M. Jones & Company	40
American Car Company	124
Total	164

Closed Trailers

Laclede Car Company	24
W & G Railroad Company	1
John Stephenson	85*
John Stephenson	41**
Total	151

Total Cable Equipment 413

All cars were single truck.

At about 11:15 p.m. on the night of September 29, 1897, tragedy struck Capital Traction. The central cable powerhouse at 14th and E Street N.W. was completely destroyed by fire. All lines except 7th Street were immediately out of service. The company's offices, shops, five grip cars, six closed trailers and one open trailer were lost.

The Capital Traction Company's annual report for December 31, 1897—after the fire—reveals the following distribution of cable cars:

*One car from this group (W & G RR 212) became Capital Traction 1512 and is still in existence as an historical relic.

**Ex-horse cars converted in company shops.

	Grip	Closed Trailer	Open Trailer
Pennsylvania Avenue	40	57	69
14th Street	29	47	50
7th Street	24	41	44
Lost in fire	5	6	1
Total	98	151	164

Obviously a loss of this magnitude is a hard one for even the best of railway properties to take, and in many instances might have put a company out of business. What happened next, however, was indeed a splendid commentary on the spirit of the Capital Traction. While the fire progressed, company officials began scouring Washington business concerns, as well as businesses up the Canal, for horses. Meanwhile, the blacksmith shop was equipping the cable trailers with whiffle trees. Metropolitan Railroad, which by this time had electrified, offered their stock of recently retired horsecars; but Capital Traction officials preferred their own methods. That cars were operating the next morning at all, let alone on schedule, gives us an example of organizational efficiency to be marvelled at even in these sophisticated times! On the following morning, within seven hours after the fire, horse-drawn cable trailers were giving service on a five-minute headway on the Avenue and four and a half minutes on 14th Street! Most of the horses acquired for the emergency were acquired from Littlefield and Alvord, a local drayage firm, or Maurice F. Talty, a Washington contractor. At the height of the emergency, 719 horses were used.

As we shall see, technology had by now advanced to the point where electrification of in-town lines was practical. There were, however, other experiments during the Washington and Georgetown/Capital Traction cable era.

Storage Battery Cars and Other Experiments

The Metropolitan resisted pressures to adopt the cable car by pleading they were not adaptable to Metropolitan's none too straight routes. Washington and Georgetown's cable system was obviously better than horse cars, and the comparison no doubt forced Metropolitan to adopt an improved form of power.

Congressional disapproval of further use of horse power was made official by statute dated August 6, 1890, which said in part "That if any such company operating a line from Georgetown or West Washington to and beyond the Capitol grounds shall fail to substitute for horse power the power herein provided for on all its lines within two years from the date of this Act, such company shall forfeit its corporate franchise." Although the Metropolitan's Board had, on September 11, 1889, decided to adopt a storage battery system, the August 6, 1890 statute was, no doubt, enacted to guarantee that Metropolitan would perform as stated. Metropolitan hired the country's leading expert, Mr. C. O. Mailloux, to supervise the installation.

On July 22, 1892, by the joint resolution of Congress, the Metropolitan was granted a one-year extension to the provisions of the August, 1890 Act, provided they place storage battery cars in service as expeditiously as possible. The Metropolitan entered the storage battery experiment whole-

Metropolitan storage battery car as a service car at P Street shops before 1905. Later, this car became Washington Railway and Electric 37. Capital Transit Library, author's collection.

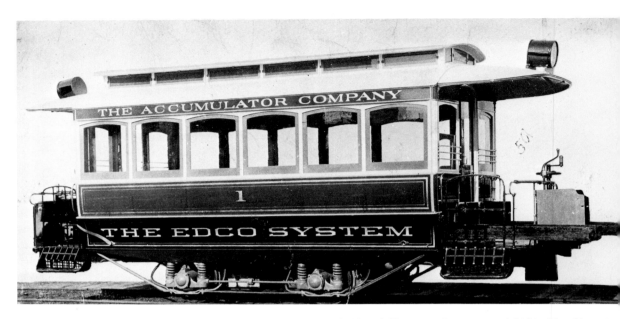

Brill-built EDCO storage battery car used on Eckington and Soldiers' Home in the spring of 1891. The Historica[l] Society of Pennsylvania.

Eckington and Soldiers' Home car equipped for Wheless surface contact experiment in what was later North Capit[ol] Street. Note long current collectors under the car and contact plate in roadway between the rails. Author's colle[c]tion.

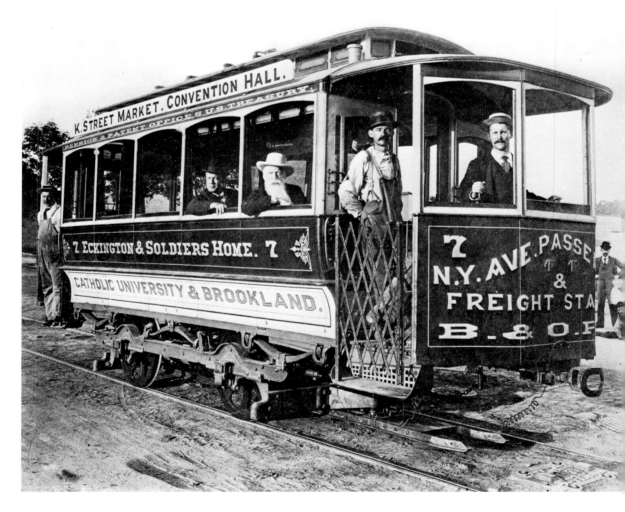

heartedly, however. In 1891, facilities were constructed at the P Street barn for generating electricity and otherwise servicing storage batteries. Similar facilities were constructed at 4 1/2 and P Street S.W. at the carbarn.

For three years, storage battery cars intermingled with horse cars. However, management was forced to the conclusion that this was not the answer to their problem. The last trip by storage battery car was on October 29, 1893. The cars later found their way to other uses: ten became closed 9th Street trailers and the other ten became service cars of various descriptions.

Eckington and Soldiers' Home Railway

The Eckington and Soldiers' Home conducted experiments in December, 1890, with the Wheless surface contact system.[3] These experiments were conducted on three-quarters of a mile of track which ran north from New York Avenue in a field which was later North Capitol Street.

Surface contact systems used energized contact plates between the tracks. The cars were equipped with long contact bars to pick up current from the contact plates. Plates were close enough together so the bars on the cars were always in contact with at least two of the plates. Magnets on the cars were supposed to energize the contact plates only while the car was over the plate. Surface contact experiments in Washington—this was only the first of three—failed essentially because no foolproof way could be found to insure that the contact plates would be dead after passage of the car.

In the closing months of 1894,[4] the Electro Magnetic Company of West Virginia, sponsored by Westinghouse and using Wheless patents, took over the surface contact experiment to no avail.

On March 13, 1891, first trips were made between 5th and New York Avenue and 15th and G Streets with two EDCO storage battery cars owned by the Accumulator Company of Philadelphia. In May or June, six battery cars (Nos. 21-26) were received from J. G. Brill Company of Philadelphia. Battery cars operated from 15th and G Streets (opposite the U. S. Treasury) to 5th and New York Avenue. There transfer was made to cars using conventional overhead power.[5]

Original reaction to the storage battery cars was, as would be expected, enthusiastic. At best, though the battery cars were slow. This, coupled with high battery maintenance and charging costs, led to their replacement by horsecars in May, 1893. The horsecars and horses were probably purchased second-hand from the Washington and Georgetown.

In 1894 the line opened electric service to Catholic University and Brookland via 4th Street. The following year, because of failure to find an acceptable method of mechanical traction, Eckington and Soldiers' Home opened its 13th and D Street line and its extension to the Pennsylvania station—with horsecars!

The Pennsylvania Station extension ran south from 5th and G Street N.W. via 5th, Louisiana Avenue, 6th, B to 7th

and B Street N.W. and reached Center Market as well as the station. Operation over 5th from F Street to Louisiana Avenue and on B Street was on Metropolitan tracks. The 13th and D Street project included trackage from 5th and G Street N.W. east to 1st Street N.W. south on 1st to C Street then east on C Street to 13th Street N.E. Cars then went north one block to D Street, then west to 4th and back to C Street. A barn was erected at the outer end of the line. A branch of this line continued east from 1st and G Streets, N.W. to North Capitol, then ran north on North Capitol to New York Avenue, thus establishing the later routing of the North Capitol Street car line.

Thirty Laclede-built sixteen foot closed horsecars were purchased for these lines. These cars, incidentally, were the first in Washington with automatic twin platform doors. Twenty of these were later converted to electric motors—eighteen for passenger service and two as sand cars. Later, all of these twenty were converted to sand cars and as such lasted up to the late 1930's. The remaining ten must have been destroyed in the car house fire of December 3, 1898.

No doubt rapid expansion, expensive and fruitless experiments, as well as a District Commissioner's order for increased headways on all lines contributed to the appointment of a receiver on September 21, 1896. W. K. Schoepf, who was later to attain fame as a midwestern interurban **magnate**, was named receiver for both the Eckington and Soldiers' Home and the Belt.*

Congress had, by an act dated June 10, 1896, directed the Eckington and Soldiers' Home (and the Belt Railway) to equip their existing horse car lines with compressed air motors. Three months were allowed to determine the practicality of the compressed air motors. If successful, the conversion was to be done within six months of the act; otherwise, the companies were to convert to underground conduit within eighteen months.

As a result of the June act, the company had ordered ten compressed air motors from H. K. Porter and Company of Pittsburgh. Then in September, receivership ensued and the court refused to authorize expenditures for the air motors.

Mr. Schoepf, still mindful of the Congressional requirement, but with no funds, worked out an agreement with the Compressed Air Power Company. Under the agreement, Compressed Air Power agreed to lend a car with a Headley-Knight compressed air system installed. Thus for about a

---

*W. Kesley Schoepf (1864-1927) became a leading figure in the industry. His first electric railway position was as chief engineer of the Rock Creek Railway. Later he was Vice President of the Eckington and Soldiers' Home and the Belt and then their receiver. From Washington he went to Cincinnati and became a major force in the vast Ohio Electric Railway. At retirement in 1925 he was president of both the Cincinnati Traction Company and the Cincinnati Car Company. He retained the latter position until his death. Electric Railway Journal, Vol. 66 (1925), p. 804; and Vol. 69 (1927), p. 887.

$500.00 expenditure for freight and a compressor, Schoepf was able to begin experiments March 10, 1897.

The first car, number 91, carried air at 2000 lbs. per square inch in thirty-four reservoirs which had to be charged once each trip at the power house which was at Eckington. In addition, the car was equipped with a coke heater to heat the air before it entered the cylinders, both to prevent freezing and for greater efficiency.

The coke heater was not satisfactory and the Receiver therefore prevailed on Compressed Air to supply another car with a hot-water heater. This second car, number 400, arrived in June and was run on regular schedules.

Mr. Schoepf stated in May that the experiments were so successful that fifteen cars were ordered. His enthusiasm wasn't matched by the public however. There were complaints of dust from the exhaust, and heat, smoke and smell from the heating device. In addition, the cars were noted for the inability to make the grade on Eckington Place at Quincy Street.

The experiment was soon abandoned probably due to poor public reception and the impracticality of having to recharge the cars each trip.[6]

The Rock Creek Railway

On June 23, 1888, a few days after the Eckington and Soldiers' Home was granted its original charter, the Rock Creek Railway of the District of Columbia was chartered. The Chevy Chase Land Company was chartered in Maryland to build the proposed Maryland portion of the line. The principal owner of both companies was Senator Francis G. Newlands of Nevada.

The Rock Creek's history is important at this point because of its construction of a conduit electric system at the city end of its line. The original charter required a substantial iron bridge, to be open to the public, not less than fifty feet wide, across Rock Creek Valley. The company also constructed a similar though smaller bridge across Klingle Valley. There were a number of route amendments to the original charter. Suffice it to say that when it was put in operation in 1892, the route was relatively simple.

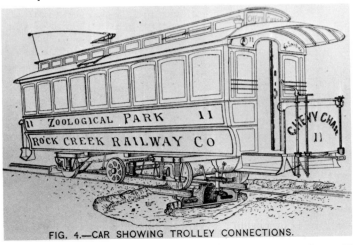

FIG. 4.—CAR SHOWING TROLLEY CONNECTIONS.

Love electric conduit system. From "Street Railway Journal", June, 1893.

The original route opened was from a point in 18th Street about one hundred feet north of U Street, up what was later 18th Street, Calvert Street, across Rock Creek Valley, and up what was later Connecticut Avenue to Chevy Chase Lake, Maryland. This opened September 16, 1892.

There was also a line on Florida Avenue running west along Florida Avenue from 18th Street to Connecticut Avenue. This portion of the road, however, was not electrified but operated with horsecars. It's probable that this was a double track shuttle operation, which could be handled with one Metropolitan Railroad horsecar.

It appears that this operation, owned by Rock Creek and operated by Metropolitan, was thought of as the first main line of the Rock Creek but, of course, never so used. The apparent configuration of the line at the east end was a double track curve north into 18th Street and joint track to a crossover. The west (or Connecticut Avenue) end of the line probably became single track before turning south into the Metropolitan line.

On March 26, 1896, Metropolitan began construction of its extension from Florida Avenue north. It was at this time that the Florida Avenue line ceased, but the exact date is unknown.

In addition to Rock Creek's main line there was a branch at the zoo which ran to the bears' den where there was a waiting shed. This branch, however, was never operated due to a severe grade which, it was felt, precluded safe oooperation.

The line was constructed with T rail on wood ties cut mostly along the right-of-way. Trolley line poles were of wood in the center of the double track line.

In May, 1893, as permitted by the charter, the line was extended east on U Street to about 150 feet east of 7th Street. At that time, Boundary Street (later Florida Avenue) was considered the city limits. Overhead trolley, was of course, prohibited, so the new extension was operated by the Love Conduit System. This required a plow pit in 18th Street for changing to underground conduit from overhead operation inbound and the reverse outbound. This was Washington's first conduit operation.

Originally, the Love system consisted of two trolley wires under the slot rail with tension springs every five hundred feet. This didn't work out too well, and they were soon replaced by U-shaped copper bars thirty-one and one-half feet long. The available description leads us to the conclusion that, although crude, this was a practical forerunner of the later Washington conduit system.

The company had two powerhouses. One, between 17th and 18th on Champlain Street N.W., was used exclusively for the conduit portion of the road. The other, at Chevy Chase Lake, generated current for the suburban portion.[7]

The Rock Creek opened service with twenty-five cars. There were twelve closed motors with Lamokin bodies. Six of them were single truckers and six were larger cars on Robinson Radial trucks. There were six Lamokin open trailers and six ex-Washington and Georgetown Stephenson closed trailers (ex-horsecars) and one double-truck freight motor.

FRANCIS G. NEWLANDS,
PRESIDENT.

EDW. J. STELLWAGEN,
VICE-PRESIDENT.

HOWARD S. NYMAN,
SECRETARY.

THOS. M. GALE,
TREASURER.

Rock Creek Railway Company,

OFFICE, 1324 F STREET NORTHWEST.

Washington, D. C., Jan. 27, 1893. , 189

General Order No. 1 .

From and after this date and until further orders,
Mr. Edward J. Stellwagen, Vice President of the Rock Creek Railway Company will have the active management of the affairs and
conduct of the business of the Company under the general direction
of the Board of Directors, and in all matters ordinarily per-
taining to the office of and requiring the action of the President
his decision shall be final and considered the same as if that of
the President.

Francis G. Newlands
President.

Rock Creek Railway's bridge over Rock Creek, which was later known as Calvert Street Bridge. From an 1893 magazine article. "Electrical World," Library of Congress.

Country terminal of the Rock Creek Ry. Note the car barn with powerhouse to the rear. This location later became known as Chevy Chase Lake. "Electrical World," Library of Congress.

Rock Creek 12 and 6 on U Street in the early '90's. Note the unusual six-wheel Robinson radial truck and, on the right, the platform, a Thomson-Houston rheostat controller. From Charles Wagner.

Rock Creek had a curious numbering system. The single truck closed motors, as well as both the open and closed trailers, were numbered 1 through 6—thus they had three cars for each of those numbers.

Under authority of an Act of Congress dated March 1, 1895, the Rock Creek Railway on September 21 acquired the assets of the Washington and Georgetown Railroad Company and changed its name to the Capital Traction Company. The primary reason for the smaller Rock Creek's acquisition of the larger and more successful Washington and Georgetown was the fact that Rock Creek's charter had the more liberal provisions on capitalization. The W & G's charter, dating from 1862, limited its capital to $500,000, too small a figure for so successful a road. Rock Creek's charter, however, had no top limit. It was easier to use this method of merger than to get Congressional approval to increase W & G's capitalization.

Operationally, however, integration of Rock Creek and W and G didn't come until the conversion of the cable lines and the conversion of the Love conduit system on U Street to the system chosen for the rest of the electric lines. This would be accomplished by 1899.[8]

Underground Conduit Perfected

When the Metropolitan's storage battery experiment failed, the road was faced with loss of their franchise because of the Congressional statute of August 6, 1890, requiring replacement of horsepower. The Board, therefore, immediately sent a petition to Congress outlining the experiment and its failure and asking for more time. They proposed to construct an underground electric system on 9th Street and, if successful, to construct a similar system on the east-west line.

The *Washington Star* had conducted and continued to conduct a campaign against overhead wires of any kind. They had considered the old Boundary of Washington (later Florida Avenue) as the limit of tolerance. The Tenallytown and Eckington lines had exceeded that limit; and Congress had been successful, again probably at the *Star's* prodding, in making the Eckington road retreat.

The Metropolitan had gotten expert testimony to back up its position that cable for its main line was impractical because of numerous curves. No explanation was offered for the failure to use cable power on 9th Street. The company then entered a period which would prove difficult because of the feeling shared by the public and reinforced by the *Star* that they were insincere.

Theodore W. Noyes of the *Star* had been travelling in Europe and seen the Budapest conduit system in operation. This discovery was duly noted in the *Star* in October, 1892, and added fuel to its campaign to make Metropolitan and others update their systems with this practical form of elec-

wo 250 HP steam engines each driving two Thomson-Houston 90 w generators at Rock Creek's original power plant at the Maryland d of the line. "Electrical World", Library of Congress.

etropolitan horsecar 27 on Rock Creek's line on Boundary Street (Florida Avenue) between Connecticut Avenue and 18th Street. Author's llection.

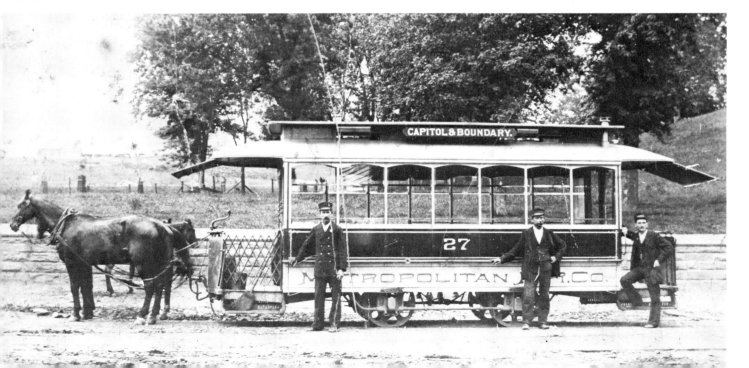

tric propulsion requiring no overhead wires.[9]

No one in this country had yet perfected a workable underground conduit system. Experiments had been carried out in Cleveland and Boston and with the Love system in Washington and Chicago. The Budapest system designed by the German firm of Siemens-Halske in 1889 had its conduit at one side of the track rather than between the two rails as it was with later systems in Washington, New York and London.

The Metropolitan Street Railway Company of New York had entered into a contract with General Electric for the installation of a conduit system. Interestingly, G.E. agreed to construct the line and allow the road to operate it for twelve months before acceptance. If the operation proved unsatisfactory at the end of that time, G.E. was to remove all its apparatus and receive no compensation.

Construction of the New York lines was commenced in September, 1894. The original route was a portion on Lenox Avenue about 4 7/8 miles long. The conduit was to be placed in the center for rather good reasons. The carriage wheel treads in America were as narrow as 3/4 inch, which is just sufficient width for the flange on the running rail. Thus, if the slot was placed next to the running rail, the width of the slot would have to exceed 3/4 inch which was impractical. It must also be remembered that New York, the first American installation, had many miles of cable track with a slot already in the middle. This fact was, of course, sufficient economic justification for the center slot.[10]

An Act of Congress dated August 2, 1894, required construction of an underground conduit system for the Metropolitan of Washington. The same Act called for the extension on East Capitol Street east around both sides of Lincoln Park to 15th and the extension northwesterly from 9th Street into Florida Avenue (old Boundary Street) to 10th and Florida.

An Act dated February 26, 1895, called for the loop at 4 1/2 and P Street S.W. (via 4 1/2, P Street, Water Street and L). It also called for the revision of trackage in Georgetown extended the loop from 35th and P Streets to 36th and Prospect. This Act also gave Metropolitan authority to contract with Rock Creek Railway for joint track on Florida Avenue between 9th and 7th. It's interesting to note that in those two blocks the new General Electric system shared the conduit with the Love system used by the Rock Creek Railway.

No doubt the Metropolitan management originated the idea for these Acts to grant authority for extensions thought necessary with the coming electrification. It must have taken an unusual amount of courage on their part to undertake the electrification even when one considers Congressional prodding.

Washington's Metropolitan started construction a month before New York's first operation, March 1, 1895. The first train operated on 9th Street for revenue service July 29, 1895.[11] Reports at the time described progress as vigorous,

and it was quite an accomplishment even though the contractors didn't have to put up with today's traffic. Temporary tracks for horsecar operation were provided on the side of the street while construction of the conduit system progressed.

The 9th Street line was a success, for construction started soon thereafter on conversion of the rest of the system. Georgetown-Lincoln Park service started June 30, 1896.[12] In connection with this electrification, a new barn was constructed at 14th and East Capitol Street. Cars destined to a loop which ran through this barn were always signed Lincoln Park.

Except for Connecticut Avenue and Boundary to Capitol cars, which were single, all Metropolitan electric operations were with two-car trains—motor and trailer. This fact called for a loop at 7th above Florida Avenue which was constructed in 1895 on the property where the Old Boundary and Silver Springs horsecar barn had been.

Each route's cars had its own distinctive color: Georgetown-Lincoln Park, green; Connecticut Avenue and Boundary Street to Capitol, yellow; and 9th Street trains were green. Destinations and routes were lettered on the side of the cars.

On September 29, 1896, a serious hurricane visited Washington. Metropolitan suffered when a portion of the new 4 1/2 Street barn's roof collapsed, resulting in severe damage to a number of the new 9th Street electric cars.[13]

The remaining history of the Metropolitan Railroad, as such, concerned two extensions. On March 26, 1896, construction began on an extension from Connecticut and Florida Avenue north along Columbia Road to 18th Street. Incidentally, this was not authorized by Congress until February 27, 1897.

On June 6, 1900, authority was granted by Congress for extension from 18th and Columbia Road to old 16th and Park via Columbia Road and old 16th Street (later Mt. Pleasant Street). This extension completed the Metropolitan's system.

Of interest is the fact that the entire system was conduit operated, and no cars had trolley poles with one exception. When the double truck "American" open cars arrived, they were pole-equipped for through operation to Glen Echo over the Washington and Great Falls.

Columbia's Cable Cars

While Metropolitan was considering the underground conduit system, so was the Columbia Railway Company. They had, in 1892, unsuccessfully experimented with a compressed air car furnished by the Hydro Pneumatic Company.

On January 4, 1893, Columbia's Board authorized a contract with the American Railway Construction Company of Chicago and an expenditure of $500,000 for installation of

Laying conduit track of the Metropolitan in the winter of 1895-6 at 5th and D Streets N.W. D Street is in the foreground and the track goes north on 5th Street along the line of buildings. From Charles Wagner.

ly 29, 1895. Brill-built Metropolitan electric train on P Street S.W. opens the underground conduit era in Washington on the 9th Street ie. Handy Studios, author's collection.

In the '90's, a Metropolitan Railroad open train turns from B Street N.E. into Delaware Avenue. Library of Congress.

Probably taken in 1896, this picture shows the interior of the new Metropolitan car barn at 4 1/2 and P Streets. This barn's roof collaps September 29, 1896. See next page. Handy Studios, author's collection.

a conduit system similar to Budapest's. The contract, however, was never signed. These events, of course, took place before General Electric's confident contract with New York's Metropolitan Street Railway.

Instead of electrification, on August 6, 1894, the stockholders authorized construction of a cable system; and on October 28, 1895, construction began.

The cable cars' short economic life has often been noted; but few examples better illustrate it than Columbia's experience. Construction of Columbia's cable line began almost three months after conduit electric operation on Metropolitan's 9th Street line.

A cable powerhouse was located at 15th and H Street N.E., and the company acquired twenty open and twenty closed cars built by John Stephenson in 1895. The cars were double-ended and operated singly rather than in trains. They were painted a striking royal blue with nickel ornamentation and silver lettering. The grips were wheel-operated rather than the usual lever. This equipment replaced forty-four horsecars and 180 horses.

On June 13, 1898, the Columbia was authorized to ex-

tend beyond 15th and H Street N.E. The Act called for a line east on Benning Road to the B & O Railroad, north along the B & O Railroad (on what later was Kenilworth Avenue) to Watts Creek. Here, one line went east under the Baltimore and Ohio and the Baltimore and Potomac Railroads to the eastern corner of the District. This end of the line became known as Chesapeake Junction* because it was the terminus of the Chesapeake Beach Railway, a steam line running excursion trains to Chesapeake Beach, Maryland. Later, Chesapeake Junction became Seat Pleasant. A branch called the Kenilworth line continued from Watts Creek along the B & O to the District line. The Act authorizing these extensions required a double trolley system. That is, the return circuit was to be via an additional overhead wire rather than through the rails. This circumstance, which applied to some but not all Washington overhead operations for a time, was an attempt to prevent electrolysis, or the corrosion of underground pipes from stray electric currents.*

When electric operation of the eastern end of the line became a fact, it seemed only sensible to have electric operation throughout. Since installation of Columbia's cable operation, conduit installations on both the Metropolitan and the Washington and Georgetown had proved successful. Therefore, despite the expense, Columbia converted to conduit operation less than four years after cable

*The electric railways in the area distinctly referred to this location as Chesapeake Junction. The Chesapeake Beach Rwy and the Baltimore and Ohio, however, used the term Chesapeake Junction to refer to the point near Kenilworth Avenue and Sheriff Road N.E. where their lines joined. Since this book deals with electric lines the former designation has been used.

terior of Metropolitan barn at 14th and East Capitol Streets. om "Street Railway Review", June 15, 1899.

*See page 136 for further information on double wire overhead.

Metropolitan's 4 1/2 and P Street barn showing roof collapse after storm of September 29, 1896. Author's collection.

Columbia Railway open grip car at the Stephenson plant. Museum of the City of New York.

Columbia Railway closed grip car 20. Frances B. Johnston Photo from Library of Congress.

One of Columbia's 60-69 series open electric cars. The picture, taken at American Car Company's plant in St. Louis, shows an American C[a] maximum traction truck. Actually these cars, at first, used Brill 27 trucks. One of Washington's most interesting group of cars, they we[re] later rebuilt to closed. One became Capital Transit 0509 which still exists as a relic. Author's collection.

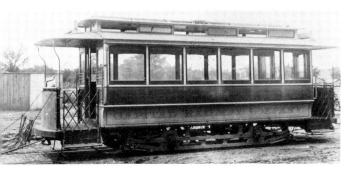

pital Railway 164 as renumbered by WRy & E Co. Potomac
ectric Power Company from Joseph J. Jessel.

pital Railway surface contact system at 8th and M Streets S.E.
vy Yard gate is on the left, and the Capital Traction car barn is
the right. Note surface contact plates between the rails in the
eground. Author's collection.

operation started! The last cable car operated July 23,
1899—it was the last one in Washington.

The cable cars were converted to electric motors, the
closed ones later became Washington Railway 200-219 and
the open ones 1300-1319.

Original operation after electrification was not a through
one. Change of cars was required at 15th and H N.E. The
electrified cable cars handled the western end of the line
while ten new double truck open motors Nos. 60-69 handled the eastern end.

Surface Contact Again—Capital Railway Company

Capital Railway made the last effort to find a substitute
for overhead trolley. Although the underground conduit
was practical at the time of its charter, March 2, 1895,
Capital felt that in a revival of the old surface contract
system they had a practical and less expensive answer.

Capital's charter called for a line (using cable, electric,
or other mechanical power) to run from a point on the

District Line near the Potomac River southeast of
Shepherd's Ferry over a route to be selected by the District
Commissioner's to the south bank of the Anacostia where
a transfer ferry would operate to the foot of South Capitol
or 1st and up the selected street to M. This route never came
into being, but the ferry operation is another of those interesting "might-have-been's."

The original Act was amended May 28, 1896. It called
for a line electrically operated underground in the city,
double overhead outside the city, from 8th and M Street
S.E. via M and 11th to the Navy Yard Bridge. At 8th and
M, of course, transfer could be made to Capital Traction.
Also authorized was a line up 11th Street to East Capitol
and a line east on Good Hope Road in Anacostia. Neither
of the latter two ever came into being. The line in Anacostia
actually followed the existing line of the A and P. It went
over the bridge and up Nichols Avenue to Congress Heights.
At that time, A and P horsecars terminated at a turntable
at the foot of Asylum Hill. Capital electric cars curved
around each side of this table to continue to Congress
Heights. Capital Railway constructed a small barn beyond
the hospital on the west side of the line—nothing pretentious, just an ordinary frame carbarn.

Capital installed a Brown Magnetic Surface Contact System from 8th to M S.E. to the Navy Yard Bridge. The
balance of the line was double wire overhead. The Brown
system was essentially similar to the Wheless system tried
on the Eckington and Soldiers' Home earlier in the decade.
Unfortunately, the contact plates sometimes remained energized after the passage of the car, creating a situation for
electrocution of horses, as well as men. This could never be
properly safe-guarded against and led to the very early
dismantling of the system. The installation contract was
dated March 22, 1897, and by January 30, 1899, the District Commissioners granted permission to open 11th and
M Streets for removal of the system.

Clearly the underground conduit system pioneered in
Washington by the Metropolitan was the solution to the
problem posed by Congress. By the end of the decade, both
the horse and the cable car would be supplanted by this
modern form of traction.

The search for underground conduit didn't slow the trolley boom on unaffected suburban lines. These were developing at a rapid pace.

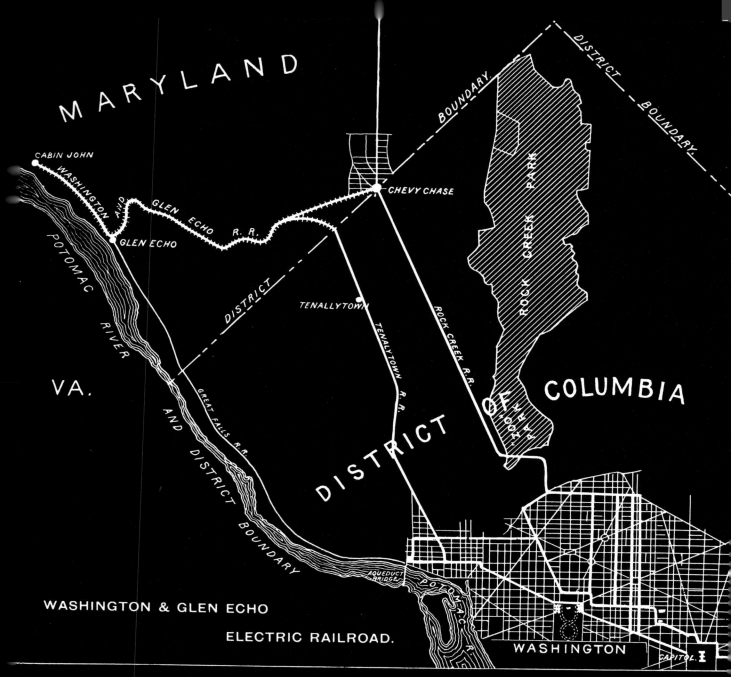

MARYLAND

CABIN JOHN

WASHINGTON AND

GLEN ECHO R.R.

GLEN ECHO

POTOMAC RIVER

VA.

GREAT FALLS R.R.

AND DISTRICT BOUNDARY

DISTRICT

TENALLYTOWN

TENALLYTOWN R.R.

DISTRICT

BOUNDARY

CHEVY CHASE

ROCK CREEK R.R.

ROCK CREEK PARK

100 FT.

COLUMBIA

OF

AQUEDUCT
BRIDGE

POTOMAC R.

WASHINGTON & GLEN ECHO

ELECTRIC RAILROAD.

WASHINGTON

CAPITOL

The Washington & Glen Echo Electric Railroad connects the upper Potomac River country, Glen Echo and Cabin John directly with the City of Washington, via the Metropolitan and Capital Traction Companies systems of roads, as shown on the above map. Glen Echo is the Rhine country of Washington, and distant seven miles from the city. Here the river, picturesque, wild and romantic, is shored by tall, abrupt, rock ribbed and forest covered hills, and filled with beautiful wooded islands, the music of the Little Falls below and the thunder of the Great Falls above. On the high bluffs, overlooking all this are the great buildings of Glen Echo, among which is the immense stone ampitheatre with its auditorium capacitated to hold 10,000 people, all happily nestling on the highland slopes and in the sylvan sounding glens. Beyond, is Cabin John Bridge, the terminal wonder attraction of the railroad. The route of the road is through a picturesque country, and a trip over it to this ideal river country and buildings and grounds, makes it one of the most fascinating of outings.

CHAPTER THREE
THE ELECTRIC CAR BOOM

The Georgetown and Tenallytown Railway Company of
the
District of Columbia

While the city lines' progress was slowed by the search for a more acceptable form of propulsion, no such restraint slowed the development of the suburban lines. At the dawn of the electric railway era, Washington's population was approximately 230,000. Transportation technology still, however, kept the population concentrated within the old boundaries of the city. Although Georgetown's separate existence had been ended in 1871, the city fathers still thought of the area north of Boundary Street (Florida Avenue) and all of Georgetown as being outside the city limits. Thus, when the Georgetown and Tenallytown was chartered, no restrictions were placed on the use of overhead trolley.

The Georgetown and Tenallytown Railway Company of the District of Columbia was chartered August 22, 1888, and was therefore one of the pioneer electric lines in the area. Its route was to be north from High Street and the Potomac River, via High Street and Tenallytown Road to the District Line. High Street and Tenallytown Road are both early names for Wisconsin Avenue.

Operation of the line commenced April 25, 1890. Original equipment consisted of a number of sixteen-foot Stephenson closed motors numbered from one up. It is not known how many cars were in this group. Original car color was light blue. This color lasted approximately five years after which it was changed to maroon. Car No. 1 had a six-window, vestibuled body and was equipped with two Thomson-Houston 20 HP motors. The Stephenson Company remarked that they were "in all their appointments the most complete and beautiful cars ever built by this company."[1]

Original Georgetown and Tenallytown track was in the middle of High Street to the present intersection of Calvert Street and Wisconsin Avenue. The line was double track north of the C & O Canal to the District Line, but at Calvert Street it moved to the east side of the road. Incidentally, at this point the name of the road changed to Tenallytown Road. The line continued to occupy the east side of the road until it reached Tenallytown Hill* (where River Road now intersects Wisconsin Avenue). Then the tracks went over to the west side of the road. These alignments continued until the 1920's when, in three projects, the "side of the road" portions were moved to the middle of Wisconsin Avenue.

Tenallytown Hill is the highest natural spot in the District of Columbia. Of course, the line started at the level of the Potomac River so the outbound trip was mostly upgrade

and, for Washington, rather severe grades. The barn and power plant were on the east side of the road at the intersection of what is now Wisconsin Avenue and Calvert Street. It was constructed on a lot about one and a half stories below street grade. The main portion was actually the second story and was a little above street level. Three tracks emerged from the barn, one from the north side turning north into the northbound main and the other two converging as they descended the ramp to join the northbound main in a southerly direction. There was a trailing crossover between the two mains to allow shifting of cars to the southbound track. The basement contained a shop which must have been reached by an elevator. On the main floor there was a transfer table at the rear.

Outside the barn building proper and to the rear of the lot was a steam power plant and water reservoir. The power plant burned Cumberland coal which came to Georgetown on C & O Canal boats. The boats ran to the end of the canal, through Rock Creek west to a dock a little west of High Street and the Potomac River. From there the coal was hauled on single-truck flat cars with sideboards behind a double truck motor coal car to the powerhouse. There, coal cars were run to the rear of the barn there there must have been a coal chute to the basement.

In the summer of 1895, one of these loaded trailers got away at the barn crossover and came to Georgetown on the northbound track. Fortunately, warning was phoned ahead—the only opposing vehicle was the usual afternoon passenger motor hauling a trailer loaded with supplies from Georgetown stores for persons living on the line. The runaway met this train between Dumbarton Avenue and N Street, and the resulting collision was the subject of conversation for many months. One of the lighter stories to come out of the accident—a store clerk wanted to know the fate of the crate of eggs he had just loaded.

The G & T suffered at least one other runaway when a

---

*The original name "Tenallytown" derived from Sarah Tenally. Miss Tenally died without heirs in the early 1800's. In 1922, the opening of a Post office brought forth a petition from a Charles Tenley who believed that Tenally was a corruption of Tenley and that the Post Office naming should correct the matter. Though the records seem to substantiate the earlier spelling, probably due to Mr. Tenley's efforts and the easier spelling of Tenleytown, the newer spelling has become official. The Traction companies used the older spelling as late as 1932 and I have followed their example. Undated (1922) newspaper clipping in the files of Robert A. Truax.

Georgetown and Tenallytown barn on the east side of Wisconsin Avenue at Calvert Street. The picture, taken probably in 1900, shows two ex-Columbia 60-69 series center aisle open motors in the barn. Potomac Electric Power Company from Joseph J. Jessel.

Georgetown and Tenallytown 9 ready for a run to Tenallytown on Wisconsin Avenue at M Street N.W. From Charles Wagner.

orgetown and Tenallytown 4. A closed platform car otherwise similar to 1 at the Stephenson plant. Which of the original cars had closed
tforms is unknown. Museum of the City of New York.

Georgetown and Tenallytown 1 at the Stephenson plant in New York City. Museum of the City of New York.

closed passenger motor got away on the hill below the canal and landed in the boathouse at the end of the street.

Shortly before the opening of the G & T, the Tenallytown and Rockville Railroad was chartered. The Maryland Assembly on March 5, 1890, authorized it to construct a road from the end of the G & T (later Wisconsin Avenue and the District Line) to what was later Alta Vista, via Rockville Pike and Old Georgetown Road. During the same period, a third road, the Glen Echo Railroad, chartered in Maryland on December 12, 1889, was placed in operation June 10, 1891. Its route was from what was later Wisconsin Avenue and Willard west to Glen Echo and Cabin John.

At Willard Avenue and Wisconsin Avenue there was a one-story pie-shaped frame transfer station known as "The Junction." The point of the "pie," so to speak, was south. Glen Echo cars used the west platform while Georgetown cars and T & R cars shared the east side. An apartment at the rear housed an Italian family who ran a refreshment stand in the stand in the station. Here, surely, was an interesting trolley center of the early days.

The Tenallytown and Rockville as chartered ran north along the east side of Rockville Pike (now Wisconsin Avenue) from the Junction to Old Georgetown Road. The route was then along the east side of Old Georgetown Road to Bethesda (now Alta Vista), a distance of 3.75 miles. At the end of the line on the west side of the road was an amusement park, Bethesda Park. The park included the usual amusements—roller coaster, merry-go-round, bowling alley, shooting galleries, etc. An 1894 guide to Washington entitled *A Glimpse at the Night Side of Washington* had this to say: "Bethesda Park Railroad. From terminus of Tenallytown Railroad northwest to Bethesda Park, 6 1/2 miles from the city, fare only 10 cents from Georgetown. Dancing at the Park every Tuesday and Thursday evenings. Refreshments, games, coaster, nine pins, etc.''

The line was single track throughout with one siding about midway on Old Georgetown Road and another at the Bethesda terminal. The company had no barn, shop or power station. Out-of-service cars were stored at the Bethesda Terminal while the car operating at night was probably parked near the motorman's home. Georgetown and Tenallytown supplied the power and conducted repairs to road or rolling stock.

In April, 1895, the *Street Railway Journal* reported that the Georgetown and Tenallytown had been bought by a syndicate including Oscar T. Crosby who started his career as an assistant to Frank Sprague on the Richmond project. His acquisition, along with Charles A Lieb, of the Georgetown and Tenallytown was the first of a series of acquisitions that eventually culminated in the formation of the Washington Railway and Electric Company. In June, 1896, the property of T & R was sold under foreclosure to Crosby for $36,500. Crosby conveyed the property to the Washington and Rockville Railway of Montgomery County (chartered September 8, 1897) on November 13, 1897. Crosby now controlled the entire route from Georgetown to Rockville. Legally speaking the Georgetown & Tenally-

town existed as a separate entity until October 27, 1926; but from an operational standpoint, it was now one with the T & P.

On September 29, 1896, a hurricane struck the Washington area. The park at Bethesda was destroyed by fallen trees and never reopened. Although there is no written proof of any cars being destroyed, Georgetown and Tenallytown cars operated the line from the time of the hurricane onward. The company's Robinson Radial car was seen after the hurricane at Bethesda on the west side of the road, a derelict.

Sharing the Wisconsin and Willard terminal with the other two roads was the Glen Echo Railroad, comprising two branches—the Tenallytown and Chevy Chase lines. It was chartered December 12, 1889, and was placed in operation June 10, 1891. The original line ran from the terminal west to Sycamore store at Walhonding and Conduit Roads. The route followed what was later Willard Avenue and Walhonding Road to the store. It was single track from the junction to the point where it joined the double track Chevy Chase-Conduit Road line. This line was rock ballasted with center poles.

From Sycamore store to Glen Echo and Cabin John the route was in line with the Washington aqueduct. The aqueduct was controlled by the U.S. Army Engineers who, in turn, supervised construction of the road in the area of the aqueduct. Engineer control over construction made progress on this portion of the line slower than the rest, so it wasn't until April 1, 1896, that operation began to Glen Echo. Operation to Cabin John began a month later.

A substantial stone car barn was erected a short distance east of the Conduit Road-Walhonding Road intersection. A powerhouse was in the rear of the building. Ruins of this building were visible up until the sixties.

On August 3, 1896, the name of this railroad was changed to The Washington and Glen Echo Railroad Company.

In July, 1897, the Chevy Chase branch opened. This line crossed the line of Wisconsin Avenue at about Oliver Street and ran cross-country to a location at about Connecticut Avenue and the District Line. There was a station there, and the track ended in a stub. Although there was no physical connection, transfer could be made with cars of the Rock Creek Railway.

The Tenallytown branch became superfluous, as will be seen by the map. The new Chevy Chase branch crossed the T & R affording transfer convenience without the extra track of the Willard Avenue route. Consequently, on November 15, 1897, operation was discontinued on the Tenallytown branch.

The Washington and Glen Echo Railroad was always closely allied with the Georgetown and Tenallytown. G & T transported coal for the Glen Echo powerhouse. Glen Echo cars were painted and repaired at the G & T barn on Wisconsin Avenue.

The fall of 1900 saw the demise of the Glen Echo Railroad as such, a rather early abandonment. That portion of the Glen Echo from Walhonding Road west to Cabin John

Jackson and Sharp-built 12 of the Washington and Glen Echo. Robert A. Truax collection.

Glen Echo car barn east of Conduit and Walhonding Roads, looking east. Handy Studios, author's collection.

survived to form the outer end of the line of that name. It had become, through Oscar Crosby's ownership, a part of the West Washington and Great Falls Road. When Glen Echo was abandoned, Crosby transferred all the remaining Glen Echo equipment to the Georgetown and Tenallytown. These were as follows:

6 Jackson & Sharp 12-bench open motors, double truck
2 Jackson & Sharp 10-bench open motors, single truck
1 Jones 8-bench open motor, ex-E & SH
1 #21 ex-E & SH closed storage battery car

At the same time, four Washington, Woodside and Forest Glen Railroad twenty-foot single-truck vestibuled closed motors were transferred to the G & T.

Now to return to the remainder of the line to Rockville. Rockville was then essentially a farming community and county seat of Montgomery County, Maryland. In discussing the Tenallytown and Rockville above we left the history at the time Crosby bought it at foreclosure and conveyed the property to the Washington and Rockville Railway Company. At that point, its northern terminal was Alta Vista (Bethesda Park).

The line was extended to Rockville and placed in operation April 8, 1900. The original terminal was at the south edge of town opposite the fair grounds. The City Council was unable to agree at first on a franchise for the company through the town. Soon, however, agreement was reached, though the exact date is not known, for the line actually was extended single track through Montgomery Avenue to the vicinity of Chestnut Lodge Sanitarium which was at the other end of town.

Some early operational problems were encountered for we find that on May 14, 1900, little over a month after opening, a car jumped the track near Halpine, two miles east of Rockville.

Early equipment of the Rockville line gave evidence of financial control which culminated in the formation of the Washington Railway and Electric Company.

First equipment was ten American double-truck center aisle open motors purchased in 1899 by the Columbia Railway for Chesapeake Junction service. These cars, Nos. 60-69, were remodeled from four-motor to two-motor, mounted on St. Louis #21 maximum traction trucks, rewired for single wire overhead in lieu of double, freshly painted and renumbered 1500-1509. The livery of dark blue with silver trim was unchanged. These were the original open motors of the line.

During the Rockville Fair each fall, 1600 series open motors, singly or coupled in two-car trains were used. The two-car train feature was a dispatching matter and not a true multiple-unit operation; two crews were used.

The first closed cars were several of the 40 series cars of the City and Suburban. These were ten-window open platform panel side cars which later became 410-419. A little later, several of the C & S 420-424 series cars were used. These were center aisle open motors remodeled to closed cars. Anacostia and Potomac 350 was regularly seen on the line, also. Spliced cars 501-506 were used in short route service to West Chevy Chase.

Still later in the same winter the four lowest numbered 1500's were remodeled to closed with the blue livery and the same numbers. In the spring of 1901, the remaining six 1500's were remodeled to closed, and all appeared in Washington Railway standard cadmium yellow and cream with

Washington Railway and Electric 508, an ex-Columbia 60-69 series open car, at Wisconsin Avenue just below M Street in Georgetown, November 4, 1907. Photo by LeRoy O. King, Sr.

black lettering, renumbered 507-516.[2] These cars served the Rockville line until the arrival in 1908 of the notable 585 series railroad roof cars.

Brightwood Electrification[3]

After failure of the Judson Pneumatic experiments, Brightwood prevailed on Congress to amend the charter to allow an overhead trolley system. This same charter

ockville line right of way south of its intersection with Route 240
out 1909. Harvey Davison collection.

amendment, dated July 26, 1892, authorized what was to become the Takoma Park branch. The following year, February 27, 1893, an act authorized another extension along Richmond Street to Rock Creek Church Road. This later became the Soldiers' Home line and Richmond Street became Upshur Street.

At Kenyon Street a line was authorized west via Kenyon and Marshall to 14th Street. This branch featured unusual construction: the poles were beside the track in the vehicle roadway instead of the usual arrangement of having poles at the side of the road with span wires. The arrangement was cumbersome even for horse and buggy days and would, of course, be hard to imagine under today's traffic conditions. No source is available to tell whether this ran as a Brightwood-14th and Kenyon shuttle or a connection between 7th and Boundary and 14th and Kenyon. This portion, however, lasted only five years, for authority for its dismantling is found under an act dated July 7, 1898.

Brightwood Railway's barn was on the east side of Georgia Avenue between Gallatin and Farragut Streets. On January 24, 1895, in an event that often seems inevitable in street railway history, this barn was destroyed by fire. This was Washington's earliest known car barn fire, though by no means the last nor the largest. The company lost fourteen cars. In May of the same year, a permit was sought to construct a new barn. This one was nine blocks north on the east side of Georgia Avenue between Peabody and Concord. This new barn was to be an integral part of the Washington traction scene until September 10, 1950, when it ceased to be an operating division. It was always known as the Brightwood Barn.

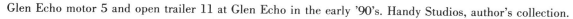

Glen Echo motor 5 and open trailer 11 at Glen Echo in the early '90's. Handy Studios, author's collection.

Washington Railway and Electric 29, ex-Brightwood 1, at the rear of the P Street shops in 1908. Phot
by LeRoy O. King, Sr.

Brightwood Railway 10 on Georgia Avenue (near Florida Avenue) in the early '90's. From Charles Wagner.

Ticket is blue on white card stock. Author's collection.

Brightwood Railway 44 at Jackson and Sharp plant. This car later became Washington, Arlington and Falls Church 77. Author's collection.

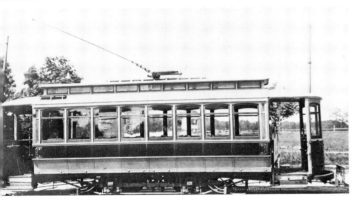

One of Washington, Woodside and Forest Glen's 1-4 series. Potomac Electric Power Company from Joseph J. Jessel.

The Washington, Woodside and Forest Glen Railway Power Company

On August 2, 1895, the Washington, Woodside and Forest Glen Railway Power Company was organized in Montgomery County, Maryland. Its purpose was to construct a line from the end of the Brightwood at the District Line to Forest Glen. It crossed the B & O at grade beside the Silver Spring Station and proceeded via Woodside to Forest Glen. The principal feature of the line was the National Park Seminary. The road crossed the grounds of this fashionable girls school which was at the site subsequently remodeled as an annex for the Walter Reed Army Medical Center.

Original equipment of the Forest Glen Road were four Brill single-truck closed motors numbered 1-4. Original color was green of the same shade as that used by Metropolitan.

As might be expected, the Forest Glen road and the Brightwood, at an early date, coordinated their operations. An act of Congress of June 29, 1898, gave the Woodside road the right to run its cars over the tracks of the Brightwood Railway.

In 1899, the two roads had together eleven motor cars and three trailers. Forest Glen cars were operated on a fifteen-minute headway and the Brightwood cars ten-minute.

The Washington Traction and Electric Company, organized by Oscar Crosby in 1899, acquired control of the Brightwood Railway and the Washington Woodside and Forest Glen by means of stock and mortgage bond ownership in substantial but not majority holdings. W T & E planned re-equipping the lines with new cars and track. The original power plant at the car barn site was replaced by two General Electric rotary transformers of 150 kilowatt capacity each. Thus, power supplied by Potomac Electric Power Company (another W T & E property) at 6500 volts was converted to 600 volts for railway use.

Although control passed to the Washington Railway and Electric Company in 1902, Brightwood Railway continued as a corporate entity until December 21, 1912, while the Forest Glen line lasted as a separate company until November 1, 1915. In order to simplify Washington Railway's corporate structure, the Brightwood was absorbed by the parent while the Forest Glen line was consolidated with the Washington Railway and Electric's wholly-owned Washington and Rockville Railway Company of Montgomery County.

Operationally, both roads were integrated with the parent in 1902. Only one Brightwood car, No. 20, was taken into the Washington Railway and Electric Company roster; however, 1-4 of the Forest Glen line were all acquired by Washington Railway.

Washington and Great Falls Electric Railway Company
West Washington and Great Falls Electric Railway Company

Three big changes in Washington's traction picture took place in the last years of the 90's: the growth of suburban lines; the adoption of underground conduit for city lines; the emergence of two large systems in place of many small ones. Rock Creek's merger with Washington and Georgetown to form Capital Traction has been recounted. The Washington and Great Falls is important as a major suburban line, but perhaps even more important is Oscar Crosby's use of it as a corporate device for merger. These merger activities culminated in the formation of the Washington Railway and Electric Company.

The Washington and Great Falls Electric Railway Company was incorporated under authority of an Act of Congress approved July 29, 1892.

The original authority called for a line from a point west of the north end of the Aqueduct bridge over Canal Road starting on an iron elevated structure and thence west on the bluff at the north side of Canal Road to Cabin John Bridge, Maryland. The elevated structure was planned to terminate in the new Capital Traction Union Terminal, and there was a door in the west wall of the building at second-floor level for entry of the Great Falls car. Much of the line was on lands of the Washington Aqueduct, and the company was required to deposit $5,000 with the Treasurer of the United States to protect the Government from any expenses incurred in the construction of the road.

An act of August 23, 1894, amended the route so that it began on top of the bluff at 36th and Prospect and continued west on the bluff rather than on the expensive elevated structure suggested by the original charter. Thus the proposed entry into second floor of the Capital Traction Union Station was eliminated. This act also required completion to the District Line in twelve months and to Cabin John by eighteen months.

Actual completion of the road to the District Line was accomplished by September 28, 1895. The line ended, for a time, in a two-track shed at that point. At the Georgetown end, the double-track line went over to the south side of Prospect Street in the rear of the 36th and M Street building which later served as D C Transit's general office. An ex-Metropolitan 9th Street closed horsecar (red dash - bombay roof) served as a waiting room at the end of the westbound track which was at the west building line of 36th There must have been a crossover west of the terminal to enable westbound cars to return to the westbound track.

On October 2, 1895, a contract was signed with the Georgetown and Tenallytown for power supply.

When the line was first opened, at one point, location now unknown, it went right through an existing and operating dairy barn—with cows on both sides of the line! This line, which later became the best known suburban line in Washington, was, by virtue of its location, one of the more scenic trolley rides in the country. After leaving 38th and Prospect and passing over the first trestle, the road entered private right-of-way high on a bluff overlooking the Potomac River. There were a number of high trestles, very few road crossings, and lots of heavy wooded countryside interrupted by delightful and impressive views of the Potomac River Valley. At Glen Echo, there was a Chatauqua—an institution as close to the trolley as the amusement park of a few years later. At Cabin John there was an amusement park, while between Georgetown and the District Line there was the International Athletic Club which featured a bicycle racetrack.

The original equipment of the line was interesting from many aspects. An original roster was:

1 - 4   25' 9-window double-truck closed motors

(two by St. Louis, two by Laconia) identical to similar cars built at the same time for West End Street Railway, Boston. The two Laconias were the only ones ever in Washington. All four cars were from a Boston order. A sign on the side of the roof just above the letterboard read, "Palisades of the Potomac." Color was brick red.

20 - 36   Standard Jackson and Sharp 10-bench single-truck open motors. Brick red.

5 - Jackson and Sharp 18' closed motor single-truck. Yellow.

Some of the 20-36 group were operated as trailers (without motors) when new. They were trailed behind similar cars with motors. Later all were equipped with motors.

As originally built the road was single track with turnouts. Curiously, the track was laid in the middle of the right-of-way rather than to one side. The passing sidings were made with "Y" switches such that the sidings were both equidistant from the center of the right-of-way.

In the early days cars were held at the District Line while an inspector counted heads to compare the number of passengers with the number of fares collected.

Congress apparently felt that, because of the involvement of the Washington Aqueduct in the route of the line, they could authorize the entire route. Some legal problem must have arisen because, before work on the Maryland portion could take place, a Maryland corporation had to be chartered. Accordingly, Jacob Clark, Lee Hutchins, Edward Baltzley, Daniel A. Grovenor and William De Welt incorporated the West Washington and Great Falls Electric Railway Company under the laws of Maryland on November 1, 1895.

June 3, 1896, was the date of an Act of Congress authorizing an extension leaving the main line at Chain Bridge and going east to the Georgetown and Tenallytown line at River and Loughboro Roads. Also provided for was a loop at the Georgetown end. Neither extension ever was accomplished. The act required electric lights from sundown to midnight at all road crossings, a feature which lasted until abandonment.

Under provisions of this act and companion legislation in Maryland, the two companies, the Washington and Great Falls and the West Washington and Great Falls, were allowed to merge. On July 1, 1896, the assets of the West Washington road were conveyed to the Washington and Great Falls Electric Railway Company. The year 1896 was also the date for construction of the Falls barn which was located just west of 38th and Prospect. Although both of those companies had included the goal of "Great Falls" in their plans and corporate titles, it remained for yet a third railway some seventeen years later to actually reach the Maryland side of the scenic falls on the Potomac.

History records that the road operated several years at a loss. In the early days of the line a contract was negotiated with the Metropolitan to provide for through tickets. Under

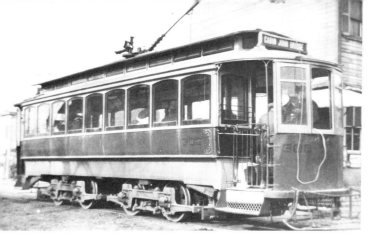

Washington Railway and Electric 300 (ex-Washington and Great Falls 1) enroute to Cabin John Bridge at 36th and Prospect Streets N.W. about 1906. Photo by LeRoy O. King, Sr.

the summer of 1909, one of the ex-Washington and Great Falls Jackson and Sharp open cars lays
er at Union Station. Photo by LeRoy O. King, Sr.

ne Falls barn in early Washington Railway and Electric days about 1908. Open car is one of the ex-Glen Echo 7-12 series
hile the closed car is one of the ex-Washington and Great Falls 1-4 series. Potomac Electric Power Company from Joseph J.
ssel.

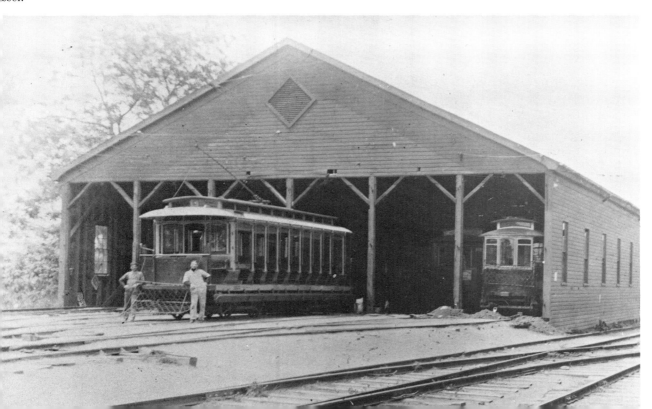

this arrangement, Washington and Great Falls sold strips of tickets for five cents, each of which had two coupons—one for each road. The Great Falls road agreed to redeem coupons collected by the Metropolitan at two and a half cents each.

Two significant events occurred in 1899: the double tracking of the W & GF as far as Glen Echo along with replacement of seven wooden trestles with steel ones; and the chartering of the Washington Traction and Electric Company in Norfolk, Virginia.

In 1899 the company sought to eliminate the inconvenience of transferring passengers between the separate lines at 36th and Prospect. A track connection was installed and on May 16, 1900, one of the classic 14-bench open cars of the Metropolitan which became later the W Rwy's 1600's made a trial run from Lincoln Park to Cabin John to inaugurate the new summer service. However, it was not until January 29, 1902, that a formal contract providing for joint operations was signed whereby cars of either company operated on through schedules in regular service. Each company collected all fares on its own cars but paid two cents for each passenger carried on the other's line.

In the fall of 1900, operation ended on the Glen Echo Railroad except for that portion running from Walhonding Road to Cabin John. This part became an integral part of the Washington and Great Falls.

On June 5, 1899, articles of incorporation of the Washington Traction and Electric Company were filed in the Corporation Court of the city of Norfolk, Virginia, and a charter secured from that Court. This concern set about to acquire through stock ownership a number of Washington properties. They were:

> The Anacostia and Potomac River Railroad
>   Company
> Brightwood Railway Company
> City and Suburban Railway of Washington
> Columbia Railway Company
> Georgetown and Tenallytown Railway Company
> Metropolitan Railroad Company
> Washington and Rockville Railway Company
> Washington, Woodside and Forest Glen Railway
>   and Power Company
> Washington and Glen Echo Railroad Company
> United States Lighting Company
> Potomac Electric Power Company

Washington Traction, on June 14, 1899, executed a mortgage to the United States Mortgage and Trust Company to guarantee payment of the principal and interest on an issue of $20,000,000 of its bonds and deposited with the Mortgage the securities of the several companies held by Stevens, Crosby and Lieb.

The Washington Traction and Electric Company then started in business by opening up an investment account comprised of stock of the subsidiary companies of a par

On a summer day, probably in 1910, Washington Railway and Electric 1606, an ex-Metropolitan 400, is about to leave Lincoln Park car house for a run to popular Glen Echo Park. Photo by LeRoy O. King, Sr.

WASHINGTON & GREAT FALLS ELECTRIC RAILWAY

FROM UNION STATION WEST WASHINGTON TO

THE PALISADES OF THE POTOMAC,

INTERNATIONAL ATHELETIC PARK,

BROOKMONT, GLEN ECHO,

AND

CABIN JOHN BRIDGE.

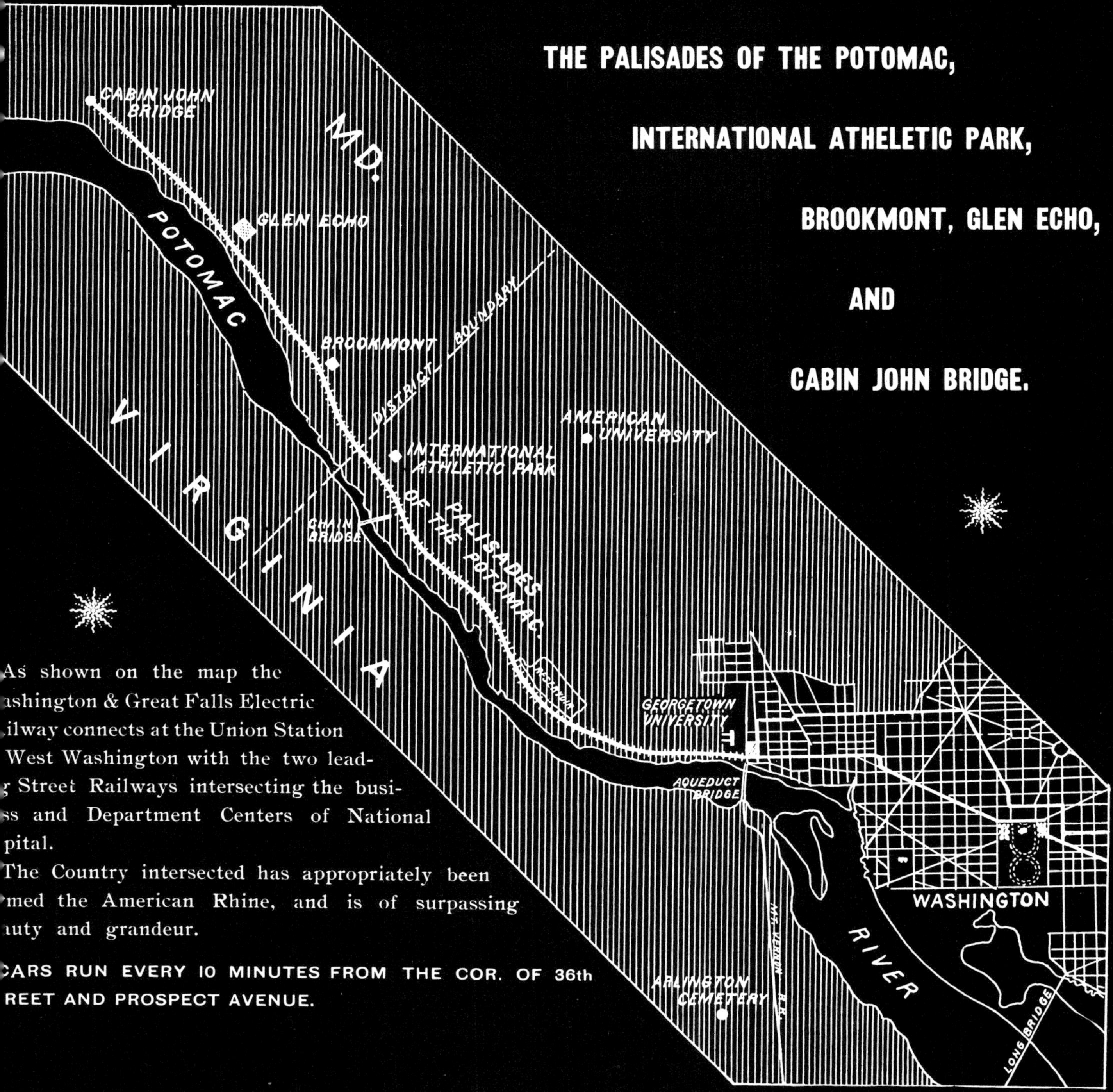

As shown on the map the
ashington & Great Falls Electric
ilway connects at the Union Station
West Washington with the two lead-
g Street Railways intersecting the busi-
ss and Department Centers of National
pital.

The Country intersected has appropriately been
med the American Rhine, and is of surpassing
uty and grandeur.

CARS RUN EVERY 10 MINUTES FROM THE COR. OF 36th
REET AND PROSPECT AVENUE.

Robert A. Truax Collection

value of $5,770,500; bonds of the face value of $1,327,000; promissory notes of a face value of $200,000. In consideration of the above, plus cash in the amount of $1,080,000, the new company issued its capital stock for $10,000,000 and 4 1/2 per cent first mortgage bonds for $12,000,000.

The company met the first year's interest (from June 1, 1899, to June 1, 1900) on the first issue of $12,000,000 of its bonds by using $540,000 of the $1,080,000 cash received from the United States Mortgage and Trust Company at the time of the issuance to that company of that amount of bonds and $2,500,000 of stock; that is, cash to pay the first year's interest on its original issue of $12,000,000 of bonds was obtained as part of the proceeds of the sale of the bonds and stocks themselves. The foreclosure suit so often referred to in the case of the Washington Traction and Electric was a result of its failure to pay the semi-annual interest on its bonds due June 1, 1901. As a result of this suit, the property of the Washington Traction and Electric Company was ordered sold under foreclosure proceeding before the United States Circuit Court at Norfolk, Virginia, on November 6, 1901.[4]

Although Washington Traction and Electric was short-lived, it did take a number of steps to integrate the system, such as the loop at F, 11th, 9th and G; connections at Wisconsin and O, Wisconsin and P and many other points as well as at 36th and Prospect as mentioned above. Through routes such as 11th and Florida to Anacostia and LeDroit Park to Wharves were set up.

The Metropolitan and the Columbia were the financially successful properties acquired. Washington Traction and Electric thus had to purchase these two properties on the owners' terms while the others were either leased or controlled through stock ownership.

Meanwhile, the Board of the Washington and Great Falls Electric Railway was active in positioning itself for eventual control of the railways involved with the Washington Traction and Electric.

An Act of June 5, 1900, allowed the Great Falls road to acquire stock in any other road and make other agreements for joint or one-management operation. The fare, incidentally, was now established at six tickets for twenty-five cents.

On January 31, 1902, the Board resolved to change the name of the company to the Washington Railway and Electric Company effective February 1, 1902. On this same date, the company entered into a contract with Samuel Lawrence (representing the Washington Traction and Electric) to purchase Washington Traction and Electric's stock holdings in the various lines listed above.

The City and Suburban Railway Company of the District of Columbia

Concurrent with the development of the Washington and Great Falls, the Eckington and Soldiers' Home was developing into a major suburban electric line. It, too, began to get involved in financial changes leading to formation of Washington Railway and Electric.

In the 90's, talk arose of a line from Washington to Baltimore, entering Washington over the lines of the Eckington and Soldiers' Home, as well as the Belt, and these two lines were purchased by the Baltimore and Boulevard Company. This company had plans which didn't materialize for a high-speed interurban between the two cities.

The Columbia and Maryland Railway was chartered March 18, 1892, by the Maryland Legislature to build a double track road from Baltimore to Washington. A subsidiary of this road, the Edmondson Avenue, Catonsville and Ellicott City Electric Railway Company, was to provide the Baltimore entrance via Ellicott City to a terminal on Saratoga Street.* The Maryland and Washington Railway was chartered by Congress on August 1, 1892, to provide entrance to Washington. They were to build from the DC line to 4th Street and Rhode Island Avenue N.E. where connection was to be made with the Eckington and Soldiers' Home.

Details are not clear, but it is apparent that the ownership of the E & SH passed from the owners of the Baltimore and Boulevard Company to those of the Columbia and Maryland and the Maryland and Washington. Indeed they may have been the same promoters.

It was later in the decade before these plans were to bear fruit; some never did. The only line from Washington to Baltimore, the Washington, Baltimore and Annapolis Electric Railroad, didn't result from these promotions.

W. K. Schoepf, who had been appointed receiver of the E & SH and Belt September 21, was also appointed receiver of Maryland and Washington on September 26. The Maryland and Washington had a right-of-way on Rhode Island Avenue from 4th Street east to the District Line and at that time owned former E & SH tracks on North Capitol, G and T Streets.

On March 3, 1897, operation of the Maryland and Washington began from the District Line (Mt. Rainier) to Florida and New York Avenues. Of course, operation from 4th Street and Rhode Island Avenue N.E. to New York and Florida Avenue was over the Eckington and Soldiers' Home and the entire route was operated with E & SH single-truck electrics, the Lacledes.

By this time the Metropolitan had already successfully installed an underground conduit system; and it would not be many months before Capital Traction, of necessity, would do the same. It is not surprising then to find that in January of 1898 preliminary surveys were begun by Mr. E. Saxton, contractor, for the electrification of the Eckington

*This road, since it was to connect with the Columbia and Maryland, was standard gauge while the rest of the Baltimore system was 5' 4½" gauge. Thus, when it became necessary in 1898 to operate the line to protect the franchise, one or more Georgetown and Tenallytown 40 series open cars were shipped to Baltimore and operated on the line. For a time they operated without relettering. *The Sun*, April 19, 1898, and Louis C. Mueller letter to LeRoy O. King, Sr., January 29, 1957.

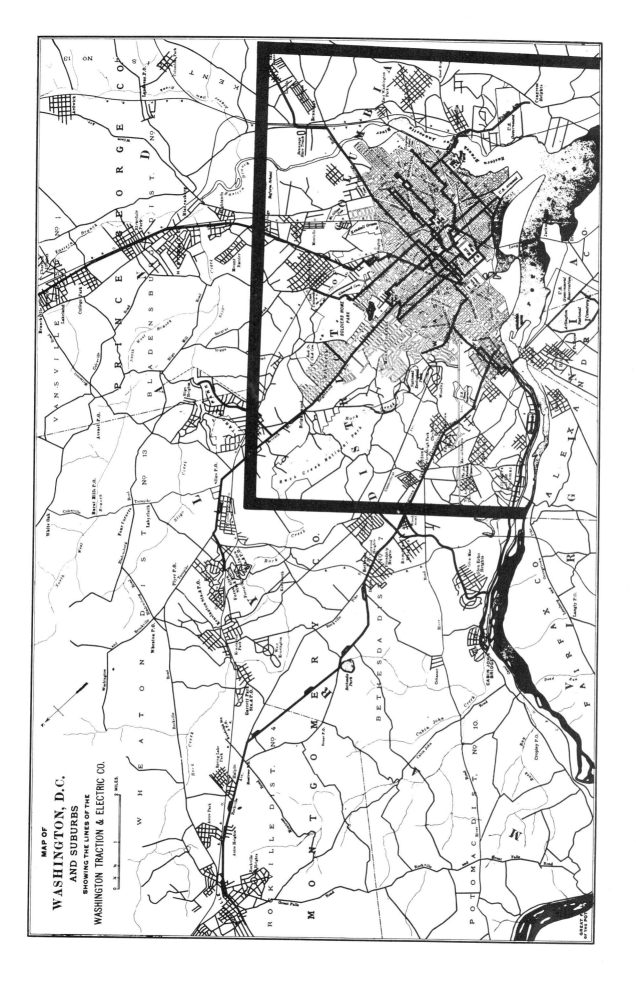

Robert A. Truax Collection

MAP OF
WASHINGTON, D.C.
AND SUBURBS
SHOWING THE LINES OF THE
WASHINGTON TRACTION & ELECTRIC CO.

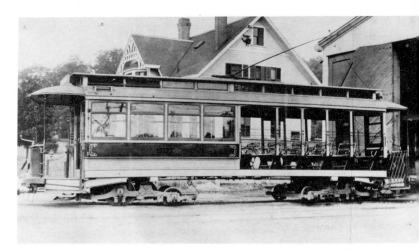

Washington Railway and Electric 907 (ex-City and Suburban 107) at Eckington barn before 1905. Barney Neuberger collection.

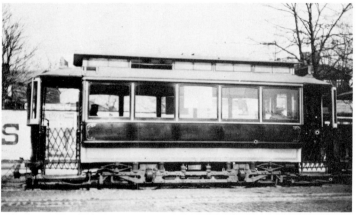

Washington Railway and Electric 8, one of the ex-Laclede-built Eckington and Soldiers' Home horsecars, as rebuilt to an electric car. Type of car used in the first operation of the Maryland and Washington. Photo by LeRoy O. King, Sr.

Treasury-bound City and Suburban 404 at the Eckington plow in 1905. Photo by LeRoy O. King, Sr.

City and Suburban half-open car enroute to the Treasury at 7th and G Streets N.W. before 1905. W.W. Buckingham collection.

and Soldiers' Home.

In 1898 the interesting name Eckington and Soldiers' Home disappeared. In June, Congress authorized the merger of the E & SH and its allied Columbia and Maryland Railway Company with the Maryland and Washington Railroad. The resultant company became known as the City and Suburban Railway Company of the District of Columbia. Thirty-five new double-truck cars were received. Some of these cars were used until the late 30's as Capital Transit 409-412.

On December 3, 1898, the Eckington car barn burned with loss of thirty cars. A fair estimate indicates that among the cars lost were seven double-deck trailers, one six-wheeler, one compressed air car, four horsecars. The balance must have been obsolete open and closed motors and trailers awaiting sale. Eight cars normally assigned to the barn were on the street at the time of the fire. There were enough cars left at the 13th and D Street N.E. barn to

keep operations intact. Those left were the single-truck Laclede motors and two other cars which later were W Ry & E Company 168 and Glen Echo 19. However, Capital Traction did lend two trains, each consisting of an open motor and closed trailer. an open motor and closed trailer.

The year 1899 was one of considerable progress for the City and Suburban. In actuality we now see the completion of the major portions of the electric lines of the railroad. Electric operation from Hyattsville to the Treasury using newly completed conduit track over the city portion of the line began May 21. Service over the conduit equipped 13th and D line began this same day. During 1899 the line was completed to the B & O station in Riverdale, and partially completed to Berwyn. For a time, the service from Riverdale to Berwyn was operated as a shuttle, using a single truck car.

In 1900, the City and Suburban, now controlled by Washington Traction and Electric, extended its North Capitol Street line via Michigan Avenue to join the older Brookland line. Original tracks via 4th Street were abandoned for regular service. However, they remained until the end of the street car era and were the best maintained yet least used tracks on the system. In addition to access from Eckington Barn to the Brookland line, the old line served for test and training purposes.

Through service to Berwyn, Maryland by the City and Suburban began about September, 1900. The delay in getting through service to Berwyn was occasioned by two problems: first, the Calvert estate was astride the route, and the estate was reluctant to grant right-of-way through the property; second, once the right-of-way problem was solved, a cut was required for this portion. It was graded once, then collapsed, and had to be redone.

Financial difficulties led to the formation of the Berwyn and Laurel Electric Railroad November 12, 1901, in order to complete that portion of the road. The independent Berwyn and Laurel operated for a time as a shuttle service

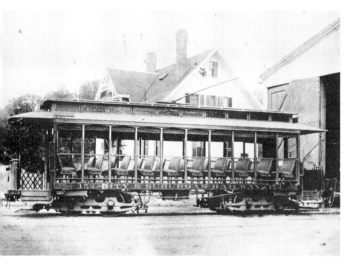

y and Suburban 152 at Eckington barn about 1900. Author's lection.

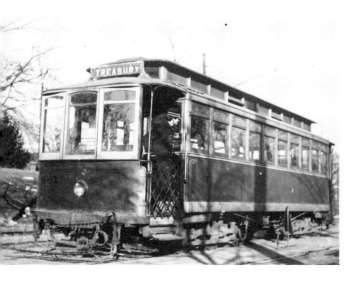

shington Railway and Electric 421 at Eckington plow pit February 15, 1907. This car and its four sisters were rebuilt from City d Suburban Railway open cars like 152 in top picture. Photo by Roy O. King, Sr.

Washington Railway and Electric 416, ex-City and Suburban 46, at Eckington pit February 15, 1907. Photo by LeRoy O. King, Sr.

from the end of the C & S line at Berwyn. Original line of the B & L was of much lighter construction than the C & S—further evidence that finances were at the root of the problem. It was single track with a stub siding at Branchville, double end sidings at Odell Road and Muirkirk and with no special work at Laurel. A substation was located at Ammendale.

Original service was hourly using yellow single truckers believed to be converted horsecars built by Laclede in 1895. C & S service was on the half-hour, so the B & L shuttle only met every other C & S car. Since the Berwyn Road owned no cars, it's apparent that C & S cars operated the B & L schedule.

Anacostia and Potomac Electrification

In Chapter One, the history of the Anacostia and Potomac was left with the Belt Railway on the verge of receivership in September, 1896. Belt and Anacostia and Potomac were still horsecar operated.

On September 21, 1896, W. Kelsey Schoepf was appointed receiver of the Belt Railway. A little over a year later, on December 24, 1897, the Court gave Belt 15 days to pay amounts due under its deeds of trust or face public auction. The Belt was unable to comply, and the American Security and Trust was ordered to sell the property at auction. On

the auction date, November 11, 1898, Oscar Crosby and N.P. Bond purchased the property for $350,000. At the purchaser's request, the property was deeded to the Anacostia and Potomac on February 7, 1899.

The Anacostia and Potomac receivership was less serious. Brought about by a suit in equity in March, 1898, by Elizabeth K. Riley, it ended January 30, 1899. The road was then returned to its stockholders by recievers H.A. Griswold and B.S. Minor.

Early in its existence, Capital Railway defaulted on payment of principal and interest on its bonds. It was, therefore, subject to sale under the terms of the deed of trust to the Washington Loan and Trust Company which was dated May 1, 1897. Washington Loan and Trust sold the property and franchises to James B. Lackey on April 2, 1900. He, in turn, on April 25, 1900, sold the road to the Anacostia and Potomac. Anacostia and Potomac now had swallowed up the two lesser roads and was under control of Crosby. It proceeded to electrify with the underground conduit system the entire trackage they wished to retain.

A good portion of the Belt disappeared as well as much of the original A & P route. May 26, 1900, saw the last horsecar operation in Washington on the Belt's LeDroit Park-Wharves line. What was to be electrified was a route

An ex-Columbia cable car, rebuilt to electric, near the end of the Congress Heights line, October 3, 1910. Library of Congress.

from 11th and Florida Avenue to Anacostia. This route used old Belt franchises on 11th Street, Metropolitan trackage rights on F and 9th, B, Missouri Avenue and 4 1/2 Streets. (Northbound cars used G Street in lieu of F between 9th and 11th.) Then A & P franchises were used to Anacostia. At that time the plow pit was at the north end of the Anacostia Bridge. The balance of the route was on two-wire overhead of the old Capital Railway.

Cars were operated from 11th and Florida to the foot of Asylum Hill in Anacostia. This location became and continued to be the one described by the destination "Anacostia." From this point up the hill to Congress Heights, a shuttle service operated. Interestingly, this shuttle required cars equipped with track brakes, the only such equipment in Washington until the streamlined cars of the 30's. This requirement arose out of an accident on this hill under the Capital Railway management. On July 10, 1898, a Capital Railway car ran away down the hill and overturned where it hit the curve that took the electric cars around the horse-car turntable.[5] The roof collapsed, killing one man and injuring a number of others. The car was a 10-bench open car, one of Capital Railway's 51-54 series.

Anacostia and Potomac bought twenty-five half-open cars from the American Car Company for the 11th and Florida to Anacostia service. The Congress Heights shuttle was operated with single-truck closed cars among which were 168 (ex-Glen Echo 21, ex-E & SH storage battery car 21)

and 169 (ex-Washington and Great Falls 5). The other line created by A & P electrification was the LeDroit Park to Wharves line. Former Belt franchises were used from 7th and W Street N.W. (LeDroit Park) to 4th and New York Avenue. Trackage rights on the City and Suburban were used to 11th and G Street N.W. A & P trackage was used for two blocks on 11th Street to E Street then Belt franchises again to the Wharves.

Four years earlier, on June 7, 1896, the Washington, Alexandria and Mt. Vernon had begun operation over Belt tracks to gain access to their terminal at 13 1/2 and E Street N.W. Their trains used underground conduit northbound from B Street South to B Street North and southbound from E Street North to B Street South on Belt right-of-way. When A & P electrified, a District of Columbia Supreme Court decision on April 25, 1900, was necessary to allow A & P to become joint owner of Mt. Vernon line conduits on 14th Street. After this decision, an agreement was reached calling for joint maintenance and an $18,000 payment to the Mt. Vernon line by the A & P. The companies also agreed that A & P would supply the power for the interurban on a three-year successive contract basis.

Trackage of the A & P, Belt and Capital not used in the new routings were dismantled.

Original summer electric equipment on the LeDroit Park-Wharves line was Metropolitan 7-bench open motors. No records exist to tell what the original winter equipment

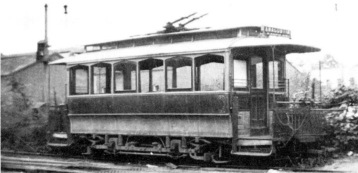

Washington Railway and Electric 168 (ex-Georgetown and Tenallytown 21) at 11th and Florida barn. This car was used for a time on the Anacostia-Congress Heights shuttle. The tall handle on the left of the platform is for the track brake required for this service after the 1898 runaway. Photo by LeRoy O. King, Sr.

Washington Railway and Electric 219, an ex-Columbia cable car, on the Congress Heights line in 1910. Photo by LeRoy O. King, Sr.

was. The half-open cars were transferred from the Anacostia line because of complaints of their noisy operation. They were later transferred to the Columbia line and the LeDroit Park line. Later, because of the high cost of converting them to full closed cars they were sold—some as far away as Boise, Idaho. The half-opens were followed on the Anacostia line by electrified ex-Columbia open and closed grip cars. These subsequently gave way to the 25-foot box cars of the 200-300 series standard Washington Railway city cars. Series 200-300 cars also followed the original equipment on LeDroit Park.

Although the Washington and Great Falls Electric bought control of Anacostia and Potomac on January 31, 1902, the corporation lasted until August 22, 1912. Shortly after the Great Falls line gained control, Congress authorized extension of the 11th Street line to its ultimate terminal at 11th and Monroe Streets.

Where applicable, conduit operation had become a reality on all lines controlled by Washington Traction and Electric by the time Anacostia and Potomac electrification was completed May 26, 1900.

Columbia line summer service was improved on April 22, 1900, by running through cars from the Treasury to the District Line. The Benning Race Track, Suburban Gardens Amusement Park and the steam-operated Chesapeake Beach Railway all accounted for increased summer traffic on this line. Probable equipment for through service was Metropolitan 1600 class cars. The Chesapeake Beach was an excursion road which ran between the District Line end of the Columbia line (then known as Chesapeake Junction) to Chesapeake Beach. In the fall of 1900, the Columbia and the Chesapeake Beach arranged for LCL freight service to all points on both roads from a terminal at 15th and H Street N.E. This service on the Columbia probably was provided by one of the ex-Metropolitan storage battery cars rebuilt for regular electric operation and modified for freight service.

Winter service continued for some years to be broken at 15th and H Street N.E. with shuttles operating from that point to both Kenilworth and Chesapeake Junction. At least

until 1903, winter service was provided by an electrified closed ex-grip car.

Progress seems always to have its price; and, in the case of the underground conduit, part of that price was the District's first plow pit electrocution. It occurred August 14, 1900, at 15th and H Street N.E.[6]

Columbia's property and franchises were purchased by Washington Railway and Electric on February 4, 1902, for $1,400,000. Metropolitan was purchased on the same day for $3,993,000. Capital Traction had been approached but refused to sell.

The next to last addition* to the basic Washington Railway System was the successor to the Berwyn and Laurel. On April 8, 1902, the Berwyn and Laurel changed its name to the Washington, Berwyn and Laurel Railroad Company. The first Washington to Laurel trip was made September 21, 1902. The Mayor and City Council of Laurel were guests on the private car Columbia which made the trip from 15th and G Street N.W., opposite the Treasury.

Final ownership integration of the Washington, Berwyn and Laurel into the City and Suburban didn't occur until 1910. On September 1, 1910, it was sold under foreclosure for $75,000 to Mr. George T. Bishop acting in the interest of the Washington, Baltimore and Annapolis. The W B & A had by then constructed a first-class, high speed interurban connecting its namesake cities. At the time, the W B & A had some idea of connecting its line with the Washington, Berwyn and Laurel by constructing a route from Annapolis Junction to Laurel. The W B & A's idea, though alive from 1901-1910, didn't materialize, as was the case of so many electric railway schemes of the day. On October 1, 1910, the road was sold by W B & A interests to Mr. Clarence F. Norment for $70,750. Mr. Norment was president of the Washington Railway and Electric Company which, by this time, controlled the City and Suburban Railway, thus completing the Maryland line.[7]

*The last addition was the Washington Interurban RR covered in Chapter V.

One of Anacostia and Potomac's "half open" cars probably near St. Elizabeth Hospital about 1900. Handy Studios, author's collection.

Anacostia and Potomac 301 at original Tenallytown barn about 1900. A sample car, never duplicated, it later became Washington Railway and Electric Company 500. Author's collection.

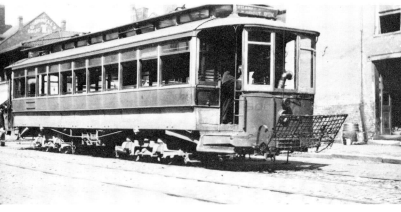

washington Railway and Electric 500 (ex-Anacostia and Potomac 301) at Wisnsin Avenue and M Streets in 1910. Photo by LeRoy O. King, Sr.

Washington Railway and Electric 169 (ex-Washington and Great Falls 5) at 11th and Florida barn about 1905. Note tall handle for track brake. Photo by LeRoy O. King, Sr.

Washington Railway and Electric 409 at Hyattsville on the Maryland line about 1914. Harvey Davison collection.

The mayor and city council of Laurel and guests pose beside "Columbia" at Laurel after the first through trip September 21, 1902. Author's collection.

A Washington Railway and Electric 420 series car at Laurel Stati about 1908. Robert A Truax collection.

G Street from the Treasury showing one of the Washington Railway and Electric Company 400-499 series cars about to leave for Berw The other car, a 300 series, dates the picture at 1903 or after. Library of Congress.

Capital Traction Electrification[8]

While Washington Railway and Electric was being formed and its components electrified, Capital Traction was electrifying its city lines. The Capital Traction's system following the powerhouse fire of September 29, 1897, comprised three separate operations. These were the unaffected electric lines of the old Rock Creek Railway, the still operable 7th Street cable line, and the emergency horsecar operation of the remainder of the system. In order to bring the system up to date, it was decided to electrify the city lines with the underground conduit system pioneered by the Metropolitan. The Rock Creek's Love conduit was to be replaced because of the improved technology of the Metropolitan system and for standardization.

The process of converting Capital Traction lines to electricity was equally as miraculous a feat of organization as the restoration of service the morning after the powerhouse fire. By July 3, 1898, electric operation of the entire property with company generated power was a reality! All this was accomplished without interruption of service. Certainly no small task!

By May 7 of the following year, the Love system on U Street had been replaced and conduit track extended to Rock Creek Loop, thus operationally combining Rock Creek and the Washington and Georgetown. It was now possible to operate the 7th Street cars from Water and P Streets to the loop at Rock Creek Bridge. Conversely, it also enabled the Chevy Chase cars to be routed down 14th Street to a switchback which would long be associated with the line at 15th and New York Avenue N.W.

Since they had been cable operated, the city lines had all the structural features necessary for conduit operations except insulators and conductor rails. Thus, conversion consisted of replacing the cable and its various sheaves, depressors, etc., with positive and negative conductor rails suitably insulated. The first insulator was installed at 14th and Park Road; on January 9, 1898, the first experimental trip operated from there south to U Street. By February 22, operation was possible to 15th and New York Avenue; by March 20, 1898, all city lines were electrified except 7th Street.

Up to now, all power was purchased from the Potomac Electric Power Company. However, on April 7, the first engine was started at the Grace Street powerhouse; by May 4, all power was obtained from the railway's own plant.

Electrification of the 7th Street line was a little more complicated than the others. Here the cable was still operating, and the work of installing the electric conductor rails had to be done without interfering with service.

D. S. Carll, who was to become a Capital Traction vice-president, maintained a journal in which he described the pulling of the cable on the 7th Street lines.[9] On May 24, 1898, all was in readiness for the change—the line was shut down at 1:00 a.m. Mr. Carll wrote:

> Arrangements were that we would cut the cable at Boundary, pulling it in two pieces, having 2 cars standing on either track at Boundary to take hold of the end of the rope so as to keep it from dragging along and interfering with the electrical installation. At south side of Virginia Avenue we had a (grip) car on either track in case any freight train should interfere so that we could drop cable and pick it up on the other car. The cable was stopped at 12:33. Cut was made in the power station at 12:45; we heard from Boundary that they were ready at 1:45. Started to pull at 1:50. First piece in house at 2:25. Started to pull in 2nd piece at 2:50. In house at 3:21. There was not a hitch in the whole operation. The end of the first piece passed in front of a freight train by about 1 1/2 min. The last piece by less than 45 seconds. We had last car that left Boundary at 12 o'clock, leave one hour earlier. We started up in the morning (with electric trains) 15 min. late.

Originally the company felt that the switch to electricity could be accomplished with seventy single truck motors. They planned to use the cable trailers with the new electric motors. Accordingly, seventy closed motors with 18-foot bodies were ordered from American Car Company, St. Louis. The seventy motors were soon supplemented by eighteen remodeled cars converted in the company shops from Stephenson cable trailers to 16-foot motors. Thirty-two motors, twenty in 1899, twelve in 1904, were ordered from Brill. Ten came from Stephenson in 1902. In 1904-05, the company ordered eleven bodies from Brill and seven from Cincinnati. These were placed on trucks of the eighteen Stephenson 16-foot motors, and they in turn were reconverted to trailers. All the motors were mounted on Lord Baltimore trucks and had two G.E. 35 HP motors.

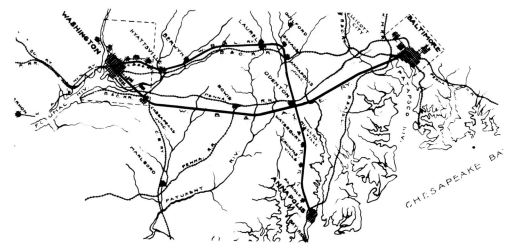

Map showing the Washington, Baltimore and Annapolis' never fulfilled plans for the Washington, Berwyn and Laurel. Author's collection.

Capital Traction electric cars on the M Street bridge over Rock Creek about 1899. Stacks in the background are at the Metropolitan's P Street shops. Compare with picture on page six. Handy Studios, author's collection.

Pennsylvania Avenue from the Treasury about 1900. In the foreground is a 14th Street line electric car. Library of Congress.

Capital Traction (ex-Rock Creek Railway) barn at Chevy Chase Lake in the summer of 1906. Photo by LeRoy O. King, Sr.

Capital Traction 11, one of the radials, at the 15th and New York Avenue turnback in 1906. Note trainman transferring fender for the return trip. Photo by LeRoy O. King, Sr.

Capital Traction's Union Station, from the southwest, about 1900. Midway in the west wall at the second floor can be seen provision for entry of Virginia cars which were to enter the station on a trestle. Note the "Union Station" sign on the tower. Author's collection.

Closed trailers were converted from cable or horsecars and mounted on Stephenson Perfection Trucks. Open motors and trailers were all rebuilt from cable equipment on hand at the time of the fire except for twenty 8-bench single truck open motors built in the company shops in the spring of 1903.

Open motors were provided, then, as follows: twenty built in company shop from J. G. Brill woodwork; thirty-seven American Car ex-open cable trailers; and forty J. M. Jones ex-open cable trailers.

This made a total of ninety-seven open motors. In addition, seventy-seven 8-bench American trailers of 1892 and fifty-five Stephenson center-aisle grip cars were converted to "electric" trailers, thus completing the open car roster of the single truck period.

The 36th and M Street Terminal[10]

An important event in the early history of Capital Traction was the construction of the massive terminal building at 36th and M Street N.W. This building, which later served as the general office of D C Transit, was built by the Washington and Georgetown. The Act of Congress of August 23, 1894, authorizing the extension west to 36th and M, required the erection of "a union station for the use of all roads that might terminate at that point."

A hillside lot, bounded by Prospect Street on the north, M Street on the south, 36th Street on the west and a line 120 feet west of 35th Street on the east was purchased from C. C. Glover and his wife. The lot selected required the excavation of 90,000 cubic yards of material, mostly rock. The hillside nature of the site, a rise of sixty feet in 250, required massive concrete retaining walls along the back and most of the east and west sides. These walls were thirteen feet thick at the base.

Waddy Wood, a prominent architect, designed a massive structure to serve as terminal for four roads. The building was 180 feet by 242 feet and three stories high. The Washington and Georgetown would use the ground floor on M Street while the Washington, Arlington and Falls Church and the projected Great Falls and Old Dominion were to come across the Potomac from Rosslyn, entering the second and third floors respectively on steel trestles. The Metropolitan Railroad would use the roof.

In early 1895, construction began. The terminal contained waiting rooms, toilets, and terminal offices for the various railways on the M Street side of the upper floors.

Because in the project (September 21, 1895) the Washington and Georgetown had merged with the Rock Creek Railway, the terminal early became identified as the Capital Traction Terminal. D. S. Carll, Chief Engineer and Superintendent of Capital Traction, was in charge of construction.

As far as Capital Traction was concerned the terminal opened May 27, 1897, and contained Washington's only cable loop, although for less than a year.

The 140-foot central tower contained an elevator for transferring passengers between the various terminals. On the roof, a central covered passageway connected the elevators with the Metropolitan Railroad on Prospect Street. Passenger rooms were handsomely finished in red oak wainscoting, delicately tinted walls, granata floors, panelled ceilings of stucco and ornate black iron grills and stair railings.

The grandeur that might have been never came to pass, for the Virginia roads never used the terminal, nor did the Metropolitan to the extent envisioned. There were to be storage tracks on the roof for the Metropolitan but all that ever existed was the covered walkway.

Capital Traction mail car 1 pulled by a closed motor at Peace Monument about 1910. Potomac Electric Power Company from Joseph J. Jessel.

Later, on October 1, 1897, after the cable powerhouse fire, the company moved its offices to the edifice. In 1906 and again in 1908, portions of the second floor were converted to office space.

Streetcar Mail Service[11]

Early in the electric car era, three railway post office routes were operated in the city. Capital Traction operated the first of these by cable from 36th and M Streets in Georgetown to the Navy Yard beginning December 23, 1895. It was known as the Pennsylvania Avenue RPO. The first mail car on this route was a rebuilt horsecar which was hauled as the second trailer in a three-car cable train. This car's heater caused a fire on April 7, 1896, near 15th and New York Avenue. While it was being repaired, its interior fittings were transferred to a regular closed cable trailer which operated the service while number one was shopped. The company, at that time, ordered number two from Brill which then became the regular mail car while repaired number one became the relief.

After the cable powerhouse fire, the mail car was horse hauled until electrification was complete. Then, until its discontinuance on June 30, 1913, Capital Traction's mail train, number 203, was made up of a single truck open or closed motor (depending on the season) and the mail car as trailer.

Metropolitan Railroad operated two RPO routes for a little over four years, from August 2, 1897, to September 14, 1901. The F Street RPO operated from Connecticut and Florida Avenues to 15th and East Capitol Streets. This service was operated with motor mail car number three which was built for the purpose by James A. Trimble.

The 9th Street RPO originally operated from 10th and Florida Avenue N.W. to 4 1/2 and O Street S.W. After the first year, the northern terminal was changed to 7th Street and Florida Avenue.

There were two mail cars for this line, both trailers. Number one was rebuilt from a 16 1/2 foot Lewis and Fowler horsecar, and number two was built for the purpose by James A. Trimble. A "no passenger" closed motor was provided to haul the mail car in winter. If, however, this motor broke down, the mail car was second trailer behind a regular revenue passenger motor trailer combination. In summer, the mail trailer was hauled behind an open motor in regular passenger service.

Mail on the Washington RPO's was picked up and discharged for the General Post Office, various branch post offices, and for steamers to Marshall Hall and Norfolk. The mail cars were all equipped with letter slots.

Reuben C. Rowzee who was the mail clerk on the Pennsylvania Avenue RPO from its beginning to its end on June 30, 1913, told an interesting story. Westbound one day in front of the White House, a man boarded the train and came into the mail car. Rowzee told him he was on the right train but the wrong car. Then he recognized President Theodore Roosevelt. The President rode with him to 36th and M Streets and discussed, enroute, all phases of the job. The President was going to meet his children at the end of the line after school so they could enjoy a walk up the canal towpath. Somewhere, near Glen Echo, a White House carriage would meet them and return them home in time for supper.

In addition to RPO cars, and extensive pouch mail service was operated beginning with a Georgetown to Bethesda route in 1893 or 1894. Pouch routes and the dates first reported in post office records were as follows:[12]

Metropolitan train at Lincoln Park car barn decorated for the October 3, 1899 parade to celebrate Dewey's victory at Manila Bay. Hand̄
Studios, author's collection.

Pouch Mail Routes		
Washington Railway and Electric (replaced Met. RR 9th St. RPO)	9th & Penna. to 7th & Florida	6-30-02
Washington Railway & Electric (after Feb. 1, 1902) Georgetown & Tenallytown	Georgetown- Bethesda, Md.	6-30-94
Brightwood Railway	7th & Florida to Brightwood (later Takoma, Md.)	6-30-95
Washington & Great Falls	36th & Prospect to Cabin John, Md.	6-30-98
City and Suburban	11th & G Sts. to Brookland	6-30-01
Capital Railway (Anacostia & Potomac after 4-25-00)	8th & M S.E. to Congress Hts.	6-30-99
Capital Traction Company	15th & F to 14th & Park	6-30-97
Capital Traction Company (after 9-21-95) Rock Creek Railway	7th & Florida to Chevy Chase, Md.	6-30-95

Post Office Department records of these services after June 30, 1905, are not readily available, so it is not known when individual routes were terminated. Since Anacostia and Potomac's pouches were transferred at 8th and M Street S.E. to Capital Traction RPO cars, it is probable that this service lasted until the end of the Pennsylvania Avenue RPO in 1913. Mail pouches were handled on the Cabin John line to Glen Echo in the 50's but it is not known how long the service lasted beyond that.

As the nineties came to a close, the electric car literally began to remake the city. Because of efficient transportation, it was no longer necessary for the breadwinner to live near his work. Suburbs grew up along the carlines and the old city boundary at Florida Avenue ceased to have meaning. Wisconsin, Connecticut, Rhode Island Avenues and Fourteenth Street, among others, were developed because of the trolley.

The trolley also led to the growth of downtown. The new mobility allowed shoppers to come from afar, and mass merchandising in the form of department stores became practical. This, in turn, led to intensive development of the F & G Street shopping area. Offices, government and commercial, located near the downtown trolley terminals. All of this was done with what today seems a sense of order, neatness, and efficiency, especially when contrasted with the sprawling, auto-dominated city of today.

CHAPTER FOUR
THE TROLLEY IN ITS PRIME

Early Electric Operation

After creation of Washington Railway and Electric, the next major development of the city's railway system was the massive rerouting brought on by service to Union Station. In the intervening period, however, both companies undertook a number of projects to extend and improve their services. Capital Traction completed, in 1901, four additions to its lines: the eastern branch, the F and G Street line, the B and O Loop, and the loop at Peace Monument.[1]

First of these was the eastern branch which was an extension in Pennsylvania Avenue from 8th Street East to 17th Street East. On January 18 at 2:40 p.m. the first trip over the line was made in 14th Street closed motor number 28 with John H. Hanna* as motorman. Mr. Dunlop,** company president, was one of the passengers. Service on this line was, at first, operated as a shuttle. A week later, the Peace Monument loop was put in operation.

The F and G Street line consisted of single track west and north on G and 25th Streets and east and south on 26th and F Streets from 17th and Pennsylvania Avenue N.W. to 26th and Pennsylvania Avenue N.W. This formed a line through Foggy Bottom as an alternate routing for Pennsylvania Avenue cars. A return loop was formed by trackage on G Street from 25th to 26th Street. This loop, for many years, was the southern terminus of Chevy Chase Lake cars. At 26th and Pennsylvania there was a west to south switch which allowed F and G Street cars to turn

---

*John H. Hanna (1876-1947) joined the engineering staff of the Washington and Georgetown Railroad in 1894 two years after graduation from Princeton. He had a prominent part in developing the electric lines of the Capital Traction Company and became president in 1926. In 1933, he became the first president of the Capital Transit Company and in 1938 became Chairman of the Board, a position he held at his death. *Star*, June 30, 1947..

**George T. Dunlop (1845-1908), after several years as director was elected vice president and manager of the Washington and Georgetown. He was prominent in the formation of the Capital Traction Company, from the W & G and the Rock Creek. He became first president of the new company. An outstanding achievement during his presidency was the recovery from the cable car power house fire September 29, 1897 which resulted in complete electrification of the city lines. The Capital Traction Company was one of the leading street railways in the country when he died as president. *Star*, February 6, 1908.

---

back instead of duplicating service to 36th and M Streets. When the line was completed May 5, 1901, through service was inaugurated from Georgetown to 17th and Pennsylvania Avenue S.E., via F and G Streets.

The B and O Loop was contracted to Mr. E. Saxton who started work March 22, 1901.[2] Before the B & O Loop, the Capital Traction's 14th Street line ran north from Peace Monument on 1st Street N.W. to C Street N.W., turning east on C Street to a point just short of its intersection with New Jersey Avenue. The Baltimore and Ohio Depot was diagonally across on the northeast corner. This is the point where later-day Mt. Pleasant cars coming out of the tunnel turned right into New Jersey Avenue.

On this same block of C Street between 1st Street N.W. and New Jersey Avenue, there was also the single-track eastbound line of the Metropolitan Railroad coming from Indiana Avenue to proceed eastward on C Street to Delaware Avenue, south on Delaware Avenue to B (Constitution), east on B to 1st Street N.E., south on 1st Street to East Capitol, and on to Lincoln Park.

In 1900-1901 the tracks on C Street between 1st Street West and New Jersey Avenue were rebuilt into a double track line for joint use of the two companies. In addition, a single track was constructed on 1st Street East between B (Constitution Avenue) and C Streets East, thus forming (with former trackage) a single track loop around the location of the Senate Office Building which would be completed in 1909.

This new trackage allowed Capital Traction's 14th Street cars to follow eastbound Metropolitan track to 1st and B Street N.E., turn north on 1st Street and return westbound on C Street to 1st Street N.W. City and Suburban track was used on C Street to Delaware Avenue, joint track with the Metropolitan to New Jersey Avenue, and then Capital Traction track.

Capital Traction's early electric operation was an interesting one which, with Washington Railway's, was unusual among large systems in this country. With the exception of the suburban line of the Old Rock Creek, operation was almost exclusively with two-car trains of single-truck cars.[3]

New closed motors along with like-new open motors and trailers (both open and closed), rebuilt from cable cars, comprised the rolling stock of the early electric operation. Colors used for route identification remained the same as in cable days:

Georgetown	Green with cream trim
7th Street	Dark yellow with cream trim
14th Street	Lemon yellow with cream trim

The numbering system of the day is of interest. For instance, this was the system on the Georgetown line:

Washington Railway and Electric Ninth Street open train, enroute to Wharves, passing the 6th and B Street N.W. Pennsylvania Railroad Station about 1905. Leonard W. Rice collection.

Capital Traction closed train in Georgetown-17th and Pennsylvania Avenue S.E. service at 15th and G Streets N.W. about 1906. Author's collection.

Baltimore and Ohio Railroad Station at the northeast corner of New Jersey Avenue and C Street N.W. about 1901. Library of Congress.

Capital Traction Stephenson 1902 car at Navy Yard car house about 1905 showing route lettering used before the advent of roll signs. Photo by LeRoy O. King, Sr.

Mixed train--closed motor and open trailer--at Peace Monument about 1910. Capital Transit Library, author's collection.

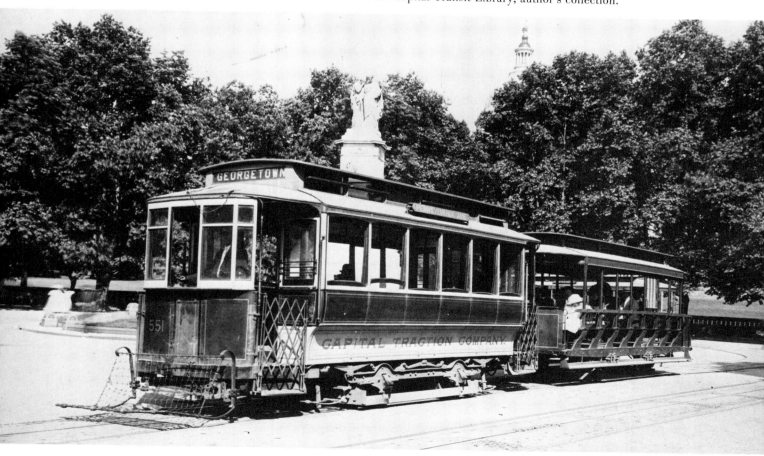

Capital Traction Station at Rock Creek Loop when new, about 1900. Columbia Historical Society.

Capital Traction open train and now unknown crew at Rock Creek Loop around the turn of the century. Felix Reifschneider collection.

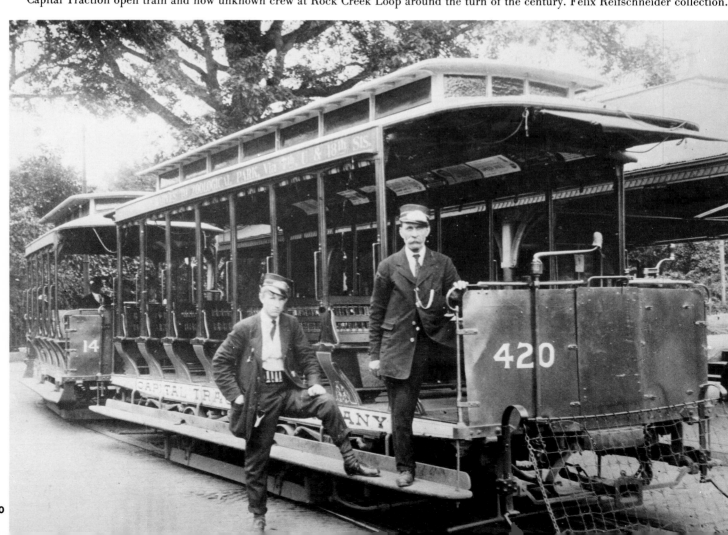

Capital Traction Station at the south side of Chevy Chase Circle about 1900. Columbia Historical Society.

201-235	Closed motors
201 up	Closed and open trailers
241 up	Open motors
299 down	Sandcars and sweepers

A train would be made up of closed motor 201 and either open or closed trailer 201. This would become the first set on the line in the morning, followed by 202 and its trailer, and so on in ascending order. Trains were punctual to a point that persons going to work could tell whether or not they were late by the car number. If the motor were disabled, the train number was that of the trailer.

Consist of these trains would be varied with the weather. Winter, of course, called for a closed motor and closed trailer; warmer weather brought closed motor, open trailer; and summer brought open motor and open trailer.

When the Brill motors of 1904 arrived, it was necessary to number them 236-40 and then 299 down duplicating the numbers previously assigned service cars.

It is interesting to think that these trains were, of course, operated with hand brakes. Motors were equipped with an efficient and quiet-operating Adams and Westlake ratchet brake handle. A brake chain connected the brakes of the trailer to those of the motor. Motormen could brake a train by using three-quarters of a turn on the handle. Two-thirds of the pressure thus generated was applied to the motor and one-third to the trailer. A wedge was driven between the faces of the Van Dorn couplers to eliminate slack and reduce the tendency to surge when starting or stopping. All this enabled an efficient and smooth stop. The trailer's brakes were used independently only when the cars were set out alone.

Interestingly, on special movements, but not in regular service, second trailers were sometimes added to trains, but in snow storms, it was customary to drop trailers. Motors in two-car trains, separately controlled of course, have been used in extra heavy storms.

On Inauguration Day 1901, while the parade was in progress, 7th Street service from Pennsylvania Avenue to the wharves was provided by two four-car trains, one on each track. There was a motor on each end and two trailers in the middle. One marvels at the coordination that that required, without benefit of intercom, color lights, or other refinements.

In 1902, the typical number of trains operated and headways were as follows:

Line	# Trains	Headway (Minutes)
Georgetown-Navy Yard (via Penna. Ave.)	20	4
Georgetown-17th & Pa. Ave. SE (via F & G)	14	3
14th Street (14th & Park-B & O Depot)	23	3
7th Street (Rock Creek Bridge-7th St. Wharves)	24	3

Chevy Chase (CC Lake-Treasury) — every 15 min. — 7:15 am-5:30 pm
Chevy Chase (CC Lake-Rock Cr. Bridge) every 15 min. 5:30 pm-Midnight

One or two extra trains per line as required in a.m. and p.m. rush hours.

Capital Traction Brill-built 801 at Union Station about 1910. Photo by LeRoy O. King, Sr.

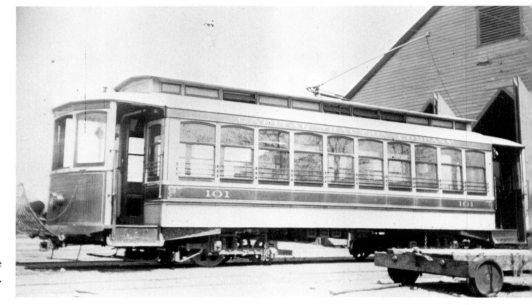

Brill-built 101 at Chevy Chase Lake barn in 1907. Photo by LeRoy O. King, Sr.

Cincinnati-built 108 at Union Station about 1910. Photo by LeRoy O. King, Sr.

During the Grand Army of the Republic Encampment in 1902 there was on the street at one time for two or more days sixty trains on Pennsylvania Avenue, forty trains on Fourteenth Street, thirty trains on Seventh Street, making a total of 130 trains on the city divisions![4]

One can't help wishing that somehow we could go back in time for a moment or two to see some of these sturdy little trains negotiate the special work at 15th and New York Avenue.

An interesting "might have been" was aired in 1904. The Great Falls and Old Dominion sought permission to construct a crosstown line from the Aqueduct Bridge in Georgetown, via M Street, to Mt. Olivet Cemetery on the far east side of town. The proposal included a request for free transfer privileges with both the Capital Traction and Washington Railway and request for permission to use Capital Traction tracks between 36th Street and Rock Creek.

Both companies vigorously fought the Old Dominion request and Capital Traction offered to build and operate such a line if it was deemed to be worthwhile. Nothing came of either proposal.[5]

In 1906-07, Capital Traction further improved its service by extension of the 14th Street line north from Park Road to Colorado Avenue and the construction of a new car barn at 14th and Decatur Street N.W. This extension was laid in its entirety with conduit track, and it was the northernmost extension of such track in the city. Until this extension, the company owned only two double truck cars, Chevy Chase convertibles 13 and 14. With the extension, the company began its commitment to a double truck car fleet.[6]

The twelve cars purchased in 1906 were as follows:

101-103	(3)	Brill semi-convertible
104-106	(3)	Cincinnati semi-convertible
801-806	(6)	Brill 13-bench open

The six closed cars were obviously samples; and, as is equally obvious from later orders, the company favored the Cincinnati cars. Although Brill was the leader of the field and would remain so until the PCC car, certainly the Cincinnati product this time was the more modern and attractive of the two. They had ten windows and were twenty-eight feet long over-all. These cars were equipped with a short platform on the front and a longer "Detroit" platform on the rear. The front platform was four feet long while the rear platform was six feet long. Although there was a definite front of the car, they were double ended, but they almost always were operated with the short platform first. This series was completed in 1907 with the purchase of 107-131, twenty-five cars from Cincinnati. Also in 1907, 807-821 Cincinnati 13-bench open motors arrived.

reet railway precedes city growth. 14th Street line extension un-
r construction July 8, 1906. Author's collection.

Attractive 14th and Decatur car house in 1914. Columbia Historical Society.

F Street west from 9th in 1908. Washington Railway 1600's and a new 300 series closed car are visible. Library of Congress.

9th Street (Washington Railway and Electric Company) open train near the turn of the century. Robert A. Truax collection.

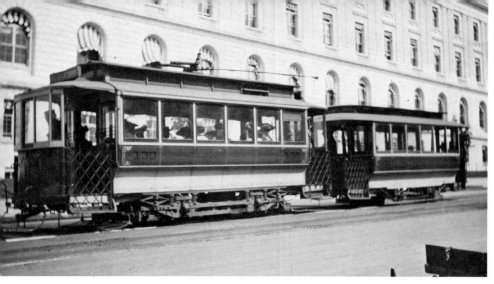

Washington Railway and Electric Company closed train (130 and 600 series trailer) in front of Senate Office Building on Delaware Avenue in 1910. Photo by LeRoy O. King, Sr.

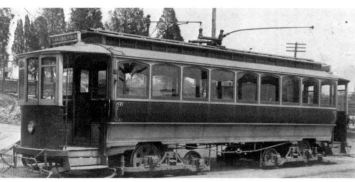

Washington Railway and Electric Company spliced car 501 (left) was built by W.T. & E. in 1900 from two Glen Echo single truckers (right). Left: Potomac Electric Power Company from Joseph J. Jessel; Right: Author's collection.

:ket is printed in light blue on buff stock. Letter "E" indicates was sold by WRY & E Co. subsidiary Georgetown and Tenally-vn. Author's collection.

The 14th and Decatur barn was opened in 1907, replacing the 14th and Park Road facility. The new barn was an outstanding one, by far the most attractive in the city. For this it received much favorable comment in the trade press of the times.

Washington Railway's immediate problem was to upgrade and standardize its heterogeneous collection of rolling stock. A 1902 roster of its equipment shows no less than forty-two different classes of cars, reflecting the varying tastes of the companies recently acquired.

A greater portion of low density routes and the inclusion of a number of financiallly weak underlying companies gave Washington Railway financial problems that Capital Traction didn't have. This fact in addition to the Railway's larger size meant that the task of standardization and improvement was much more difficult than it would be for Capital Traction. As a stopgap, Washington Traction in this period had produced some less-than-attractive rebuilds.

In 1903, the company began a program of acquiring a group of cars that would be the backbone of the system for a decade; some of them would be part of the Washington scene until the mid-1930's. A total of 155 new double truck twenty-five foot nine-window, closed motors were ordered from various builders as follows:

Year	No. Cars	Builder	Car Numbers
1903	40	Laclede	304 - 343
1904	25	Kuhlman	344 - 368
1905	25	Cincinnati	369 - 393
1905	25	Cincinnati	275 - 299
1906-7	40	St. Louis	235 - 274

In 1907-08 this first group of new cars was enlarged by twenty-five larger but similar St. Louis built cars.

The design of all these new cars along with the first double truck cars Capital Traction bought was no doubt influenced by a March 3, 1905 act of Congress requiring closed platforms. This requirement was enacted to protect motormen from inclement weather. One wonders why management itself didn't have some compassion without a prod from Congress. Yet, more than one motorman complained that windows for his protection were an insult to his manliness. New York City motormen, when faced with the same circumstance, claimed that vestibules interfered with their work.

From a cracked glass plate Washington Railway and Electric Company 500 in "Seeing Washington" sightseeing service about 1904. Car is probably at 15th and G Streets N.W. Robert A. Truax collection.

Operations weren't always smooth. Motorman E. S. Colvin blamed fog for his failure to reduce speed before rounding the curve at 4th and T Streets N.E. The accident, which happened at 7:27 a.m. October 17, 1904, killed one and injured 30. Leonard W. Rice collection.

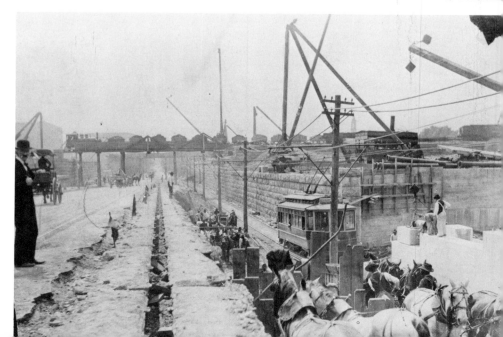

Construction scene on the H Street underpass behind Union Station in 1905. Note the car operating by double wire overhead. Author's collection.

For a few years near the turn of the century, the Seeing Washington Car Company leased Washington Railway cars for organized sight-seeing trips. The Seeing Washington Car Company was a franchised operation of the American Sight-seeing Car and Coach Company which conducted similar operations in Denver, Salt Lake City, Boston, Charleston, Los Angeles and New York. For this operation, the Railway first furnished Metropolitan 700 class cars. Later, 500 or City and Suburban 400-419 class cars were used. By 1905, the cars were replaced by Seeing Washington automobiles.

Union Station

The most far reaching changes ever wrought by a single project on the operations of both Washington Railway and Electric and Capital Traction were as the result of the construction of Union Station. Prior to construction of Union Station, Washington was served by two railroad stations, the Baltimore and Ohio at New Jersey Avenue and C Street N.W. and the Philadelphia, Baltimore and Washington Railroad station (later Pennsylvania Railroad) at 6th and B Street N.W. In addition to P B & W Railroad trains, all southern trains used the 6th Street station.

The primary motivation for a new station was that the P B & W station made an inexcusable clutter on the mall in front of the Capitol.

HENRY J. MAYHAM.   EDWARD K. SOMBORN.   WILLIAM C. AMOS.

Seeing Washington Cars
Observation
DAILY AND SUNDAY TOURS OF
WASHINGTON.
25 MILES OF SIGHTSEEING.

OPEN CARS IN SUMMER.   CLOSED CARS IN WINTER.

EXPERT GUIDE ON EACH CAR.
1000 POINTS OF INTEREST EXPLAINED EN ROUTE.
Cars Leave 1419 G Street, each day
10 a.m., 12 noon, 2 and 4 p.m.
ROUND TRIP 50 CENTS.
Seeing Washington Car Co.
1419 G Street, N.W., WASHINGTON, D.C.
Telephone 749-3.   WILLIAM C. AMOS.
General Manager.

Union Station contemplated new approaches from the northeast for Pennsylvania trains as well as a tunnel under 1st Street East for trains from the south. B & O approaches, while modified, weren't nearly so drastic since their station was not far from the present location of Union Station. The station itself was of monumental stature and proportions designed to meet all future needs of railroads entering Washington. That the designers succeeded, incidentally, is attested by the statistics of World War II passenger traffic when daily totals of 100,000 and more passengers were not uncommon.[7]

Even if street cars were never to serve the station, the mere fact of its location was to have a far reaching effect. The Columbia line ran behind the station in H Street. It had to be interrupted for the construction of the lengthy underpass known as the H Street Subway, which ran under all the tracks of the station. While this was being done, Columbia line cars were detoured north of the final route but within the confines of the retaining walls of the cut. Through the detour cars used overhead double wire trolley, necessitating a plow pit at either end of the detour.

Steam railroad tracks at 7th and Virginia Avenue S.W. were elevated while the street was depressed to effect a grade separation in connection with Union Station 1st Street tunnel approaches. While this was going on, 7th Street trains of the Capital Traction used overhead "trollers" across the detour. These were plugged in on the side of the car while the plows, of necessity, were removed and replaced at each side of the detour. Practice differed from that of the Columbia line primarily because of lack of poles on Capital Traction trains.[8]

The first B and O train into the new terminal arrived on October 27, 1907, while the first Pennsylvania train left the station November 17, 1907. Each road closed its old terminal on those respective dates.[9]

Street railway service for the benefit of the old stations was discontinued as they closed, but it would not be until June 24, 1908, that any service to the new station would be offered. This sad state of affairs must be laid at the door of an uncompromising Congressional District Committee.

This committee apparently felt that Union Station was of such a monumental nature that its appearance could not be spoiled by mere street cars operating in its plaza. Also, Representative Madden of Illinois let it be known that it would be useless to consider any track extension without the universal transfer. The notion of universal transfers was then a new and daring idea and the traction companies fought it tooth and nail. Particularly outspoken was General George H. Harries,* Vice President of the Washington Railway. On the subject of universal transfers he pointed out

*George Harries (1860-1934) was one of the most colorful characters associated with street railways in the District. Born in Wales, one time Texas Ranger and *Star* Reporter. As a reporter for the *Star* he dressed as a vagrant to get arrested to expose conditions in the District jail. Became President of the Metropolitan RR in

that since his road had 145 miles of line and the Capital Traction had only forty-four, "we would do all the carrying and they'd get all the money"—not an illogical thought at that.[10]

On the idea that the appearance of the station plaza shouldn't be spoiled by streetcars, outspoken General Harries asked whether the Union Station was a monument or other sacred edifice. If it was, he would like to see it carefully roped off and strewn with flowers on fete days. If it was not, he would be overjoyed with an agreement whereby his company and the Capital Traction Company could get their cars within a mile or so of the general area of the station.[11]

After much acrimonious debate, an act enabling construction of Union Station trackage was passed on May 23, 1908, without the universal transfer provision.

On June 8, 1908, the Capital Traction Company and the Anacostia and Potomac River Railroad entered into a contract providing for joint construction and ownership of Union Station trackage. Washington Railway and Electric Company guaranteed performance of A & P since, of course, they controlled it.

Each company appointed two representatives who would select a competent engineer to be in charge. Together the five men would carry out the project. D. S. Carll, Second Vice President and J. H. Hanna, Chief Engineer, represented Capital Traction, while C. S. Kimball, Engineer of Maintenance and Ways, and J. T. Moffett, Superintendent of Transportation of the Washington Railway, represented Anacostia and Potomac. Mr. William B. Upton, who was not connected with either company, was the fifth member.[12]

The companies were authorized, as a temporary expedient during the project, to use double wire overhead trolley on a double track shuttle between the plaza and existing rail lines at Delaware Avenue and C Streets.

Enthusiastic press reports greeted the first operation of the shuttle June 24, 1908. No fare was charged for the two-minute ride, provided by Capital Traction 130 operating in both directions on one track and Washington Railway 288 on the other.

To serve Union Station, enabling legislation authorized the following lines:[13]

Joint (Cost Shared Equally)

1. Massachusetts Avenue, New Jersey to Union Station.
2. Union Station Loop and sidings (including switch tower).
3. Delaware Avenue, Union Station to C Street N.E. (including switch tower).
4. 1st Street East, East Capitol to B Street S.E.

1896, Vice President of the Washington Railway and Electric in 1900. Resigned in 1911 to become associated with H. M. Byllesby & Co. Engineers. Commanded D.C. Regiment of National Guard in the Spanish American War earning a Brigadier General's commission. Also served as Brig. Gen. in World War I. *Brills Magazine*, May, 1910; *The Star*, January 9, 1952.

Union Station Plaza, October 4, 1908. Author's collection.

Capital Traction Union Station shuttle car 130 at Delaware Aven and C Street N.E., October 11, 1908. Author's collection.

Washington Railway and Electric Company 288 at Delaware Av nue and C Street N.E., October 11, 1908. Author's collection.

5. C Street, New Jersey to 1st N.W.

A & P Railroad

1. 1st and E Street S. E. North to 1st and B Street S.E.

In addition, the following extensions to Capital Traction lines were authorized.

Capital Traction

1. From 7th Street and Florida Avenue N. W., east to 8th Street East, south on 8th to connect with company's line at 8th Street and Pennsylvania Avenue S.E.
2. From New Jersey and Florida Avenues, south on New Jersey to Massachusetts Avenue.
3. From Union Station Plaza via F Street to 8th and F Street N.E.
4. A loop at 7th, T Street, and Florida Avenue N.W.

Appropriate contracts with the Pennsylvania and Baltimore and Ohio, owners of the Washington Terminal, on March 15, 1909, were entered into to govern operations on their property, the Plaza.[14]

Operation to the station began December 6, 1908. Connections necessary had been made without interruption to normal service.[15]

The new Union Station Plaza had a unique signal system which was the forerunner of others about town but peculiar to Washington. The system included five signal towers. One tower was at each end of the four tracks in front of the station, one at Delaware Avenue and C Street, one at 1st and B Street S.E. and one at the F Street, North Capitol and

Union Station switch tower as later used at 14th and New York Avenue N.W. in the 40's. Capital Transit Library.

Massachusetts Avenue intersection.

These towers, installed by the American Automatic Switch Company, contained switches and miniature diagrams to allow the tower operator to control switches. Motormen were apprised of the towerman's intention by red or green lights under a grating in the track. The system also provided appropriate interlocking devices to prevent collision.[16]

Pre-War Improvements

The Union Station project was large enough to overshadow other events of the same period. On February 8, 1908[17] Washington, Baltimore and Annapolis interurban trains began operating over the Columbia line from its eastern end to a terminal on Washington Railway property at 15th and H Street N.E. The terminal was known as White House Station. This, of course, generated traffic for Columbia cars which already enjoyed connections with Chesapeake Beach steam trains at Chesapeake Junction.

A rider to the bill enabling Union Station trackage was responsible for the city's first motorbus operation. Sixteenth Street had been served by a fleet of ancient horse drawn omnibuses known locally as Herdics, after their designer Peter Herdic. Congress was anxious to force modernization of this operation with then novel motor-buses.[18]

Accordingly, the owners, Metropolitan Coach Company, replaced the Herdics beginning January 17, 1909, with six new motor-buses. The bodies, built by the Brill Company, were mounted on two ton Mack chassis. The route was from 15th and U Street N.W. to 22nd and G Street N.W. via 16th Street, Massachusetts Avenue, 15th Street, H. Street, Pennsylvania Avenue, 17th Street and G Street. The round trip of two and a half miles took fifteen minutes and the fare was five cents.[19] The venture wasn't successful, perhaps due to the primitive nature of the vehicles and went out of business August 13, 1915.[20]

Meanwhile, both street car companies embarked on ambitious rolling stock programs. These programs were interesting because of the variety of car styles purchased and because they would replace the single truck trains with more modern double truck cars.

Purchases in 1908 included Capital Traction's Cincinnati semi-convertibles (132-143) and Washington Railway's incomparable "Rockville" cars (585-589).* Then in 1909, the "Pay as You Enter" car was introduced in Washington. This concept was a replacement of a fare collection system which required the conductor to work his way through the car hoping to pick out the new passengers and ask for their fare. Under the PAYE car plan, passengers paid their fares to the conductor as they entered the rear platform.

*Though referred to as "Rockville" cars by Washington fans, only seven (593-599) were originally assigned to the Rockville line while eight (585-592) were assigned to the Maryland (Hyattsville, Riverdale, Laurel) line. LeRoy O. King, Sr., "Washington Railway and Electric 585-599," *Headway Recorder*, February, 1960.

This ticket was printed on buff stock with light green pattern on front. Letteri[...]
and picture on reverse were black except for the ticket number which was re[...]
Author's collection.

Typical horse-drawn "Herdic" at Madison Place N.W. about 1897. Handy Studios, author's collection.

Washington's first public transit busses looked like this one. Metropolitan Coach Company's 9 was actually one of the second order of six Brill coaches mounted on Mack chassis. From Brill's Magazine.

Washington Railway 300, working the outer end of the Columbia Line, at Washington, Baltimore and Annapolis' White House Station [a]out 1908. Most city trips terminated in the loop in front of the station then. Library of Congress.

[In] the waning days of single-truck operation, this group of commuters hurry onto an ex-Columbia cable car in front of Woodward and [Lo]throp's on G Street about 1916. Library of Congress.

596, one of Washington Railway's majestic "Rockville" cars at 4 switch in 1908. Note MU jumper box under center front window. Harvey Davison collection.

FLOOR PLAN OF A PAY-AS-YOU-ENTER CAR

PAY FARE HERE COND'R ON OFF OFF OFF MOTORMAN OFF ONLY

The arrows show the movement of passengers entering and leaving the car

ELEVENTH STREET LINE COMMENCING
SUNDAY, MAY 16, 1909

PAY-AS-YOU-ENTER CAR *of the*
Anacostia & Potomac River Railroad Company

Brochure announcing introduction of PAYE service on 11th Street. Reverse, not shown, gave instructions to passengers. Car shown in tuscan red and cream colors applied to PAYE cars. Capital Traction had a similar brochure for their 14th Street service. Author's collection.

Capital Traction Cincinnati-built PAYE car 177 at Union Station in 1910. Photo by LeRoy O. King, Sr.

Washington Railway and Electric (Anacostia and Potomac Railroad Company) PAYE car 16 at Union Station in 1910. Note Anacostia and Potomac Railroad Company on platform knee--a condition that ended in 1911 with the final transfer of Anacostia and Potomac assets to Washington Railway and Electric Company. Photo by LeRoy O. King, Sr.

Interior of Washington Railway and Electric Company PAYE car 52. Brill photo, author's collection.

Capital Traction introduced PAYE service on 14th Street with newly acquired Cincinnati cars 151-170 on February 21, 1909.[21] Washington Railway followed on May 16, 1909, with service on the 11th Street line using newly acquired Brill built 1-50.[22] Later in the year, Capital Traction added nineteen cars to their PAYE fleet, bring the total to thirty-nine.

Following quickly the PAYE idea came the improved "Pay Within" idea. The very nature of the PAYE fare collection system slowed car loading since passengers had to pay while they boarded the car. On Pay Within cars, the conductor's position was moved further inside the car to the front of the rear platform. Thus passengers would board the rear platform before paying fares with a consequent speeding up of the loading process. Capital Traction's splendid Cincinnati built 1-15, acquired in 1909, were the first Pay Within cars. These were followed later (1912) by five identical cars numbered 16-20.

Increased use of double truck cars and line extensions rendered Capital Traction's Grace Street power plant inadequate. In 1910, because the site at Grace Street prohibited additions, a new facility was constructed on the southwest corner of Wisconsin Avenue and K Streets.[23]

In 1910 and 1911, the 36th and M street Union Terminal was extensively remodeled to permit handling and storage of double truck cars. Much of the steel structure was either replaced or strengthened, a car elevator was installed, as were transfer tables on the first, second, and third floors.

The office portion of the building was redone, and the upper floors on the street side of the building were extended out to the building line to provide additional office space.[24]

The remaining Washington Railway PAYE cars (51-100) came in 1911. In the same year, fifty 14-bench open car bodies, Washington's last, were ordered. These cars, numbered 1650-1699, were delivered in 1912 and used trucks and electrical equipment of 51-100. Exchange of equipment between 51-100 and the 1650's, while a saving in capital outlay, certainly added substantial annual expenses.

Air brakes were rare in the city in 1910. Only Capital Traction 1-15 and Washington Railway 585-99 and 507-16 were so equipped. In that year Capital Traction began equipping 807-815 with air brakes. In the fall of 1912, Capital Traction decided to so equip all their double truck passenger cars and by October, 1913, had completed the project.[25]

Perhaps sensing the logic of Capital Traction's decision, the Public Utilities Commission issued an order July 19, 1913, requiring all cars weighing sixteen short tons or more to be equipped with air brakes before December 1, 1914.[26] Washington Railway, however, didn't substantially complete the equipment of their fleet until 1915 when cars 2-15, 41-49, and 51-100, along with a number of 1600 series open cars and 425-449 were air brake equipped.[27]

Washington Railway's roster was depleted by fire on February 11, 1912.[28] The two floor car storage area of the

Handsome Capital Traction 1, the company's first Pay Within car, at Chevy Chase Lake about 1910. Author's collection.

36th and M Street Union Terminal during 1910-11 remodeling. Note Great Falls and Old Dominion terminal at left. Capital Transit Library, author's collection.

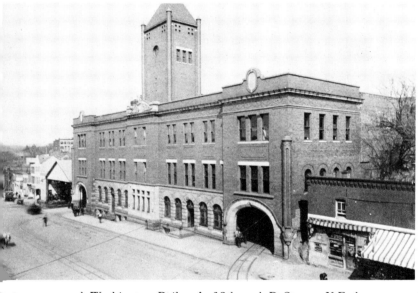

36th and M Street building in 1914 after remodeling from an abortive Union Station to a three-story car house. Note interurban station at left. Columbia Historical Society.

ty-two cars and Washington Railway's 13th and D Streets N.E. barn were destroyed on the night of February 11, 1912. Author's ection.

A Washington Railway and Electric Company center-door, northbound on 9th, while a 300 runs west on G Street in 1913. Library Congress.

Capital Traction trains were all replaced by double-truck cars less than five years after this 1908 scene. Handy Studios, author's collection

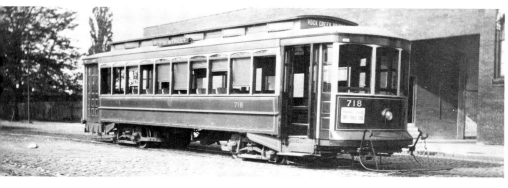

One of Capital Traction's 150 Jewetts at 7th Street barn, These sturdy cars, the backbone of the fleet, served well for over 30 years. Photo by LeRoy O. King, Sr.

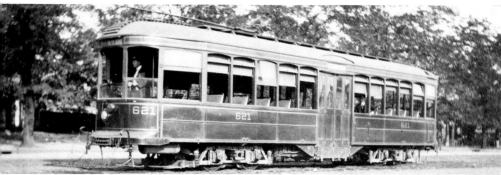

Washington Railway and Electric 621, one of the Brill-built center-door cars. Designed by Mr. W. A. Wenner, Washington Railway and Electric's master mechanic, they were known as "Washington" cars. They were duplicated for other properties only twice--one car to Perth, Australia, and two for the Buffalo (New York) and Williamsville. Photo by LeRoy O. King, Sr.

apital Traction Jewett 740 northbound on 7th Street N.W. at Massachusetts Avenue in 1918. Note lady traffic officer. U.S. Signal Corps.

13th and D Street N.E. carbarn and sixty-two cars were destroyed by fire. Losses included twenty-four of the 300 class cars and the remainder of the 1300 class of open cars. Grover Crown, night foreman, discovered the fire which was presumed to have been started by a short circuit in car 333. Employees got three cars out, but one of these was badly damaged. The portion of the building housing the substation was spared and survived another fifty years.

Capital Traction offered assistance but Washington Railway operating personnel solved the rolling stock shortage next day by rearranging schedules and equipment. This was done by decreasing service on all lines by only ten trips a day. The barn was never rebuilt, but the lot was used for minor open storage throughout the streetcar era.

Major rolling stock additions were made by both companies in 1912-13. Most unusual was Washington Railway's fleet of center entrance cars. The first of these was Brill built sample number 650 which made its trial run April 25, 1912. Experience with 650 led to orders for sixty more center doors which arrived in late 1912 and in 1913. Thirty were from Brill, twenty from St. Louis, and ten from Southern. Completing the center door fleet were ten heavy suburban versions, from Brill and Southern, and Southern built 1000, a double deck car. Originally the company had plans for using the double decker as a sightseeing car but the car didn't meet standards and after forty months of experimental use, was converted to single deck car 661.[29]

Capital Traction in the same period received 150 Jewett built Pay Within cars and five suburban cars (21-25) which were Brill versions of Cincinnati built 1-20. The Jewetts became the backbone of Capital Traction's fleet.

Acquisition of these new cars by both companies allowed compliance with an I. C. C. order issued October 28, 1912, which effectively ended operation of single truck trains. The order required a conductor on each vehicle after February 1, 1913. Both companies had complied by January 31 of that year.

In 1909, Washington Railway established an interesting but short-lived crosstown routing.[30] In order to better serve residents of the northeast section of the city who wanted to go to Anacostia, service was started May 1 on a line from 4th and T Street N.E. to 1st and E Street S.E. via Union Station. Series 200 ex-Columbia cars were used on this line. Prior to inauguration of this service, passengers who wanted to go from northeast to points on the Anacostia line had to go all the way to 11th and G Street N.W. to transfer. The line was soon replaced, however, by routing alternate Anacostia cars via Union Station. Cars carried small metal signs under the right-hand front vestibule window reading "Via Union Station" or "Via Center Market" as appropriate.

The Washington, Baltimore and Annapolis relocated their terminal from White House Station to 15th and New York Avenue on March 1, 1910.[31] A series of new Niles interurbans, lighter than the original AC cars, entered service on the line concurrent with a change from AC to DC on February 15, 1910. These changes, along with heavy rebuilding of the Columbia line, prepared the way for the interurban to reach the heart of downtown. Since 15th Street and New York Avenue was the throat of the Capital Traction system as well as the terminal for the Columbia line, street loading of W B & A trains would, in a few years, cause intolerable traffic congestion.

Women's Lib in 1913: Capital Traction Pennsylvania Avenue services were delayed over two hours for a Suffragette parade March 3, 19 C.W. Witbeck collection.

In addition to extending the North Capitol Street line to Brookland, Washington Railway double tracked their line on Nichols Avenue in Anacostia from Talbert Street to Congress Heights. Through service from 11th and Monroe Street N.W. to Congress Heights started November 12, 1911.[32]

On December 3, 1911, Washington Railway started through service from Brightwood and Forest Glen to the Wharves in place of the former terminal at 9th and Louisiana.[33] Major track renewal on 9th Street was undertaken culminating in renewal of the complicated underground conduit crossing at 9th and G Streets. The cost of replacement of this crossing in 1912 dollars was $40,000.[34]

Capital Traction improved service on its Chevy Chase Lake line by adding through service from the lake to 7th Street Wharves to already existent service every fifteen minutes to 15th Street and New York Avenue.

Inaugural Service

Washington's big event has always been the Presidential Inaugural. Pennsylvania Avenue, the traditional route of inaugural parades, is closed to traffic both on the Avenue and across it. This fact always leads to special and interesting arrangements.

Some observations on the 1913 Inaugural, which was on March 4, may be of interest. Washington Railway for the benefit of the many out-of-towners, equipped many of their cars with extra wood-backed paper signs outlining routes.

For example, on eastbound Lincoln Park cars the sign read:

"Union Station Capitol Library"

The reverse side of the sign used on westbound cars to Georgetown read:

"F Street Connecticut Ave. Georgetown"
Westbound cars to Mt. Pleasant carried a similar sign reading:

"F Street Connecticut Mt. Pleasant"
Extra trips were operated on the following routes, among others:

Connecticut and S to Lincoln Park
11th and Monroe to Union Station (return via City Hall)
Mt. Pleasant - Union Station
At peak periods for both inbound and outbound inaugural traffic W B & A furnished ten-minute headway of limited trains, some of them two cars. Capital Traction provided no extra routings but did, of course, increase service on regular routes.

Express Service

A new concept appeared on the Washington scene in 1914—that of express service on some of Washington Railway's longer routes. Through cars on longer routes stopped only at fire stops and intersecting rail lines until they reached the outer end of the line.

The term "Express" was something of a misnomer. The "Limited Stops" theory was intended to relieve overcrowding of cars bound for distant destinations by reserving them for those who needed them and forcing intermediate passengers to take the trippers which cut back during rush hours. Obviously, there was no time gained.

ound Washington Railway and Electric Company center-door car crossing the Baltimore and Ohio Railroad in Silver Spring, Maryland, on Forest Glen Line about 1915. Handy Studios, author's collection.

Connecticut Avenue, south from Bradley Lane, about 1915. Note marker lamp placement on one of Capital Traction's 1-20 series. Library of Congress.

Even though the service was widely publicized, a number of patrons were incensed at being passed up by the express cars. Nonetheless, Washington Railway and Electric Company with PUC's blessing tried it out for a number of years after experimentation on the Brightwood line.

A PUC order dated June 29, 1914, formalized express service for all cars leaving downtown points indicated between 4:00 and 6:15 p.m. on the following lines:[35]

Tenallytown - F Street Line	5th and F Streets to Wisconsin Avenue & P Street
Rockville Line	Wisconsin Avenue & M Street to District Line
Brightwood Line	9th Street and Louisiana Avenue to Soldiers' Home Jct.
Maryland Line	15th and G Streets to District Line
Glen Echo Line	5th and F Streets to 36th and Prospect Street N.W.

Included in the order were all the cars of both the W B & A and the Washington-Virginia. All cars, in express service, except those of W B & A and Washington-Virginia, were required to have a sign beside the entrance with the word "Express."

The service was, at first, enthusiastically received; in response to request of citizen groups, the service was expanded November 1, 1915, to include the Columbia Line from Treasury to 15th and H Street N.E.

Washington Railway was authorized in 1914 to construct a branch off the Wisconsin Avenue line at Macomb Street.

Pennsylvania Avenue, looking east from 26th Street N.W. July 1916. By July 15, completion of track changes would allow full of the new bridge over Rock Creek. Author's collection.

The line, a real estate venture, ran through virtually open country west to the District Line via Macomb Street and Massachusetts Avenue. Track and roadway crews had it in operation as far as Nebraska Avenue by May 27, 1914, and to the District Line by September 24.[36]

Another more important extension opened for service July 28, 1915[37] when trackage was completed on 14th Street from F Street to Pennsylvania Avenue. This trackage together with trackage rights over the Washington-Virginia from B Street south to Water Street and the construction of a double track turn-off from 14th into Water Street permitted service to the Bureau of Engraving and improved service to the Department of Agriculture.

Final pre-war extension was the Portland Street branch off the Anacostia-Congress Heights line. This line, completed in May, 1915, allowed service to the new Washington Steel and Ordnance Company plant at Giesboro Point on

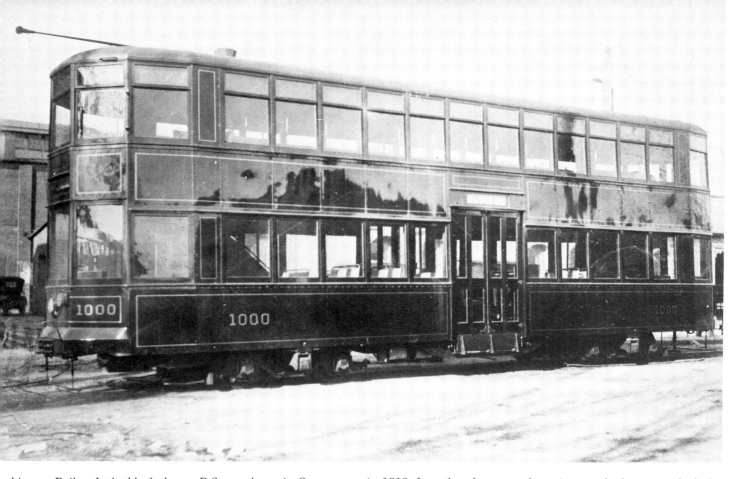

ashington Railway's double-decker at P Street shops, in Georgetown, in 1913. Less than four years later, it was rebuilt to a single-decker 1. Leet Brothers photo, author's collection.

route to Anacostia, Washington Railway's 10 eastbound on F Street N.W. waits for 615 on its way to Wharves before following it south 9th. Note double trolleys on 10. C.W. Witbeck collection.

the Potomac. At the same time, a single track extension to the Congress Heights line was added from Nichols and Alabama to Nichols and Upsal Streets, and conduit construction was extended across the Navy Yard bridge into Anacostia to Nichols Avenue and Talbert Street.[38]

Both Washington Railway and Capital Traction endured a rough but short strike of operating employees, over wages, in 1916. Cars continued to operate, but many were damaged by flying objects thrown by the strikers. The strike lasted two days and gave rise to this quaint statement in the Washington Railway's 1916 annual report:

> The Company absolutely refused to recognize the irresponsible organization known as the Amalgamated Association of Street Railway and Electric Employees.[39]

Capital Traction's extensions of this period were more modest. In 1916, the loop around the GAR monument at 7th and Pennsylvania was put into service and the M Street bridge over Rock Creek was vacated in favor of a more direct route across the new Pennsylvania Avenue Bridge.[40]

Service on 1st Street East was affected by two unusual problems in connection with the steam railroad tunnel serving Union Station. While the tunnels were under construction, 1st Street cars ran alongside the enormous excavation. When the tunnels were completed, a design defect in the ventilation system caused billowing clouds of steam locomotive exhaust to surge out of the manhole covers atop the tunnel. While the problem was soon corrected, it was no doubt an imposing sight for the street car patrons.

Now, another problem presented itself. Ground settlement, three feet or more, had occurred in 1st Street over the tunnels. For two years the street car tracks were left without paving. Jacks were placed under the tracks to compensate for the settling, and barriers were erected on each side of the tracks to keep vehicular traffic from falling into the ditch. Despite concern for the expense involved on the part of the traction companies, the costs were borne by the railroad.

Double Wire Overhead

Little known is the fact that several of Washington's trolley lines used double wire overhead. The idea, fully used in this country only in Cincinnati, was first required on the Columbia line extension in 1898.[41]

The purpose of double-wire overhead was to prevent electrolytic damage to underground pipes and conduits believed to be caused by stray electric currents flowing from poorly bonded rail return systems. Mr. MacFarland, then a District Commissioner, probably brought the idea with him from his native Ohio. Quite often, in the early days, even large double truck cars used one pole or, in the case of double wire, one set of poles. At the end of the line, conductors walked the poles around the car. With double poles this created a problem in geometry. Poles, side by side, when "walked" around often became hopelessly tangled. The first solution, adopted by both the Columbia and the A & P, was to mount both trolley bases on a single swivel. Later, Columbia and Capital Traction adopted staggered trolleys.

Columbia's operations were the most interesting of the double-wire lines primarily because at the line's two junctions there were no frogs. Conductors on Kenilworth cars had to swing their trolleys to the branch at Kenilworth Junction, and since W B & A cars enjoyed the through wires at the District Line, conductors on Chesapeake Junction cars had the same problem when entering the stub siding there. W B and A trains, using the Columbia line to their terminal at 15th and New York Avenue N.W., used three current collection methods. From the Treasury to 15th and H Street N.E., underground conduit; from there to the District Line, double wire; and, on their own line, single wire.

The Anacostia and Potomac inherited double wire operation from the provision for it in the original Capital Railway charter.

The Washington and Old Dominion was required to use double wire for their line over Aqueduct Bridge. In addition, three suburban lines (to be described in the next chapter) used it. These were:

> The Washington and Maryland Railway
> The East Washington Heights Traction Railroad Company
> The Washington Spa Spring and Gretta Railroad Company.

Washington Railway's Wisconsin Avenue line had double wire all the way to Rockville, and the Brightwood line had it to the District Line. Apparently, it was, in these cases, installed during a reconstruction project anticipating a directive which never came and neither line ever used it.

Washington's double wire program lasted until 1922 when PUC approved discontinuance. The wires remained for years until major maintenance made their removal economical.

On the eve of World War I, Washington's street railway system was virtually complete. However the trolley, still the dominant transport vehicle, was beginning to show signs of competition from the automobile. Capital Traction revenue passenger totals dropped over two million between 1913 and 1915. After 1915, wartime growth of government activity reversed the trend for a time, but the heyday was over.

A pre-World War I view, looking north at the intersection of Wisconsin Avenue and Old Georgetown Road in Bethesda, Maryland. Rockville Line cars turned off Wisconsin Avenue to Old Georgetown Road here. Library of Congress.

Conduit track being installed on 14th Street beside the Willard Hotel by Washington Railway and Electric Company in 1915. Columbia Historical Society.

Washington Railway 333, victim of a serious encounter, details unknown, being towed to the barn for repair about 1920. The scene is on the Columbia (Benning) line and shows the staggered trolley arrangement required by double wire overhead. Library of Congress.

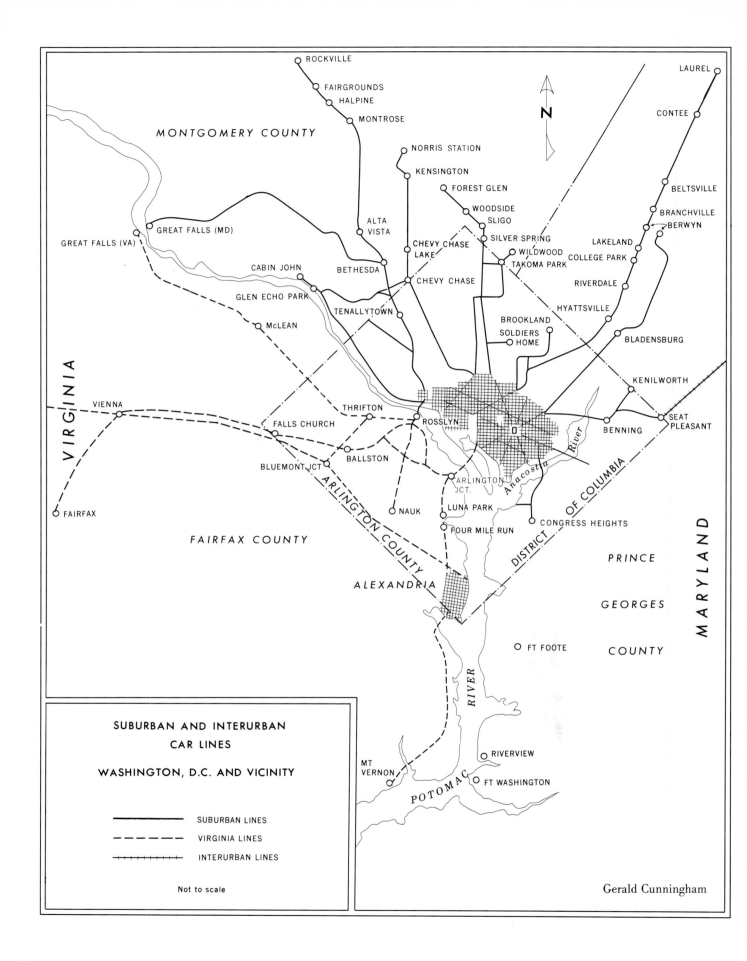

ROCKVILLE

FAIRGROUNDS
HALPINE
MONTROSE

LAUREL

CONTEE

MONTGOMERY COUNTY

N

NORRIS STATION

KENSINGTON

FOREST GLEN

BELTSVILLE

BRANCHVILLE
BERWYN

WOODSIDE
SLIGO

ALTA
VISTA

GREAT FALLS (MD)

CHEVY CHASE
LAKE

SILVER SPRING

WILDWOOD
TAKOMA PARK

LAKELAND

COLLEGE PARK

GREAT FALLS (VA)

CABIN JOHN

BETHESDA

CHEVY CHASE

RIVERDALE

GLEN ECHO PARK

TENALLYTOWN

HYATTSVILLE

McLEAN

BROOKLAND

SOLDIERS
HOME

BLADENSBURG

KENILWORTH

VIRGINIA

VIENNA

THRIFTON

FALLS CHURCH

ROSSLYN

BENNING

SEAT
PLEASANT

BALLSTON

BLUEMONT JCT

ARLINGTON JCT.

Anacostia River

DISTRICT OF COLUMBIA

MARYLAND

FAIRFAX

NAUK

LUNA PARK

FOUR MILE RUN

CONGRESS HEIGHTS

FAIRFAX COUNTY

PRINCE

ALEXANDRIA

GEORGES

COUNTY

FT FOOTE

RIVER

RIVERVIEW

MT
VERNON

FT WASHINGTON

POTOMAC

SUBURBAN AND INTERURBAN
CAR LINES

WASHINGTON, D.C. AND VICINITY

—————— SUBURBAN LINES

– – – – – VIRGINIA LINES

+++++++++ INTERURBAN LINES

Not to scale

Gerald Cunningham

94

CHAPTER FIVE
SOME SMALL INDEPEND-
ENTS

A number of interesting small lines served the outlying areas of Washington. While they were for most of their history nominally independent, they were closely tied to the city transit picture by virtue of equipment exchanges, operational tie-ins, or management connection. Included here are:

The Washington and Great Falls Railway and Power Company

The Kensington Railway

The Baltimore and Washington Transit Company

The Washington, Spa Spring and Gretta Railroad Company

The East Washington Heights Traction Railroad Company of the District of Columbia

The Washington and Great Falls Railway and Power Company[1]

West of present day Bethesda, Maryland, in the direction of Great Falls is one of Washington's finest residential areas. Included in the area is the Congressional Country Club. It was for the purpose of original development of this land that a charter was sought to construct the Washington and Great Falls Railway and Power Company line from Wisconsin Avenue at Bradley Lane to Great Falls.

The charter was granted May 29, 1912; and the line was placed in operation July 2, 1913. The single track line was ten and two-tenths miles long, comprising six signal blocks whose limits coincided with turnouts at Offutt, Wilson, Kefauver, Bradley and Lynch. Movements were governed by Nachod automatic signals, which incidentally were of a more advanced design than any of the manual signals used on other suburban lines. They permitted following but not opposing moves. Cars kept to the main line sidings except where meets were required. One thousand feet east of Bradley there was a temporary stub siding to a quarry. The line had a maximum grade of 5 per cent with many curves. The longest tangent was three quarters of a mile.

The line left a junction with the Rockville line at Bradley Lane in Bethesda and ran on the north side of the road (except for a short distance west of Edgemont) to the Country Club. There it crossed to the south side continuing to the intersection of Bradley Lane and River Road. From there it ran cross country to Great Falls. The trip took forty-three minutes.

nallytown car house in 1914. Left to right are Washington Railway and Electric Company 595, 505, 422 (probably) and 500. 505 was at at time in Great Falls service as indicated by its sign "5th and F N.W." Columbia Historical Society.

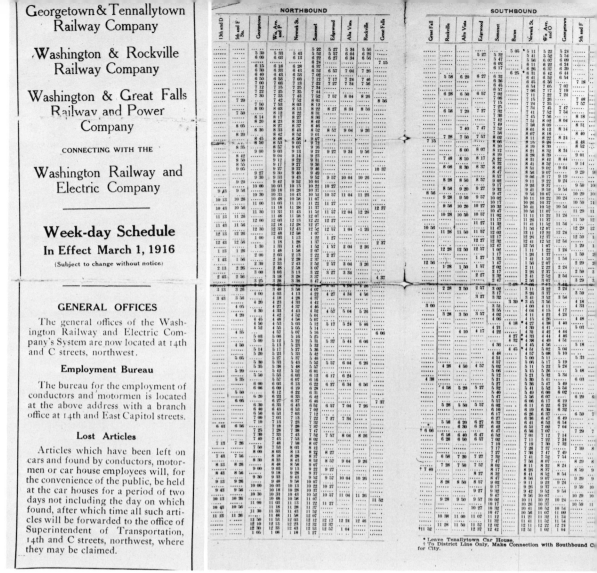

Georgetown & Tennallytown Railway Company

Washington & Rockville Railway Company

Washington & Great Falls Railway and Power Company

CONNECTING WITH THE

Washington Railway and Electric Company

Week-day Schedule
In Effect March 1, 1916
(Subject to change without notice)

GENERAL OFFICES

The general offices of the Washington Railway and Electric Company's System are now located at 14th and C streets, northwest.

Employment Bureau

The bureau for the employment of conductors and motormen is located at the above address with a branch office at 14th and East Capitol streets.

Lost Articles

Articles which have been left on cars and found by conductors, motormen or car house employees will, for the convenience of the public, be held at the car houses for a period of two days not including the day on which found, after which time all such articles will be forwarded to the office of Superintendent of Transportation, 14th and C streets, northwest, where they may be claimed.

Robert A. Truax collection

In the early days of operation the line was operated as a shuttle from the junction to Great Falls. It was always operated by Washington Railway and Electric Company for the account of the Great Falls road. For instance, on July 20, 1913, the line was being worked by one car, Washington Railway and Electric Company 422. On the same day there was a work train on the line with a W Ry & E Company 1700 class open trailer. On November 5, 1913, through service to downtown Washington was started. Service was maintained by 501-509 series cars. Service was offered from 5th and F every hour and a half. Through service was offered at least through 1918, but shortly after that the line was reduced to a franchise run from Wisconsin Avenue and Bradley Lane to Great Falls. Probably a W Ry & E Company 100 class single trucker was used for this.

The *Evening Star* reported that service was discontinued midnight February 12, 1921; but the Maryland Public Service Commission didn't approve removal of tracks until October 26, 1926.

The Kensington Railway[2]

The Kensington Railway had its southern terminal at Chevy Chase Lake. This line had its beginning in the Chevy Chase Lake and Kensington Railway which was chartered in September, 1894. The line, which began operation May 30, 1895, consisted of a single track line starting on the west side of Connecticut Avenue just south of the B & O Georgetown branch crossing at Chevy Chase Lake and running to the bank in Kensington. The line stopped just short of the road which crossed the B & O Metropolitan branch west of Kensington Station. On the south end there was a short stub siding just north of the B & O at Chevy Chase Lake and a through siding, known as Ray's Turnout, about midway on the line and just north of its crossing of Rock Creek. The line typically followed the contour of the land and, of course, had many curves. Original equipment consisted of two Jackson and Sharp closed motors built in 1895.

Power was supplied by Capital Traction as was equipment and line maintenance. As was so often the case, early history of the company was not too successful. It was sold at foreclosure in 1902 to the Kensington Railway, chartered in the same year.

The Montgomery Electric Light and Railway was chartered in April 11, 1902, to extend the Kensington eventually to Ellicott City, a suburb of Baltimore! The Montgomery Company's name was changed to Sandy Spring Railway March 23, 1906. At this point, all the stock and bonds of the Kensington Railway were purchased by Mr. Robert H. Phillips, representing those in control of Sandy Spring. This purchase was apparently in furtherance of the Baltimore extension plan.

The new owners immediately began the slow process of extending the line—along Howard Avenue to the highway bridge crossing the B & O at the west end of town. Two cars were added to the roster in 1908, a 1700 series Washington Railway open trailer to aid in construction and a new double truck semi-convertible from Stephenson, Number 11.

By 1910, construction had been completed to the bridge. Remaining progress was at a snail's pace. It wasn't until sometime in 1915 that the railway's bridge across the B & O was finished. Crossing the trestle, the single track followed a northeasterly course approximately three-quarters of a mile to a terminal known as Norris Station. This portion of the road was completed in 1916.

At the insistence of Kensington citizens and with their agreement to finance by bond issue the repair and improvement of the tracks. Capital Traction agreed to operate through service to downtown Washington. The lease was signed May 14, 1923; and operation by Capital Trac-

tion using Kensington Railway schedules commenced August 1, 1923.

Operation through to Potomac Park began November 11. Later cars went to 26th and G Street N.W., but, when the F & G Street line was abandoned in 1931, the southern terminal again became Potomac Park.

Shortly after Capital Traction operation began, a new turnout was constructed on the Kensington Branch as it was then known. This was "North Chevy Chase Turnout" and was located about a block west of the point where the line crossed Connecticut Avenue Extended in Kenilworth.*

During Capital Traction operation, their equipment was used. Kensington Number 11, the Stephenson 1908 car, was stored in the Chevy Chase Lake barn. The remaining equipment was stored at Norris Station where it fell prey to vandals and the weather.

Capital Traction operated the line for exactly ten years. They returned the property to the owners on August 1, 1933, along with three operable cars: Capital Traction 1 and 2, of the 1909 Cincinnati group, and 3 which was one of the 1898 American group.

*This Kenilworth was in what is now known as North Chevy Chase and is not to be confused with the other Kenilworth on the Columbia line at the east side of the District.

Kensington Railway's first 1 at Chevy Chase Lake about 1905. Photo by LeRoy O. King, Sr.

Kensington Railway 1 on trestle over Rock Creek about 1900. Montgomery County Historic Society.

Kensington Railway 3 and one of the two Cincinnatis' at the end of the line after abandonment. Photo by Stephen D. Maguire.

Right: Kensington Railway map. Adapted from U.S.G.S. Quadrangle map by G.F. Cunningham.

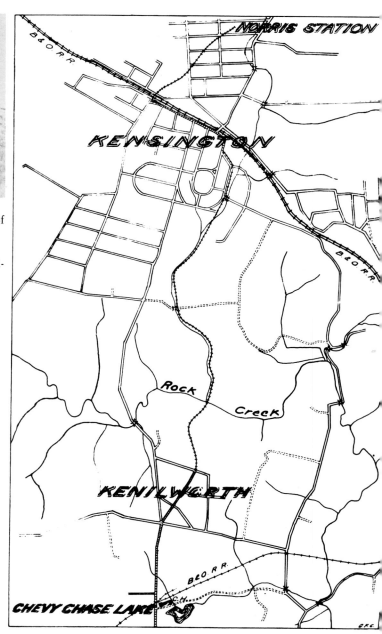

The road was to operate independently for just over two years. Lack of power caused abandonment when Capital Transit abandoned Connecticut Avenue in September 1935. At this time Capital Transit returned 11 but not in operating condition; it had been stored in the Chevy Chase Lake barn since the beginning of Capital Traction's Lease.

Mr. Phillips did attempt to find ways to continue, but Kensington cars would have been no match for new through Capital Transit buses.

Baltimore and Washington Transit Company

In 1894, the Baltimore and Washington Transit Company was chartered with the pretentious aim of constructing a line from the 4th and Butternut Street Terminal of the Brightwood Railway to Baltimore via an Ellicott City connection with a Baltimore line.[3] But like many similar projects, its name was far more impressive than its accomplishments.

In September, 1897, the line was placed in operation. The original route was from 4th and Butternut south on 4th to Aspen, thence to Laurel Avenue, Carroll Avenue,

Left: Wildwood terminal of the Baltimore and Washington Transit near what was later Elm and Heather Avenues in Takoma Park, Maryland. From the *Star*. Right: B. & W.T. 1, derelict on February 16, 1907. Photo by LeRoy O. King, Sr.

Ethan Allen Avenue to Jackson Avenue, and then across country to what is now Heather and Elm Streets in Takoma Park, Maryland.

We know that the line originally had two Jackson and Sharp open motors, but we have no record of any closed motors as original equipment. One wonders if there were many passengers in these early days because it wasn't until May 27, 1900, that the line served any destination that would attract significant patronage. On that date, Wildwood Park was opened. Advertisements of the era tell us of a dancing pavilion, vaudeville acts and "excellent cuisine," in a beautiful sylvan setting. A typical vaudeville act in those days included J.K. Wilson in minstrel melodies, J.J. Claxton, baritone, Daly Brothers, horizontal bars, Loretta Findley, soubrette and Harry Hanlein, Hebrew jesting. As an aside, maybe TV isn't so bad after all.

It's probable that the line relied on the Brightwood Railway for some equipment. Cars destined for Wildwood could be seen at 7th Street and Florida Avenue, but they were definitely Brightwood cars.

The line was far from successful. Wildwood Park may have been a drawing card for several summers, but only in summer. Wildwood Park itself had much competition from similar ventures at Cabin John, Bay Ridge and the variety of parks reached by river—Marshall Hall, Norley Hall, River View to name a few. It's easy to imagine that Wildwood lost its glamor, and the B & WT couldn't survive on meager summer traffic alone.

At any rate, we know that in February, 1907, the property was derelict. The two Jackson and Sharp bodies were mere hulks, the trolley wires gone, and in many cases the rail gone.

After so resounding a failure in the midst of the trolley boom, it must have taken some gambling spirit to revive the project. On May 30, 1910,[4] the line was reopened, but with two gasoline cars rather than electric.

The reopened route was, however, somewhat different from the original one. The single track line, with turnouts, started at the end of Capital Traction's 14th Street line.

Beginning at 14th and Kennedy Streets, N.W., it ran east on Kennedy to 3rd, north to Aspen, and then by way of the original line to Laurel and Carroll Avenues. The balance of the old route to Wildwood remained unused.

The gasoline cars, built by Stephenson with Brill trucks, were single truck with center doors. Each had forty HP Sintz-Wallen Marine engines designed to give a twenty mph speed at 600 RPM.[5] They were numbered 4 and 5 and painted "Pennsylvania" red.

Brill repossessed 4 and had advertised it for resale in July, 1911.[6] It was subsequently resold to Sioux Falls, South Dakota, as an electric car, their 17.

By August 28, 1911, two Edison Beach storage battery cars were operating on the line.[7] One of these, an eighteen-foot single truck car, was sold to the B & W and became their second 4.

In 1913, ownership of the Baltimore and Washington Transit Company changed. During that year the contractors constructing the road instituted foreclosure proceedings. Simultaneously they obtained control of the Baltimore and Ocean City Railway Company as a device to legalize their puchase at foreclosure of the B & WT Company. The Baltimore and Ocean City at the time owned only a charter. They purchased the B & WT for $20,500 and transferred its assets to the Baltimore and Ocean City Railway Company.

The Baltimore and Washington Transit Company seemed destined to failure. At 2:04 a.m. September 16, 1913, the barn, storage battery car 4 and gasoline car 5 were destroyed by fire.[8] The barn was a one-story frame structure on Blair Road. The loss was estimated at $14,800. With this disaster, of course, operations ceased for the time being.

However, it was hard to keep the B & WT down. In 1914, under a new corporate name, the Washington and Maryland Railway Company electrified its entire line. The *Star* dates the beginning of this electric operation as August 18, 1914. In November, 1914, Capital Traction car 324

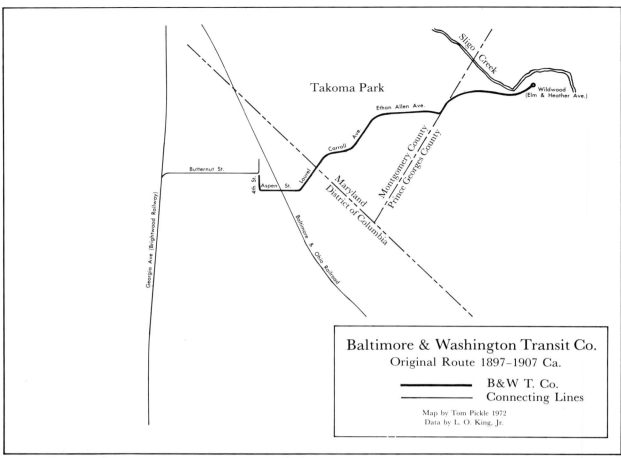

Baltimore & Washington Transit Co.
Original Route 1897–1907 Ca.

———————— B&W T. Co.
———————— Connecting Lines

Map by Tom Pickle 1972
Data by L. O. King, Jr.

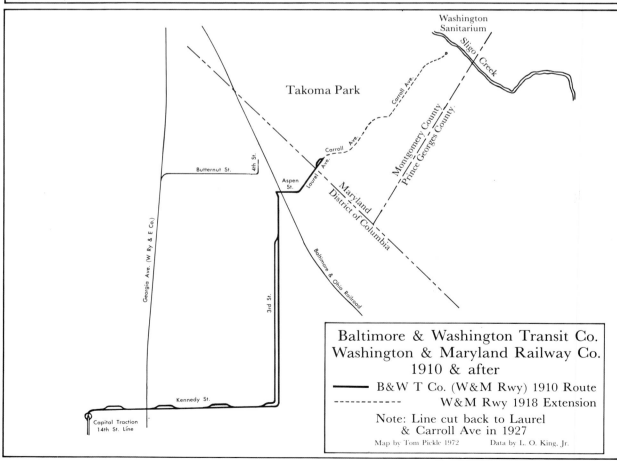

Baltimore & Washington Transit Co.
Washington & Maryland Railway Co.
1910 & after

———————— B&W T Co. (W&M Rwy) 1910 Route
- - - - - - - W&M Rwy 1918 Extension

Note: Line cut back to Laurel
& Carroll Ave in 1927

Map by Tom Pickle 1972   Data by L. O. King, Jr.

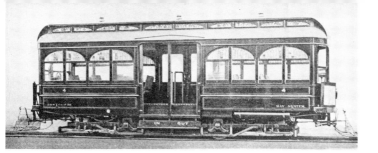

B. & W. T. Co. 4, one of the two Stephenson gasoline cars. Author's collection.

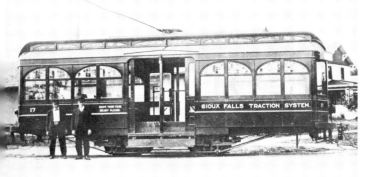

Sioux Falls (North Dakota) Traction electric car 17, ex-B.& W.T. Co. 4. Barney Neuburger collection.

Washington & Maryland 34, new in 1916, it was sold in 1918 to become Indiana Union Traction Company 30. Author's collection.

with double trolley was seen at 14th and Kennedy.* On one end there was a "14th and Kennedy" sign and the other end a "Takoma Park" sign.[9]   The car was operated by one man and gave half-hourly service. At the time, the road stopped approximately two hundred feet beyond the District Line.

Later, two cars, 597 and 598, were bought from Capital Traction. This made a total of three cars. Payments must have been hard to come by for the Traction Company repossessed 597-8 late in 1915.[10] It's probably that Capital Traction did not repossess 324 at the time because they were trying to make Washington and Maryland realize the seriousness of their debt, not to put them out of business. Before the year was out a lease arrangement for the three cars was arranged. The line was, after all, a feeder to the larger company. Apparently, a Capital Traction 8-bench open car, probably 72, was also leased. One such car, with double trolleys, was observed at 14th and Kennedy bound for Takoma circa 1914.

In 1916, the company acquired an additional car, a new one from the Cincinnati Car Company.[11] It was a single truck steel Cincinnati, numbered 54. It's apparent that the intent was to number the other three cars 51-

*Washington Railway & Electric Company car records indicate that their single truckers 123 and 153 were to be rented to the W & M in September, 1914. Available evidence suggests that this arrangement, if consummated, was of short duration.

53. In December, 1916, the Washington and Maryland entered into negotiations for its lease by Capital Traction. It was agreed that before the lease was to be consummated, the W&M would extend their line to the grounds of the Sanitarium of the Seventh Day Adventists. The new extension followed Carroll Avenue to its intersection with Sligo Branch. On May 2, 1918, the extension having been completed the Capital Traction Company took over the line under a ten year lease. By May 10, Capital Traction cars were handling the service off the 14th Street line.[12] Number 54 was sold immediately to the Indiana Union Traction Company becoming their 30.[13]

In December, 1921, Capital Traction's one-man safety car 300 was assigned to the Maryland portion of the line.[14] The service was protected by single truckers 315 and 316. Then, on November 17, 1922, the double overhead wires were discontinued in favor of standard single wire trolley system. A sidelight to this, the surplus poles and retrievers removed from cars 621-645 were installed on cars 139-143 and 171, 189. This allowed certain runs of the New Jersey Avenue line to be extended from Rock Creek bridge to Cleveland Park.

During the ten year lease period, Capital Traction acquired stock ownership of the line. During that time, in August, 1927, the Maryland portion of the line was abandoned, ending single truck passenger operation by Capital Traction. The corporation lasted until March 5, 1936, when it was dissolved by Capital Transit. A little over a year later, when the Takoma line quit in April, 1937, the final end came for an unbelievably tough little enterprise.

The Washington, Spa Spring and Gretta Railroad Company[15]

The Washington Spa Spring and Gretta had ambitious plans. Rumored ultimate terminals were to be Baltimore and Gettysburg—the latter to be reached via Frederick, Maryland. The road was incorporated in Maryland on February 14, 1905, and its charter ratified by the Mary-

Capital Transit 815 leaving Takoma terminal at Laurel and Eastern Avenues shortly before abandonment in 1937. Witbeck Photo from Charles J. Murphy.

land General Assembly on April 6, 1908. The original name, Washington, Spa Spring and Gretta Railroad Company, was as picturesque as its plans were ambitious.

An Act of Congress dated February 18, 1907, and subsequently amended authorized extension into the District of Columbia. It was not until August 27, 1910, however, that the road was placed in operation between 15th and H Street N.E. and Main and Sand Streets in Bladensburg. The line was single track with turnouts as required. Double wire overhead was used and power was purchased from the Washington Railway and Electric Company. The original barn and shop were located at 806 Bladenburg Road N.E.

Mr. Robert H. Phillips, owner of the Kensington Railway, had an interest in this line. Undoubtedly because of this, the Capital Traction Company, though not a connecting line, aided in maintenance and management.

Original equipment consisted of three cars from the Union Railway, New York City. These were purchased, secondhand, by Mr. Fayette Johnson who was at the time barn foreman at Capital Traction's Chevy Chase Lake barn. Two of the cars, 20 and 21, were deck roof single truck closed motors with closed platforms. Number 10 was a conventional ten-bench open motor. These three cars were green, but we have no record of builder or make of trucks.

Another and fourth car, 25, was former Capital Traction 20 in red and cream livery. This was a nine-bench, single truck Stephenson open motor car which had been built for the Rock Creek Railway in 1894. The late Mr. Johnson had recalled that this car with its G.E. 800 motors was so fast that it was felt advisable to slow it down, and this was done before it was put in service for its new owners.

A new Federal* storage battery car for the road was in the Pennsylvania Railroad freight yard October 26, 1910. This car was bought to determine the feasability of its use on a yet to be built extension from Bladensburg to Berwyn Heights.

Experiments must have been successful. The company sought and got permission from the Public Service Commission of Maryland on October 9, 1911, to sell $50,000 in bonds to finance the extension, which was to be about four miles. On March 28, 1912, permission was gained for sale of another $50,000 issue to finance cars and other equipment.

The record of a Maryland Public Service Commission

*The Federal Storage Battery Car Company, Silver Lake, New Jersey, built battery cars popularly called "Edison-Beach" cars. The name of the firm was changed circa 1912 to the Railway Storage Battery Car Company. E. Harper Charlton, "Railway Car Builders of the United States and Canada," *Interurbans*, Los Angeles, 1957, p. 29.

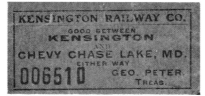

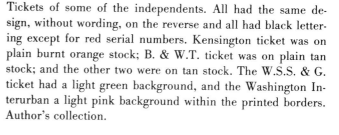

Tickets of some of the independents. All had the same design, without wording, on the reverse and all had black lettering except for red serial numbers. Kensington ticket was on plain burnt orange stock; B. & W.T. ticket was on plain tan stock; and the other two were on tan stock. The W.S.S. & G. ticket had a light green background, and the Washington Interurban a light pink background within the printed borders. Author's collection.

hearing on December 16, 1912, explains the purpose of the two bond issues. Some items were:

1. Construct a three-quarter mile extension from the present end of the track to Branchville Road at Berwyn Heights.
2. Reconstruct the last four miles of line. (This portion had been constructed by a contractor named Hampton who defaulted on the work. Although he was paid $50,000 for completed portion of work, the track was rough with several dangerous grades. It was proposed to cut some of these grades down.)
3. Acquire property and construct a terminal at 15th and H Street N.E.
4. Construct trestle work over the Eastern Branch at Bladensburg to raise the tracks above the high water mark.
5. Acquire four storage battery cars at $9,000 each plus shipping. (As of December 16, 1912, three were on hand and the fourth expected momentarily.)
6. Make track improvements, ballasting, etc.

In April, 1912, 10, the second storage battery car arrived. The road then announced its intention to convert the entire line to storage battery. In a trade journal article of the period, obviously composed by Federal Storage Battery public relations men, 8 per cent grades and the fact of only 800 feet of level track were cited, prematurely, as conquered obstacles of the efficient battery cars.

The extension was placed in operation in 1912 making a total mileage of 8.44 miles, 2.89 in the District of Columbia and 5.55 in Maryland. On October 12, 1912, the name was changed to the Washington Interurban Railway Company. By this time two Washington Railway 100 series cars, 124 and 161, worked from 15th and H Street N.E. to Bladensburg while 12 storage battery car worked the extension. A new barn had been built on the east side of Bladensburg Road opposite the gate to Mt. Olivet Cemetery. Number 20 and original 10 (an open motor) were derelict, 21 had been scrapped, and 25 converted to a dirt car. Storage battery car 10 had been returned to the factory while the road had acquired an additional storage

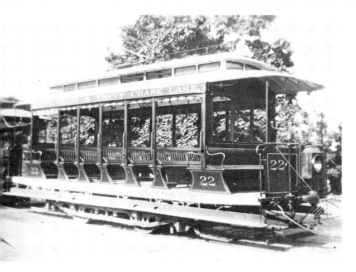

pital Traction 22 at Chevy Chase Lake about 1905. W.S.S. & G. 25 was similar. Photo by LeRoy O. King, Sr.

.S.S. & G.RR storage battery 11 on the line in 1910. Author's llection.

103

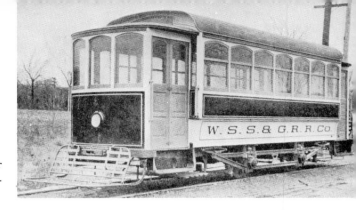

W.S.S. & G. RR storage Battery car 11 about 1910. Lee Rogers collection.

One of the 1912 Federal storage battery cars of the Washington, Spa Spring and Gretta. Author's collecti

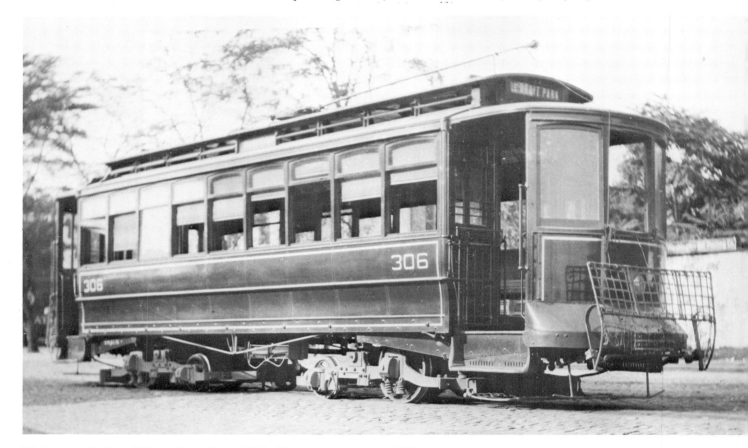

Washington Railway 306 on Water Street S.W. (Maine Avenue) about 1910. It was this type of car which Washington Railway and Elect Company converted to one-man in 1920. The first of these one-man cars operated over the Washington Interurban. Photo by LeRoy O. Ki Sr.

battery car 11. The line's complete operation by storage battery cars had not materialized.

Like many trolley lines, this one was planned to encourage real estate growth along its line. Under the name of the Bladensburg Development Company, the railroad owned real estate for development purposes. The territory served was, unfortunately for the W SS & G, already well served by the Baltimore and Ohio's line to Baltimore and the well-established Maryland line of the Washington Railway and Electric Company. The population was hardly sufficient to support two electric lines plus whatever local service the Baltimore and Ohio might wish to provide.

Complaints against the line indicate that the service offered was primitive at best. As we have seen, regular trolleys were operated as far as Bladensburg, storage battery cars to Brownings Road (Riverdale) and as of May, 1913, no service at all beyond Riverdale. The change at Bladensburg between the trolley and the battery car required a hundred-foot walk along the track, there being no acceptable platform arrangement.

On October 6, 1913, the Washington Railway agreed formally to operate the line, and from then on operation was with 200-300 class Washington Railway cars. Washington Railway physically connected the line to theirs by means of a switch on the White House Station loop at 15th and H Street N.E. and electrified the entire line.

From December 1 to 15, 1913, Washington Railway operated, experimentally, through cars from 15th and H Street N.E. to Berwyn. Their conclusion was that patronage was insufficient. Service returned to an unsatisfactory state as evidenced by additional complaints in April, 1914. Since no turnout and no terminal existed at Bladensburg, passengers still had to put up with changing cars which met head-on at Bladensburg School. When cars were late, these meeting places might be anywhere. A complainant noted that, "On every trip Berwyn to Bladensburg, trolley off wire

two to ten times. Conductor must take seat at center window of rear platform, engaged continuously in replacing trolley along rough stretch of track."

On or about June 15, 1914, the Railway Storage Battery Car Company foreclosed on its mortgage, forcing receivership. The franchises were sold to Gustave Herre on December 23, 1915. To effect the transfer, Herre and his associates formed the Washington Interurban Railroad Company January 27, 1916. Washington Railway's subsidiary, the Washington and Rockville, acquired ownership of the Washington Interurban by stock purchase effective March 20, 1916.

Washington's first one-man safety cars operated over this line. Washington Railway converted a number of the 200 series cars to one-man, the first in 1920.

The company at an early date was proven uneconomical. The Public Service Commission of Maryland approved bus substitution from Berwyn Heights to East Riverdale effective June 11, 1921. Permission to remove track was not approved, however, until September 19, 1923.

Although abandonment was fought by the public served by the line, its demise seemed inevitable. In 1922, Congress appropriated money for paving Bladensburg Road. The company's contribution was to be $152,000. This was in addition to a $7,523 claim by the District of Columbia arising out of replacement by the District of the center poles with span wire construction in 1914. Clearly, these expenditures were beyond the means of the company which, therefore, applied for permission to substitute buses.

The District of Columbia Public Utilities Commission on April 11, 1923, and the Maryland Public Service Commission on May 10, 1923, authorized respectively bus substitution from 15th and H Street N.E. to the District Line and from the District Line to Bladensburg. Buses replaced street cars on April 22, 1923. Remaining, however, was the Bladensburg School/East Riverdale segment which, curiously,

Washington Interurban's less-than-pretentious waiting station at 15th and H Streets N.E. Brick building in the upper left corner is the Columbia barn. Shannon collection, Columbia Historical Society.

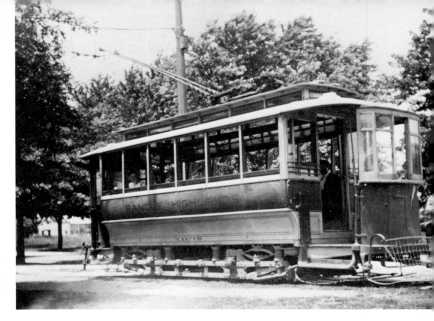

One of East Washington Heights Traction's two ex-Washington Railway and Electric Company cars at 17th and Pennsylvania Avenue S.E. about 1905. Photo by LeRoy O. King, Sr.

operated between two buslines until its substitution was authorized by the PSC April 4, 1925.

The East Washington Heights Traction Railroad Company of the District of Columbia[16]

From 17th and Pennsylvania Avenue S.E. across the Anacostia River for a distance of .72 mile ran the East Washington Heights Traction Railroad Company of the District of Columbia. One can't resist the remark that the length of the name almost exceeded the length of the line.

The basic purpose of the company was to provide transportation facilities for the Randle Highlands real estate development. Arthur E. Randle, president of the East Washington, and the United States Realty Company of Washington together owned 75 per cent of the stock.

The road had its beginning in an Act of Congress approved June 18, 1898. The company was organized July 15, 1898. The route was to begin at 17th and Pennsylvania Avenue S.E., cross the Anacostia River on a company-constructed trestle and proceed along Pennsylvania Avenue to Branch Avenue. Branches were called for as follows:

1. Along Minnesota Avenue to Harrison Street.
2. North along 28th Street and Anacostia Road to East Washington Park.
3. Along Branch Avenue to Bowen Road to Good Hope Settlement.
4. From Branch Avenue and Bowen Road to the District Line.

A charter amendment of April 30, 1900, authorized connection with the Columbia Railway at Benning. The amendment also granted trackage rights over the still non-existent road by the Washington and Marlboro Railroad Company. This road was chartered to connect the area with the Chesapeake Beach Railroad (a steam line) at Marlboro, Maryland. Nothing ever came of the proposition, however.

An amendment of July 1, 1902, provided for the use of the Pennsylvania Avenue bridge and also, for the second time, extended the original two-year time limit for construction of the road.

Construction finally began in May, 1905. The only portion ever constructed ran from the terminus of the Capital Traction at 17th and Pennsylvania Avenue S.E. across the bridge and along Pennsylvania Avenue to the other side of Minnesota Avenue. There was one siding midway between the end of the bridge and the east end of the line. At the east end of the line on the south side of the avenue was a two-car capacity unpainted car barn. The line was laid with eighty-six-pound rail, had double overhead trolley and used power purchased from the Capital Traction Company.

At approximately 4 p.m. August 31, 1905, Capital Traction tested the lines and turned on the power. Two identical ex-Washington Railway cars, 25 and 27, opened the line. These were motorized ex-Belt horsecars. These were turned over to Capital Traction at 1st and B Street N.E. and delivered by Capital Traction to the East Washington at the Anacostia River Bridge.

The line was place in operation at 12:22 p.m. September 1, 1905; the first round trip took ten minutes. At a date unknown, the line acquired two standard eighteen-foot closed motors from Capital Traction to replace the original equipment. The 1916 Public Utilities Commission report noted that "the division superintendent is also motorman and conductor at a salary of $2.00 a day; he received in addition $10.00 a month as superintendent."

The history of the line was rather uneventful and, as early as January, 1923, the PUC, in response to complaints by residents, was seeking ways and means of effecting a change. After a number of solutions were reviewed, the PUC issued an order on May 17, 1923, calling for East Washington substitution of bus service for the rail line and an extension of the bus service into Randle Highlands. The order also required settlement of tax indebtedness to the District. Failure to substitute buses and settle the tax matter by August 1, 1923, would be sufficient justification to revoke the order and authorize others to operate over the route. East Washington could not comply and, on November 1, 1923, the PUC ordered Capital Traction to provide bus service. The last car of this little line ceased operation at 10 a.m. December 1, 1923.

CHAPTER SIX
THE TWENTIES

World War I

The entry of the United States into World War I made increased demands on many traction properties, and Washington's were no exception. Many changes to traction lines were proposed to suit wartime conditions, but our participation in the war was too short for many of the proposals to be effected.

The Portland Street extension in Anacostia, essentially a wartime venture, was completed before we entered the war. Capital Traction's Potomac Park loop, designed to serve numerous wartime temporary buildings near its terminal at 18th and Virginia Avenue, was not operating until June 1, 1918,[1] and really couldn't be said to be complete until April 15, 1919. On this date Washington Railway cars began operating over the Potomac Park loop via connecting tracks on 17th Street from H to Pennsylvania Avenue. Although it is probable that war conditions called for this last line, it was not authorized until November 20, 1918, nine days after the armistice.[2]

One of the major effects of the war, aside from the influx of a multitude of new government workers, was the shortage of skilled personnel available for operation of the street railway system. Many, of course, went to war, while others left for higher paying jobs. This led to service and maintenance shortcomings.

By February, 1918, the Senate had become sufficiently interested in real and imagined shortcomings in streetcar service to ask John A. Beeler, New York consulting engineer, to make a survey of the situation.

Among other points, Beeler's study revealed that an eastbound Capital Traction car traveling from 15th and New York Avenue to 14th and Pennsylvania Avenue (about three blocks) made no less than seven established stops. This was changed to three, at locations which served until the end of the streetcar era.[3]

Since 1910, Washington, Baltimore and Annapolis interurban trains had been using a stub terminal at 15th and New York Avenue, the downtown end of the Columbia line. Beeler felt that storage of interurbans between runs at the end of the line, loading times of up to six minutes per train at 14th and New York Avenue, and delays caused by alleged faulty maintenance were all reasons to force the W B & A to return immediately to the use of White House Station at 15th and H Streets N.E.[4] This recommendation was not carried out, but it did lead to the establishment of a new off-street terminal for the interurban at 12th and New York Avenue N.W. in January, 1921. The Beeler report is responsible for the preservation of some rather impressive statistics. For instance, on February 28, 1918, from 4:30 to 6:00 p.m., Beeler's checkers observed 172 Washington

Railway cars and 178 Capital Traction cars passing 14th and H Street N.W.[5] Considering the variety of car types and destinations, this would certainly have been an interesting hour and a half for a traction fan!

The war was responsible for the purchase of one of Washington's most outstanding groups of cars. Fifty cars, numbers 700-749, were ordered by Washington Railway in 1918 from G. C. Kuhlman Car Company, Cleveland, Ohio. Capital Traction followed with an almost identical group of twenty cars (numbers 26-45) from the same builder. In 1919, Washington Railway ordered fifteen more (750-764) and Capital Traction forty more (46-85); both orders in this instance, however, went to Brill in Philadelphia.[6] The similarity of these 125 cars was no doubt due to wartime restrictions. No other group of Washington Railway and Capital Traction cars were so nearly alike.

The second Eckington car house fire occurred on February 24, 1919. This one was reported to have started with a short circuit in car 589 which, along with thirty-two others, was destroyed. The insurance money for this fire was used to purchase 750-764.

One-Man Cars

After the war, Washington Railway turned to the one-man safety car as a solution to increased wage costs. Typically, Washingtonians fought the idea largely on safety grounds. Operation of a vehicle the size of a street car required the motorman's full attention, so the argument went, and his attention could not safely be diverted by fare collection duties. Nevertheless, Washington Railway, taking advantage of safety devices then available, converted twenty-eight of its 200 class cars to one-man safety cars. The first of these operated on the Bladensburg Road line in 1920. By 1921, one-man cars were being operated on the Wisconsin Avenue line, the LeDroit Park line and the 11th and Monroe-North Capitol Street line.

By 1923, thirty-two additional cars of different series had been remodeled for one-man service. This, along with the purchase of ten new one-man cars, brought the total to seventy. At this point, public dislike of them caused the Public Utilities Commission to forbid further rebuildings.

Capital Traction, for its part, had only one experience with the one-man idea. Their 300, one of the 1902 Stephenson single truck motors, was assigned to Pennsylvania Avenue on April 10, 1921, and transferred to the Maryland section of the Takoma line in December of that year. Unlike 324 which had been operated by one man on Kennedy Street, 300 was equipped with folding doors and appropriate safety control devices.[7] Capital Traction must have been less than satisfied, for it was removed

Spanish American War veterans' parade in the early '20's, passes the Treasury at 15th and Pennsylvania Avenue N.W. Note new Capital Traction 83 followed by two 600 series Jewetts. Library of Congress.

15th Street N.W. looking north from the south lawn of the Treasury during World War I. At that time, Capital Traction cars still h fenders. Library of Congress.

...ooking south from 15th and New York Avenue N.W. in 1918. This was the busiest junction on the Capital Traction system. The auto was ...ginning to cause the traffic problem which, it was thought, would be solved when the streetcars were abandoned. Library of Congress.

...th Street just below New York Avenue about 1920. Note the MU jumpers on Washington Railway and Electric Company 734 and the ...urred Washington, Baltimore and Annapolis interurban crossing in front of the Georgetown center-door car. Library of Congress.

In the early '20's, Washington Railway and Electric Company 268, a one-man car, runs north on 14th at C Street N.W. The track entering from the left is from the Mt. Vernon line terminal at 12th and Pennsylvania Avenue N.W. Library of Congress.

Two Washington Railway and Electric Company 1600's cross 11th Street at F N.W. in the '20's. Note the "Jitney", an early form of unregulated competition. Library of Congress.

Washington Railway and Electric Company 68, in 11th Street-Anacostia service, loads passengers on 9th Street just below Pennsylvania Avenue just before 1920. Library of Congress.

Washington Railway's safety message was carried, in the early '20's, on ex-open car 1639 which had been rebuilt for the purpose in 1918. Library of Congress.

Capital Traction 681 westbound on Pennsylvania Avenue just west of 7th about 1920. Note W.Ry. & E. Co. car crossing at 9th Street in the background. Library of Congress.

9th Street, north from Pennsylvania Avenue, about 1914 with W. Ry. & E. Co. center-door in the distance. Compare the number of autos in this picture with those in other pictures on these two pages. Library of Congress.

111

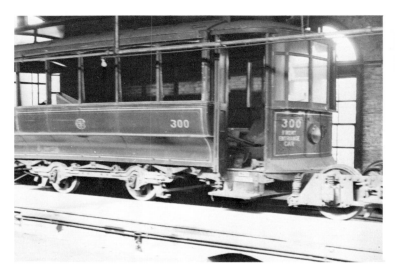

Left: Capital Traction one-man car 300 at 14th and Decatur barn in 1939. Robert S. Crockett. Right: Interior of 300 as one-man c[...]
Author's collection.

Interior of Capital Traction 79 shows the style for streetcars in the early '20's. Rattan seats were typical. W.Ry. & E.Co. 750's were simil[...]
The Historical Society of Pennsylvania.

from the active roster in 1924, although it wasn't scrapped until 1940.

Train Operation

Washington Railway and Capital Traction both began experimenting with the larger double truck cars operated in trains. Washington Railway, in 1918, had ordered fifty 700's partially equipped for proposed hauling of closed trailers rebuilt from open cars. Partial equipment included Tomlinson couplers and multiple-unit jumper boxes. Beginning in July, 1919, Washington Railway experimented with multiple-unit operation of certain of the new cars. In the following spring, experiments turned to the motor-trailer idea. It was decided to rebuild a number of the 1650 calss "Narragansett" open car bodies into closed cars. The first of these, 1071 and motor 749 were operated on various East Capitol Barn (Lincoln Park)—Fourteenth and "F" and East Capitol Barn—Georgetown schedules to gather data on energy consumption, passengers carried, and platform hours. On the basis of these runs, the company's engineers recommended the adoption of the motor-trailer train idea as opposed to the multiple-unit train of two motor cars.

As a result of these experiments, motor cars 742-749 were equipped to haul trailers. In addition to 1071, another "Narragansett" became trailer 1073. Because this type of operation was extremely limited by the WRy & E Co's track system, the engineers now considered the possibility of train operation on stub end lines. This necessitated a control trailer instead of a plain trailer.

Thus, by 1923, 1071 and 1073 had been converted to control trailers and two additional "Narragansetts" were converted directly to control trailers 1079 and 1080. In addition to control equipment, four jumper cables instead of two between the cars were required. With electric switches to operate, the lead car, and thus, both cars had to have a plow. This made necessary a cut over switch placed on the rear platform of the motor car to switch from one plow to another.[8]

By this time (1923), the decision was made to limit the trains to four in number. Of the eight motors equipped for trailer haul, only five (745-749) were later revised for service with the control trailers. Two other "Narragansetts", apparently originally slated to become trailers, were converted directly to motor cars 801 and 802 in 1921 and 1922 respectively. Years later, all of the Kuhlman 700's still carried two round patches over the headlight, a reminder of the original idea of equipping all fifty cars for train operation.

These trains were successfully used, in rush hour principally, on the Mt. Pleasant line. One train was assigned to the Maryland line for a short period, however. Except for this operation which lasted up to the early Thirties, Washington Railway had no known double truck train operation, although the "Rockville" cars were delivered equipped for multiple-unit operation. In the winter of 1936-37, after a couple of years in storage, the four trailers were rebuilt and equipped with newly-acquired trucks and motors to become **Capital Transit Motor Cars 914-917.**

Capital Traction's train experiment was more complicated. Cars 26-45, purchased in 1918 were equipped with train operation. However, Washington's underground conduit system gave rise to complications with train operation not encoutered in other cities. These complications led to engineering work which took until 1924 to solve.

Capital Traction's first multiple-unit train operation, in revenue service, began in early 1924—a morning rush hour trip from 14th and Decatur to the Navy Yard. A "High School Special" leaving Rock Creek Loop at 8:25 a.m. and running down 7th Street was among the trains operated in 1924.

By November 1925, train operation had reached its maximum extent. Three trains were operated on 14th and Decatur—Union Station and 14th and Decatur—Potomac Park schedules in both the morning and evening rush while two trains were operated morning and evening between Rock Creek Bridge and 7th Street Wharves. Of the original group of twenty cars, only twelve, numbers 26-37, were finally equipped to operate these services, ten for the five trains and two for spares.[9] By 1931, only seven cars were equipped for train operation and the equipment on these was removed that year.

The short term of multiple-unit train operation was due to two factors: complexity and increased automobile traffic. In Washington's underground conduit system, positive and negative supply were both taken from the underground rails. This fact required breaks, called "deadmen", in the underground rails at crossings and switches to avoid direct contact between positive and negative rails. Cars had to cut current and coast over "deadmen" to avoid serious and possibly damaging arcing.

Since both positive and negative supply was taken from the underground, the system could be sectionalized. If a ground occurred in one section, the polarity was reversed until the problem was solved. While this was an advantage, it enormously complicated Capital Traction's train operation as did the current cut-off problem at "deadmen".

Capital Traction attempted multiple-unit operation with K controllers. In other words, all eight motors of a train were controlled directly from a single controller with one plow. Because polarity might change momentarily, two live plows (one for each car) would cause a short circuit by bridging sections of opposite polarity.

The use of only one live plow to a train led to more problems too complex for a rule book to correct. If a motorman missed cutting current at a deadman with a single two or four motor car, it could be damaging, but much more so with the increased amperage of an eight motor train. The live plow had to be on the leading car since a live plow on the second car would activate automatic switches under the train with consequent derailment. When reversing ends, the rules called for extreme care to insure that the live plow was cut out before the other plow was cut in, lest a short circuit occur.

Increased auto traffic required cars with faster acceleration and braking, a need which largely ruled against train

Washington Railway and Electric two-car train in a publicity shot at 1st and East Capitol Streets in 1923. 1703 was a control trailer bu... from an open car which, in 1936, was converted to Capital Transit motor 915. Author's collection.

W.Ry. & E. Co. control trailer 1079 heads a two-car train southbound at Dupont Circle and P Streets N.W. on the Mt. Pleasant-Lincoln Pa... line about 1923. Robert A. Truax collection.

Capital Traction multiple-unit train at Water (Maine Avenue) and O Streets S.W. Note that the cars are equipped with trolley boards and hooks but no trolley poles. Library of Congress.

nother picture at 15th and New York Avenue looking south. This one, about 1930, shows, at the upper left, the only known view of a pital Traction MU train in operation. Author's collection.

operation on city streets.

Incidentally, the Washington, Baltimore and Annapolis interurban, operated two-car trains with much less complication. It avoided Capital Traction's problems by utilizing true multiple-unit control. In other words, the only electrical link between two cars was the control circuit, not the entire power supply. And, of course, they could afford to put up with the traffic problems in exchange for the real advantage of train operation when they reached private right-of-way.

The Blizzard of 1922[10]

A major event in the history of the city, as well as for the traction companies, was the blizzard of 1922. It began at 4:00 p.m., Friday, January 27, and continued for twenty-eight hours. The snow started with such ferocity that street car service was severely affected by 9:00 p.m., as were railroad schedules. For much of the period, snow fell at the rate of an inch an hour. This was the first blizzard to befall Washington since the advent of the motor car; and, in the words of one writer, traffic was "demoralized."

The rapidity of the onslaught along with the large number of abandoned autos caused early capitulation of the city to the blizzard.

Washington Railway had twenty-two sweepers ready for service, but by the time they were really needed, ten were burned out and half of the rest were caught among the stalled vehicles in the streets.

When the snow stopped, twenty-six inches had fallen; and in many places drifts of five feet were common. On top of that, alternate melting and refreezing of the road surface led to almost impossible ice conditions.

In the midst of all this hardship, at about 9:00 p.m., Saturday night, the roof of the Knickerbocker Theater at 18th and Columbia Road collapsed while the second show was in progress. Ninety-six persons lost their lives while 125 were injured. Caring for this problem, which included calling out the Marines, further delayed recovery from the storm.

Even as late as Tuesday a trip in from Chevy Chase, seven miles, required transferring five times and a total walk of a mile or more.

After six days of Herculean efforts, the city returned almost to normal. Ironically, a temperature change on the seventh day removed more snow than all the efforts by men and machines of the preceding six days. Washington didn't

Ninety-six lost their lives when the Knickerbocker Theater roof collapsed from snow on January 28, 1922. Car 725 is actually on northbound track on Columbia Road enroute to Mt. Pleasant although its sign is set for Lincoln Park. Library of Congress.

Washington Railway heavy center-door cars caught in the blizzard on January 28, 1922, at 22nd and Rhode Island Avenue N.E. Note motorman's door on 577. Mike Lavelle collection.

n January 28, during the 1922 blizzard, this was New York Avenue west from 14th Street. The long line of cars is on the W.Ry. &E. Co. lumbia line. A lone Capital Traction car is in the right background. Library of Congress.

A spectacular wreck at the intersection of Washington Railway's 9th Street and F Street lines in 1921. On 9th Street are two W.Ry.&E. 1-100 series cars, while the car marked "Mt. Pleasant" is one of the 425 series. Witbeck Photo. Author's collection.

see another storm to match this one until 1966.

Early Bus Operation

The motorbus became important in the Twenties. The traction companies saw it as a supplement to rail service and as a replacement for marginal trolley lines. By the end of the decade, though, it would be a major factor in the city's transit picture. The unsuccessful Metropolitan's Coach Company's operation was the first motorbus operation in the city. In 1921, however, the Washington Rapid Transit Company established successful operation on 16th Street. The company operated two routes south from 16th Street and Columbia Road: one to Potomac Park and one to 8th Street and Pennsylvania Avenue. The operation boasted fifteen buses.[11]

The following year, Capital Traction and Washington Railway started joint operation of the Woodley Road Bus line.[12] In 1923, the Carnegie Institute on Connecticut Avenue asked Capital Traction to substitute buses for street cars north of Rock Creek Bridge from 1:30 to 5:30 a.m. The request allowed the Institute to conduct experiments which were interfered with by trolleys.[13] Capital Traction found buses more economical for "owl" service and continued it.

Regular bus services were established by both traction companies throughout the decade. Some of these replaced electric car operations such as Randle Highlands and the Washington Interurban while others opened new territories. Capital Traction introduced the "Chevy Chase Coach Line," a deluxe extra-fare service from Chevy Chase to downtown in 1925.[14] Of course, the Washington Rapid Transit prospered from the growth of the suburbs north and east of their 16th Street trunk line.

Although most extensions were now bus service, streetcar service was extended to Rosslyn, Virginia, over the new Key

W.Ry.&E.Co. bus of the mid-'20's. This is a Yellow Coach in fr of the Pan American Union Building. Author's collection.

Bridge on December 1, 1923.[15] The District required the company to collect a half cent per passenger bridge toll and special tickets were sold for this. The opening of Key Bridge meant the establishment of a new terminal for the Washington and Old Dominion on the Virginia side of the river. Their terminal was on the west side of the Capital Traction loop while the Washington-Virginia Railway cars had their terminal on the east side. Neither line had physical connection with each other or with the Capital Traction.

Recreation by Trolley

A number of recreational activities in the twenties still generated nonrush hour traffic for the trolleys.

There were steamboats for holiday and weekend trips down the river: the *St. John* to Colonial Beach, the *Charles McAllister* to Marshall Hall and the *E. Madison Hall* to

Connecticut Avenue, looking south at Cathedral Avenue in 1930. Bus is one of Capital Traction's Chevy Chase coaches. U.S. Bureau of Public Roads.

rare view of a Washington Railway 300 on Massachusetts Ave-e near Nebraska in 1923. Photo by Conant Emmons.

Riverview. The Norfolk and Washington Steamboat Company operated nightly voyages to Norfolk, Newport News and Old Point Comfort while the Baltimore and Virginia operated the unlikely route from Baltimore to Washington. When a steamboat arrived at 7th Street Wharves, there waiting for it was a selection of cars to most parts of the city over the lines of both the Capital Traction and the Washington Railway.

On weekends and holidays steam roads serving Union Station operated low fare excursion tours to many nearby East Coast points. The Chesapeake Beach Railway still operated summer excursion trains which added traffic to the Columbia line.

Finally, in the twenties, there were still a number of amusement parks: Great Falls Park on the Old Dominion, Luna Park (at Four Mile Run) and Arlington Beach (virtually where the Pentagon is), on the Washington-Virginia, Glen Echo on the Washington Railway's Cabin John line, Suburban Gardens on the Washington Railway's Columbia line, and Chevy Chase Lake on the Capital Traction.

Glen Echo, typical of many amusement parks, offered an escape from the heat of the city in addition to the usual exciting rides. The Park gave away its traction company background to the careful observer. All the electrically operated rides were operated by obsolete street car controllers, and in some cases tickets were "rung up" on a rather familiar fare register.

A fitting end to all the wonderment seemed to be a ride in one of the open cars usually found in quantity at the gate when it was time to go home. The cars literally flew through the wooded right of way on the bluff overlooking the Potomac, depositing the rider back in the city—cool, tired, and ready for bed.

Gradually the automobile became the means of transport to recreational activities and later, for a time, the recreation itself.

Early Abandonments

Many of the early abandonments occurred in the Twenties, victims to both overbuilding and the advent of the auto. We have already noted the abandonment of service on the Washington and Great Falls Railway and Power's line in 1921, the demise of East Washington in 1923, and the ultimate abandonment of the Bladensburg line in 1925.

Symptomatic of the times was Capital Traction's takeover of both the Washington and Maryland line to Takoma in 1918 and Kensington Railway operations in 1923. The Washington and Rockville Railway, though not an operating property, was a corporate subsidiary of Washington

Railway and Electric in 1924. In that capacity, on May 16, 1924, the Washington and Rockville Railway Company (successor to the old Washington, Woodside and Forest Glen) applied to the Public Service Commission of Maryland for permission to substitute motorbus service for the existing rail service north of the Baltimore and Ohio Railroad in Silver Spring. The principal cause of this request was the pending grade separation project at Silver Spring. The Commission at first denied the request but did go on record as permitting the use of one-man safety cars by the company after relocating the tracks under the Baltimore and Ohio. The order also permitted temporary bus service while the grade separation was in progress.

While the project was being carried out, the PSC granted service extensions in the Silver Spring-Forest Glen area to Washington's new and expanding bus company, Washington Rapid Transit Company.

Because of the Washington Rapid Transit extensions and Washington and Rockville's still earnest desire to cut the rail line at the District Line, the matter was again submitted to the PSC in March of 1926. This time the company asked to abandon the substitute bus service because Washington Rapid Transit service was adequate. Again, they asked approval to abandon the carline. This time, permission was granted to abandon the bus service, but resumption of rail service was to be postponed for one year. A year later, March 7, 1927, abandonment of rail service was finally approved. The line ended then at Georgia and Eastern Avenues, just over the Maryland line. The cars, however, displayed Georgia and Alaska Avenue destination signs.

In this period, service to Laurel, Maryland, was also abandoned. The City and Suburban Railway of Washington, another nonoperating Washington Railway and Electric subsidiary, applied to the PSC of Maryland in the spring of 1925 for permission to abandon their line from Branchville

to Laurel. It's interesting to note that during the hearings **Mr. Ham, Washington Railway and Electric Company** President, admitted that service beyond Branchville had been operated as a shuttle for about three years. Actually, shuttle service had begun in April, 1921. There were twenty-seven departures from Branchville, alternate ones turning back at Beltsville; thus in the final years only about fourteen daily trips were made to Laurel. Morning and evening rush hours, however, saw a few through trips from Laurel to the Treasury.

The PSC, in effect, compromised with the railway and authorized discontinuance of rail service from Beltsville to Laurel upon establishment of a Laurel-Hyattsville bus service and retention of Beltsville to Branchville as a shuttle car line. This was accomplished July 1, 1925. The track from Beltsville to Laurel remained in place until 1930 when it was removed, thus ending another dream of a Baltimore rail link.

The never successful Macomb Street line out Massachusetts Avenue was abandoned on May 13, 1925, with the establishment of the Massachusetts Avenue bus line.[16]

With the end of World War I, the steel plant at the foot of Portland Street in Anacostia ceased to be important. Streetcar service dwindled to what apparently was a franchise run of two trips a day. As a result of a hearing before the Public Utilities Commission, service was abandoned December 25, 1926. The PUC Order 654, which required that tracks be kept intact, termed it a temporary suspension. The track and overhead was removed in December, 1931.

North American Company

In 1925, the North American Company, a holding company, began acquiring, by stock purchase, control of the Washington Railway and Electric Company. Since the Washington Railway owned all the stock of the Potomac

Left: Connecticut Avenue south from Chevy Chase Lake showing Capital Traction tracks in the mid-twenties. Bureau of Public Roads. Right: Connecticut Avenue north from the Bureau of Standards in the early twenties. From C.B. Kipps Ara Mesrobian collection.

16th and U Streets before traffic lights, about 1925. The streetcar is a Capital Traction Jewett; the bus belongs to the Washington Rapid Transit Company. Potomac Electric Power Company from Joseph J. Jessel.

W.Ry.&E.Co. 118 in olive paint scheme, ready for an eastbound trip at 15th and New York Avenue N.W. Author's collection.

Electric Power Company, this would have a marked effect on the future of Washington street railways after World War II. At the same time North American bought the Washington Rapid Transit Company and substantial, though minority, interest in Capital Traction.[17]

New Cars

Beginning in 1923, the Washington Railway began acquiring its 100 series cars. These were all deck roof double-end cars, similar to but smaller than the 700's. Many were equipped with trucks and electrical equipment from scrapped cars. Numbers 101-110 were one-man and assigned to 4 1/2 Street car house for service on 11th-Anacostia while 111-129 were two-man and assigned to the Columbia line. There were seventy-seven cars in all, but the fifteen ordered in 1926 and the final twelve ordered in 1928 were fully equipped by Brill with the latest comforts of the day, including leather seats and four motor trucks. They were advertised as "deluxe cars" and were one-man. The exterior paint scheme was cream with a blue stripe below the windows, quite a contrast from the olive drab of other Washington Railway and Electric Company cars. Because of this paint scheme, they were known informally as "the blue stripe cars." These were the finest pre-streamlined era cars on the system, but surely among the last deck-roof cars built

in the country and therefore not as modern as they could have been, at least from a style point of view. The first fifteen (160-174) were equipped with Golden Glow headlights and whistles for service to Alta Vista, while the newer cars (175-186) without these extras went to 11th Street. On a number of occasions they could be seen in Rockville although normal service to that distant point was by the 593-599 class "Rockville" cars.

Although Capital Traction didn't enter the new car market, they did make an important contribution in 1930. On September 17 of that year, the Board authorized the subscription of $10,900, payable over a three-year term, to the Electric Railway Presidents' Conference Committee. It was this committee that later developed the PCC car.[18]

In 1931, Capital Traction completed modernization, begun in 1928 of the sixty four-motor cars purchased in 1918-19 by installing new leather seats, improving the air brakes, shunting the motor fields (to speed them up) and giving them an entirely new and modern exterior paint scheme of grey and green.[19] At the same time Washington Railway rebuilt 594-597 to one-man cars. A 1928 rebuilding gave these cars a modern look when bulkheads were removed and air operated folding doors and luxurious new leather seats were installed. The 1931 rebuilding added one-man safety control features and treadle operated rear

Looking north from above the intersection of 14th and F Street N.W. A W.Ry.&E.Co. 425 series turns east into F Street, a 1600 series open car turns north into 14th, while a 700 is southbound on 14th in the near background. Potomac Electric Power Company from Joseph J. Jessel.

14th Street south from New York Avenue. Note four tracks on both 14th Street and New York Avenue. Double-track curve in right foreground is Capital Traction 14th Street line. W.Ry.&E.Co.'s Columbia line crosses 14th while the tracks continuing down 14th lead to the Bureau of Engraving and F Street. Library of Congress.

Southbound W.Ry.&E.Co. 719 crosses Capital Traction 14th Street tracks to enter four-track section between H Street and New York Avenues in the mid-twenties. Potomac Electric Power Company from Joseph J. Jessel.

Northbound W.Ry.&E.Co. open car 1620 about to turn left into H Street while Capital Traction Chevy Chase Lake car prepares to continue North on 14th Street. Library of Congress.

New York Avenue and 15th Street N.W. looking east. On the left are two Capital Traction cars while on the right, a W.Ry.& E.Co. Columbia line car, loads for a return trip about 1925. Library of Congress.

New York Avenue and 15th from the Treasury roof in the early twenties. Capital Traction's double-track "Y" is in the left foreground. A Columbia line car loads on the right side of New York Avenue. At the right is a W.Ry.&E.Co. center-door nearing the end of track on G Street. Note also the ex-Union Station switch tower at the far left. Library of Congress.

From 1898 to the merger in 1933, Washington street railways had to pay the salaries of traffic policemen at street railway crossings and intersections. Capital Traction spent as much as $50,000 a year for this requirement. This picture is at 14th and Pennsylvania Avenue. Capital Traction 70 is in the background. U.S. Bureau of Public Roads.

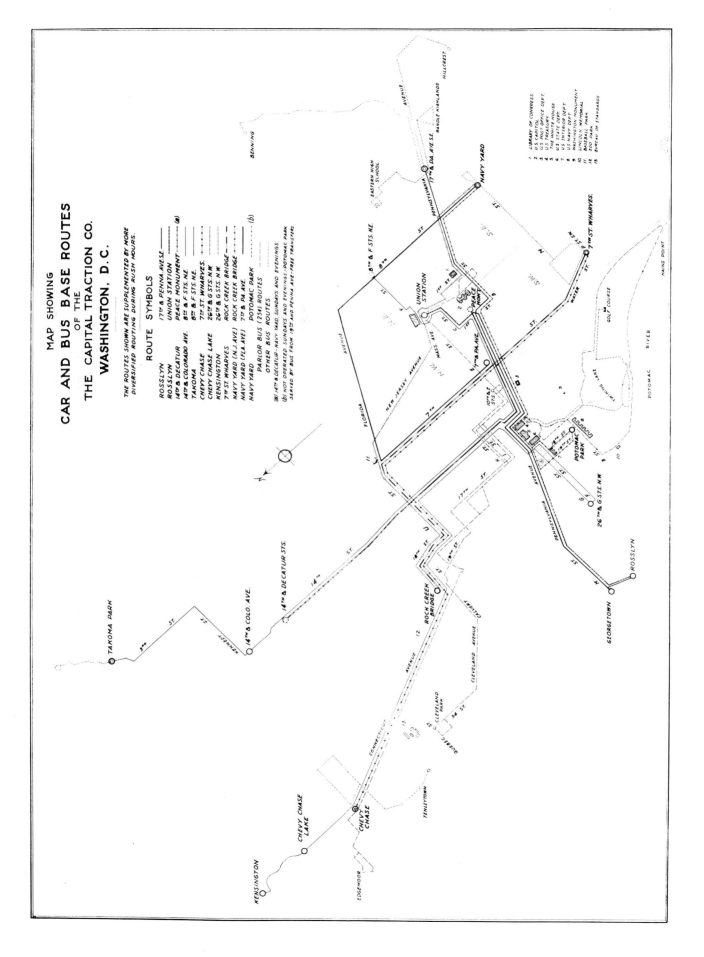

MAP SHOWING
CAR AND BUS BASE ROUTES
OF THE
THE CAPITAL TRACTION CO.
WASHINGTON, D. C.

THE ROUTES SHOWN ARE SUPPLEMENTED BY MORE
DIVERSIFIED ROUTING DURING RUSH HOURS.

ROUTE SYMBOLS

ROSSLYN	17TH & PENNA. AVE S.E.
ROSSLYN	UNION STATION
14TH & DECATUR	PEACE MONUMENT — (a)
14TH & COLORADO AVE.	8TH & F STS. N.E.
TAKOMA	8TH & F STS. N.E.
CHEVY CHASE	7TH ST. WHARVES.
CHEVY CHASE LAKE	26TH & G STS. N.W.
KENSINGTON	26TH & G STS. N.W.
7TH ST. WHARVES	ROCK CREEK BRIDGE
NAVY YARD (N.J.AVE.)	ROCK CREEK BRIDGE
NAVY YARD (FLA.AVE.)	7TH & PA. AVE.
NAVY YARD	POTOMAC PARK — (b)

PARLOR BUS (25¢) ROUTES
OTHER BUS ROUTES

(a) 14TH & DECATUR-NAVY YARD, SUNDAYS AND EVENINGS.
(b) NOT OPERATED SUNDAYS AND EVENINGS—POTOMAC PARK
SERVED BY BUS FROM 19TH AND PENN A AVE—FREE TRANSFERS

1. LIBRARY OF CONGRESS.
2. U.S. CAPITOL.
3. U.S. POST OFFICE DEPT.
4. U.S. TREASURY.
5. THE WHITE HOUSE.
6. U.S. STATE DEPT.
7. U.S. INTERIOR DEPT.
8. U.S. NAVY DEPT.
9. WASHINGTON MONUMENT.
10. LINCOLN MEMORIAL.
11. BASEBALL PARK.
12. ZOO PARK.
13. BUREAU OF STANDARDS.

Above: Looking south on W.Ry.&E.Co.'s lower 14th Street trackage with two 300's crossing Pennsylvania Avenue while a Capital Traction 26-85 series waits on Pennsylvania. Below: The same intersection but looking east from Pennsylvania into E Street. A W.Ry.&E.Co. 1-10 series is entering E Street while in the foreground are a Capital Traction 600 and one of their 104-131 series. Across the intersection is C.T.Co. 26-85 series car. Both photos from U.S. Bureau of Public Roads.

W.Ry. & E.Co.'s deluxe "Blue Stripe" 160, purchased in 1926, on East Capitol Street beside the Lincoln Park car house. 160-174 were one-man cars and featured comfortable leather seats. Author's collection.

Rebuilt Capital Traction 48 at Union Station in 1933. Leather seats, higher speeds, improved braking, and a new grey and green paint scheme made these very attractive cars for their time. Photo by Leonard W. Rice.

back of the Eckington barn in the late twenties. The variety of cars for W.Ry.&E.Co.'s Maryland and Brookland lines shown here is what de trolleys interesting. From left to right are 585 class railroad roof cars, heavy center-doors, 50 series one-man cars, small center-doors d 400's dating from City and Suburban days. Library of Congress.

F Street east from 14th about 1925. W.Ry.&E.Co. 602 is bound for Georgetown. Library of Congress.

F Street looking toward 14th in 1931. The "new" National Press Building is on the left. U. S. Bureau of Public Roads.

Overleaf: Compare this map of all trackage in 1925 with Capital Traction route map on Page 125.

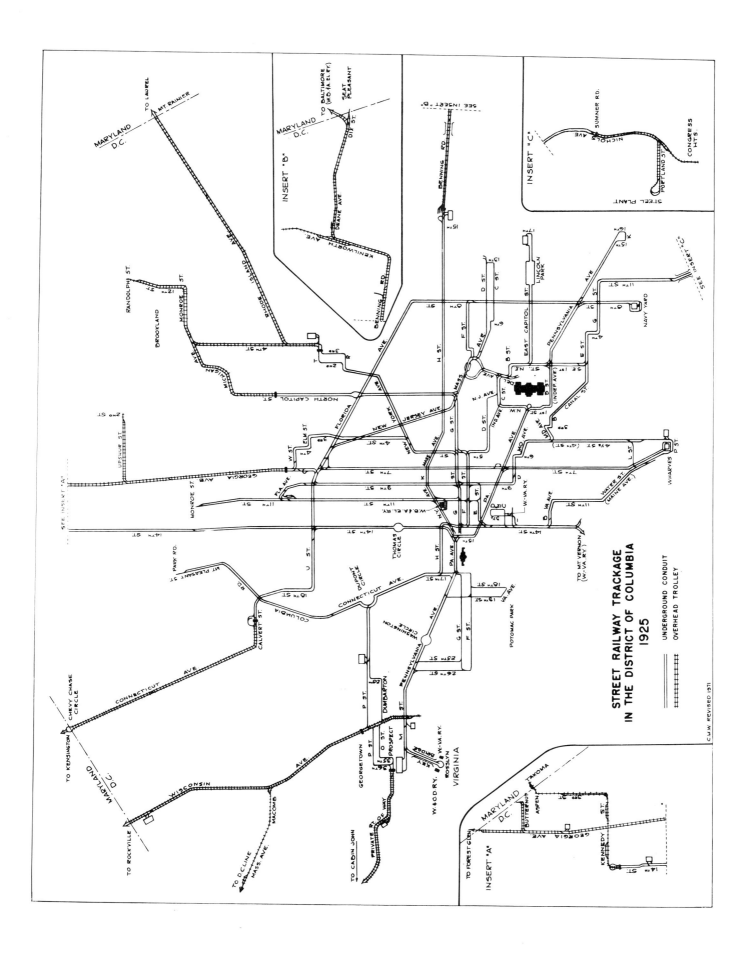

STREET RAILWAY TRACKAGE
IN THE DISTRICT OF COLUMBIA
1925

UNDERGROUND CONDUIT
OVERHEAD TROLLEY

C.M.W. REVISED 1971

INSERT "A"

INSERT "B"

INSERT "C"

W.Ry.&E.Co. 712 and Capital Traction 631 share a platform at Union Station about 1930. North Jersey Chapter, N.R.H.S.

Lorain (Ohio) Street Railroad 201 at Lorain in the early thirties. Similar to Capital Traction's contemplated 1931 order. Author' collection.

exits. When finished, these cars received the blue stripe paint scheme and held down the Rockville schedules.[20]

Buses for F and G Street Line

Both the F and G Street line west of 17th Street and the Pennsylvania Avenue S.E. extension of the Capital Traction, built in 1901, were in need of complete rebuilding by 1930. Estimates indicated an investment of $365,000 to rehabilitate F and G Street versus a total of $86,000 for removal of tracks and purchase of necessary buses. Since traffic to "Foggy Bottom" was not heavy, bus replacement was ordered and carried out in 1931 under authority of PUC Order 910 dated April 2, 1931. Buses were substituted May 3.

On the same day, buses were substituted for all owl cars, and the Navy Yard-18th and Virginia Avenue car line was abandoned. Chevy Chase cars then terminated at 18th and Virginia Avenue (Potomac Park).

Although service was light on the F and G Street line, it was not on the Pennsylvania Avenue S.E. extension; and it was, therefore, decided to rebuild these tracks in 1931. Incidentally, a waiting station was added at 17th and Pennsylvania Avenue S.E.[21]

Union Station Plaza Rebuilding

An Act of Congress dated March 4, 1929, provided in 1930 for the extension of the Capitol grounds to the Union Station Plaza. This area then contained numerous unsightly stucco temporary office buildings erected during World War I, a not-too-attractive view for the traveler to the nation's capital in the days when a very high proportion of them arrived by train.

Congress' motive was to replace this view with one which provided an uninterrupted parklike setting for the Capitol Building. Streetcars were not to mar the view and, accordingly, were placed underground in a tunnel with a fountain on top. This tunnel still stands and is now used by DC Transit buses.

The plan required removal of tracks from Delaware Avenue, C Street and B Street and relocating them on 1st Street East and across the Capitol grounds in a location a little north of C Street, partly underground.

All of this, which was estimated to cost the two companies about $370,000 was conceived and planned without consulting either company. After the plan was announced, the companies did succeed in getting a Senate hearing to present alternate proposals, but no changes were made in the bill. Work began on the project May 26, 1931, and the new tracks were put in service October 11.[22]

During the depths of the Depression, Washington was affected somewhat differently from the rest of the country. Since Washington is not a factory town, it was not overwhelmed with unemployed factory workers; but there were unemployed and many of them entered the taxi business to earn a living. In 1931, there were five thousand taxis in Washington offering a twenty cent rate, for as many as four passengers, throughout downtown. As a result, the number of traction passengers slid precipitously.[23] Some solution to the cab problem was reached a few years later by increased regulation.

In 1931 the Capital Traction Board approved the purchase of thirty-five new cars of the most up-to-date type obtainable.[24] The order was not placed, however, because of favorable Congressional action on a long-sought merger. Blueprints prepared by St. Louis Car Company indicate a Peter Witt car very similar to, but larger than, those of the **Lorain (Ohio) Street Railroad**.

After over five years of investigation and hearings, the Senate passed a resolution December 22, 1932, permitting merger of Capital Traction Company, Washington Railway and Electric Company and the Washington Rapid Transit Company. This was followed by House approval January 5, 1933, and Presidential signature on January 14. A long sought objective was accomplished, and a new era in Washington transit opened on the effective date of the merger of Capital Traction and Washington Railway and Electric, December 1, 1933.[25] The inclusion of Washington Rapid Transit in the new company was delayed until a subsequent merger of June 10, 1936.[26]

BEFORE AND AFTER REROUTING

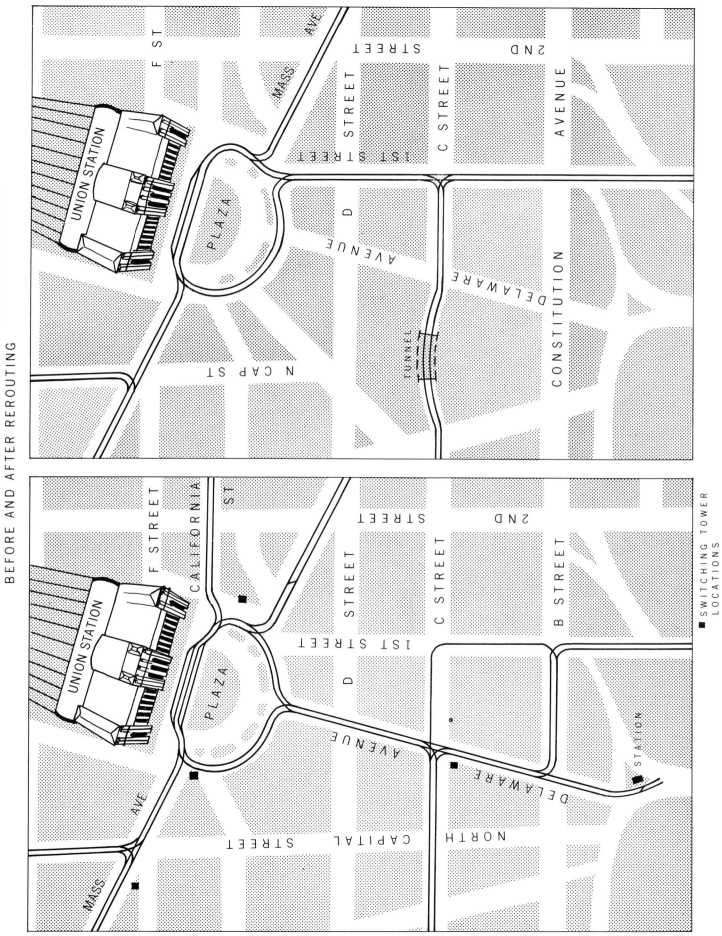

ORIGINAL LAYOUT

FINAL LAYOUT

■ SWITCHING TOWER
   LOCATIONS

Pennsylvania Avenue east from the Treasury in 1929. Capital Traction cars fight for space with ever-increasing numbers of autos. It was solve this problem that streetcars gave way to busses in 1962. Library of Congress.

CHAPTER SEVEN
CAPITAL TRANSIT ERA

With the formation of Capital Transit Company in December, 1933, all street railways in the District were under one management for the first time. John H. Hanna of Capital Traction became president and W. F. Ham of Washington Railway and Electric Company was elected Chairman of the Board of the new company.

The automobile and bus had forced the decline of the trolley by the time Capital Transit came into being. Evidence of the decline, in addition to the abandonments already recounted, could be seen in the plight of nearby suburban and interurban electrics. The Mt. Vernon line had been reduced to a mere overflow carrier to Alexandria for A B & W buses and the Washington, Baltimore and Annapolis, the Great Falls branch of the Washington and Old Dominion, the Kensington and the Arlington and Fairfax would not last long after 1933.

The Roosevelt Administration brought a marked increase in government employment which resulted in substantial growth of Washington and its Maryland and Virginia suburbs. Total revenue passengers (rail and bus) for the system increased from 81.6 million in 1933 to 172 million in 1940.[1] Part of the increase was due to fare revisions by Capital Transit. A one dollar weekly pass, good for unlimited riding on all city lines,[2] a twenty-five cent all day Sunday pass and, for the first time except for a short period in 1919, transfers were free and universal. Thus, while transit companies in most of the nation were suffering from the Depression, Capital Transit enjoyed growth.

The new company faced a number of major problems. Rerouting of car lines, merging shop facilities, and modernization of rolling stock were among them.

Because of contemplated improvements to Constitution Avenue, Capital Transit was ordered to abandon the Ninth Street line. Abandonment of Ninth Street line trackage below Pennsylvania Avenue forced abandonment of the Anacostia line trackage as far east as First and E Street S.E.[3]

In its first year, the company brought about another change in the 36th and M Street building. The old Union Terminal was selected as general offices for Capital Transit. The closed passageway on the roof of the building, originally for transfer to Metropolitan Railroad cars, was removed, and the roof over the central portion of the building was removed to form a light well for office space created from remaining third floor car storage space.[4]

*William T. Ham (1870-1949) served Washington Traction interests nearly fifty years. President of Washington Railway and Electric Company (1918-1935), Chairman of Board Capital Transit (1922-1937), Director (1937-1949). *Star*, May 29, 1949.

Also in the first year, Washington Railways' shops at 2411 P Street N.W. were abandoned; and all shop operations were concentrated at Washington Railway's former Wharves' carhouse at 4th and P Street S.W. and the former Capital Traction shops at 3222 M Street N.W.[5]

Calvert Street & P Street Bridge Projects

Replacement of two bridges over Rock Creek Valley contributed to the problems faced by the company in its first year. The larger of the two, Calvert Street Bridge, carried tracks of the ex-Capital Traction Connecticut Avenue line while P Street Bridge carried the ex-Washington Railway Cabin John, Wisconsin Avenue and Georgetown lines. Both bridges were steel trestles with wooden floors, a design fashionable before the turn of the century.

The Calvert Street Bridge replacement was the more complex and interesting project of the two. Built by the Rock Creek Railway in 1891, it was 750 feet long, 130 feet high and weighed 1,200 tons. Since trolley traffic on Connecticut Avenue was too important to be interrupted and a temporary trestle was too expensive, it was decided to move the existing bridge and use it for a detour. After appropriate ramps were built to the new bridge location, the old Calvert Street Bridge was to be moved eighty feet downstream.[6]

Pier footings of the bridge were dug out and each footing was placed on rollers atop parallel rails running south to the new location. A number of cables were then run to horse-operated windlasses mounted downstream. Work began at 4:30 a.m., June 7, 1934. While work was in progress, the two ends of the car line were joined by shuttle buses. Cars on the west side used a temporary crossover to turn back while cars on the east side used Rock Creek Loop.

At 5:00 a.m., June 9, ex-Capital Traction Company car **28 bound for Chevy Chase Lake became the first car to** use the newly moved viaduct—a courageous but uneventful feat. Though the new bridge was designed for streetcars using underground conduit, the Connecticut Avenue line was abandoned before it was completed.[7] The decision might well have been influenced by the possibility of extending conduit operation to Klingle Bridge just south of Macomb Street.

The old P Street Bridge was of the same general construction as Calvert Street although not nearly as long or high. The solution here was to build a temporary trestle to serve as a detour. Cars over the single conduit track bypass were controlled by a typical Washington Railway and Electric Company red light signal system. As was the Calvert Street bridge, the new P Street Bridge was designed to restore (conduit) streetcar tracks; but the P Street line was abandoned before the new bridge was completed.[8]

Rock Creek Bridge as constructed in 1891, looking east. Compare with view below and note where bridge h been strengthened. Robert A. Truax collection.

Thirty-sixth and M Street Union Station as Capital Transit main office in 1937. Capital Transit Company.

Looking east over Rock Creek Valley, this photo shows the meth devised for moving the bridge downstream in 1934. Capital Trar Company.

At the east end of the Calvert Street (Rock Creek) bridge, work is in progress constructing track to meet the new bridge site. Rock Creek loop is in the background. Capital Transit Company.

At the west end of Calvert Street bridge, north end Connecticut Avenue line cars used a temporary turnback for two days while the bridge was moved. The Twin Coach shuttle bus at right took passengers around the detour. Capital Transit Company.

Takoma bound WRy&ECo center door about 1933 on Constitution Avenue just east of 9th Street, N.W. The steelwork in the background is the Archives Building. Gerald Cunningham collection.

"Blue Stripe" car from Wisconsin Avenue line crosses temporary P Street bridge. P Street shop in background. Author's collection.

732, bound for Cabin John, waits its turn to cross the temporary P Street bridge in 1934. Witbeck Photo, Charles Murphy collection.

⸱th Street north from F in 1931. Note four-track network in upper left background. An inbound Maryland line car and an outbound ⸱ookland car cross at G Street. Northbound Rockville car indicates picture was taken in the evening rush since that service usually ⸱rminated in Georgetown. Potomac Electric Company.

Brill 1003 in a publicity shot in front of the White House in 1935. Historical Society of Pennsylvania.

St. Louis 1051 on Pennsylvania Avenue at 15th Street N.W. in 1939. Photo by George Votava.

Interior of Brill 1001 looking forward (left) and looking to the rear. Although controller handle was provided, cars were operated with f control. Note the farebox at the center door indicating two man operation. Historical Society of Pennsylvania.

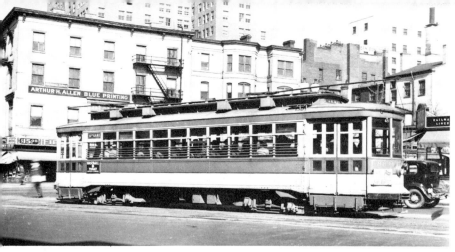

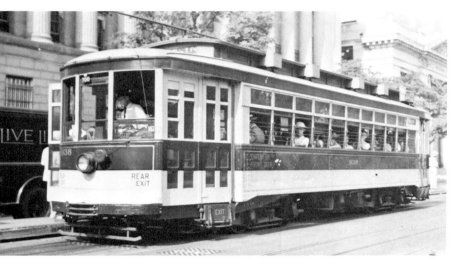

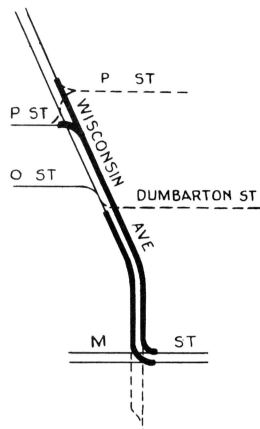

Top: Capital Transit 88 (ex W Ry & E Co 128) on New York Avenue at 14th with experimental green and cream color scheme. Author's collection.

Above: Capital Transit 968, an ex W Ry & E Co "Blue Stripe" car on ex Capital Traction trackage on Pennsylvania Avenue just west of 15th Street N.W. in 1939. Jeffrey Winslow.

Above right: Revised track layout in Georgetown. Heavy line indicates new conduit track while dotted line denotes abandoned track. From 1934 Beeler study. Author's collection.

New Cars, Bus Substitutions

Capital Transit inherited a well maintained but old fleet of streetcars. The only modern cars were the twenty-seven "Blue Stripe" cars bought by Washington Railway in 1927-28.

As 1935 began, the plans developed by transit company and PUC engineers began to be put into effect. Many of the first moves called for rail abandonment on a scale not yet seen in Washington. There were five major bus substitutions in the year:

1-7-35	LeDroit Park line in its entirety
6-16-35	P Street line (Dupont Circle to Wisconsin Avenue)
7-16-35	Anacostia Congress Hts. (1st & B Street S.E. to Congress Hts.)
8-4-35	Rockville line (District line to Rockville)
9-16-35	Connecticut Avenue (Rock Creek Loop to Chevy Chase Lake)

Coincident with the abandonment of Connecticut Avenue, the independent Kensington line quit, being replaced by Capital Transit buses.[9]

Sad times, indeed, for the traction fan! And, as if that weren't enough, on August 21, 1935,[10] the last Washington, Baltimore and Annapolis train left Washington forever.

Work was in progress on a number of track projects that soon would bear fruit. The trackage on Wisconsin Avenue in Georgetown was rebuilt with conduit from P Street south to a turnoff into M Street to allow Cabin John and Tenleytown cars to use M Street instead of P Street.

Capital Traction almost ordered thirty-five new cars, but put it off pending a merger. Now that the merger was a fact, Capital Transit ordered twenty new cars. The Electric Railway Presidents' Conference Committee was at work perfecting an entirely new vehicle, and Capital Transit's specifications were to incorporate as many of those features as possible into the new design. Ten cars of riveted construction were ordered from Brill and ten of welded construction were ordered from St. Louis.

In May, 1935, the ten new Brill-built cars arrived with considerable favorable publicity.[11] Immediately nicknamed "streamliners," these cars were far ahead of anything yet seen on rails, accelerating faster than an auto, and sporting a new electric blue (turquoise), tan and grey paint scheme.

Inbound Chevy Chase Lake car and a 700 bound for Chevy Chase Circle on 18th Street at Columbia Road in 1934. Witbeck photo, author's collection.

F Street looking east at 13th in 1934. Note car 178 destined for Congress Heights. Witbeck photo, author's collection.

Capital Transit one man car 359 (ex W Ry & E Co 86) enroute to the Bureau of Engraving at 14th and Pennsylvania Avenue in 1934. U. S. Bureau of Public Roads.

Carl Mydans took this picture of motorman Tom Marshall on a Cincinnati "Chevy Chase" car contemplating some unknown delay. Note unusual controller handle under motorman's right arm. Library of Congress.

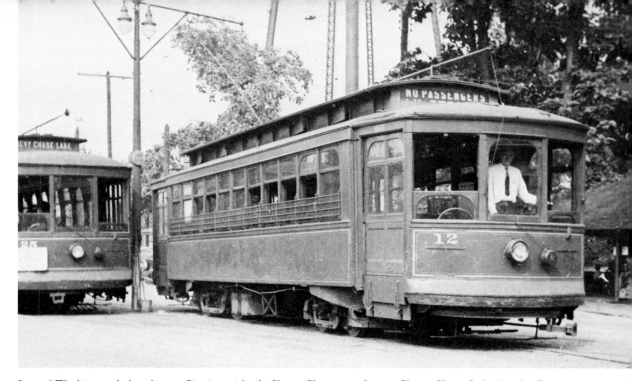

One of Washington's handsome Cincinnati built Chevy Chase cars leaves Chevy Chase Lake for the Benning scrap track in this melancholy scene. Brill 25 waits in the background to finish out the last day of the Connecticut Avenue line September 14, 1935. Photo by Robert A. Truax.

A pulled plow caused this backup on Eighteenth Street just below Columbia Road on a Winter evening in 1935. Witbeck photo, author's collection.

Open car 1604 crosses 29th Street on P Street in Georgetown about 1934. Photo by T. J. Wingfield.

vernment workers board cars at the Bureau of Engraving on 14th Street for the trip home in 1939. Library of ngress.

A delay on Pennsylvania Avenue just west of Peace Monument in 1935. Witbeck photo, author's collection.

They immediately entered service on the Rosslyn-17th and Pennsylvania Avenue S.E. line. The ten St. Louis cars entered service on the same line in the summer.[12]

Abandonments, along with the acquisition of twenty new cars allowed the scrapping of a number of older vehicles. In 1935, eighty-two cars were scrapped, including twenty-nine open cars. In addition to the twenty new cars, the company acquired two locomotives for freight service at the **Potomac Electric Power Company's Benning Power Station.**[13]

Capital Traction's K Street power plant was closed.* Potomac Electric Power Company then supplied all the transit company's electric power.[14]

The major track project was the elimination of four track operation on 14th Street and New York Avenue. Almost as important, however, were the straightening of the Potomac Park Loop by bringing cars straight up 18th Street to Pennsylvania Avenue and the elimination of the stub end in G Street by connecting the G Street tracks with 15th Street trackage.

The 14th Street and New York Avenue trackage was used by the two busiest lines in the city and, of course, it was all complex underground conduit construction. The work was completed, after months of preliminary work, on July 19, 1936, without interrupting service except to turn back Columbia line cars through the then abandoned Washington, Baltimore and Annapolis Terminal. This track change brought about many novel new routings. The Pennsylvania

Avenue routing, started in 1862 with horse cars, was now replaced by a routing from Rosslyn to Seat Pleasant.[15]

To those interested in the street railway, it was unusual and interesting to see Washington Railway cars on M Street, Capital Traction cars on the Mt. Pleasant line and other oddities such as revised paint schemes, new cars, and buses in the sanctuary of the trolley.

Here is a brief review of the reroutings occasioned by the

Aerial view of 14th and New York Avenue during the 1936 four track elimination project. 14th Street runs from top to bottom of the picture. The Columbia line crosses in the right foreground. From Transit Lines.

*The K Street Power Plant remained an empty landmark on the Georgetown waterfront until demolished in October, 1968. The *Star,* October 11, 1968.

Looking south on 14th Street at New York Avenue during the 1936 reconstruction. Witbeck photo, author's collection.

TRACKAGE DIAGRAMS
VICINITY OF 15TH AND NEW YORK AVENUE

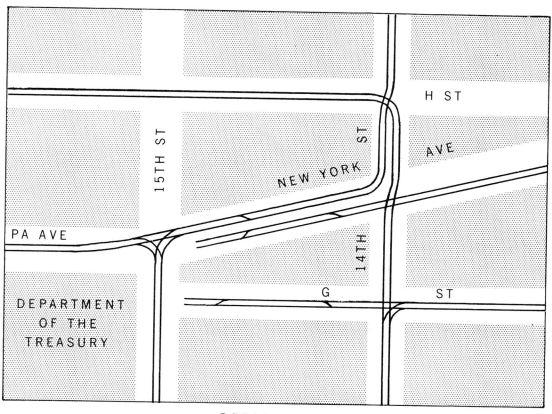

BEFORE 1936

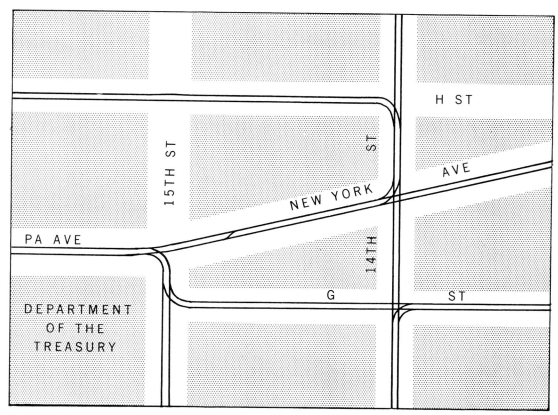

AFTER 1936

trackwork and abandonments of 1935-36. First efforts at reroutings downtown (July, 1936):

1. 14th Street cars went straight down 14th Street to the Bureau of Engraving, or left into Pennsylvania Avenue at 14th as required.
2. Columbia line cars went to Washington Circle via Pennsylvania Avenue.
3. Brookland Cars went to Potomac Park.
4. Cabin John, Glen Echo, Friendship Heights cars to M Street in Georgetown and to various destinations via Pennsylvania Avenue.
5. Maryland line cars looped downtown by running west on F Street to 14th then east on G Street.
6. Mt. Pleasant-13th and D N.E. cars were routed via Pennsylvania Avenue and G Street rather than H, 14th and F. Mt. Pleasant-Lincoln Park cars remained on old route via H and 14th and F.[16]

These route changes were temporary. They were the original ideas resultant from the major trackage changes in the 15th, 14th, New York and Pennsylvania Avenue areas. In a change so drastic, some problems developed, and the July reroutings were amended in November, 1936. It is a credit to the schedule and traffic men to note that the November, 1936, changes were in essence the routings that lasted until the end of the streetcar in Washington. The company's publication, "Transit News" of November 22, 1936, reproduced on page 149 shows the new routings. Incidentally, this was the first use of route numbers by the company.

A number of interesting "might have been's" were proposed and rejected while planning the abandonments and reroutings of 1935-36. Many of these plans contemplated continuation of the Connecticut Avenue car line. Fred A. Sager, chief engineer of the Public Utilities Commission, proposed these solutions:

1. Route Chevy Chase Circle cars south via 18th and Columbia Road, then via Mt. Pleasant line to 17th and Pennsylvania N.W., over Pennsylvania Avenue to G Street and then via Maryland line to 4th Street and Rhode Island Avenue N.E.
2. Chevy Chase Lake cars via the same route except they would follow Mt. Pleasant route to 3rd and Indiana.
3. An alternate terminal for Chevy Chase Circle cars would be via Mt. Pleasant line to Lincoln Park.[17]

John A. Beeler, then consultant to the Public Utilities Commission, proposed these routings for the Connecticut Avenue lines:

1. Chevy Chase Circle cars to 18th and Columbia thence via Mt. Pleasant line to 15th and H, then south on 15th to Pennsylvania Avenue to a 6th and Pennsylvania Avenue terminal.
2. Chevy Chase Circle cars use regular route to 11th

and U Streets then downtown via 11th Street to a new loop at 11th, E, 10th and D Street N.W. (to be shared with the 11th Street line).
3. Chevy Chase cars would use Taft Bridge to effect a junction at Connecticut Avenue and Columbia Road with the Mt. Pleasant line.[18]

The 18th and Columbia Road connection was taken seriously because the special work for the double track turnout was actually purchased. It remained a number of years beside the Wisconsin and K Street powerhouse and was eventually taken away for scrap. The Taft Bridge proposal was almost immediately forgotten for two reasons. First, provision for underground conduit would have required structural alteration to the bridge floor and, second, engineers doubted that the bridge could carry the extra burden of street car operation.

Other suggestions of interest:

1. The abandonment of "Maryland" line trackage from 5th and G Street to New York Avenue and North Capitol Street. Thus Maryland line and North Capitol cars would share trackage to New York Avenue and North Capitol Street.
2. Rerouting of cars around both sides of Dupont Circle rather than having the intolerable problem caused by northbound cars operating in opposition to traffic around the west side of the circle. (a refinement of this plan was actually realized some years later).
3. A new east-west trunk line from the Bureau of Engraving east via C Street and Maryland Avenue out to 3rd Street, north on 3rd to C Street North. Here it would meet the Pennsylvania Avenue line which would be rerouted east of 7th Street on C Street to 1st Street East. Trackage in Pennsylvania Avenue east of 7th Street and west of 1st Street would have been abandoned. In addition this scheme proposed a line south from Taft Bridge on Connecticut Avenue, Florida Avenue, down 22nd Street to E Street. The line would have then followed E Street (with a tunnel under the Ellipse) to join the Pennsylvania Avenue line at 13th, E and Pennsylvania Avenue.[19] Such a line would undoubtedly have made as much of a change in the streetcar scene as the Union Station project of an earlier day.

The abandonment of the Rockville line created the need for the first of Capital Transit's many attractive rail-bus transfer stations. An interesting sidelight to the abandonment is the story of the line's terminal relocations during the summer of 1935. It will be remembered that cars of this line used Wisconsin Avenue and M Street as a southern terminal and that operation was with overhead wire. The project to extend conduit track on Wisconsin Avenue into M Street was begun April 15, 1935. The Rockville cars then

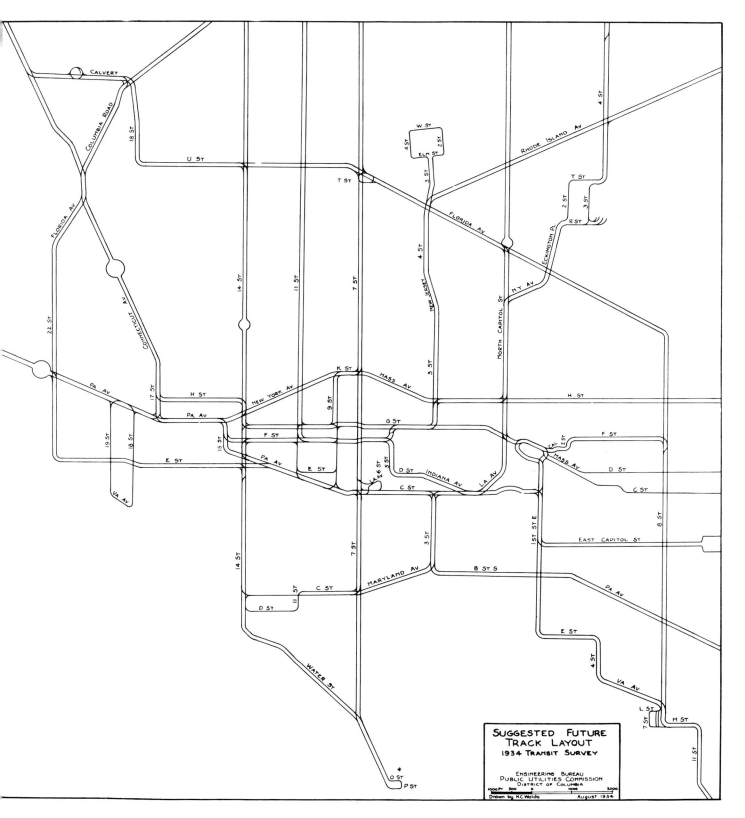

interesting "might have been". This map represents the District of Columbia PUC's 1934 future view of Washington's street car system. ...npare with 1948 map on page 173. Author's collection.

Sixty days before service ended to Wisconsin Avenue and M Streets in April 1935, one man 964 was photographed on Wisconsin just below M about to begin a northbound trip. Photo by George Votava.

Between June 16 and August 4, 1935, when the line was abandoned, southbound Rockville cars terminated at the District line. 423 served as a temporary terminal for the latter part of this time. Photo by J. B. Yeabower, M. J. Lavelle collection.

At abandonment of the Rockville line, Capital Transit built this rail-bus transfer station at Wisconsin and Western Aven (Friendship Heights). Capital Transit photo, author's collection.

STREET CAR REROUTINGS—DOWNTOWN DISTRICT
Effective November 22, 1936

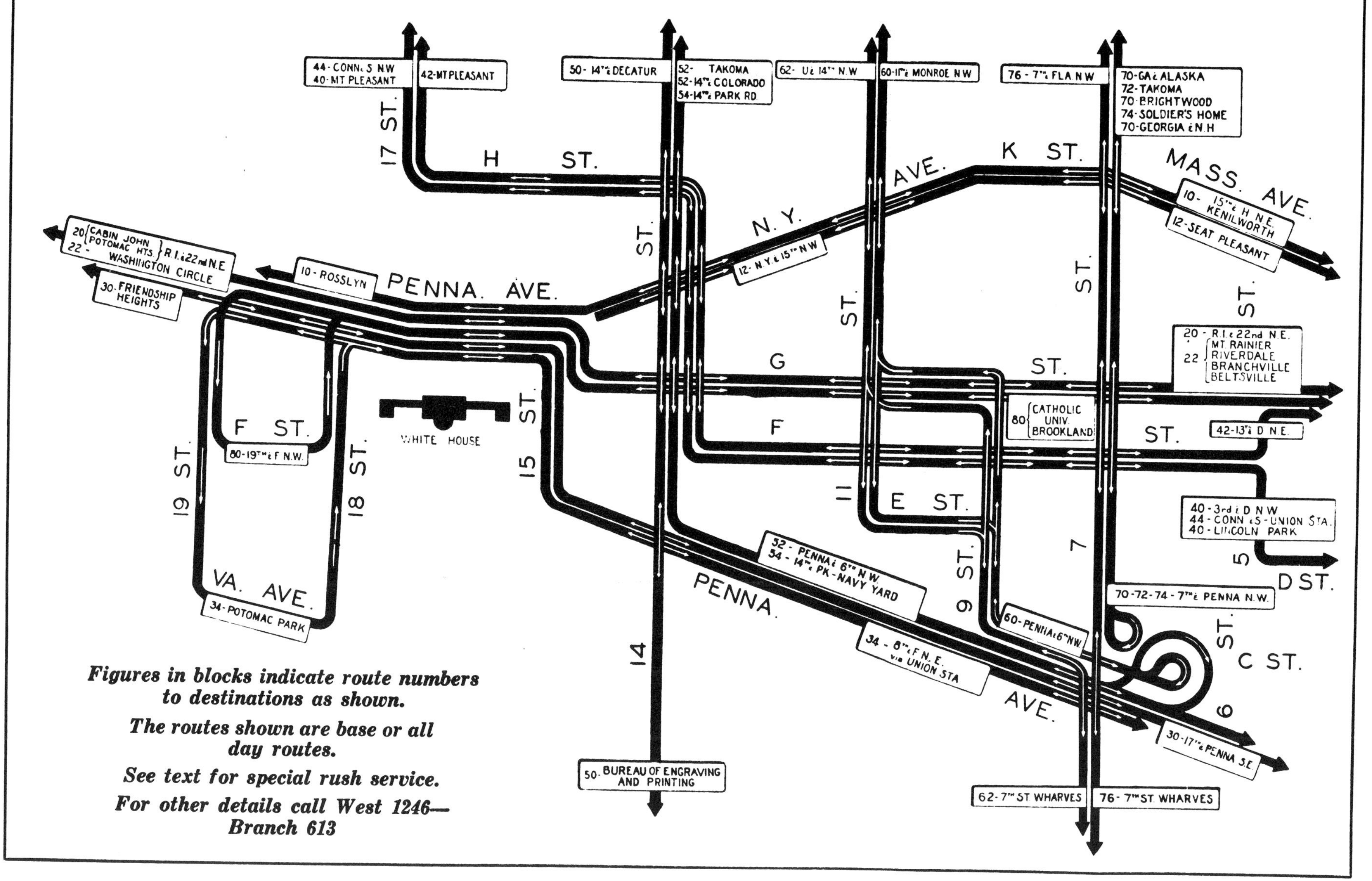

MASS. AVE.

10 - 15ᵀᴴ H N.E. KENILWORTH
12 - SEAT PLEASANT

70 - GA. & ALASKA
72 - TAKOMA
70 - BRIGHTWOOD
74 - SOLDIER'S HOME
70 - GEORGIA & H

20 - R.I. & 22ⁿᵈ N.E. MT. RAINIER RIVERDALE BRANCHVILLE BELTSVILLE
22 -

42 - 13ᵀᴴ D N.E.

40 - 3ʳᵈ & D N.W.
44 - CONN. & S - UNION STA.
40 - LINCOLN PARK

D ST.

76 - 7ᵀᴴ & FLA N.W.

60 - 11ᵀᴴ & MONROE N.W.

62 - U & 14ᵀᴴ N.W.

K ST.

AVE.

N.Y.

12 - N.Y. & 15ᵀᴴ N.W.

52 - TAKOMA
52 - 14ᵀᴴ & COLORADO
54 - 14ᵀᴴ & PARK RD.

50 - 14ᵀᴴ & DECATUR

H ST.

42 - MT. PLEASANT

44 - CONN. & S N.W.
40 - MT. PLEASANT

17 ST.

C ST.

G ST.

F ST.

E ST.

9 ST.

CATHOLIC UNIV. BROOKLAND
80 -

7

70 - 72 - 74 - 7ᵀᴴ & PENNA N.W.

60 - PENN & 6ᵀᴴ N.W.

30 - 17ᵀᴴ & PENNA S.E.

76 - 7ᵀᴴ ST. WHARVES

62 - 7ᵀᴴ ST. WHARVES

6

32 - PENNA & 6ᵀᴴ N.W.
34 - 14ᵀᴴ & PK. - NAVY YARD

34 - 8ᵀᴴ & F N.E. via UNION STA.

PENNA.

AVE.

14

50 - BUREAU OF ENGRAVING AND PRINTING

PENNA. AVE.

15 ST.

WHITE HOUSE

18 ST.

10 - ROSSLYN

F ST.

80 - 19ᵀᴴ & F N.W.

19 ST.

VA. AVE.

34 - POTOMAC PARK

20 - CABIN JOHN POTOMAC HTS. R.I. & 22ⁿᵈ N.E.
22 - WASHINGTON CIRCLE
30 - FRIENDSHIP HEIGHTS

Figures in blocks indicate route numbers to destinations as shown.

The routes shown are base or all day routes.

See text for special rush service.

For other details call West 1246—Branch 613

From Capital Transit's "Transit News", author's collection.

149

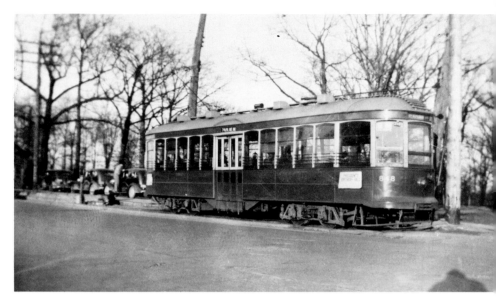

Capital Transit 848 at Georgia and Alaska Avenues in the mid-thirties. Barney Neuburger collection.

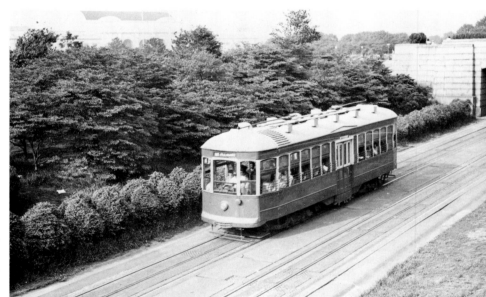

Mt. Pleasant bound sample center entrance car, Capital Transit 884, leaving the Union Station Plaza tunnel in the mid-thirties. Photo by Jeffrey Winslow.

Pennsylvania Avenue looking west from in front of the Treasury about 1937. Photo by Jeffrey Winslow.

A 700, bound for Friendship Heights, in the 1900 block of Pennsylvania Avenue N.W. March 13, 1939. Photo by Robert Crockett.

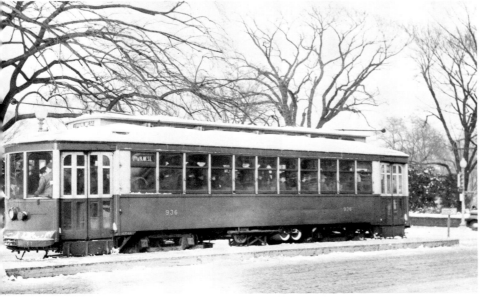

Capital Transit 936, one of the Brill "Chevy Chase" cars, eastbound on B Street S.E. in the Winter of 1940. Photo by S. P. Davidson.

An ex Capital Traction 131 series car working on ex W Ry & E Co trackage on G Street at Thirteenth N.W. The car is eastbound, enroute to Eckington. Photo by W. W. Buckingham.

965 in the rain on Pennsylvania Avenue near 19th Street. Photo by W. W. Buckingham.

New York Avenue and 15th Street in 1937. Two Brill 1000's pass while a Maryland line center door enters G Street. The bus at right on the F & G Street line. Library of Congress.

terminated at a point just below Q Street on Wisconsin Avenue. A temporary surface trailing crossover was installed there for the purpose of turning the cars back. By June 16, the new conduit track in Georgetown was complete, the P Street line was abandoned, and the Rockville line's terminal again moved—this time to the District Line. Here a temporary shelter in the form of Capital Traction single truck motor 315 was installed. The car was freshly painted in bright apple green and chained to the track. It soon proved too small and was replaced by a double truck car, Capital Transit 423 which was similarly painted.[20]

By August 4, the new terminal at Wisconsin and Western Avenues (Friendship Heights) was ready for operation. Montgomery Bus Lines (a Capital Transit subsidiary) took over from the handsome "Rockville" cars. The then new 1000 class single end cars were assigned to the Wisconsin Avenue line, where they remained throughout their entire service. When the P Street line was abandoned June 16, temporary substitute bus service was given by extending the West End Bus Line north from Foggy Bottom into Georgetown. Earlier in the year on January 7, the LeDroit Park car line (4th and New York Avenue to 7th and W Street) was abandoned. On August 4, the P Street bus line was created to serve the territory of the P Street and LeDroit Park car lines and at the same time furnish a much needed crosstown service.[21]

The Washington Rapid Transit Company was acquired in 1936. This successful bus property, using 16th Street as its trunk line, was presided over by Mr. Edward D. Merrill who then became vice president and general manager of Capital Transit.[22]

After considerable argument with the Public Utilities Commission, the company was allowed to make the twenty streamliners one-man in 1936. In the same year, fifty cars were purchased second-hand from Providence, Rhode Island, to replace thirty of the Washington Railway's older one-man cars (Capital Transit 337-366) on the Brookland line. As with other cities, the carmen's union and the riding public conspired against the inevitable approval of one-man cars. The advent of the Providence cars, of which forty-five were one-man, brought forth the rule not to be broken until the War, that no additional one-man cars could be operated unless they exceeded specifications of the streamliners. The one-man Providence cars were thoroughly rebuilt and were painted with the new electric blue color scheme heretofore reserved for the streamliners. The twenty-seven cars purchased in 1927-28 were also modernized, with new motors and improved braking and control; and they also came out of the shops in the new colors. Four additional two-man cars were added to the roster by remodelling Washington Railway's four trailers (1071 et al.) into motors 914-917.[23]

Subsequently, all one-man cars used the electric blue, tan and grey paint scheme while two-man cars were painted apple green with a broad cream stripe around the windows. All service cars were painted dull maroon except the two rail grinders which were orange and the Benning locomotives which were black.

Finally, in 1936 the Takoma line was abandoned, and a new loop and transfer station was erected at 14th Street and Colorado Avenue.

PCC Cars

On August 28, 1937, the first of forty-five new Electric Railway Presidents' Conference cars (1101) entered service on 14th Street, with appropriate publicity.[24] These were the "last word" in electric railway transportation. Although one of the ideas behind the PCC car was standardization, Washington's departed from standard in two minor respects. Because of restrictive transfer table clearances, they were one window shorter than usual and they were the only such cars to operate on conduit track.

Additional PCC car orders followed quickly. Mt. Pleasant was equipped with fifty in 1938 while the District portion of the Maryland line and the Georgia Avenue line shared thirty-eight in 1939. In 1940, thirty-four more arrived while sixty-five came in 1941.

The coming of the PCC's, all of which were single ended, required the building of turning facilities to replace stub end tracks in many places. Loops were constructed at Mt. Pleasant, Mt. Rainier, the Bureau of Engraving and at Georgia and Eastern Avenues. At Soldiers' Home and at Takoma Park, Y's were constructed. When the Maryland line was first equipped with PCC's, they operated only as far out as the new loop at Mt. Rainier. Service in Maryland was performed as a shuttle using conventional cars.

Each order of new cars allowed retirement of older cars. Large numbers of cars were scrapped at Benning yard in 1937, '38 and '39. The last of Washington's open cars, except 1614, were scrapped at Benning yard in 1937. Number 1614 continued on the roster until 1946 for use as an advertising car.

In addition to rolling stock activity, several interesting but not necessarily related events should be noted. Most important of these was a change in company management. Mr. Ham, Board Chairman, resigned from that position, although he remained on the Board. On March 10, 1937, Mr. J. H. Hanna was elected Board Chairman and Mr. E. D. Merrill was elected president.[25]

1938 Events

Service on the relatively unimportant 8th and F N.E. car line was discontinued in 1938.[26]

During the year, the Arlington and Fairfax submitted to the PUC a variation of the old 1904 Washington and Old Dominion crosstown trolley idea. By this time, the delapidated trolley line had been purchased by the Evans Products Company. Evans took down the trolley and equipped the road with auto railers. These vehicles were small buses with extra retractable flanged wheels to guide them over the rails. At rail end, the flanged wheels were retracted and the auto railer took to the highway. Evans, of course, hoped to use the road as a demonstration project for its auto railers. Therefore, they sought and won PUC approval to run them, as buses, from the end of their track in Rosslyn to down-

505, an ex Providence, R.I. car, shortly after entering Capital Transit service, in "electric" blue and gray color scheme on Virginia Avenue. Photo by George Votava.

In 1940, 504, an ex Providence car southbound at the plow pit on North Capitol Street. The motorman is testing the hand brake. Photo by Gerald Cunningham.

14th and Main Avenue S.W. in the evening rush in 1940. U.S. Bureau of Public Roads.

523 and 871 at Union Station about 1940. Photo by Jeffrey Winslow.

the last days of the Takoma line, 1936. Southbound 823 approached the plow pit while workmen build track for the new 14th and
lorado terminal loop. Witbeck photo, Charles Murphy collection.

The PCC Car Comes to Washington

The finest public transportation vehicle Washington has yet to see (1972) was the Electric Railway President's Conference Car (PCC). Fast, quiet, comfortable and without noxious fumes, it came first to the Fourteenth Street line, then the Mt. Pleasant line and eventually, to the entire system. These pages show sample views of the early models, all products of the St. Louis Car Company.

Upper left: 1181 of the second order on its first run on the Mt. Pleasant line on East Capitol Street just East of 1st in 1938. Witbeck photo, author's collection.

Lower left: Builder's photo of 1203 (1939 order) on 1st Street at East Capitol. St Louis Car Company photo, author's collection.

Below left: 1112 on 14th Street. One of the first (1937) order, this car had "Blinker" doors, standard to PCC's but a claims problem in Washington. The doors were rebuilt in 1947 and 1948. Photo by Roy S. Melvin.

Below right: 1134 on arrival at Benning in 1937. Photo by Churchman Johnson.

Bottom: 1151 westbound on East Capitol Street at 1st in 1938. The U.S. Supreme Court is in the background. Witbeck photo, author's collection.

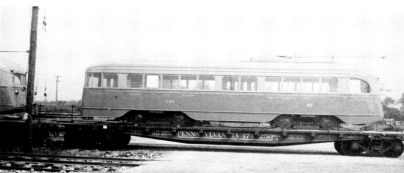

Mt. Pleasant loop at Mt. Pleasant Street and Park Road N.W. April 25, 1941. 1101 is about to leave for 13th and D N.E. Photo by Leonard W. Rice.

Arlington and Fairfax Auto-railer at Rosslyn. Capital Transit sought and won an injunction in 1938 prohibiting their use as road vehicles from here to downtown. Photo by Churchman Johnson.

Bottom: In 1937, the last open cars for passenger service were scrapped. 1614 remained, but as an advertising car. Here is a classic shot of 1612 on 1st Street at East Capitol in the early 30's. Felix Reifschneider collection.

Below right: Independence Avenue trackage nearing completion in November, 1940. Houses in the background later were removed as part of the street widening project. Photo by LeRoy O. King, Sr.

Below left: Special work in Independence Avenue at 7th under construction in March 1941. Photo by Ed Schell.

town Washington, duplicating Capital Transit service. Capital Transit won an injunction prohibiting the duplication, however, and the plan was dropped.[27]

S.W. Mall Line and Benning Barn.

While new terminals and loops had been completed in 1940 at both Rosslyn and 17th and Pennsylvania Avenue S.E., the biggest project of the immediate pre-war period was the construction of the Southwest Mall car line. This new streetcar facility was made necessary by the construction of a group of new government buildings south and west of the Capitol. It was a double track route on Independence Avenue between 7th and 1st Street West. Included in the project was a loop for eastbound cars on 3rd, D and 2nd Streets with the track of the loop placed next to the curb for easy loading. The line opened March 16, 1941, and cost in excess of $400,000.

Routes 30 and 54 cars were sent over the new line instead of continuing on Pennsylvania Avenue, and Route 70 cars were terminated at S.W. Mall loop instead of continuing to 7th Street wharves. Additional evening rush hour service was operated from the new loop to Mt. Pleasant and 11th and U Street N.W.[28] The new line caused increased activity at 7th and Pennsylvania and, to alleviate that problem, one of the old "Union Station" switch towers was installed.

The new 110-car Benning barn, destined for a short life,

was opened in November, 1941. Constructed on company property at Benning Road and Kenilworth Avenue, it was designed to serve the needs of the east end of the Benning car line and, therefore, to allow conversion of the old Columbia barn to a bus garage.

World War II

Metropolitan Washington's population which had grown from 571,900 in 1920 to 968,000 in 1940, would grow to an astounding 1,462,000 by 1950. Wartime population growth, coupled with gasoline shortages, created for Capital Transit a mammoth job to perform. At the same time, wartime maintenance problems and personnel shortages created serious obstacles to the performance of that job.

Fortunately, at the time of Pearl Harbor, the company's physical plant was in excellent shape. There were large numbers of new buses, 252 new cars purchased since the merger, and the track and roadway throughout the system had been kept in top condition.

Personnel was probably the worst problem. Many employees went off to war. These had to be replaced, of course, with inexperienced people. In the case of motormen, some were replaced with women.

Since transit in the Capital was of critical importance, the Government, during the war, authorized a number of improvements. Major among these was the acquisition of addi-

Motorman Lloyd Frazier of eastbound 808 was killed and sixteen passengers were injured in this spectacular crash with northbound 953 at 7th Street and Massachusetts Avenue N.W. The accident happened shortly after midnight March 26, 1941. Both cars were rebuilt. Author's collection.

Pennsylvania Avenue looking west from 9th Street in March 1941. Photo by Robert Crockett.

894 about to start a trip to Riverdale from 19th and F Street N.W. in November 1940. Photo by Robert Crockett.

One man 956 at the end of the Takoma Park line (4th and Cedar Streets N.W.) July 27, 1940. Photo by Gerald Cunningham.

1338 and another PCC lay over at the loop at 11th and Monroe Streets N.W. Photo by Leonard W. Rice.

tional PCC cars. Sixty-seven arrived in 1942 and, to take full advantage of them, new loops were constructed at 11th and Monroe Street N.W. and at 12th and Quincy Street N.E. (Brookland).

At 14th Street and Maine Avenue S.W., the busy Bureau of Engraving loop required trolleys to make a left turn against auto traffic entering Washington on busy U.S. 1. To alleviate this problem, an underground loop terminal at the Bureau of Engraving was constructed. During construction of this facility, cars used a temporary loop built on the east side of 14th Street on the lawn at the northeast corner of 14th and Independence Avenue S.W.

Chronic manpower shortages forced the Public Utilities Commission to relent on its prohibition of additional conventional one-man cars. Authority was granted to convert fifty-two cars in 1943 and an additional sixty-nine in 1944. Most of these were 700 class cars.

A double-track branch off south to east at 14th and U Streets was constructed in 1943 to allow routing some 14th Street cars away from the congested area of downtown 14th Street. Loops were constructed at McLean Gardens on Route 30 and at Glen Echo on Route 20 to allow short routing of cars on those lines, thereby helping the still critical manpower situation.[29]

Additional PCC's arrived as the war came to a close. Sixty-five in 1944 and 125 in 1945-6, the last of the fleet arriving in January, 1946. A "Y" was constructed at the end of the Kenilworth line in 1944, and a loop at Seat Pleasant in 1945 allowed use of PCC's on those lines.[30] As additional PCC's arrived and as the war began to progress favorably, the company resumed scrapping of conventional cars; fifty-three in 1944 and ninety-five more in 1945.

An idea of the enormous impact of the war, with the consequent growth of Washington's population and its enforcement of transit patronage because of gas rationing can

A candid view of a PCC at 14th and New York Avenue in the late 'hirties. Author's collection.

100 bound for Rosslyn at Kenilworth Junction on December 8, 1940. Seat Pleasant line goes to the right in the background. Photo by Gerald Cunningham.

eft: Northbound 1453 leaves Bureau of Engraving Tunnel bound for 14th and Decatur in the Forties. Photo by Robert Crockett. Right: 187 in the tunnel-loop at the Bureau of Engraving in 1961. Photo by Harold Buckley, Jr.

be seen by comparing revenue passenger data for 1940, 1942, 1944 and 1945. A trend away from the peak can be seen in the 1945 data even though the war was on for most of that year. Data for 1950 has been added to the table below to show, in comparison, how quick the trend away from public transit would be.

Year	Population (Metro Washington)	Total Passengers Carried		
		Rail	Bus	Total
1940	968,000	164,166,385	86,127,241	250,293,626
1942		274,679,449	180,137,379	454,816,828
1944		336,004,507	199,491,360	535,495,867
1945		255,507,589	155,780,650	411,288,239
1950	1,462,100	191,208,326	160,340,416*	351,548,742

(All data from Capital Transit Annual Reports)

Post War Capital Transit

When the war ended, the auto returned. The automobile again assumed its role of enticing passengers away from public transit and of increasing traffic congestion.

Capital Transit aggressively looked for ways to keep its service attractive at war's end: their rail fleet was one of the most modern in the nation. Except for the "cut back" Seat Pleasant to 15th and New York Avenue service which required double end cars, all base service was furnished with streamliners or PCC cars.

Maintenance standards—car, bus and track—were high. Among the post-war rolling stock programs was one to bring all PCC's to the standards of the newest ones.

Maryland line service was improved in 1946. Loops were constructed at Branchville and Riverdale allowing the replacement of shuttle service with through PCC car service to Branchville. Incidentally, PCC's were the first cars on the Maryland line without whistles. In an effort to improve service to the area served by the Benning line (the old Columbia Railway), the company proposed bus substitution

*Increase for Bus passengers due to Benning line conversion in 1949

in 1946. Although the company had a good case, as will be seen later, the Public Utilities Commission denied permission largely because of concern over the possibility of future gasoline shortages.

The company had on its staff a competent group of traffic engineers who worked with District of Columbia traffic authorities to find ways to increase transit speeds.

Two Capital Transit employees demonstrate the war time "stand-sit" seat idea. Designed to increase seating capacity it was, fortunately, applied only to car 824. Capital Transit photo, author's collection.

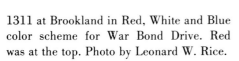

1311 at Brookland in Red, White and Blue color scheme for War Bond Drive. Red was at the top. Photo by Leonard W. Rice.

ove: M Street at Wisconsin Avenue looking east in 1943. Wartime gas rationing didn't solve this traffic jam. U.S. Bureau of Public ds. Below: 14th Street south from New York Avenue in 1943. Capital Transit photo, author's collection.

BELIEVING that the people of Metropolitan Washington are deserving of the best possible transit service at the lowest possible fare, Capital Transit has helped pioneer and initiate the evolution of the modern street car and bus. Washington was the first city in the country to operate the modern streamlined street car. It now has more streamlined cars in proportion to cars operated than any city in the world.

And now Capital Transit is proud to present for its patrons' approval additional forward steps in the development of more attractive, comfortable and convenient transit vehicles.

Among these advancements are:

Interior and Exterior Color Styling
Improved Ventilation
Fluorescent and Indirect Lighting
All-Electric Car
New Destination Signs
Car Full Sign
Automatic Bus Transmission

The most dramatic of the new developments, perhaps, is dynamic color styling. The four interior color combinations have been designed by outstanding color stylists.

The mechanical improvements, destination signs, lighting, etc., were subject to a great deal of research and experimentation. In addition to Capital Transit engineering skill, the resources of the largest manufacturers of transit equipment and accessories in the country were behind the developments. They incorporate advancements hurried by the war and the theories of peacetime planning.

Although tomorrow's transit vehicles may be considered by many to be here today, public preference will determine the final choice. Capital Transit is YOUR service. The entire population rides street cars and buses and if advancements in color styling, destination signs and other recent developments are to be incorporated in the equipment on the street, the public must express its approval. Your cooperation is requested in the final determination.

COLOR STYLING

INTERIORS: The interior and exterior color schemes were determined by the most outstanding color stylists and industrial designers in the country.

A great deal of work and thought were put into the styling before the final sketches were submitted. A number of scientific factors were considered in addition to pleasing appearance and functional use. The color stylists worked independently and then in cooperation with each other before the final results were produced.

The selection of the interior color schemes was motivated by the necessity of choosing cool hues because of the generally warm temperature in and around Washington.

EXTERIORS: Two cars have been given a different exterior appearance. The present exterior colors on the street cars were selected by a leading artist when the first streamlined car was placed in service some years ago. The bluish-green color is symbolic of the electric

arc. However, the new exterior color designs were achieved through a functional method. A quick recognition is a dominant requirement, therefore the colors have been chosen from the high-visibility region of the spectrum.

IMPROVED VENTILATION

Capital Transit has been experimenting with street car and bus ventilating equipment for some time. However, the practical lessons learned in the experiments led to the presently designed equipment installed in car No. 1158. Fresh air is drawn into the car through the monitor roof along the entire length of the vehicle. The air is baffled to remove moisture and diffused through the car by three fans located in the ceiling. The fans are capable of changing the air at the rate of 12,000 cubic feet or four complete changes per minute, six times more rapidly than that now in effect. The action results in positive circulation and will provide more passenger comfort through "evaporative cooling".

INTERIOR LIGHTING

The adaptation of fluorescent lighting to transit vehicles seems a natural sequence in lighting progress. Pleasing and acceptable in modern design, fluorescent lighting has been used for the first time in a streamlined street car. Shadows are eliminated with a resulting lessening of eye strain in addition to a cheerfulness suggestive of the finest salons.

One car has also been equipped with total indirect lighting.

Both methods of lighting provide even intensity throughout the car insuring plenty of light for easy reading.

ALL-ELECTRIC CAR

The doors and a phase of the braking equipment, particularly, on street cars are now operated pneumatically. It is believed that a more positive action, providing for even greater safety, can be obtained by the use of electric motors on these devices. On car No. 1487 the propeller shaft brake has electric control and the doors and windshield wiper are also operated independently by their own motors. While this improvement will not be visible to the public, it is a definite contribution to a further modernization of what are already the most advanced transit vehicles to be found anywhere in the world.

DESTINATION SIGNS

For some time a special committee of Capital Transit people have been studying and experimenting to provide the public with more information on destination signs. The newly designed front destination sign retains the route number which has been found the easiest way for the regular rider to identify the route. The center section has been developed to show information as to the route the vehicle travels. The right section of the sign contains the destination. The route number and destination have yellow lettering on a black background. Scientific tests prove that this color combination has the best visibility.

Rear route signs have been relocated and redesigned to increase the visibility range for those passengers approaching the vehicle from the rear.

CAR FULL SIGN

Being passed up by street cars and buses with capacity loads has been a source of annoyance to passengers. To overcome this and to indicate to the prospective passenger that no more room is available, a flashing "Car Full" sign has been incorporated in the upper right hand corner of the vehicle, next to the destination sign. The signal is turned on by the operator when his vehicle is loaded and automatically the sign flashes "Take next car, please". The flashing light and the lettering will be an indication to the passenger that the vehicle cannot accommodate him.

AUTOMATIC BUS TRANSMISSION

Automatic transmission was reaching perfection on the private automobile prior to the restrictions brought about by the war. Since then manufacturing designs and practical application on war equipment have added to the progress. The very latest automatic transmission designs have been incorporated by the White Motor Company in the bus on exhibit. It frees the operator from gear shifting action and the selection of speeds is automatic. It will give the passenger a smoother ride as the vehicle moves through the speeds necessary for maximum performance.

TRANSIT'S

Cavalcade of Progress

F St. between 14th and 15th St., N. W.

Created and Presented

By Capital Transit Co. For the Street Car and Bus Patrons of Washington, D. C.

New

INTERIOR AND EXTERIOR COLOR STYLING

IMPROVED VENTILATION

INTERIOR LIGHTING

ALL ELECTRIC CAR

NEW TYPE DESTINATION SIGNS

AUTOMATIC BUS TRANSMISSION

And other advancements designed to increase the comfort and convenience of transit vehicles.

Folder of three 3x7 inch panels, blue ink on buff stock, reduced to fit page. Author's collection.

verleaf: Capital Transit's folder for their "Cavalcade of Progress" exhibit held November 3-4, 1945. Three PCC's, each in a different terior and exterior design, and a White bus made up the exhibit which was on the south side of F Street between 14th and 15th. A poll of ser preference was a feature and it resulted in retention of the current blue and tan paint scheme. Above left: The exhibit showing 1487 eft) in carmine red and light blue, 1158 (center) in standard color and 1502 (right) in tan with dark red stripes. Photo by Ed Schell. Above ght: Carmine and blue 1487 at Mt. Pleasant in March 1946. Photo by Robert Crockett.

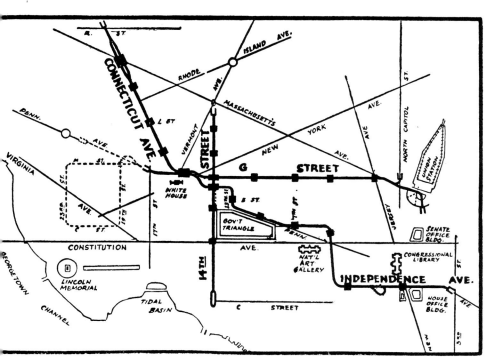

Map showing $56,000,000 street car subway system proposed by the District Commissioners in 1946. From the Evening Star.

1218 leaving Mt. Ranier loop at 34th and Rhode Island Avenue in the Forties. Photo by Jeffrey Winslow.

The District, in an effort to solve the downtown traffic problem, engaged the Griener DeLeuw Engineering firm to make a study which was completed in December, 1946. The basic part of their plan was a comprehensive downtown streetcar subway system which would have taken streetcars off the streets in all the downtown "core" area. Other interesting suggestions included these:

1. Connect the 7th-Georgia line with the end of the 11th Street line to divert some outer Georgia Avenue area traffic directly to the F & G Street shopping area.
2. Connect the Maryland line to the North Capitol Street line at North Capitol Street and Rhode Island Avenue. This would allow elimination of the old Eckington and Soldiers' Home trackage via 5th Street and New York Avenue.

If the subway plan had been developed, it would have been a very expensive proposition for Capital Transit if only because of the need to lay a large amount of new conduit track. Nothing, however, came of any of these proposals.

Capital Transit, and, indeed, the entire transit industry lost two of its outstanding personalities in 1947 and 1948. Mr. Hanna died in 1947, and Mr. Dalgleish* followed in 1948. Both men had spent their lives in Washington's public transportation industry, and both had given themselves freely to the industry as a whole as well. Both occupied important positions over the years in the affairs of the American Transit Association. In addition to his duties as president Mr. Merrill became chairman of the board in 1947.

*Robert H. Dalgleish (1875-1948) began his career as an electrician for the Eckington and Soldiers' Home in 1894. Later he served as electrician for the Rock Creek and chief electrician for Capital Traction. In 1915 he became chief engineer for Capital Traction and later held the same position (until retirement in 1946) for Capital Transit. He was a former president of the engineering section of the American Transit Association and a leader in the design of the PCC car. *Star*, September 23, 1948.

Overleaf: High point of street car design, 1576 of Washington's la PCC order (1945) poses for a company photograph at Rossly Virginia. Capital Transit photo, author's collection.

M Street, looking east, at Wisconsin Avenue in the evening rush March 31, 1948. One man 734 has left Georgetown Barn for a rush ho trip on Route 30. U.S. Bureau of Public Roads.

Benning Line Abandonment

Again, authority was sought to substitute buses on the heavily traveled Benning car line. Hearings on the matter lasted over a year. At the time, the Rosslyn-Benning line consisted of base day service as follows:

Rosslyn - Kenilworth

Washington Circle - Seat Pleasant

These were supplemented by the following rush hour routes:

Washington Circle - Kenilworth Junction

15th and New York Avenue N.W. - Kenilworth Jct.

Potomac Park - Seat Pleasant[31]

There were a number of problems with service on the line which forced the company to seek some solution. First, service to this fast growing area needed, in peak hours, headways of less than sixty seconds. Plow pit changes at 15th and H Street N.E. ruled against this since they averaged sixty seconds. Second, eastbound movements at 15th and New York Avenue regularly caused cars to be lined up as far back as 17th Street and beyond in evening rush hours. Often Benning line cars, on reaching the intersection, would find the traffic signal set for a turn down 15th Street, or 15th Street cars would find the light set for New York Avenue. Third, substantial numbers of Benning line passengers were transferring at 8th Street East for Florida Avenue and U Street destinations, a fact which meant that a number of the cars causing congestion at 15th and New York were really not needed there.

When the Public Utilities Commission denied the company's original application to abandon the line, they had directed the company to develop plans which would have alleviated the problems. Specifically, PUC asked for prompt submission of the following Plans:

1. Turn around facilities near Kenilworth Junction including bus to rail transfer facilities
2. Turn around facilities in the vicinity of the Benning Viaduct (Benning Road and Kenilworth Avenue)
3. Track connection at 8th and H Street N.E. to permit operation from the eastern end of the line to the U Street area
4. Develop plans for a turn around in the vicinity of 14th Street and New York Avenue N.W. (company plans show a loop in two lots just west of the New York Avenue Presbyterian Church)

In addition, the Commission had also ordered the company to commence reconstruction of the line from 2nd and H Street N.E. to 14th and H Street N.E.[32]

Plans and cost comparisons developed by the company enabled them to convince the Commission that bus substitution was the practical answer. Authority for the change was granted October 15, 1947.

The last Benning cars ran in the early morning hours of May 1, 1949.[33]

At the same time, the division office at 36th and M Streets was closed after fifty-four years. Some cars remained stored until May, 1950, when they, too, were removed, and the 36th and M Street property became solely an office building.[34]

The western terminal of North Capitol Street cars was changed from 19th and F Street N.W. to Rosslyn to serve that end of the line.[35]

The Benning abandonment ended the need for double ended cars; the system was now all PCC although a number of conventional cars were held in reserve. Incidentally, the last two-man car had operated in Washington on 14th Street on January 5, 1948.

Dupont Circle Underpass

The final major construction project in Washington's street railway history was the massive Dupont Circle underpass. Since Dupont Circle was at the intersection of two

The Benning line. Below left: Westbound 942 leaves H Street underpass in back of Union Station October 10, 1948. Center: Eastbound 1359 on Benning Road near Kenilworth Avenue October 17, 1948. Benning Power Plant in background. Bottom right: PCC 1400 and Providence 510 at Kenilworth and Deane Avenue N.E. (Kenilworth Junction) April 26, 1949. PCC is on Kenilworth line. All photos Edward S. Miller.

Looking west on Pennsylvania Avenue from 17th Street N.W., this photo, taken in July 1948, shows a typical evening delay which was one of the causes of the Benning abandonment. Photo by W. W. Buckingham.

Benning line, looking east, just east of Kenilworth Junction. Yard in the background is where Capital Transit electric locomotive picked up coal cars for delivery to Potomac Electric Power's Benning power plant. Author's collection.

major thoroughfares and because the streetcars still went both directions around one side of the circle, it was the focus of intolerable traffic congestion. The project consisted of a double track trolley tunnel in line of Connecticut Avenue from N Street to S Street and a separate vehicular tunnel. At the station under the circle, car tracks followed the layout of the outer edge of the circle to save patrons walking from the center of the circle to bus transfers on the street above.

During construction, Connecticut Avenue cars ran on a $225,000 conduit equipped detour across the circle and on the sidewalks. The first street car operated through the tunnel northbound November 2, 1949. The tunnel was completed with the opening of the southbound track December 14, 1949.[36] Connecticut Avenue service was considerably improved at a total cost of $600,000 to Capital Transit.

Earlier in the year, on July 31, another segment of the Washington Berwyn and Laurel disappeared when the picturesque Branchville-Beltsville Maryland shuttle was abandoned.

Wolfson Management

Louis Wolfson of Jacksonville, Florida, ended long-time North American Company control of Capital Transit on September 12, 1949, by acquiring from North American approximately 45 per cent of the outstanding shares of Capital Transit.[37] North American control of Capital Transit arose through their control of Washington Railway and Electric Company which, in turn, controlled the Potomac Electric Power Company. The Public Utility Holding Company Act required North American to divest itself of either Capital Transit or PEPCO; and they, of course, chose to retain PEPCO.

Wolfson, attracted by Capital Transit's strong financial statement, gave North American the opportunity to comply with the act.

At the same time that Wolfson gained control, Wolfson, J. A. B. Broadwater and two others of the Wolfson group replaced four Capital Transit directors. Mr. Broadwater became vice president and chairman of the executive committee. By 1950, A. G. Neal, PEPCO President and the last link with North American Company, resigned as director. Mr.

Below left: Construction scene, looking north from N Street in March 1949, showing temporary tracks on the sidewalk. Below right: Look north from the south side of the circle showing first temporary track through the center of the circle. Both photos by Ed Schell. Bottom South portal of tunnel June 12, 1956. Photo by LeRoy O. King, Sr. Bottom right: Sweeper 025 descending north ramp February 14, 19 Photo by Edward S. Miller.

Merrill retired to be replaced as president by Mr. Broadwater and as chairman of the board by Mr. Wolfson.[38]

Wolfson management viewed the inflated surplus of the company as stockholders' property. Funds for equipment and plant renewal should, they felt, come from profits. Accordingly, dividends in amounts not seen in many years by traction stockholders were declared by the Wolfson Board.

At the same time, Capital Transit effected economies in maintenance of the car and bus fleet and sought fare increases. These changes, in marked contrast to the conservative approach of the old management, gradually lost the goodwill of both the Congress and the Public Utilities Commission.

The final straw came in the summer of 1955. The carmen went on strike for higher wages and management refused to negotiate without a commitment from the Public Utilities Commission for a fare increase. By daring to put the PUC in this position, the Wolfson group so angered Congress that they enacted Public Law 389 which gave the District Commissioner the right to settle the strike and revoked the company's franchise effective August 14, 1956. The Commissioner's settlement of the forty-five day strike included wage increases as well as fare increases. This settlement, if offered earlier, could have avoided the whole problem.[39]

In addition to revoking Capital Transit's franchise, Public Law 389 specified that the new operator would have to provide an all-bus system. Senator Wayne Morse, of Oregon, then Chairman of the Senate District Committee, felt that large numbers of people would clamor for the franchise and October, 1955, was set as the time for accepting bids. The nationwide plight of the transit industry coupled with the high-handed revocation of Capital Transit's franchise are both probable reasons for the lack of a single bid.

The search for a buyer continued. Since the Government wished to find someone who would not buy Capital Transit rail equipment, the newspapers began pointing out as August neared that a sufficient number of buses simply couldn't be obtained. Finally, O. Roy Chalk, a New York financier who also owned controlling interest in Trans Caribbean Airways, was interested in taking the operation over.

DC Transit and Abandonment

Despite Congressional wishes not to use any Capital Transit Company equipment, the Chalk management purchased it and assumed operation of the property under the corporate title of DC Transit on August 15, 1956. A condition of DC Transit's charter was the elimination of streetcars.

Almost immediately after DC Transit's arrival on the scene, August 26, 1956, the already planned abandonment of Key Bridge trackage to Rosslyn took place. Route 80, North Capitol Street, from then on terminated at 19th and F in rush hours and at Washington Circle in non-rush hours.

First evidence of the change was, however, new names on the equipment, in virtually the same style—*DC Transit* in lieu of *Capital Transit*. Cars and buses were lettered to show "an affiliate of Trans-Caribbean Airways." Trans-Caribbean

"... Upset By Radio Commercials On Streetcars? Try Dr. Shmoogle's Soothing Stomach Syrup ..."

In 1948, as a source of extra revenue, Capital Transit agreed to allow Radio WWDC-FM to install and operate radios in street cars and buses. There was background music with commercials. Installation and maintenance was at WWDC's expense and about 500 sets were installed. Public reaction, as evidenced by the cartoon, made the project shortlived. Cartoon from "The Herblock Book" (Beacon Press, 1952).

July 31, 1949, the unique Branchville-Beltsville shuttle was abandoned. Below left: Inbound 369 crossing U.S. 1. June 30, 1949. Note ...enary across highway. Below right: 369 nearing U.S. 1 crossing, inbound, December 24, 1947. Both photos by Robert Crockett.

DE-BUNKING THE BUNK
ABOUT STREET CAR CONVERSION

District Commissioner Samuel Spencer has stated that streetcars cost 50 per cent more to operate than buses.

District Commissioner Robert McLaughlin has stated that streetcars cost 40 per cent more to operate than buses.

Engineer Commissioner Thomas Lane in a radio interview stated that a public hearing on the transit riders' desire to continue streetcars would be "idle discussion" and would not be held.

Public Utilities Commissioner Robert Weston has stated that conversion to all-bus would result in savings of $2,900,000 in transit operating expenses.

And, NOW . . . Edward Roberts, an "expert" retained by the Public Utilities Commission, has testified before the House Subcommittee on Transportation, Interstate and Foreign Commerce Committee, that had Capital Transit operated an all-bus system in 1955 it would have saved $2,940,000 in operating expenses based upon a "study" he made in July, 1955.

If it were possible to save $2,940,000 annually, the Company would have long ago petitioned the PUC to convert

HOW MUCH UNINFORMED BUNK DO THE DISTRICT AND PUC COMMISSIONERS AND THEIR "EXPERT" THINK THE TRANSIT RIDING PUBLIC WILL SWALLOW?

HERE ARE THE FACTS: Both Mr. Spencer and Mr. McLaughlin made their statements based on the average cost per bus mile as opposed to the average cost per streetcar mile. They both neglected to mention that most of Capital Transit's bus miles are operated in less congested, higher average speed areas than are streetcars. *What they forget to mention under the same standards is that streetcar income per mile is almost 100 per cent greater than bus income per mile. And that the bus lines as a whole lost in excess of $1,049,000 in 1955 while the streetcar lines showed a profit of $1,573,000.*

Commissioner Weston's statement that $2,900,000 would be saved in operating expenses was evidently based on "expert" Roberts' study made in July although he did not disclose the source. Mr. Weston evidently saw fit to take credit for arriving at this conclusion himself, passing over the contrary opinions of Company officials on the basis that "none exist."

Now, as for "expert" Roberts:

Mr. Roberts' transit operating experience was confined to a small transit operation in Queens, New York, several years ago. Mr. Roberts "experted" in the 1954 Capital Transit rate case for the Commission. He advocated the present weekly permit. He "experted" that 2,800,000 weekly permits would be sold and would produce $7,212,000 in revenue. Actually, 1,909,000 permits were sold and produced $4,188,000 in revenue. "Expert" Roberts was wrong by almost 1 million in the total of weekly permits sold and over $3,000,000 in error as to revenue. *How wrong can an "expert" get?*

The Commissioners have stated they had "expert" advice that private capital would come forward to take the place of Capital Transit Company. "Expert" Roberts provided the Commissioners with a long list of prospective operators of a Washington Transit System. To date not one individual or group with any substance has come forward that could be considered as serious. *How wrong can an "expert" get and still be paid from public funds?*

Now, "expert" Roberts comes up with a figure of $2,940,000 savings in operating expenses if buses are substituted for street cars. He testified that several cities in the United States had converted. He failed to mention that in those cities which have been converting the equipment was old and/or the rail badly in need of repair or in a dangerous condition as compared to Washington's modern streetcars and excellent maintenance and repair. He stated that most of the remaining streetcars in the United States are in cities where they are not physically replaceable by buses because they run partially in subways, tunnels and over bridges. He knows that Chicago, Baltimore, Philadelphia, to name just a few cities, operate streetcars on the surface. *How much further down the blind alley can the public be led in relying on this type of "expert" advice?*

And, "expert" Roberts testified that his report to the Public Utilities Commission only dealt with the economics of conversion because the Gilman report, made at the insistence of the PUC and which advised the retention of streetcars and their conversion on a gradual basis, did not deal with this phase of the situation. How could "expert" Roberts have known what the Gilman report would contain when his (Roberts') report was made in July and Gilman's report was made in September? The Gilman report, buried by the PUC although made at their insistence, did not contain the conclusions needed to meet the Commissioners' executive decision.

To get back to "expert" Roberts $2,940,000: His "analysis" is made on various "assumptions." He did not consider local experience factors. He assumes that buses, when substituting for streetcars, will operate ½ mile per hour faster over the same routes as street cars. There is no basis for his "assumption." If he assumed 5 miles per hour faster, he would have had us make more money than we could haul to the bank in one day. The facts are that if buses are substituted on the present streetcar routes they will not operate any faster because neither will move any faster than traffic will allow.

"Expert" Roberts also "assumes" in general that bus operating expenses and taxes will be the same per bus mile on motorized streetcar routes as the average similar expenses per bus mile on all present bus routes. And, this, when he knows that the average cost per mile for presently operated buses is in free movement areas. He backed up Commissioners Spencer's and McLaughlin's false premise used when they stated streetcars cost 50 per cent and 40 per cent more per mile to operate than buses. "Expert" Roberts' "assumed savings" come to 38 per cent.

"Expert" Roberts is full of "assumptions": It makes any informed criticism of his "analysis" almost factually impossible. But how far can the "expert" and the city officials go to fool the public?

Actually, an unbiased examination of all the expense factors indicate there is very little difference, if any, in the operating expenses of streetcars vs. buses.

The above facts do not take into consideration the wishes of the public. The strong public feeling for retention of Washington's streetcar system is very real. The Federation of Citizens Associations took cognizance of it when it resolved that the decision of the Commissioners was "precipitous" and that a public hearing should be held to determine public preference. So far, the District and Public Utilities Commission Commissioners have chosen to ignore the Federation's expression.

WE THINK IT IS ABOUT TIME FOR THE PUBLIC OFFICIALS, WHOSE ACTIONS AND LEADERSHIP LED TO THE PRESENT TRANSIT MESS ON "EXPERT" ADVICE, TO GET DOWN TO THE REALITIES OF THE SITUATION AND RESPOND TO THE PUBLIC DESIRES AND NEEDS. THERE IS STILL TIME FOR THEM TO ABANDON THE "FOOL THE PUBLIC" ATTITUDE AND APPROACH THE PRESENT CRISIS FACTUALLY AND WITH REGARD FOR THE PUBLIC INTEREST. OTHERWISE THERE MAY NOT BE ANY TRANSIT SERVICE ON AUGUST 15, 1956.

Commissioner Spencer (testifying before the House Committee of the District of Columbia) said:

". . . by and large, their maintenance (Capital Transit's) as I understand it, has been very good and their service on the whole has been satisfactory . . ."

Commissioner McLaughlin (testifying before a Senate Sub-Committee) said:

". . . It will be observed that the Company has not, in any post-war year, even when adjusted to give full effect to the tax refund related to accelerated depreciation, earned the fair rate of return allowed by the Public Utilities Commission."

Engineer Commissioner Lane (testifying before a Senate Sub-Committee) said:

". . . I have no complaint about the behavior and acts of officers in any regard. They have been friendly and good. Our letter makes no mention of any inefficiency of the Company's operations during the recent period because we are not charging any such deficiency . . ."

Capital Transit Co.

Full page ad placed in the Evening Star, March 1, 1956 by Capital Transit to counter the street car conversion propaganda of the District of Columbia government. Author's collection.

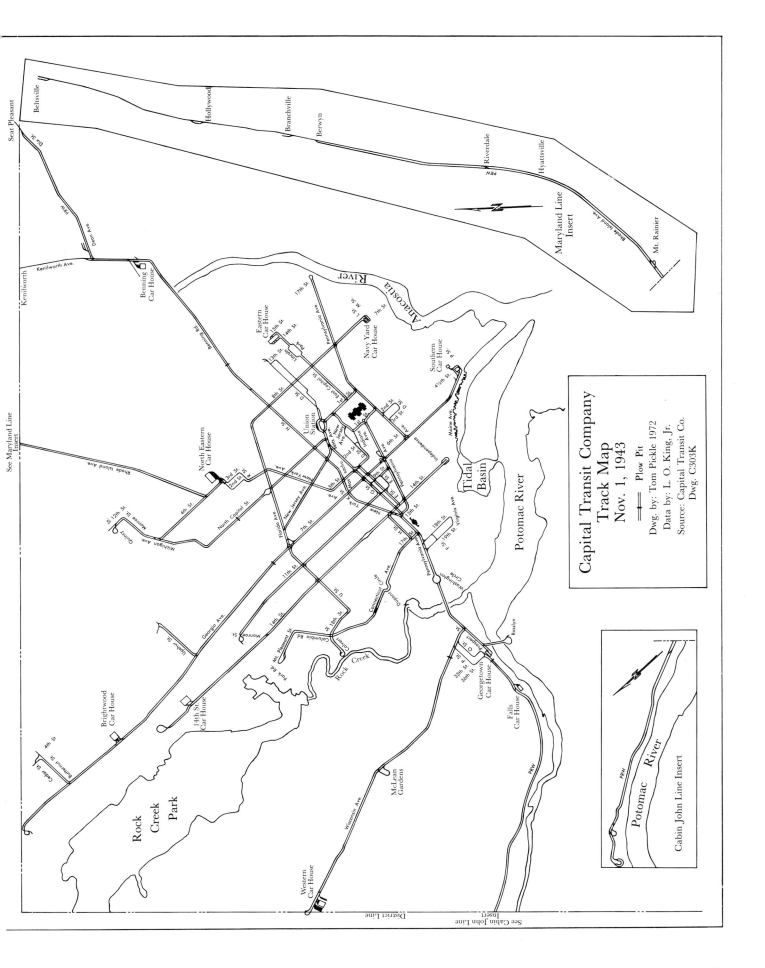

Capital Transit Company
Track Map
Nov. 1, 1943

Plow Pit

Dwg. by: Tom Pickle 1972
Data by: L. O. King, Jr.
Source: Capital Transit Co.
Dwg. C303K

Cabin John Line Insert

Maryland Line Insert

See Maryland Line Insert

See Cabin John Line Insert

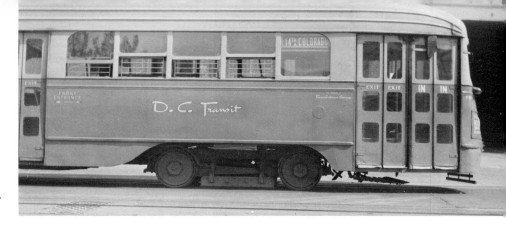

DC Transit's lettering style. Photo by Le-Roy O. King, Sr.

Above: Pouch mail from Cabin John and Glen Echo being transferred to U.S. mail truck at 36th Street an Prospect Avenue N.W. March 21, 1951. Below: 1505 southbound at Connecticut Avenue and M Street N.W. Ma 23, 1961. Both photos by Edward S. Miller.

PCC's fill the lead tracks at Tenleytown barn on June 2, 1955 during the strike that caused revocation of Capital Transit's franchise. Photo by LeRoy O. King, Sr.

bove: 1152 leaving Calvert Bridge loop about 1950. Capital Transit photo, author's collection. Below: 099 waits r Riverdale bound 1327 to clear before running out the Maryland line. The picture is on Rhode Island Avenue ar 34th Street N.E. (Mt. Ranier). Photo by Edward S. Miller.

Some snow scenes Top: Delay on F Street at 14th January 26, 1961 caused by pulled plow in the foreground. Photo by Richard Kotulak. Center: 8th and Pennsylvania Avenue S.E. February 14, 1960. Left to right are cars 1489, 1438, and, on 8th Street, 1582. Photo by Edward S. Miller. Bottom: Sweeper 08 northbound on 14th Street at F in the Winter of 1960-61. Note broom for sweeping platform. Photo by Paul Dolkos.

Below left: 1565 at 19th and Pennsylvania Avenue N.W. December 4, 1957. Below right: 1554, 1564 and 1563 delayed at 36th and P Streets N.W. on February 16, 1958 following a fourteen inch snowfall. Both photos by Richard Kotulak. Bottom: 1475 crossing Rock Creek at Pennsylvania Avenue February 16, 1958. Photo by Ara Mesrobian.

1470 inbound at 48th Avenue, Berwyn, Maryland September 21, 1957. Photo by Richard Kotulak.

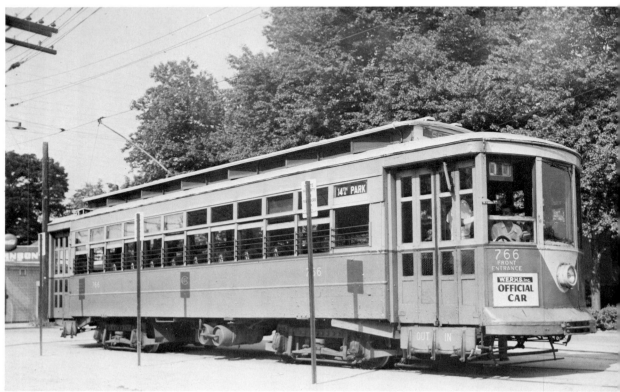

Above: Venerable 766 on a fan trip at Branchville, Maryland June 3, 1951. Photo by Leonard W. Rice. Below: 1111 Navy Yard car barn in DC Transit's new colors April 24, 1960. Photo by Edward S. Miller.

ove left: 1553 outbound on Cabin John line at Reservoir Road May 24, 1959. Above right: 1583 on Pennsylvania Avenue S.E. near 13th
reet June 27, 1959. Both photos by Richard Kotulak. Below left: 1300 at Wisconsin Avenue plow pit August 1, 1959. Note automatic pole
ching device on roof. Author's collection. Below right: 1149 at Wisconsin Avenue plow pit about 1955. Barney Neuburger collection.

e silver sightseer on an evening fan trip on 1st Street S.E. near Independence Avenue August 22, 1961. Photo by
ward S. Miller.

179

Tragedy, January 27, 1962. Photos by (left) Joseph Saitta and (right) Harold Buckley. Below: Author's collection.

JANUARY 28, 1962

CONVERSION TO BUS OPERATION

14th STREET CAR LINE   –   ROUTES 50, 54, 54

U STREET CAR LINE   –   ROUTES 90, 91, 92

SCHEDULE: Same basic schedules and frequency of trips will be maintained.

ROUTE: Buses will follow street car routes with the EXCEPTION of Route 50 at the Bureau of Engraving

BUREAU OF ENGRAVING

Operation through underground tunnel will be DISCONTINUED

Buses will operate from the intersection of 14th and Independence Avenue, S. W.

    East on Independence Avenue
    South on 12th Street
    West on C Street to bus stand east of 14th Street

Returning: West on C Street
    North on 14th Street
    and over existing route

For further information call FEderal 7-1300

D. C. TRANSIT SYSTEM, INC.

Airways was another of Chalk's holdings.

A new paint scheme appeared, very dramatic in appearance. Basically, it was the old electric blue overlaid with a pattern using white on the roof and upper body, then cream with an orange stripe.

The new management, between 1957 and 1960, completely refurbished the inside and outside of the 36th and M Street property. Ceilings which had been built to clear streetcars were lowered and accoustically treated, fluorescent lighting was installed, and the building was completely air-conditioned. The magnificent Union Terminal now had a new lease on life as a modern functional office building.

The Chalk management made proposals to retain some rail lines. For instance, a plan was advanced to make 7th-Georgia a high-speed trolley line by separating the right of way from vehicular traffic and closing some cross streets; but it came to no avail. The Silver Sightseer, an air-conditioned rebuild of PCC 1512, may have been a subtle attempt to convince the authorities of the advantages of trolleys, although it was officially denied that this was the case.

At any event, the end was beginning. Many citizens' groups objected as effectively as possible in a voteless society against what one newspaper called the "arbitrarily decreed conversion." But a blind Government will won out and the first major conversion came September 7, 1958.

Routes 80 and 82, the North Capitol and Maryland lines respectively, were abandoned September 7, 1958.[40] With them went memories of such resounding corporate titles as Eckington and Soldiers' Home and Washington, Berwyn and Laurel. Trolleys no longer served Mt. Rainier, Brookland, Riverdale, Branchville or Eckington; and the name "Maryland Line," a once meaningful bit of local color, disappeared. Needless to say, Eckington Barn ceased to exist as an operating barn and became instead a storage depot for the 1000's and surplus PCC's.

January 3, 1960, saw the next major installment, larger in scope and therefore more dramatic. The abandonment closed Cabin John (20), Tenleytown-Pennsylvania Avenue (30), 7th-Georgia (70) and rush hour service to Potomac Park and S.W. Mall.[41] Since this included the last overhead trolley lines, the plow pit was relegated to history.

Now the system was down to a shell of its former self. The remaining system was so small as to be uneconomic, particularly when it was known it must go. Only the best remaining cars and two barns, Lincoln Park and Navy Yard, were used. No major repairs were necessary since there were plenty of extra cars. Seventh Street barn had been closed when the Georgia Avenue line was discontinued; 14th and Decatur was turned into a bus garage; and the Friendship Heights barn was torn down to make a bus parking lot. Both shops, M Street and 4th Street, continued in use.

Because of the uneconomic aspects of operating the small remaining 1960-61 system, the company advanced the date of final abandonments. On December 3, 1961, buses took over Mt. Pleasant (long the busiest line) and 11th Street.[42] The expensive and long-awaited Dupont Circle underpass became a white elephant. This abandonment meant the end of Washington Railway and Electric Company lines. The remaining Capital Traction lines, too, had not long to go. On January 28, 1962, buses replaced the 14th Street and the U Street lines;[43] and Washington became an all-bus town.

Some Washington trolleys operated later in Fort Worth, Texas; Barcelona, Spain; and Sarajevo, Yugoslavia. Several are relics; one was sold to General Electric, and the rest were scrapped or sold for non-transit use.

For almost one hundred years, streetcars had been a part of Washington. While the bus was then thought to be more practical, the last streetcar took with it a majestic air that the bus will never attain.

A melancholy reminder of Washington street car abandonment, 050 performs its last duty removing track from the Cabin John line February, 1960. Photo by Paul Dolkos.

the day before President Truman's Inaugural, PCC's at Benning were swapped for double end cars from other barns so the Benning line ld operate from the 15th and New York Avenue crossover. Above: January 20, 1949, 900's and 500's were backed up on New York nue at 14th, during the parade, waiting their turn at the crossover. Below: On the morning of January 20, before the parade, 1348 passes Presidential reviewing stand at the White House. A close look at both photos will reveal American flags on the cars - a longtime custom National holidays. Photos by Edward S. Miller.

Top left: Burning plow in conduit track. Kodachrome by Catherine Murphy. Top right: 303-1512 at Washington Cir on a fan trip, September 14, 1952. Kodachrome by Ara Mesrobian. Bottom: 729 inbound on Michigan Avenue at Street N.E. in 1941. Kodachrome by Ed Ball, Charles Wagner collection.

p: 1000's at Tenleytown car house, March 2, 1952. Bottom: 1577 at Wisconsin and Garfield, inbound, April 5, 59. Both Kodachromes by Ara Mesrobian.

The Tractioneers, a local fan group, participated in a trip on September 11, 1949, to advertise Transit Progress Day exhibits the following day. Capital Transit photo, author's collection. Bottom left: 1555 leaves Glen Echo, outbound, about 1959. Top right: 1544, inbound at Glen Echo in September, 1958. Below right: Inbound route 30 car on Wisconsin Avenue just below 36th Street January, 1960. Three photos by Paul Dolkos.

Top: 1139 advertising a Defense bond drive at Union Station September 23, 1951. Kodachrome by Ara Mesrobia
Bottom: 1260 at Wisconsin and Western Avenues about 1950. Kodachrome by author.

p: Sweepers on Maine Avenue February 14, 1960. Kodachrome by Ara Mesrobian. Bottom: Eckington car house
out 1956. Kodachrome by M. J. Lavelle, author's collection.

Above: 1260 inbound from Riverdale, Maryland October 10, 1955. Photo by Paul Dolkos. Below: 371 at Beltsville Road on the Beltsvil[le]-Branchville (Maryland) shuttle June 14, 1949. Photo by Edward S. Miller. Facing page: 1230 at Branchville loop October 10, 1955. Ph[oto] by Paul Dolkos.

Top: 1512, the Silver Sightseer on a fan trip at Mt. Pleasant about 1958. Kodachrome from author's collection. Bottom
DC Transits colors at Union Station April 19, 1959. Kodachrome by Ara Mesrobian.

op: Pennsylvania Avenue from the Treasury, April 18, 1959. Kodachrome by Ara Mesrobian. Bottom: 766 at 1st and ast Capitol Street about 1960. Kodachrome by Ed Miller. Charles Wagner collection.

Above: 1053, on a June 1959 fantrip, passes the Department of Commerce on 14th Street, northbound. Below: Mt. Pleasant loop September 1961. 1548 (left) is in regular service while 1512 is on a fan trip. Both photos by Paul Dolkos.

Above: 1512 and 1503 at Connecticut Avenue and Columbia Road, April 9, 1960. Below: 1556 enters the Union Station Plaza Tunnel, April 23, 1960. Both photos by Edward S. Miller.

APPENDIX 1
EQUIPMENT ROSTERS AND NOTES

Introduction to Rosters

The rosters following represent all known data on the electric cars of Washington. Information on horse and cable cars is included in the text and in picture captions. These rosters are the result of many years work by the leading authorities on the subject. Their notes, along with standard references, official records, and previous rosters form the basis of these data.

Information has been checked and rechecked against all known references. Where data cannot properly be verified, I have used the word "probable." Many of the electric cars had two or more owners in their active life. Therefore, when remodeling or reequipping was done, it has been detailed in the roster of the company doing the work. Rosters have been cross referenced so that cars having more than one owner can be followed to disposition date. Rosters have been tabulated as follows:

Roster of Early Electric Cars 1888-1916
Capital Traction Company Passenger Cars 1895-1933
Washington Railway and Electric Company Passenger Cars 1902-1933
Capital Transit Company - DC Transit Company Passenger Cars 1933-1962
Service Equipment: Capital Traction Company, Washington Railway and Electric Company, Capital Transit Company and DC Transit Company

General Roster Notes

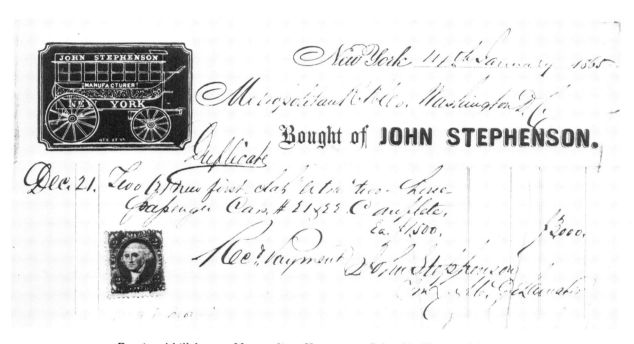

Receipted bill for two Metropolitan House cars. Columbia Historical Society.

Facing page: 14th and Colorado about 1960. Photo by Paul Dolkos.

ROSTERS OF EARLY ELECTRIC CARS (ALL CARS SINGLE TRUCK UNLESS NOTED)

Car Number	Type Car	Builder	Date	Notes

Washington Railway and Electric Company Predecessors

Anacostia & Potomac River R.R. Co. Color — Yellow (see note at end of Rosters of Early Electric Cars)

Car Number	Type Car	Builder	Date	Notes
100-124	Half Open Motors (Double Truck)	American	'00	Wason-21 trucks. Became WRy&E Co 910-934
301	11-window Closed Motor (DT)	American	'00	Became WRy&E Co 500

Capital Railway Company Color — Green

Car Number	Type Car	Builder	Date	Notes
51-54	10 Bench Open Motors	St. Louis	'97	Peckham 7B Trucks. To WRy&E Co 1419-1422
55-58	18' Closed Motors	St. Louis	'97	Originally had Dupont Truck, Lorain Motors & Control; later had Peckham 7B Trucks. To WRy&E Co 164-167

City and Suburban Railway of Washington Color — Olive Green (entire body), Gray roof and Gold Lettering for Double Truck Cars. Single Truck Cars — Orange with Silver Lettering

Car Number	Type Car	Builder	Date	Notes
1-20	16' Closed Motors	Laclede	'95	Motorized E&SH Horsecars. To WRy&E Co 1-18 and 503
30-39	28' Closed Motors (Double Truck)	American	'98	Acquired for Laurel Service. To WRy&E Co 400-409
40-49	28' Closed Motors (DT) Open Platform	American	'98	To WRy&E Co 410-419
100-109	Half Open Motors (DT)	Laclede	'98	To WRy&E Co 900-909
150-154	Center Aisle Open Motors	American	'98	Converted to Closed Motors and Renumbered by WRy&E Co in 1902 to WRy&E Co 420-424

Columbia Railway Color — Dark Blue, Silver Lettering

Car Number	Type Car	Builder	Date	Notes
26 et al	20' Closed Motors	Stephen'n	'95	Ex Cable Conv. to Elec 1899. To WRy&E Co 200-221. Exact Columbia Rwy Numbers unknown
57 et al	9 Bench Open Motors	Stephen'n	'95	Ex Cable conv. to elec 1899. To WRy&E Co 1300-1321. Exact Columbia Rwy numbers unknown
60-69	Center Aisle Open Motors (DT)	American	'99	Originally had Brill 27 Trucks & 4 G.E. 1000 Motors. Enclosed about 1902 and renumbered by WRy&E Co to 507-516
06-015	Sweepers	McG-Cum	'99	10 Sweepers purchased by Columbia for entire Wash Trac & Elec System. To WRy&E Co. Same numbers

Eckington and Soldiers' Home Railway Color — Red with White Dash. Later Orange with Silver Lettering except 146 et al Yellow

Car Number	Type Car	Builder	Date	Notes
1-3	Closed Motors (Open Platform)	Brill	'88	
4-7	Closed Motors — Vestibuled	Brill	'89	
8-14	Double Deck Trail	Brill	'89	
?	10 Window Closed Motor	Brill	'90(?)	Mounted on Robinson Radial Truck
21-26	Closed Storage Battery	Brill	'91	21 to Wash & Glen Echo 21 & to WRy&E Co 168
146 et al	Open Trailer	Unknown		Ex Wash & Geo RR. Number of cars unknown

Note: Roster of E&SH fragmentary. SRJ Directory (1891) lists 12 4-Wheel Box, 1 6-Wheel Box, 10 4-Wheel Open, 15 Motors, 8 Trail. Most of early equipment destroyed 12-3-98 in Eckington Barn fire. A compressed air car was among those destroyed.

Georgetown and Tenallytown Railway Co. Color — Light Blue, Later Maroon

Car Number	Type Car	Builder	Date	Notes
1 up	16' Closed Motors	Stephen'n	'90	Number of cars unknown but less than 10. Originally had Stephenson Trucks, later Manier and later Peckham. Four (at least) had closed Platforms
31-39	7 Bench Open Motors	Gilbert	'90	Probably 5 cars — odd numbers only

Horse Cars 1720, 1762, 1779 and 1828. One used temporarily on Standard Gauge Baltimore End of Columbia & Maryland Rwy

No.	Type	Builder	Year	Notes
50	Open Freight Motor	Brill	'90	Ex Brightwood Open Motor
—	Four Wheel Sweepers	Unknown		Open (Gondola) Body with Mast for Trolley Pole. Revolving brooms, numbers unknown. Two cars
—	Open Parlor Trailer	Dewitt (Wash DC)		Ex-Brightwood. Equipped with Rattan Chairs and Awning. One car
—	Double Deck Open Motor	Unknown		Open Top Deck. Probably owned by Glen Echo RR.
—	Motor Coal Car (Double Truck)	Unknown		
—	Trailer Coal Cars	Unknown		One or more cars

At abandonment of Glen Echo RR (Fall, 1900) Passenger Cars of G&T replaced by the following:

No.	Type	Builder	Year	Notes
1-4	20' Closed Motors	Brill	'95	Ex Wash. Woodside & Forest Glen 1-4. Became WT&E 740's, then WRy&E Co 296-299, Later 222-225. Brill 21E Trucks
7-12	12 Bench Open Motors (DT)	J&S	'96	Ex Glen Echo 7-12. To WRy&E Co 1510-1515
13-14	10 Bench Open Motors	J&S	'96	Ex Glen Echo 13-14. To WRy&E Co 1400's
19	8 Bench Open Motor	Jones	?	Ex E&SH, Ex Glen Echo, Scrap 1902
21	18' Closed Motor	Brill	'91	Ex E&SH 21, Ex Glen Echo 21, to WRy&E Co 168
—	16' Closed Motor	Laclede	'91	Ex Brightwood 1. To WRy&E Co 746, later 29. Had Brill 21E Truck in 1908

The Tenallytown & Rockville Railroad Color – Brown

No.	Type	Builder	Year	Notes
1	Closed Motor	Newb. Pt.	'91	Had Robinson Radial Truck (six wheel) Scrap 1896
2	Closed Motor	Unknown		Six Window–Deck Roof Car, details unknown
?	8 Bench Open Trailer	Brill	?	Similar to 1; may have been Glen Echo 11

Washington & Glen Echo RR of the District of Columbia Color – Lemon Yellow (1-6 were, for a time, white)

No.	Type	Builder	Year	Notes
1-6	16' Closed Motors	Brill	'91	Four cars used to make WRy&E Co spliced cars 501-502 in 1900. 2 demolished in collision with 7 on 6-6-00. Both presumed scrapped.
7-12	12 Bench Open Motors (DT)	J&S	'96	2 West 60 HP Motors, J&S Trucks. Became G&T 7-12 in 1900, later WRy&E Co 1510-1515
13-14	10 Bench Open Motor	J&S	'96	Became G&T 13 & 14 (1900), later WRy&E Co 1400's
19	8 Bench Open Motor	Jones	?	Ex E&SH, acquired 1900. To G&T in 1900
21	18' Closed Motor	Brill	'91	Ex E&SH Storage Batt Car 21. To G&T 21 and WRy&E Co 168

The company also owned two (at least) 8 bench Open Trailers numbered 7 & 11 by Brill '91.
Presumably both out of service when 7-12 arrived in 1906

Metropolitan Railroad Color: Georgetown – Green; Boundary – Yellow; Ninth Street – Green w/Carmine Dash
Ninth Street Line

No.	Type	Builder	Year	Notes
1-16	6 Bench Center Aisle Open Motor	Brill	'95	To WRy&E Co 1000 series
37	16' Closed Motor	Stephen'n	?	Motorized Horse Car. To haul Mail Car. To WRy&E Co 088
101-123	16' Closed Trail	American	'95	To WRy&E Co 600-622
124-128	16' Closed Trail	Brill	?	Ex Horse. To WRy&E Co 623-627
129-133	16' Closed Trail	Trimble	?	Ex Horse. To WRy&E Co 628-632
134-135	16' Closed Trail	Lew & Fow	?	Ex Horse to WRy&E Co 633-634

Note: Numbers on Met 124-135 assumed. Known to be in 100 series and subsequent WRy&E Co numbers are known

No.	Type	Builder	Year	Notes
200's	8 Bench Open Trail	Brill	'95	Number of cars unknown. To WRy&E Co 1900's
200's	8 Bench Open Trail	Amer	'95(?)	Number of cars unknown. To WRy&E Co 1900's
200's	7 Bench Open Trail	Trimble	'90(?)	Number of cars unknown. To WRy&E Co 1800's

Metropolitan Railroad (continued)

Georgetown-Lincoln Park Line

No.	Description	Builder	Year	Notes
301 up	18' Closed Motors	American	'96	Green for Georgetown. To WRy&E Co 100's
356 up	18' Closed Motors	American	'96	Yellow for Boundary. To WRy&E Co 100's
350	Spliced Closed Motor (DT)	Co. Shop	'00	Built from two of 300's. To WRy&E Co 506

Note: Total cars in 300 series — 66. Exact Met RR numbers unknown except 301, 356 and 350. See WRy&E Co 100-163 and 506

No.	Description	Builder	Year	Notes
201 up	7 Bench Open Motors	American	'96	Green for Georgetown
241 up	7 Bench Open Motors	American	'96	Yellow for Boundary

Note: 200 Series Motors to WRy&E Co 1100-1167. Exact Met RR numbers unknown

No.	Description	Builder	Year	Notes
201 up	5 Bench Center Aisle Open Trail	American	'96	Yellow for Boundary
251 up	5 Bench Center Aisle Open Trail	American	'96	Green for Georgetown

Note: 200 series Trailers. To WRy&E Co 1700-1764. Exact Met RR numbers unknown

No.	Description	Builder	Year	Notes
400-449	14 Bench Open Motor (DT)	American	'99	Not painted for line identification. Cadmium Orange and Cream with Black Lettering. To WRy&E Co 1600-1649
700-739	Closed Motors (DT)	Stephen'n	'99	Painted as above St. Louis 21 Trucks, 2 G.E. 57A Motors, K10 control. Sold summer 1901. 20 to Birmingham (Ala) 400-420, 3 to Richmond (Va): 182, 184 & 186 (Met RR 720-22); 4 to Danville (Ill) — Met RR 723 & 725-727) Danville 146 (ex Met 727) to Peoria, Ill in 1928. 739 to Lewisville & Reedsville (Pa). L&R may have bought three more. One became Wilkes Barre Ry 160. Probably nine to Binghamton (N.Y.) 302-310
1	Mail Car Trailer	Lew & Fow	?	Rebuilt from Horse Car — Co. shops 1897
2	Mail Car Trailer	Trimble	'97	Sold by WRy&E Co (1911) to Jefferson City (Mo) Bridge & Transit Co
3	Mail Car — Motor	Trimble	'97	To WRy&E Co 092
?	Sweeper - Open Platform	Brill	'95	Lost in 2-11-12 13th & D N.E. Barn fire WRy&E Co 01
100-101	Sweeper	Brill	'95	100 Built 1897. To WRy&E Co 02 & 03
198-199	Sweeper	Brill	'95	To WRy&E Co 04 & 05

Brightwood Railway Color — Green — Same as Met RR
(Roster of this company is fragmentary and based largely on available photographs)

No.	Description	Builder	Year	Notes
1, 7	16'-6 Window Closed Motors	Laclede	'93	Number of cars unknown. WRy&E Co 29 (only BRwy car to WRy&E Co one of this class)
10	16'6 Window Closed Motor	Unknown	(?)	No data other than photograph
32	7 Bench Open Trail	Pullman	'92	Ex Belt Horse. Number of cars unknown
39, 44	9 Bench Open Trail	J&S	'95	8 cars. Some motorized by Brightwood. One of Motors to Wash Arlington & Falls Church 77
——	Vestibuled Open Motors	J&S	'95	4 cars - no other details
50	4 Bench Open Motor	Brill	'90	To G & T 50
——	Open Party Car	Dewitt		To G & T

WRy&E Co 087 & 089 (converted Met RR Horse or Battery cars) used for light freight service on Brightwood Rwy. St Rwy Journal Directory (Dec 1895) lists 14 Motors, 10 Trail & 3 others. Original barn destroyed by fire 1-24-95. No record of cars destroyed.

Washington, Woodside & Forest Glen Railway & Power Co Color — Green — Same as Met RR

No.	Description	Builder	Year	Notes
14	20' Closed Motors	Brill	'95	To WRy&E Co 206-209, later 222-225

No.	Description	Builder	Year	Notes
1-2	25' Closed Motors (DT)	Laconia	'95	To WRy&E Co 300-301
3-4	25' Closed Motors (DT)	St. Louis	'95	To WRy&E Co 302-303
5	18' Closed Motor	J&S	'95	To WRy&E Co 169
18	Snow Plow	Stephen'n	'99	To one of WRy&E Co 047-049 group
20-36	10 Bench Open Motors	J&S	'95	To WRy&E Co 1400-1418 (less 2 cars) numbered 20-36 (conjecture), but known to have been numbered in 20's and 30's

Washington, Spa Spring & Gretta Railroad Color: 10, 20 & 21 Green, 25 Red and Cream. No other data
(After 1912 — Washington Interurban Railway Company)

No.	Description	Builder	Year	Notes
10	10 Bench Open Motor	Unknown		Ex Union Railway, New York City
20, 21	16' Closed Motor	Unknown		Ex Union Railway, New York City
25	9 Bench Open Motor	Stephen'n	'95	Ex Capital Traction 21, Ex Rock Creek 7
10-12	Closed Storage Battery	Federal	'10	11 (1910) 10 & 12 (1912). 10 returned to builder 1912. 11 & 12 retired 1913

Washington and Great Falls Railway and Power Company
(This road owned no rolling stock. Operated by WRy&E Co with their equipment. See text.)

Capital Traction Company Predecessors
Rock Creek Railway Color — Maroon until 1909
(after 1895 Capital Traction Company — Chevy Chase Line)

No.	Description	Builder	Year	Notes
1-6	16' Closed Motors	Lamokin	'92	Peckham 8B Truck, T-H 30 HP Motors, D81 control. 1&4 destroyed Power House fire 9-29-97. Replaced by CT Co 201 & 205 which were renumbered 1 & 4. In 1905 these replaced by (then) New Cinn S.T. Motors.
7-12	26' Closed Motors	Lamokin	'92	Robinson Radial Truck. 2-50 HP T-H Motors. D-81 control (later K-2). Vestibuled 1905. 3 retired 1907, rest 1912.
1-6	9 Bench Open Motors	Brill	'95	Peckham Trucks, West Motor and control. To CT Co 23-28
7-9	9 Bench Open Motors	Steph	'95	Peckham 8 c Trucks, K-2 control. 7 had G.E. 800 Motors, 8 & 9 had T-H. To CT Co 21, 20 & 22 respectively. 21 to WSS&G 25 in 1910
10-13	9 Bench Open Motors	Brill	'95	Peckham Trucks, West Motors & control. To CT Co 29-32
1-6	16' Closed Trailers	Unknown		Ex Wash & Geo Horse Cars. Retired: 1 (1905) 3 (1906) & 2 (1911). Four to work cars. See DCTS service car roster.
1-6	7 Bench Open Trailers	Lamokin	'92	Peckham Trailer Truck

After the 1895 merger of Rock Creek and W&G, cars (in addition to 1 & 4 above) were transferred from City Lines to Chevy Chase line as follows:

No.	Description	Builder	Year	Notes
7-15	8 Bench Open Trailers	Americanf	'92	Trans. from City Lines 1898
16-17	6 Bench Open Trailers	Steph	'92	Ex Grip cars. Trans from City Lines 1905
33	8 Bench Open Motor	American	'92	Ex CT Co 238. Motorized and trans from City Lines 1898
34	8 Bench Open Motor	CT Co	'98	Ex CT Co 41. Trans from City Lines 1898
35-36	8 Bench Open Motors	CT Co	'03	Built from Brill Woodwork in Co Shop
13-14	28' Convertible Motors (DT)	Brill	'04	To CT Co 144 & 145 after 1909. See CT Co Roster
101-103	Semi Convertible Motors (DT)	Brill	'06	Trans from City Lines 1907. See CT Co Roster

In 1909 with the arrival of Cincinnati Semi-convertibles 1-15, all of the above except 13-14 (convertible) and 101-103 were stored at 14th & Decatur until scrapped in 1912. All cars transferred to Chevy Chase Line until and except the 1907 transfer of 101-103, were repainted to maroon. Until abandonment of Connecticut Ave. CT Co 1-25 and double truck open motor (Chevy Chase cars) were Dark Green while remaining Capital Traction cars were an altogether different shade of Green.

Rock Creek Railway (continued)

Work Equipment

No.	Type	Builder	Year	Notes
501	Snow Sweeper	Brill	'05	To Capital Traction 7 & Capital Transit 037
1000	Vacuum Cleaner Car	W&GRR		Used to clean car interiors
1001	Freight Motor	Unknown		Peckham 8B Truck, 2 50 HP Motors, K Control. Originally a summer party car. To Cap Trac Line Car 31
1002	Freight Motor (DT)	J&S	'92	Peckham 100 Truck, 4 West 30 HP Motors, West Rheostat Control. To Cap Traction and Cap Transit
1003-08	Dump Cars	Unknown		
1009-10	Flat Cars	Unknown		
1011-12	Snow Scrapers	Unknown		
1013	Sand Car	Unknown		Open Flat Trailer

Kensington Railway Color – Maroon & Cream, later Orange & Cream

No.	Type	Builder	Year	Notes
1	Closed Motor	J&S	'95	Peckham 8A Trucks, K-2 Control
2	Closed Motor (DT)	J&S	'95	Brill 23 Trucks, K-2 Control
11	Semi-Convertible Motor (DT)	Steph	'08	Brill 27G1 Trucks, K-10 Control. Similar to Wash Arlington & Falls Church 217-222 and may have been part of same order
1714	5 Bench Open Trailer	Brill	?	Ex WRy&E Co 1714. Used as a Tool Car
21	Flat Car			

On August 1, 1923, when operations were assumed by Capital Traction, 11 was stored in the Chevy Chase Lake Barn. Other equipment was stored at the end of the line where it steadily deteriorated. When Capital Traction Lease was terminated August 1, 1933, the following (in addition to 11) were turned over to Kensington Ry.

No.	Type	Builder	Year	Notes
1-2	Semi-Convertible (DT)	Cinc	'09	Ex Capital Trac 1 & 2 – See CT Co Roster
3	18' Closed Motor	American	'98	Ex Capital Trac 316

All cars scrapped (21 – probable) at abandonment 1935

Baltimore and Washington Transit Company Color – Brown
(after 1914 Washington and Maryland Railway Company)

No.	Type	Builder	Year	Notes
1-2	8 Bench Open Motors	J&S	'97	No benches on Platforms. Derelict 1907
4-5	Center Entrance Closed	Brill	'10	Painted "Pennsylvania" Red. These were gasoline powered. 4 repossessed and resold by Brill in 1911 to Sioux Falls (S.D.) Traction. Became their electric car 17.5 destroyed in 9-16-13 car barn fire.
2nd 4	Closed Storage Battery	Federal	'11	Destroyed in 9-16-13 barn fire
71	8 Bench Open Motor	CT Co	'03	Leased from Capital Traction
324	18' Closed Motor	Brill	'99	324, 597 & 598 (CT Co numbers) leased from Capital Traction 1914-1916. 1906-1909 Cap Trac renumbering lost builder data on 597-98
597	18' Closed Motor	See note		
598	18' Closed Motor	See note		
54	Closed Motor	Cinc	'16	To Indiana Union Traction 30 in 1918

Independent – East Washington Heights Traction Railroad Company of the District of Columbia

No.	Type	Builder	Year	Notes
—	16' Closed Motors (2 Cars)	Pullman	'92	Ex Belt, Ex WRy&E Co 19-28 series. Painted Yellow and unnumbered
—	18' Closed Motors (2 Cars)	?		Ex Capital Traction Motors, Numbers unknown. Painted Green and unnumbered. The Ex Cap Traction Motors replaced the Ex WRy&E Co cars. Date unknown

Where color is shown, it is taken from a series of notes completed January 21, 1963 by LeRoy O. King, Sr. from his memory and notes taken during his life. Color given is the prevailing color which was generally applied to upper side body panel, dash, and letterboard on closed Cars. Again generally, lower side panels, the area below windows on platform and the roof were white. On open cars, seat end panels, dashes, and area over bulkhead window had prevailing color. Sills and roof generally white.

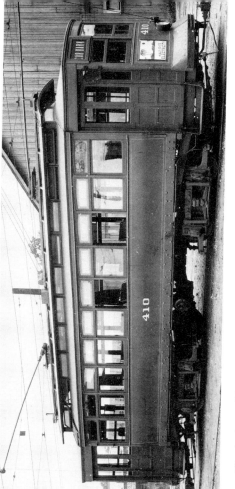

Birmingham (Ala.) Electric 410, an ex Metropolitan 700. Alvin Hudson collection.

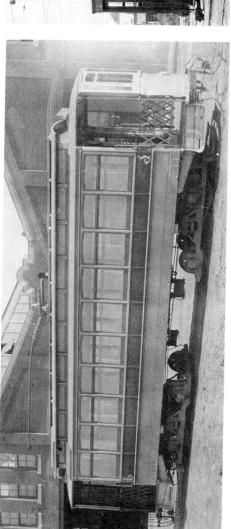

Metropolitan RR 700 at Lincoln Park car house about 1900. Robert A Truax collection.

Danville (Illinois) Street Railway 145, ex Metropolitan 726 in 1913. Charles Gammel collection from Paul Stringham.

Illinois Power and Light (Peoria) 146. Ex Danville 146 ex Metropolitan 727. Paul Stringham collection.

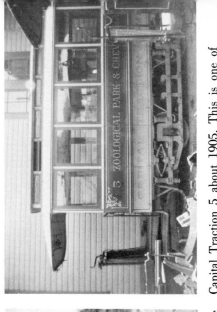

Kensington Rwy 2 at Jackson and Sharp Plant in Wilmington, Delaware. Howard E. Johnson collection.

Capital Traction 5 about 1905. This is one of Rock Creek's Lamokin built closed motors 1-6. Photo by LeRoy O. King, Sr.

Capital Traction 26 (Brill '95), ex Rock Creek 4. Right: Capital

Wilkes Barre Railway 160 about 1920. Ex Lewisville (Pa.) and Reedsville, ex Metropolitan 700. Richard Kotulak collection.

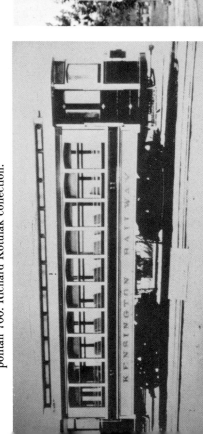

Capital Traction (ex Rock Creek) 11 at Chevy Chase Lake about 1905. Photo by LeRoy O. King, Sr.

Center: Capital Traction I (ex 201).

Kensington Rwy 11. Author's collection.

Left: Capital Traction I (ex 201). Center: Capital Traction 26 (Brill '95), ex Rock Creek 4. Right: Capital

Capital Traction 4 (Cincinnati 1905) at Chevy Chase Lake in 1905. Photo by LeRoy O. King, Sr.

One of Rock Creek's 1-6 series open trailers. Capital Traction photo, author's collection.

Left: Capital Traction 4 (ex Rock Creek closed trailer 4, ex W & GRR horse car). Right: Capital Traction freight motor 1002 (ex Rock Creek 1002). Both photos taken about 1905 at Chevy Chase Lake by LeRoy O. King, Sr.

CAPITAL TRACTION COMPANY – ELECTRIC CARS
(See also Rock Creek Railway)

Single Truck Cars

All single truck motors had Lord Baltimore Trucks, 2 G.E. 1000, 35 HP Motors and K-8, 9, or 10 Control. All single truck trailers had Stephenson Perfection trucks. All single truck cars had 30" Wheels.

No. of* Cars	Builder	Date	Weight	Seats	Length O/A	Body Length	Remarks
Closed Motors							
70	Amer.	1898	19990	26	25'6"	18'	One car exists as relic (303) and another as 0522 now at Nat Cap Museum of Transport
18	Steph	1892	---	24	---	16''	Converted from cable trailers in 1898. Reconverted to electric trailers in 1904-05
20	Brill	1899	19990	26	25'6"	18'	Trucks and elec equip to 1904 Brill and 1905 Cincinnati Bodies
10	Steph	1902	19990	26	25'6"	18'	1 car later 300, experimental safety car Sligo Run line
12	Brill	1904	19990	26	25'6"	18'	
11	Brill	1904	19990	26	25'6"	18'	Bodies only. Trucks and electric equip from 16' Stephenson cars
7	Cinc	1905	19990	26	25'6"	18'	Bodies only. Trucks and elec equip from 16' Stephenson cars
Closed Trailers							
58	Steph	1892	---	24	---	16'	Ex Cable Trail. To Electric Trail 1898
18	Steph	1892	---	24	---	16'	From 16' Stephenson Motors (above)
27	Co. shop	1902	---	24	---	16'	Ex Stephenson Horse, Ex Cable Trail, re-roofed Bombay to Deck — Co. Shops
24	Laclede	1890	---	24	---	16'	Orig Cable Trail 7th St Line (Nos. 1–24). Converted to Elec Trail 1898 Nos. 301–324 as Elec Trail
1	Co. Shop	1898	---	24	---	16'	Rebuilt W&G RR from Jones Built Horse to Cable Trail in 1890. To Electrical Trail — Co. Shops 1898. Was 325 to 1906. Then 1325
Closed Trailer Mail Cars							
1	Steph	1870's	---	---	---		Ex W&G Horse. Mail Trailer 1895—1913. Later mounted on tires and used as T&R office. Now at Nat Cap Museum of Transp.
1	Brill	1896	---	---	---		Built as Mail Car used to 1913. Donated to Chevy Chase Recreation Center 1923
Open Motors							
37	Co. Shop	1898	---	8-Bench	---		From 1892 American Cable Trailers
20	Co. Shop	1903	---	8-Bench	---		Woodwork from Brill. Assembled Co. Shop
40	Co. Shop	1898	---	8-Bench	---		From 1890 J.M. Jones Cable Trailers
Open Trailers							
77	Amer.	1892	---	8-Bench	---		Ex Cable Trail
55	Steph.	1892	---	6-Bench	---		Ex Center Aisle Cable Grip cars

Notes:

In the days of single truck train operations Capital Traction numbered cars by lines rather than make or other criteria. Therefore for at least a momentary distribution by maker, see tables below.

Note on original numbers of Capital Traction Single Truck Electric Cars

Pennsylvania Avenue (green livery)
Closed motors — 201 up
Open motors — 241 up
Open & closed trailers — 201 up
Sweepers & sand cars — 299 down with sweepers first, followed by sand cars

Thus: Train 201 included closed motor 201 and either open or closed trailer 201.
Summer trains (open motor and trailer) would match motor 241 with trailer 201.
Train numbers followed one another in numerical sequence except for trippers.

14th Street (yellow livery)
Closed motors and open and closed trailers numbered from 1 up.
Open motors 40 up and sweepers 99 down with sand cars following.

7th Street (yellow livery)
Closed motors and open and closed trailers numbered from 300 up.
Open motors 331 up.

Distribution of Closed Motors:

	American 1898		Brill 1899 & 1904		Stephenson 1902		Cincinnati 1905		Total
	# Cars	Car No.	# Cars	Car No.	# Cars	Car No.	# Cars	Car No.	
Pa. Ave.	30	201-215 221-235	12	216-218 236-238 290, 295-299	4	291-294	4	219-220 239-240	50
14th St.	24	1- 24	13	25-37	4	91- 94	1	319	41
7th St.	16	301-316	18	317-318 320-331 390, 393, 394 & 396	2	391-392			37
Chevy Chase							2	1 & 4	2
	70		43		10		7		130

Note: This tabulation is transitory since cars were continually shifted from line to line and renumbered.

Distribution of Closed Trailers:

	Stephenson 1892		Co. Shop 1902		Stephenson 1892 (ex-motors) 16'		LaClede 1890		Washington & Georgetown Horse	
	# Cars	Car No.	# Cars	Car No.	# Cars	Car No.	# Cars	Car No.	# Cars	Car No.
Pa. Ave.	30	201-232	10	219-220 236-243	6	218-220 238-240	—	—	—	—
14th St.	28	1- 28	13	27- 39	5	28 (No record of others)	—	—	—	—
7th St.	—	—	4	326-329	5	320 (No record of others)	24	301-324	1	325
Chevy Chase	—	—	—	—	2	1 & 4	—	—	—	—
	Total – 58		27		18[1]		24		1	

Note 1: 1892 Stephenson ex-motors were converted to trailers on arrival of eleven 1904 Brills and seven 1905 Cincinnatis. Numbers shown are as motors. No record of change.

Distribution of Open Motors:

	American 1892		Co. Shop 1903 (Brill Woodwork)		J.M. Jones 1890	
	# Cars	Car No.	# Cars	Car No.	# Cars	Car No.
Pa. Ave.	30	241-270	8	258-260 278-282	—	—
14th St.	5	51- 55	6	67- 72	20	31- 50
7th St.	—	—	4	361-364	20	321-340
Chevy Chase	2	33(ex 238) 34(ex 41)	2	35, 36	—	—
	37		20		40	

Distribution of Open Trailers:

	American 1892		6-Bench Stephenson 1892	
	# Cars	Car No.	# Cars	Car No.
Pa. Ave.	32	201-232	18	214-220 234-244
14 St.	25	1- 25	14	23, 24 27- 37 39
7th St.	20	301-320	21	315-319 321-336
Chevy Chase	—	—	2	16, 17

Renumbering in 1906.

Hunter roller signs made the use of color for different lines obsolete. Hence green became standard, and single truck cars were were renumbered in the following plan:

	Pa. Ave., F&G Sts. from 36th & M	Pa. Ave. from Navy Yard	7th Street
Closed Motors	501 up	551 up	301 up
Closed Trailers	1501 up	1551 up	1301 up
Open Motors	201 up	251 up	401 up
8 Bench Open Trailers	1201 up	1251 up	1401 up
6 Bench Open Trailers	1249 down	1299 down	1499 down

All single truck trains withdrawn 1-31-13 because of PUC order requiring a conductor for each car after 2-1-13. Capital Traction, due to public demand, operated a number of open trains in summer 1914; attempted to get waiver from PVC of one conductor per car requirement but failed, and operation discontinued, ending revenue service of single truck trains.

Capital Traction Company   Known Disposition of Single Truck Cars

Notes: These records are not complete but are based on official records or photographic evidence. The number of cars shown (quantity) are known to have been sold to the property indicated. Car numbers, both for Capital Traction and for the buying company, are quite incomplete and, where shown, are only those known. Thus, in many instances, the quantity of cars shown will exceed the car numbers indicated.

Types of cars are abbreviated as follows:
Closed Motor CM   Closed Trailer CT   Open Motor OM   Open Trailer OT

Company and Location	Number & Type	Capital Traction Numbers	Their Numbers
Alabama City, Gadsden & Attalla Rwy Co. Gadsden, Ala	2 CM	536, 529	
Algiers (La) Rwy Light & Power	3 CM	519, 520, 560	23
Allentown (Pa) and Reading Traction	1 CM	1560	
City and Suburban Rwy, Brunswick, Ga	1 CT	1245	
	1 OT		
Charlottesville (Va) & Albemarle Rwy	2 CM	533, 568	
Compania de Electricidad y Tranvias Aquascalientes, Mexico	2 OM	259, 260	
	2 OT	1208, 1260	
Danville (Va) Traction & Power Co.	2 CM	591, 593	
East Carolina Rwy, Tarboro, N.C.	5 CT	1514, 1521, 1526, 1552 & 1554	
	4 CM	531, 563	
Ensley (Ala) Street Rwy Co	1 CM	585	
Fernandina Florida	2 OM	47, 209	
	2 OT	1404, 1410	
Five Mile Beach Elec Rwy., Wildwood, N.J.	3CM	562	17, 18 & 19
Frederick (Md) RR	2 CM	29–32	50, 51
	6 OM		78–82
Fries Mfg & Power Co., Winston-Salem, N.C.	6 CM	335, 532, 518, 565, 556 & 569	
Goldsboro (NC) Street Rwy	2 CM	544, 545	
Grafton (W Va) Traction Co	2 CM	1504, 1505 & 1510	7 & 9
	3 CT		
Hagerstown (Md) Railway Co.	5 CM	317, 318, 320, 321 & 516	
Huntsville (Ala) Rwy Light & Power	7 CM	501, 504, 507, 508, 509, 521 & 588	12, 13 & 14
Kentucky Traction & Term, Lexington, Ky	5 CT	1506, 1508, 1523, 1528 & 1578	13–19
Knoxville (Tenn) Rwy and Light	5 CT	326, 327, 571, 28 & 573	
Laurel (Miss) Light and Rwy Co	4 CM	227	
	1 OM	590	
Laurel Park Street Rwy Co., Hendersonville, N.C.	1 CM	31 & 1483	
	2 OT		

Lincoln (Ill) Street Railway	1 CM	211, 218, 219 & 223
Maysville (Ky) St Rwy & Transfer	4 OM	1210, 1214, 1216, 1217, 1289, 1290 & 1291
	7 OT	559
Moncton (New Brunswick) Tramways	1 CM	
Mt. Vernon (Ohio) Elec Co	3 CM	503, 517 & 526
Newport News (Va) and Old Point Comfort Rwy & Electric Co.	7 CM	1–7
Norway (Me) and Paris Street Rwy	1 CM	1297
Quakertown (Pa) & Delaware River RR	1 OT	1501 & 1517, 1566
	3 CT	572
Radford (Va) Water Power Co	1 CM	23 & 27
St. Petersburg (Fla) and Gulf	2 OM	312 & 575
Shamokin (Pa) & Edgewood Elec Rwy	2 CM	3 & 6
Shenandoah Traction Co (Staunton, Va)	1 CM	
Stone Harbor (NJ) RR	4 CT	200 & 205
United Electric Company, Denison, Ohio	1 CM	5
Washington (Ind) Street Rwy	2 OT	1296 & 1298
Yarmouth (New Brunswick) Light & Power	2 CM	328 & 330

Capital Traction single truck cars used by other properties in the Washington area:

Washington and Maryland
3 closed motors, Capital Traction numbers 324, 597 & 598; 1 open motor, Capital Traction number 72 (probably); Circa 1914
Washington, Spa Spring & Gretta
1 open motor, Capital Traction member 20 (en-Rock Creek Railway); W.S.S.&G. number 25 in 1900
East Washington Heights Traction Railroad
2 closed motors ex-Capital Traction 1898 American Car Company; numbers and date unknown – estimate 1912
Kensington Railway
1 closed motor ex-Capital Traction number 316 (1898 American); Kensington number 3 – 1933

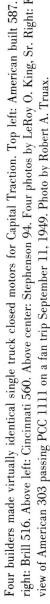
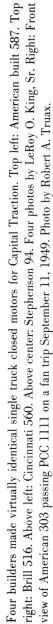

Four builders made virtually identical single truck closed motors for Capital Traction. Top left: American built 587. Top right: Brill 516. Above left: Cincinnati 560. Above center: Stephenson 94. Four photos by LeRoy O. King, Sr. Right: Front view of American 303 passing PCC 1111 on a fan trip September 11, 1949. Photo by Robert A. Truax.

Capital Traction closed trailers, all ex cable trailers. Far left: Platform of Stephenson 227. Left above: Stephenson 206. Right above: Ex horse, ex cable, by Stephenson. Bombay roof replaced by deck roof in company shops 1902. Left: 320, an 1890 Laclede. Four photos by LeRoy O. King, Sr.

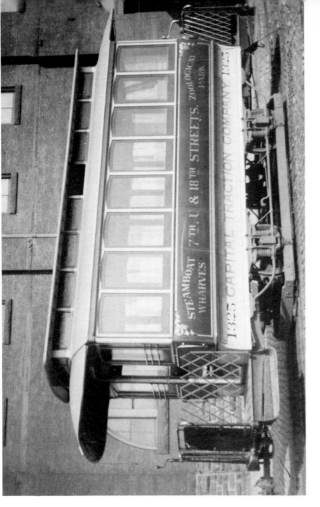

Company built closed trailer 1325 (ex 325) at Seventh Street barn.

American open motor 257 at Georgetown.

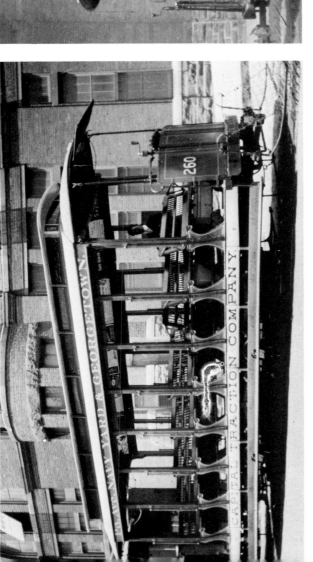

Brill open motor 260 at the Navy Yard.

Jones open motor 404 at Seventh Street barn.

American 8 Bench open trailer (ex cable trailer) at Navy Yard barn.

Stephenson 6 Bench open trailer (ex cable grip) at Navy Yard barn.

Closed train. Motor 585 and trailer 1502 at Navy Yard barn.

Mixed train. Closed motor 521 and open trailer 1241 at Union Station.

All photos on pages 212-213 taken 1905-1910 by LeRoy O. King, Sr.

Mail Car 1 at Georgetown about 1906.

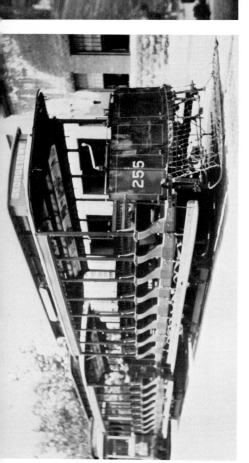

Capital Traction American open train at Navy Yard about 1910.

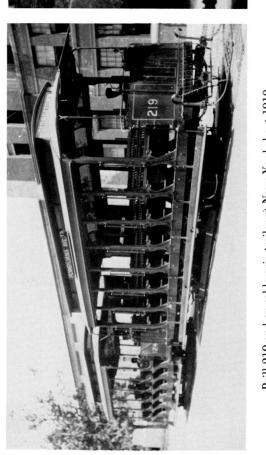

United States Railway Post Office

Mail Car 2 at Georgetown about 1906. Four photos by LeRoy O. King, Sr.

Brill 219 and ex cable grip trailer at Navy Yard about 1910.

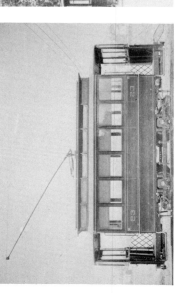

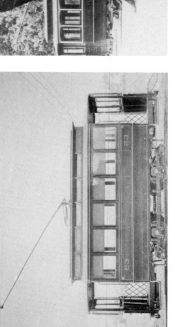

Capital Traction cars sold to (left) Denison, Ohio (S. D. Maguire collection), (Center) Allentown (Pa.) and Reading (Howard P. Sell collection) and (right)

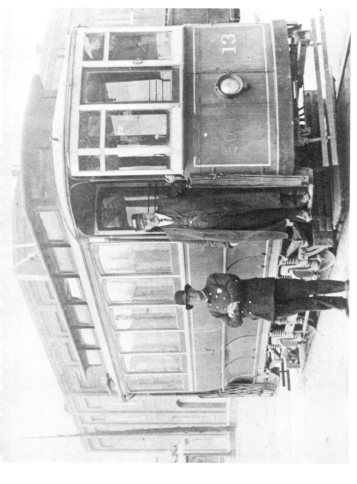

Above: Winchester (Kentucky) Traction 13, ex Capital Traction 504. David J. Williams collection. Below: Five Mile Beach Electric (Wildwood, N.J.) 19 at Georgetown shop. Capital Transit Library, author's collection.

A Unique Opportunity to Buy in Washington, D. C.

30 Trains—Must be Sold

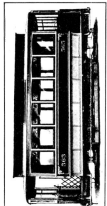

Trail Cars

Restrictions passed by the Commission in the National Capital caused the withdrawal of all single-truck motor and trail cars in Washington.

This is the biggest opportunity we have ever seen offered to buy practically new cars at ridiculously low figures. The cars are not being sold because of their condition. They are in splendid physical condition. An inspection will convince you.

The finest single-truck cars we have ever offered. **Some are practically new.**

Can sell motor or trail cars separately. Motor equipment and trucks in splendid condition. Can paint, letter and number to your standard. **Folding vestibule doors if you desire.**

MOTOR CARS

Built by J. G. Brill Co., American Car Co. Length over posts, 18'; over all, 26' 6". Mahogany interior. Longitudinal slat and plush upholstered seats; electric heaters; Pantasote curtains; electric bells and push buttons, portable vestibules, Van Dorn couplers, etc.

Trucks—Lord Baltimore, 6' 6" wheelbase, 30" wheels, 4" axles.

Equipment—Two G. E. No. 1000 motors, K-9 controllers. Circuit breakers, etc.

TRAIL CARS

Built by J. G. Brill and Pullman Cos. Length over posts, 15' 4"; over all, 23' 10".

Trucks—Brill and Pullman; 6' wheelbase; 30" wheels; 3¼" axles; 2¼" tread.

Longitudinal rattan seats, cherry finish; curtains; platform gates; electric heaters; Van Dorn couplers, etc.; complete.

Can be shipped immediately.

Ridiculously low price.

20—18' Closed Cars

Built by J. G. Brill and American Car Co.

Longitudinal rattan or plush covered seats, veneered ceiling, 10-light circuit, curtains, portable vestibules, platform gates, Consolidated heaters, Van Dorn couplers, sand boxes, etc.

Trucks—Brill 21-E or 21-A, Peckham 7-B or Bemis; 6' 6" or 7' wheelbase; 30" or 33" wheels; 2¼" tread; ¾" flange; axles 3¾".

Equipment—G. E. No. 1000, No. 800, or West. No. 3 motors; K or K-10 controllers.

These cars are in excellent condition, would not need painting, and are complete in every detail, ready for immediate operation. Very low price.

Trade magazine ad. Charles Murphy collection.

CAPITAL TRACTION COMPANY – DOUBLE TRUCK ELECTRIC CARS

Number	Builder	Date	Trucks	Motors	Control	Weight	Seats	CT No.*	Remarks
Double Truck Closed Motors									
1- 15	Cinc	'09	Std 050	4WH101B2	K29B	48267	44	914-926	1 & 2 to Kensington Rwy 8-1-33
16- 20	Cinc	'12	Std 050	4WH101B2	K29B	48267	44	927-931	
21- 25	Brill	'13	Std 050	4GE200C	K29B	49202	44	932-936	
26- 45	Kuhl	'18	Brill 77E1	4GE247D	K66A	44800	48	765-784	Originally MU. See notes 1, 2, 3
46- 85	Brill	'19	Brill 77E1	4WH514	K40AR2	44000	48	785-825	See note 3
101-103	Brill	'06	Brill 39E1	2WH101B	K9	31796	40	101-103	Brill sample DT car - Detroit Platform. See notes 4 & 5
104-106	Cinc	'06	Brill 39E1	2WH101B	K9	32201	40	104-106	Cincinnati sample DT car – Detroit Platform. See notes 4 & 5
107-131	Cinc	'07	Brill 39E1	2WH101B	K9	33284	40	107-131	See notes 4 & 5
132-143	Cinc	'08	Brill 39E1	2WH101B	K27A	33744	40	132-143	See notes 4 & 5
144-145	Brill	'04	Brill 22E	2GE1000	K9	26750	44	—	Were Chevy Chase 13 & 14 – convertibles. Permanently closed & renumbered 1909. 144 to Hagerstown & Frederick 102 in 1911 or 1912. 145 to Instruction car 1001
151-170	Cinc	'09	Std 045	2WH306	K27A	36621	38	151-170	Original PAYE cars & orig had longitudinal seats. See note 5
171-189	Cinc	'09	Std 045	2WH306	K27A	36621	40	171-186 / 144-146	PAYE Cars. See note 5
601-620	Jewett	'10	Brill 39E	2WH306	K27A	35172	40	187-206	
621-700	Jewett	'11	Brill 39E	2WH306	K27A	33857	40	207-286	
701-750	Jewett	'12	Brill 39E	2WH306	K27A	33857	40	287-336	
Double Truck Open Motors									
801-806	Brill	'06	Brill 22E	2WH101B	K9				800's were 13 Bench Open Motors. Twelve were re-equipped for Chevy Chase service in 1900. Headlights removed and replaced with portable arc lamps; air brakes & vestibules fitted. Withdrawn from service about 1919. Returned for Shrine convention 1923 & summer of 1929. 812 to advertising car 12-15-24. All scrapped by Capital Transit in 1935.
807-821	Cinc	'07	Lord Balt	2WH101B	K9				

*Capital Transit Number

Notes on Double Truck Cars:

1. All cars equipped with Van Dorn couplers except 26-45 which had Tomlinson couplers while MU equipped. Capital Transit equipped all with Hedley anticlimber & bar coupler (WRy Standard).
2. 26-45 (20 cars) all originally MU equipped. MU equipment removed prior to 1924 from 26-33. By 1931, 7 cars (39-45) retained MU equipment which was removed that year.
3. 26-85 rebuilt. Motors shunted, new brakes, floors, leather seats & new green and gray color scheme; 63-68 in 1928. Remainder in 1931. None had trolleys when

4. Brill 22E Trucks on 101-103 and Lord Baltimore Trucks on 104-143 changed to Brill 39E; 15 cars in 1919, 15 in 1920, and 13 in 1921.

5. Cars 1-85 & 601-750 were built as Pay-within Cars. Remaining double truck closed cars (except 144 & 145) converted and rebuilt to Pay-within as follows:

Car Numbers	Date	Detail of Rebuilding
101-103	After 1910	Bulkheads removed & folding doors & steps added
104-131	1910	Bulkheads removed & folding doors & steps added
132-143	1919-1921	Rebuilt 1909 to PAYE. At that time bulkheads altered and equipped with air front sliding doors & folding steps. 1919-21 to PW-Bulkheads removed and equipped with rear air operated folding doors and steps.
151-170	1919-1921	Bulkheads removed, air operated rear doors and steps installed
171-189	1919-1921	Bulkheads removed, air operated rear doors and steps installed

6. Except for cars 1-25 & 144-145, Capital Traction cars were not trolley equipped when new. The company had only two trolley operations — Connecticut Ave. beyond Rock Creek Loop & the old Washington & Maryland Line to Takoma. As suburban service grew, large numbers of cars were trolley equipped. Some, however, were never so equipped. They were as follows:

104-106	151-170	
107-131	601-609	
132-138	661-719	

101-103 trolley equipped 1907 but trolleys removed in few years. 144-145 trolleys removed about 1909.

7. 1-25 were first cars' factory equipped with air brakes. 101-143, 151-187, 601-750, & 801-821 originally had hand brakes only. All were air brake equipped 1912-1913.

8. All double truck closed motors except 1, 2, 144 & 145 to Capital Transit Co.

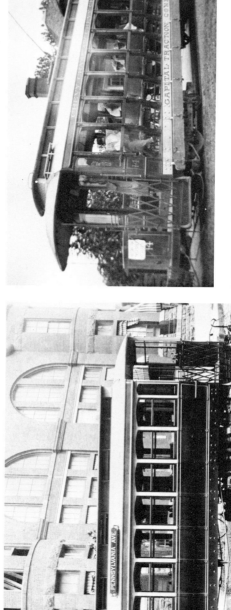

Top right: Capital Traction Convertible Car 14 at Chevy Chase Lake about 1905 without vestibule.
Bottom right: Same car and location about 1906 with vestibules. Above: 144 (ex 13) at the Navy Yard about 1910 after being permanently closed. All photos by LeRoy O. King, Sr.

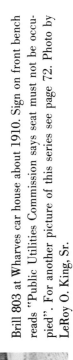

Capital Traction Double Truck open cars.

Brill 803 at Wharves car house about 1910. Sign on front bench reads "Public Utilities Commission says seat must not be occupied". For another picture of this series see page 72. Photo by LeRoy O. King, Sr.

Above: Front and side views of Cincinnati 811 before vestibules added about 1910. Below: Front and side views of same series after vestibules added about 1910. Front views at Chevy Chase Lake. Capital Transit Library, author's collection. Side views at Rock Creek Bridge by LeRoy O. King, Sr.

Double Truck Closed Cars

Numbers	Builder	Date	Trucks	Motors	Control	CT No.*	See Note	Remarks
1-50	Brill	'08-'09	Brill 39E	2GE210	K27A	1-70	1	1st PAYE cars
51-100	Brill	'10	Brill 39E	2GE210	K39A	1-70	2	1st P-W cars
101-110	Brill	'22-'23	Peck 14D5	2WH93A	K27A	337-366 / 367-376	3	1 Man Safety
111-125	Brill	'23	Peck 14D5	2WH93A	K27A	71-85	4	(Bodies similar on all Cars 101-186)
126-132	Brill	'23	Peck 14D5	2WH306C	K27A	86-92	4	
133-140	Brill	'23	Peck 14D5	2WH93A	K27A	93-100	4	
141-142	Brill	'24	Brill 27GE1	4WH101B	K31A	825-826	5	
143-146	Brill	'24	Brill 27GE1	4GE200K	K31A	827-830	6	
147-150	Brill	'24	Peck 14B3	2GE57	K27	147-150	7	
160-174	Brill	'26	Brill 76E1	4GE265A	K31A	937-951	8	1 Man Safety
175-186	Brill	'28	Brill 76E1	4GE265A	K81A	952-963	9	1 Man Safety
235-274	St. Louis	'06	Peck 14D5	2WH101B	K27A	414-418	10	(235-299 similar)
275-299	Cinc	'05	Peck 14D5	2WH101B	K27A		11	
300-301	Laconia	'95	Peck 14B3	?	?	—	12	Ex W&GF 1 & 2
302-303	St. Louis	'95	Peck 14B3	?	?	—	13	Ex W&GF 3 & 4
304-343	Laclede	'03	Peck 14D5	2WH101B	K8	419-420	14	(304-393 similar and similar to 235-299)
344-368	Kuhlman	'04	Peck 14D5	2WH101B	K8	421-425	15	
369-393	Cinc	'05	Peck 14D5	2WH101B	K8	409-410	16	
400-409	American	'98	Peck 14B	2GE57	K8	411-412	17	Ex C&S 30-39
410-419	American	'98	Peck 14B	2GE57	K8	—	18	Ex C&S 40-49
420-424	American	'98	Peck 14B	2GE57	K8	—	19	Ex C&S 150-154
425-449	St. Louis	'07-'08	Peck 14D5	2GE57	K8A	426-448	20	
500	American	'00	Peck 14B3	2GE1000	K7	0500	21	Ex A&P RR 301
501-502	Co. Shop	'00	St. Louis	?	?	—	22	See 507-516
501-509						—		
503	Co. Shop	'00	St. Louis	?	?	—	23	
504	Co. Shop	'00	St. Louis	?	?	—	24	
505	Co. Shop	'00	St. Louis	?	?	—	25	
506	Co. Shop	'00	Peck 14B3	?	?	—	26	
507-516	American	'99	St. L. 21	2WH101B	K31	0509	27	Ex Col Ry 60-69
575-579	Southern	'13	Bald 73-20K	4GE201G	K40A	896-900		
580-584	Brill	'12	Br27MCB1	4WH306G	K40A	901-904	28	(Heavy Suburban Center Entrance)
585-599	Brill	'08	Br27El	4WH306G	K40A	905-913 / 964-967	29	"Rockville" cars
600-629	Brill	'12-'13	Baldwin 48-14-H2	4WH323A	K31A	834-863	30	Center Entrance

* Capital Transit Number

Numbers	Builder	Date	Trucks	Motors	Control	CT No.	See Note	Remarks
630-649	St. Louis	'12-'13	Baldwin 48-14-H2	4GE200A	K31A	864-883	30	Center Entrance
650	Brill	'12	Brill 27GE1	4WH323A	K31A	884	31	Sample Cen. Entrance
651-660	Southern	'12-'13	Baldwin 48-14-H2	4GE200A	K31A	885-894	30	Center Entrance
661	Southern	'13	Baldwin 60-25N	4GE236B	K31A	895	32	Ex Double Deck
700-744	Kuhlman	'18-'19	Brill 76E	4GE200K	K66A	700-744	33	(700-764 similar & similar to CT 26-85)
745-749	Kuhlman	'18-'19	Brill 76E	4WH101B	K66A	745-749	34	
750-764	Brill	'19	Brill 76E	4WH101B	K40AR2	750-764	35	
800	American	'99	Brill 27GE1	4WH101B	K31A	831	36	Ex "Columbia"
801-802	Brill (WRy &E)	'12	Brill 27GE1	4WH101B	K40AR	832-833	37	

Double Truck Half Open—Half Closed Motors

Numbers	Builder	Date	Trucks	Motors	Control	CT No.	See Note	Remarks
900-909	Laclede	'98	Peck 14D3	?	?	—		Ex C&S 100-109 Sold 1905
910-934	American	'00	Peck B3	2WH49	K-10	—	38	Ex A&P 100-124

Double Truck Closed Trailers

Numbers	Builder	Date	Trucks	Motors	Control	CT No.	See Note	Remarks
1071 et al	Brill (WRy&E)	'12	Peck 14B	1WH306	K66A	1071 et al	39	Control Trailers

Double Truck Open Motors

Numbers	Builder	Date	Trucks	Motors	Control	CT No.	See Note	Remarks
1495-1499	American	'98	Peck 14B	2GE57	K8A	—	40	Ex C&S 150-154
1500-1509	American	'99	St. Louis 21	2WH101?	?	0509	41	Ex Columbia 60-69
1510-1515	Jackson & Sharp	'96	St. Louis	2WH?	?	—	42	Ex Glen Echo 7-12
1600-1649	American	'99	Peck 14B3	2GE57A	K8A	1600-1649	43	Ex Met RR 400-449
1650-1699	Brill	'12	(See Note)			1071 et al	44	

Single Truck Cars

Note: All single Truck Cars acquired in 1902 merger. None purchased new by WRy&E Co. All withdrawn from revenue service by 1-31-13. A number were sold. Some became service cars & remainder scrapped in early 20's. See also roster of original owner & service car roster.

Number	Builder	Date	Remarks
Closed Motors			
1-18	Laclede	'95	Ex C&S 1-20. 2 cars used to make spliced car 503. 1 sold (1909) to Princeton (W. Va.) Power Co.
19-28	Pullman	'92	Ex Belt Horse. 25 & 27 sold (1905) to East Wash Hts Trac RR
29	Laclede	'92(?)	Ex Brightwood 1. Orig numbered 746 by WT&E
100-163	American	'96	Ex Met RR 300's. 2 GE 1000 motors & K10 control. 2 used to construct spliced car 506. 3 sold (1911) to Jefferson City (Mo.) Bridge and Transit Co, their 10, 11, and 12. 131, 135, 148 & 140 believed sold (1918) to Northumberland County (Sunbury, Pa.) 140 is certain. 100,120,126

125, 126-130, 132 & 133 sold or scrapped prior to 1/1/17 & 121 & 123 sold 1914; 121, 134, 137 & 140 sold 1917. Following to work cars (then renumbered with "0" preceding old number): 122 & 124 (1917), 125 (1916), 127 (1915); 141, 143, 145 & 153 (1923) and 152 (1922). Balance scrapped 1920-1922 except 107 sold (3/12/11) to Great Falls & Old Dominion for Rosslyn-Georgetown Bridge Car. Prior to conversion to work car, 152 used as passenger car on Macomb Street line.

164-167	St. Louis	'97	Ex Capital Ry 55-58. Peckham 7B trucks, 2 GE1000 motors. 166 to Princeton, W. Va. 1909
168	Brill	'91	Ex Wash & Glen Echo 21, Ex E&SH storage batt car 21. Brill 21E trucks
169	Jackson & Sharp	'96	Ex Wash & Great Falls 5
200-221	Stephenson	'95	Ex Col Ry grip cars 1-22. Converted to motors 1899. Brill 21E truck. 203 to wreck car 0203 in 1923, to CapTran 0203, and scrap 1938
222-225	Brill	'95	Ex WW&FG 1-4. Orig renumbered 740's, then 296-299, then 222-225. 4-9-07 all shipped to Warren (Pa) St. Rwy. 222 & 223 became Warren 8 & 9. Other numbers unknown

Closed Trailers

600-622	American	'95	Ex Met RR 101-123. 613 & 615 sold (1915) to Bristol (Tenn) Trac. Co.
623-627	Brill	?	Ex Met 124-128 ex horse
628-632	Trimble	?	Ex Met 129-133 ex horse
633-634	Lewis & Fow	?	Ex Met 134-135 ex horse. 635 & 636 Sold (1915) to Queen's Run Fire Brick Co.
635-644	Pullman	'92	Ex Belt horse. 643 sold to North Beach Rwy., Chesapeake Beach, Md.

Open Motors

1000-1035	Brill	'95	Ex Met RR center Aisle 1-36. 2 GE800 motors, K control. One or more sold to Salisbury, N.C.
1100-1167	American	'96	Ex Met RR 200's. 1106 & 1123 to Pt. Pleasant & Bayhead (N.J.) about 1912. North Beach Rwy (Ches. Beach, Md) had one. 1124 to flat trailer 065 in 1917
1300-1321	Stephenson	'95	Ex Columbia cable grip. Brill 21E trucks. Those remaining destroyed 2-11-12 barn fire at 13th & D St. N.E.
1400-1418	Jackson & Sharp	'96	Ex Glen Echo 13 & 14 and Ex W&GFE Ry 20's & 30's. Some Peckham 7B & some Brill 21E trucks. 1401 sold about 1908 to Ocean City (NJ) Rwy — their 22
1419-1422	St. Louis	'92	Ex Capital Ry 51-54. Peckham 7B trucks. 1422 lost in 2-11-12 barn fire 13th & D N.E. 1419 sold (1921) to Stone Harbor (NJ) RR

Open Trailers

1700-1764	American	'96	Ex Met RR 200's, 1700-1743, Baker trucks. Rest had Brill trucks. One, at least, sold to North Beach Rwy (Ches. Beach Md)
1800-1809	Trimble	'90(?)	Ex Met RR 200's. Some to flat cars — see service cars 054-065 & 069
1900's	Brill	'95	Ex Met RR 200's. Number of cars unknown
1900's	American	'95	Ex Met RR 200's. Number of cars unknown.

Notes on WRy&E Co. Roster

1. 1,32-50 converted to Pay Within beginning 1912. Air brake equipped 1914-15. 36 got Peckham 14D5 trucks & WH93A motors in 1922 when 39E trucks & GE 210 motors trans to 101, 23, 24, 94-100 in similar exchange of trucks and motors with 102-110 about 1926.

2. Similar to 1-50. Air brake equipped 1915. 50-64 & 79-93 to 1 Man safety cars and exchanged K39 control for K27 from cars 20-49 beginning 1922.

3. 101 placed in service with 39E trucks and GE210 motors from 36. Balance similarly equipped as noted under note 1. 14D5 trucks, motors and control from 426-435.

4. 2 man cars. 14D5 trucks from 371-393 and others.

5. 2 man cars. Trucks, motors and control from 501-509 series. 141-142 had LB2 controller handles for GE automatic line breakers. These were the only 2-man cars in Washington so equipped.

Notes on W Ry & E Co. Roster (continued)

6. 2 man cars. Trucks and control from 501-509 series but motors from 745-749 series.

7. 2 man cars. Trucks and motors from 1645, 1647, 1648, and 1649 which were then stored.

8. First cars with "Blue Stripe" paint scheme. Bought for Anacostia Line and thus were not equipped with whistles and "Golden Glow" headlights. Equipped with "Golden Glow" headlights and whistles for suburban service.

9. Same as above except for Wisconsin Avenue service. Equipped with "Golden Glow" headlights.

10. 235-244, 246, 247, 250, 257, 266 and 270 lost 2-11-12 in fire at 13th and D Street N.E. barn. 245, 248 and 249 renumbered to 257, 266 and 270. Second 270 burned 5/28/18. 252-254 (PAYE) scrap 1931-1933. Balance to 1 man safety 1920-1921 and scrap 1927-1928 except 273 was scrapped by Cap Tran 1934.

11. 275-82 to 1-man safety 1921. 278 lost 1927, 275-277 and 279-282 scrap in 1928. 283-293 scrap 1931-1933. 294-299 to Cap Tran 413-18 and scrap 1935.

12. Only Laconia cars in Washington. 301 sold in 1910 to Wash. Balt & Annapolis. 300 scrapped before 1913.

13. Scrapped before 1913.

14. Probably originally had K8A controls and W49 motors. 323, 325, 327, 331, 333-335 and 338 lost 2-11-12 in 13th & D N.E. barn fire. Renumbered: 324 to 331, 326 to Cap Tran and scrap 1934. 369-70 lost 1919 Eckington barn fire. 371-373, 375-76, 378-79, 381-82 and 386-87 scrap 1931-1933. 388-91 scrap 1930. 383-85 to Cap Tran and scrap 1934.

15. 345, 351, 353, 354, and 356-67 lost in 2-14-19 Eckington barn fire. 352 and 355 to Cap Tran 419 and 420. Balance to scrap 1930-32.

16. 378 had Taylor single truck installed experimentally 1917. In 1923, 371-393 gave up trucks to 101-140 series and, in turn, received trucks from 304-343 series. 369-70 lost 1919 Eckington Barn fire. 371-373, 375-76, 378-79, 381-82 and 386-87 scrap 1931-1933. 388-91 scrap 1930. 383-85 to Cap Tran and Scrap 1934. 392-93 to Cap Tran 424-425 and scrap 1935. 374, 77, and 80 to Cap Tran 421-23 and scrap 1935.

17. Probably originally had 4 West 49 motors. Had K7 control and 2 GE57 motors in 1913. By 1924 all remaining equipped as shown. 400, 402, 404, and 406 lost in 1919 Eckington barn fire. 401 lost to fire 12-31-27. 405 and 407 scrap 1934. 409 to Cap Tran 0409. 403 and 408 to Cap Tran 409 and 410.

18. Had Sjoberg portable vestibules. Probably originally had 2 West 49 motors. In 1913 410 had K7 control and 2 GE57 motors; 411-419 K8 control and 2W93A motors. 1924 all equipped as shown. 410, 412, 414, 416, and 417 lost in 1919 Eckington Barn fire. 413 lost to fire 12-31-27. 411 and 415 scrap 1934. 418 and 419 to Cap Tran 411 and 412.

19. Ex WRy&E Co 1495-99 open motors. Rebuilt 1902 to closed with Brill portable vestibules. Probably originally had 2 West 49 motors. In 1913, 420-22 had K8 control and WH101B motors; 423 had K7 control and 2W93A motors; 424 had K7 control and 2 GE57 motors. By 1924, all equipped as shown. 424 lost to fire at Riverdale 8-12-24. Balance scrap 1934.

20. Similar to, but one window longer than, 235-99 and 304-93. Air brake equipped 1915. 426-435 received Peckham 14B3 trucks, K8A control and GE57 motors from 1600's in 1922-23. 425 to 1-man safety 1925. 444 and 446-449 had WH101B motors. 445 lost in 1919 Eckington barn fire. 425 scrapped 1934. 449 to Cap Tran 445. Balance to Cap Tran — same numbers.

21. Originally had 2W95A (60 HP) motors K8 control. To work car 0500 in 1925.

22. Spliced from 4 of Glen Echo 1-6. Motors WH101B motors. Originally 750 class (WT&E). 501 was 753. 501 rented to Great Falls & Old Dominion as bridge car (Georgetown to Rosslyn). Both scrap 1912.

23. Spliced from 2 ex C&S 1-20 series by WT&E. Scrapped 1912.

24. Spliced from 2 ex Brightwood 1-6 series by WT&E. Scrapped 1912.

25. Spliced from 2 ex Capital Ry St. Louis cars by WT&E. Scrapped 1912.

26. Spliced from 2 ex Met RR 300 class (one was 350) by Met RR. Scrapped 1912.

27. One car presumed lost by fire 1910. Remainder renumbered 501-509, remodeled with new Brill 27GE1 trucks and 4 WH101B motors, all in 1912. 506 burned 10/30/18 at Mass. & Western Aves. 503 scrapped 1922. Remainder, except 509 to storage 1924 and scrap 1927. 509 to work car 0509 with Peckham 14B trucks and 4GE 1000 motors from "Columbia" in 1923. Trucks and elec equip 501, 502, 504, 505, 507, & 508 to 141-146 (except 143-146 got 200K motors from 745-749). Trucks and elec equip 506, 509 & 503 to 800, 801, & 802 respectively.

28. 581 lost Eckington barn fire 2-24-19.

29. Originally had WH Unit control, WH12 master controller and West 101B motors. Control to K40A in 1910 and to 306 motors probably 1910. 586 and 589 lost in 1919 Eckington car house fire. 594-97 to 1 Man and controllers exchanged for K66A from 700-703 in 1931. This group had RR roof and "Washington" window arrangement.

30. 620-629 had GE 200A motors, 600-649 and 651-660 virtually identical center entrance cars. Sunken vestibules rebuilt to floor level all cars 1915.

31. Sample center entrance car originally had 3 part doors on each side. Replaced 1915 with standard 2-part door arrangement. Sunken vestibule rebuilt to floor level

32. Ex 1000 center entrance — double deck to single deck 1911.

33. Originally had Tomlinson couplers and MU jumper boxes. Not operated in train service and equipment removed 1929-30. 700-703 received K40A control in 1931 exchange with 594-597. K40A's too high for 1 Man operation of 594-597.

34. Used to haul 1071 group trailers. Originally had GE200K motors but received WH101 motors before 1924 from 764 and 501-509 series.

35. Bought with insurance money from 2-24-19 Eckington barn fire. Motors salvaged from same fire. 764 had GE200K motors from 745-749 group.

36. Ex Baltimore City Pass Rwy "Maryland". Acquired by WT&E in 1900 and renamed "Columbia". Originally had Peckham 14B trucks, GE 1000 motors and K7 control. In 1916 remodeled — enclosed platforms, lavatory and toilet added and redecorated. Mounted on Brill 27GE1 trucks from 506, converted to straight passenger and redesignated 800 in 1921.

37. Converted from open motors 1682 and 1686 to closed motors in Co. shop 1921 and 1922 respectively. 801 was 1 man 1923-31 and had K66A control; 802 originally had K31A control. Trucks and motors from 501-509 series.

38. Sold 1909-12 to: St. Petersburg (Fla) and Gulf (3), Lancaster (Pa) and York Furnace (2), Norfolk (Va) and Atlantic Terminal, Boise (Idaho), Wausau (Wisc) (2), and Angola (Ind) Rwy and Power. Some may have gone to Seoul, Korea. At least one (their 33) went to Southern Public Utilities, Winston-Salem, N.C.

39. 4 cars — 1071, 1073, 1079 and 1080 — rebuilt Co. shops 1920-21 from open motors 1671, 1673, 1679 and 1680 respectively. 1071 and 1073 originally straight trailers with two doors only at diagonally opposite corners equipped with 3rd door and as control trailers in 1923. 1079 and 1080 originally had four doors and control equipment. All equipped with 1 WH 306 motor for shifting. 1071 had Peckham 14B3 trucks from 1600 class open car. Remainder had Peckham 14B trucks from C&S 400's lost in 2-24-19 Eckington car barn fire.

40. 10 Bench Center aisle. Rebuilt to closed 420-424 in 1902.

41. 12 Bench Center aisle. Rebuilt to closed in 1902-03 and renumbered 507-516.

42. Scrapped prior to 1913.

43. 1614 to advertising car (1933), 1623 to instruction car (1921), & 1639 to advert car (1922). All three to Cap Tran. 1638 to advert car (1923) and scrap 1930. 1602, 04-05, 07-10, 12-13, 15-22, 24-26, 29-32, 35, 36, & 40-44 to Cap Tran. Balance scrap 1921-30.

44. Brill "Narragansett." Exchanged trucks and electric equipment annually with closed 1-100 class. 1682 and 1686 remodeled to closed 801-802 in 1921 and 1922. 1671, 1673, 1679 and 1680 to closed trailers 1071, 1073, and 1079 and 1080 in 1920. Remainder scrapped 1926-27.

Washington Railway & Electric 302 (ex W & GF 3) at P Street shops June 20, 1908. Photo by LeRoy O. King, Sr.

W Ry & E Co's first standard double truck cars, loosely called the 300's, were from several builders. This one, 345 by Kuhlman in 1904, is at Union Station about 1910. Photo by LeRoy O. King, Sr.

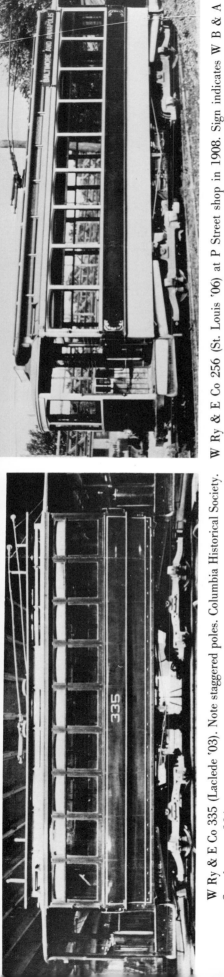

W Ry & E Co 335 (Laclede '03). Note staggered poles. Columbia Historical Society. See also page 104.

W Ry & E Co 256 (St. Louis '06) at P Street shop in 1908. Sign indicates W B & A connection. Photo by LeRoy O. King, Sr.

Above: W Ry & E Co 433 (St. Louis '07) at Union Station 1910. Photo by LeRoy O. King, Sr. Below: Capital Transit 432 (ex W Ry & E Co 432) at 14th and Water Street S.W. about 1933. Author's collection.

Above: Capital Transit 392 (ex W Ry & E Co 392) about 1934. Photo by Harold D. Forsyth. Below: Capital Transit 435 (ex W Ry & E Co 435) at Benning 1937. Photo by Edgar Gilchrist.

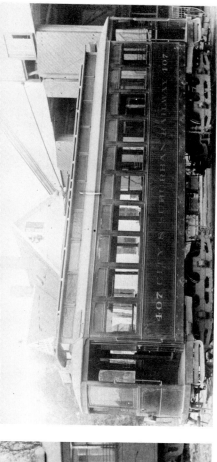

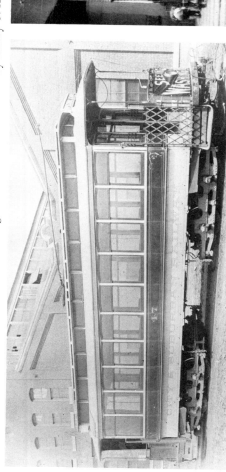

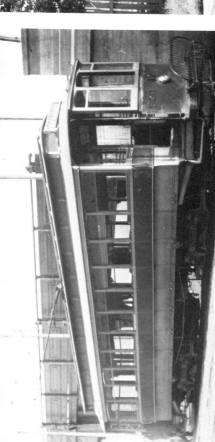

Above left: 409 (ex C & S 39) being scrapped at Benning 1938. Photo by Edgar Gilchrist. Above right: C & S 407 (W Ry & E Co 407) at Eckington about 1905. Author's collection. Below left: C & S 47 (W Ry & E Co 417) at Lincoln Park barn about 1903. Robert A. Truax collection. Below left: W Ry & E Co 413 (ex C & S 43) at Eckington barn about 1910. Photo by LeRoy O. King, Sr. See also page 54 and 55.

Left: W Ry & E Co 500 (ex A & P 301) at Eckington about 1908. Photo by LeRoy O. King, Sr. Right: Capital Transit 0500 (ex W Ry & E Co 500) at Eckington about 1945. Author's collection. See also page 59 and 76.

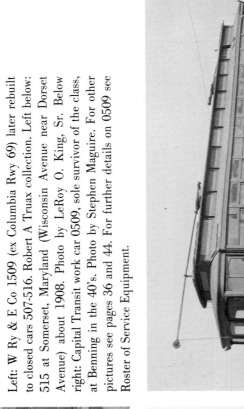

Left: W Ry & E Co 1509 (ex Columbia Rwy 69) later rebuilt to closed cars 507-516. Robert A Truax collection. Left below: 515 at Somerset, Maryland (Wisconsin Avenue near Dorset Avenue) about 1908. Photo by LeRoy O. King, Sr. Below right: Capital Transit work car 0509, sole survivor of the class, at Benning in the 40's. Photo by Stephen Maguire. For other pictures see pages 36 and 44. For further details on 0509 see Roster of Service Equipment.

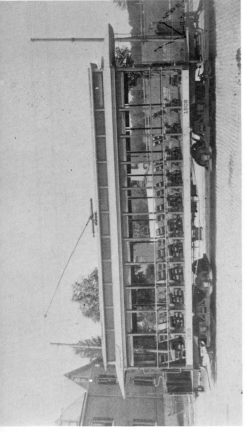

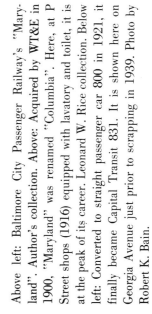

Above left: Baltimore City Passenger Railway's "Maryland". Author's collection. Above: Acquired by WT&E in 1900, "Maryland" was renamed "Columbia". Here, at P Street shops (1916) equipped with lavatory and toilet, it is at the peak of its career. Leonard W. Rice collection. Below left: Converted to straight passenger car 800 in 1921, it finally became Capital Transit 831. It is shown here on Georgia Avenue just prior to scrapping in 1939. Photo by Robert K. Bain.

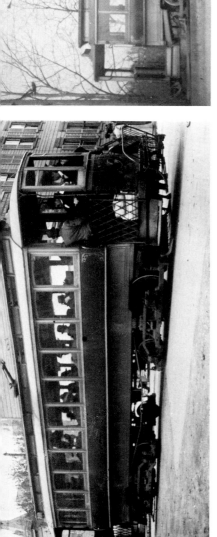

Left: Spliced car 504 at 36th and Prospect Avenue. Right: Spliced car 505 at Somerset, Maryland. Both photos about 1908 by LeRoy O. King, Sr. For details see W Ry & E Co roster notes 22-26. See also page 75.

Anacostia and Potomac half-open cars 100-124 (American 1900) were short lived in Washington obviously because they were not adaptable to the climate. By 1909, then W Ry & E Co 910-934, the owners began selling them far and wide. Left: W Ry & E Co 927. Robert A. Truax collection. Below left: Painted and lettered as St. Petersburg (Fla.) and Gulf 32, this half-open was photographed at P Street shops in 1908. Photo by LeRoy O. King, Sr. Below right: Southern Public Utilities 33 at Winston-Salem, North Carolina about 1935, another ex A & P half-open. David Burnette collection.

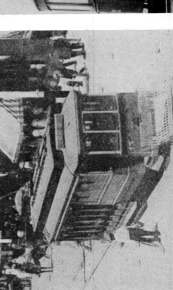

A & P half-opens on other properties. Left: Boise (Idaho) Traction 1919. Author's collection. Center: Lancaster (Pa.) and York Furnace bought two. Open sections were used to make double truck open car 31 while closed sections were used for 21 shown here. J. D. Denney collection. Right: Wisconsin Public Service 100 at Wausau in 1940. Barney Neuburger collection.

Orange and cream 1600's were, for many years, the harbinger of summer. In 1935, 1641 enroute to Cabin John was caught at 15th and Pennsylvania Avenue. Photo by George Votava.

City and Surburban half-opens were numbered 100-109 and built by Laclede in 1898. They became W Ry & E Co 900-909 and were sold 1905. No data on buyers. Author's collection.

Above: End view of 1608, about 1908, before installation of vestibules. Photo by LeRoy O. King, Sr. Above right: 1642 and 745 at Mt. Pleasant in the 30's. Photo by Harold D. Forsyth. See also pages 50, 143 and 158.

Right: 1650-1699, Brill "Naragansett" (1912). Four were converted to closed trailers 1071, 1073, 1079 and 1080 and two to closed motor 801-802. Photo by LeRoy O. King, Sr. For further detail see W Ry & E Co roster notes 39 and 44 and text page 113. .

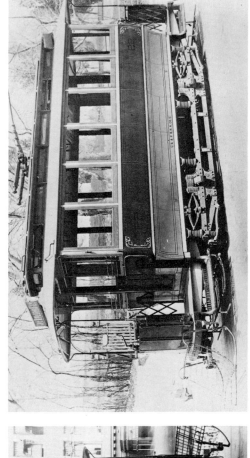

W Ry & E Co 1514 at P Street shops about 1908. Photo by LeRoy O. King, Sr.

One of W Ry & E Co 1-18 series about 1905. Photo by LeRoy O. King, Sr.

W Ry & E Co 22 about 1909. Potomac Electric Power Company from Joseph J. Jessel.

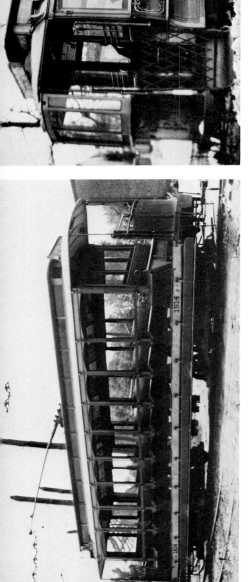

One of W Ry & E Co 19-28 series about 1909 on 6th at Pennsylvania. Robert A. Truax collection.

Left: W Ry & E Co 166; Center: W Ry & E Co 220. Both photos about 1906 by LeRoy O. King, Sr. Right: W W & F G 61, later W Ry & E Co 222, later Warren (Pa.) Street Ry 8. Author's collection.

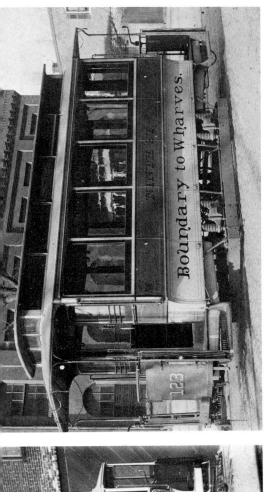

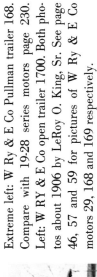

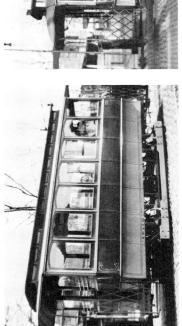

W Ry & E Co Motor 118 at P Street shops 1908. Photo by LeRoy O. King, Sr.

Metropolitan trailer 123, later W Ry & E Co 622. Robert A Truax collection.

Left: W Ry & E Co Brill trailer 625. Center: Trimble trailer 632. Right: Lewis and Fowler trailer 634. Three photos about 1905 by LeRoy O. King, Sr.

Extreme left: W Ry & E Co Pullman trailer 168. Compare with 19-28 series motors page 230. Left: W RY & E Co open trailer 1700. Both photos about 1906 by LeRoy O. King, Sr. See page 46, 57 and 59 for pictures of W Ry & E Co motors 29, 168 and 169 respectively.

Metropolitan trailer 205 (Trimble), later W Ry & E Co 1700 series. Robert A Truax collection.

W Ry & E Co Brill trailer 1909 about 1906. Photo by LeRoy O. King, Sr.

Left: W Ry & E Co trailer 1919 (Brill) at P Street shops. Right: W Ry & E Co motor 1420 at Lincoln Park Barn. Both photos about 1906 by LeRoy O. King, Sr.

Left: W Ry & E Co Brill motor and American trailer. Right: Metropolitan American motor and trailer. Later W Ry & E Co 1100 and 1900 series

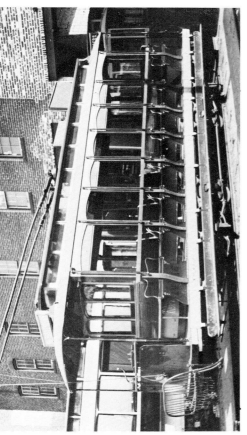

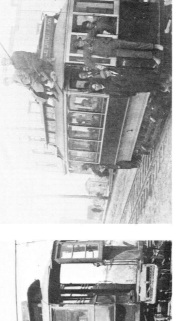

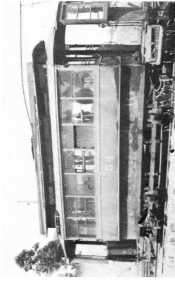

Left: W Ry & E Co 1300 in Anacostia about 1908. Right: W Ry & E Co 1418 at P Street shops 1908. Both photos by LeRoy O. King, Sr.

Some W Ry & E Co single truck cars on other properties. Left: Northumberland County Ry. (Sunbury, Pa.) 149 (ex 100-163 series) Howard E. Johnston collection. Center: Washington, Arlington and Falls Church 54, an ex Metropolitan horse car. Photo by LeRoy O. King, Sr. Right: Princeton (W. Virginia) Power Company 1, an ex 1-18 series. Note Washington destination. Stephen D. Maguire collection.

Extreme left: Unique tractor hauled train at North Beach, Maryland. Car is an ex W Ry & E Co 1700. Author's collection. Left: Ex Metropolitan mail trailer 2 painted and lettered for the Jefferson City (Mo.) Bridge and Transit Company at P Street shops 1911. Photo by LeRoy O. King, Sr.

233

CAPITAL TRANSIT COMPANY – DC TRANSIT COMPANY ROSTER OF PASSENGER CARS

Number	Builder/Date	Trucks	Motors	Control	Length	Width	Height	Weight	Seats	See Note	Was*	Remarks
1-70	Brill '08 '10	Brill 39E	2GE210	K39A	42'4-1/2"	8'1-1/2"	12'1-1/2"	37400	37	1	W1-49 65-78 94-100	
71-100	Brill '23	Brill 39E	2GE210	K27A	42'11"	8'3"	12'4-1/2"	36930	44	2	W 111-140	Sample DT cars Scrap '38
101-103	Brill '06	Brill 39E	2WH101B	K9	40'2"			31800	40	–	C 101-103	Scrap 116 (1937) Rest 1939
104-131	Cinc '06 '07	Brill 39E	2WH101B	K9	39'2"			31800	40	–	C 104-131	
132-143	Cinc '08	Brill 39E	2WH101B	K27A	41'8"	8'7"	12'5"	32000	44	3	C 132-143	
144-146	Cinc '09	Std 045	2WH306	K27A	42'8"	8'7"	12'6-1/2"	35100	44	–	C 187-189	Scrap 1945
147-150	Brill '24	Bald 48-14-H2	4GE200A	K40AR2	42'11"	8'5"	12'6"	38830	44	4	W 147-150	Same series as 144-146
151-186	Cinc '09	Std 045	2WH306	K27A	42'8"	8'7"	12'6-1/2"	35100	44	5	C 151-186	
187-336	Jewett '10-'12	Brill 39E	2WH306	K27A	41'8"	8'8-1/4"	12'6-1/2"	33600	44	6	C 601-750	1 man safety Scrap 1936
337-366	Brill '10-'11	Brill 39E	2GE210	K27A	42'4-1/2"	8'1-1/2"	12'1-1/2"	35300	43		W 50-64, 79-83	
377-408	See Note											Numbers reserved for W 1600's which see
409-412	Amer '98	Peck 14B	2GE57	K8	38'8"	8'8"	12'5-1/2"	35600	*40	–	W 403,408 418 & 419	Scrap 1935
413-425	Various '06-'07	Peck 14D5	2WH101B	K27	37'6"	8'3"	11'6"	31500	34	7	W-Various	Scrap 1935
426-448	St.L '07 '08	Peck 14B3	2GE57	K8	41'10-1/2"	8'2"	11'7-1/2"	37130	38	8	W-Various	
501-550	Os-B '22 '23	OsB 30-64	4GE265A	K35	41'0"	8'2-1/2"	11'5-1/2"	33500	44	9	——	"Providence" cars
700-764	Kuhl '18 '20	Brill 76E	4GE200K	K66A	43'11-1/2"	8'7-1/2"	12'7-1/2"	44800	48	10	W 700-764	
765-784	Kuhl '18	Brill 77E1	4GE247	K66A	43'11-1/2"	8'7-1/2"	12'7-1/2"	44800	48	11	C 26-45	
785-824	Brill '19	Brill 77E1	4WH514	K40AR2	43'11-1/2"	8'7-1/2"	12'7-1/2"	44800	48	11	C 46-85	
825-830	Brill '24	Brill 27GE1	4WH101B	K40AR2	42'11"	8'5"	12'6"	44300	44	12	W 141-146	Scrap 1939
831	Amer '99	Brill 27GE1	4WH101B	K31A	41'11-1/2"	8'1-1/4"	12'0"	41800	46	–	W 800	
832-833	Brill '12	Brill 27GE1	4WH101B	K66A	44'1"	8'4"	12'6-1/2"	48500	48	–	W 801-802	833-K40AR control
834-863	Brill '12 '13	Bald 48-14-H2	4WH323A	K31A	41'8"	8'2-3/4"	11'6"	39500	48	13	W 600-629	Scrap 1947 Center Entrance

Car Numbers	Builder / Year	Truck	Motor	Control	Length	Width	Height	Weight			Car No.	Remarks
		48-14-H2		K31A		8'2-3/4"	11'6"	40100	14	48		Center Entrance
884	Brill '12	Brill 27GE1	4WH323A	K31A	'41'8"	8'2-3/4"	11'6"	38900	15	52	W 650	Center Entrance
885-894	Southern '12-'13	Bald 48-14-H2	4GE200A	K31A	41'8"	8'2-3/4"	11'6"	40400	16	48	W 651-660	Center Entrance
895	Southern '13	Bald 60-25N	4GE236B	K31A	42'7-1/2"	8'7-3/4"	11'6"	48060	—	48	W 661	Orig double deck. Scrap 1938
896-900	Southern '13	Bald 73-20K	4GE201G	K40A	46'8"	8'7"	12'3/4"	50000	—	54	W 575-579	Heavy Center Entrance, 900 Scrap 1937 Balance 1938
901-904	Brill '12	Br 27MCB1	4WH306G	K40A	46'6"	8'7-1/2"	11'10"	49000	17	54	W 580, 582-584	Heavy Center Entrance Scrap 1938
905-913	Brill '08	Brill 27E1	4WH306G	K40A	45'10"	8'8"	12'1"	53100	18	48	W 587 et al	RR Roof "Washington" window
914-931	Cinc '09 & '12	Std 050	4WH101B	K29B	43'8"	8'7"	11'5"	48200	19	44	C 3-20	"Chevy Chase" cars
914-917	Brill '12	Brill 27F	4WH101B	K35	44'1"	8'4"	12'6-1/2"	51000	—	48	W 1071 et al	
932-936	Brill '13	Std 050	4GE200C	K29B	44'4"	8'10-1/2"	12'7-1/2"	49000	20	44	C 21-25	
937-963	Brill '26	Brill 76E1	4GE1198B1	K35	42'11"	8'5"	12'6"	41600	21	49	W 160-186	"Chevy Chase" cars. Scrap 1944
964-967	Brill '08	Brill 27E1	4WH306G	K66A	45'10"	8'8"	12'1"	53100	19	48	W 594-597	RR Roof "Washington" window
1071 et al	Brill '12	Peck 14B	1WH306	1-K66A	44'1"	8'4"	12'6-1/2"	35240	19	48	W 1071 et al	
Open Motor Cars												
801-806	Brill '06	Brill 22E	2WH101B	K9							C 801-806	Never operated by Cap Tran Scrap 1935
807-821	Cinc '07	Lord Balt	2WH101B	K9							C 807-821	Never operated by Cap Tran Scrap 1935
1602 et al	Amer '99	Peck 1433	2GE57	K8	42'2"	8'8-3/4"	11'10"	33140	22	65	W 1600 class	
Streamliners and PCC Cars												
1001-1010	Brill '35	Brill 97E1	4WH1426L	West Va.	43'7-1/2"	8'4"	11'1/2"	35000	23	49	---	
1051-1060	St. Louis '35	Capital 70	4GE1193	PCM	43'7-1/2"	8'4"	11'1/2"	34750	23	49	---	

CAPITAL TRANSIT COMPANY – DC TRANSIT COMPANY ROSTER OF PASSENGER CARS

Number	Builder Date	Trucks	Motors	Control	Length	Width	Height	Weight	Seats	See Note
1101-1122	St. Louis '37	Clark B2	WH1432	Automatic Floating	44'0"	8'4"	11'1/8"	33000	50	24
1123-1145	St. Louis '37	"	GE1198F1	"	"	"	"	"	"	"
1146-1175	St. Louis '38	"	WH1432	"	"	"	"	34240	"	—
1176-1195	St. Louis '38	"	GE1198F1	"	"	"	"	"	"	—
1196-1213	St. Louis '39	"	GE1198F1	"	"	"	"	"	49	—
1214-1233	St. Louis '39	"	WH1432B	"	"	"	"	"	"	25
1234-1250	St. Louis '40	"	GE1198F1	"	"	"	"	35020	"	—
1251-1267	St. Louis '40	"	WH1432D	"	"	"	"	"	"	25
1268-1284	St. Louis '41	"	GE1198F3	"	"	"	"	"	"	—
1285-1302	St. Louis '41	"	WH1432D	"	"	"	"	"	"	25
1302-1317	St. Louis '41	"	GE1198F3	"	"	"	"	"	"	"
1318-1332	St. Louis '41	"	WH1432D	"	"	"	"	"	"	"
1333-1366	St. Louis '42	"	GE1198F3	"	"	"	"	"	"	—
1367-1399	St. Louis '42	"	WH1432D	"	"	"	"	"	"	—
1400-1431	St. Louis '44	"	GE1198F3	"	"	"	"	36360	"	—
1432-1464	St. Louis '44	"	WH1432D	"	"	"	"	"	"	—
1465-1501	St. Louis '45	"	WH1432D	"	"	"	"	35740	50	25 & 26
1502-1539	St. Louis '45	"	GE1220A1	"	"	"	"	35760	"	27
1540-1564	St. Louis '45	"	GE1220A1	"	"	"	"	35640	"	28
1565-1589	St. Louis '45	"	WH1432HE	"	"	"	"	"	"	25

NOTES

1. 2-19 and 50 had K27 control. 1-42, 51-53 scrap 1937; 45, 50, 55-60, 62-65, 67-80 scrap 1938; 43, 44, 46-49, 54, 61 and 66 partially scrapped about 1940. Reassembled and returned to service for WWII and scrap 1944.

2. 39E trucks and GE210 motors from stock resulting from scrap of 337-366 and 2-35 in 1936-37. Scrap 1947.

3. 138, 141 and 142 had 2 WH306 motors. 132-138 scrap 1945. Rest 1946.

4. 147-150 Peckham 14B3 trucks replaced by Baldwin 48-14-H2 trucks from scrapped center door cars in 1938. Converted to 1 man (single end) 1945. Scrapped 1952.

5. 151-154 weight 34960 lbs. and had WH101B motors. All scrapped 1945.

6. 187-195 and 247-286 scrap 1945; 196-219 and 287-305 scrap 1946; balance scrap 1947.

7. Were W294-299 (Cincinnati '05), W352 and 355 (Kuhlman '04) and W374, 377, 380, 392 and 393 (Cincinnati '05).

8. Were W426-444, 449, 446-448, 436-449 weight 35,000 lbs. and WH101B motors. 436-448 scrap 1935. Remainder 1937.

9. 50 cars bought second hand from United Electric Rwys Providence, R.I., in 1936. Rehabilitated with new gears, seats and interior lighting. 501-544 replaced 337-376 and 964-967 as 1 man cars. 545-550 − 2 man to 1945. Then (except 549 destroyed by fire 1944) 1 man single end. 544 − 2 man 1940-45 to allow operation of 1 man 713. 550 had Baldwin 14-48-H2 trucks (from Center Entrance car) until 1944 destruction of 549, then it received 549's Osgood-Bradley trucks. Remainder scrapped 1949-50.

10. 750-764 built by Brill − weight 46000 lbs., 4 WH101 motors, and K40AR2 control. 742, 744-749 had 4 WH101B motors and K66 control. 743 had 4 WH306 motors and K66 control. 713 to experimental 1-man single end semi-streamlined in 1940. 700-712 and 714-735 to 1-man (single end) 1945. 736-764 scrapped 1948; 700-735 scrapped 1950.

11. 765-784 originally Cap Trac MU. Bodies similar to WRy&E Co 700-764. 765 and 824 had GE200K motors probably from 742 and 744 which then got WH101B motors 765-816 to 1 man (single end) 1944. 817-824 to 1 man (single end) 1945. 765 scrapped 1950. 767-824 scrapped 1952. 766 stored to March, 1970, when donated to Nat. Cap. Museum of Transport, Wheaton, Md.

12. 827-830 − weight 41800 lbs. and 4 GE200K motors. All to 1 man (single end) .945. Scrap 1952.

13. 853-863 had 4GE200A motors. 838, 842, 845 & 854-858 scrapped 1938. 839, 840, 859, 862 and 863 scrap 1939, remainder scrap 1944.

14. 875, 877 and 879 scrap 1938. Remainder 1944.

15. Sample Center Entrance car. To Branford Museum 1944.

16. 887-891 scrap 1938. 892 scrap 1939. 885, 886, 893 and 894 scrap 1944.

17. W587, 588, 590-593, 598 and 599 scrap 10-38. See also Cap Tran 964-967.

18. 3-15 built 1909. Rest 1912. Probably only two actually renumbered. Scrap 1935.

19. Control trailers 1071, 1073, 1079 and 1080 converted to motor cars 914-917 in 1936. See also 832-833 and comments in WRy&E Co Roster re 801, 802 and 1071 et al. See also text on Train Operation.

UER—CT Co Numbers

CT Co	UER	CT Co	UER	CT Co	UER	CT Co	UER	CT Co	UER
501	2056	511	2094	521	2135	531	2126	541	2021
502	2083	512	2055	522	2080	532	2145	542	2053
503	2033	513	2131	523	2067	533	2148	543	2127
504	2073	514	2039	524	2084	534	2092	544	2146
505	2144	515	2088	525	2043	535	2054	545	2130
506	2050	516	2133	526	2091	536	2142	546	2089
507	2037	517	2059	527	2038	537	2070	547	2141
508	2012	518	2029	528	2086	538	2047	548	2132
509	2125	519	2136	529	2093	539	2085	549	2011
510	2044	520	2041	530	2009	540	2049	550	2058

Notes (continued)

20. 952-963 built 1928 and had K81A control. New motors (same as PCC) and gears in 1936.
21. "Rockville" cars. 1 man to 2 man 1937. Scrap 1939 except 964 scrap 1941. See also Cap Tran 905-913.
22. Were to be renumbered 307-408 but never done. Ex 1600 class open motors — WRy&E Co 1602, 04, 05, 07-10, 12-22, 24-26, 29-32, 35-36. and 40-44. 1605, 08, 13, 22, 24, 26, 29, 35 and 36 scrap 1935. Balance 1937 except 1614 used as advertising car from 1933 and scrapped 1946.
23. 1000 class "streamliners" were experimental. Brill cars were riveted; St. Louis cars welded. 1010 and 1060 originally equipped with resilient wheels. All scrap 6-59 except 1053 which was saved as a relic and donated March, 1970, to Nat Cap. Museum of Transport, Wheaton, Md.
24. 1101 seated 54; 1112 seated 49. 1101-1145 had "Blinker" doors which were replaced 1947 and 1948.
25. 1266 equipped with automatic (motor driven) trolley retriever May, 1945. In 1953 and 1955 the following PCC's were so equipped: 1214-33, 1286-91, 1293, 1294, 1296-1300, 1302, 1318-32, 1467-71, 1565-87 and 1589.
26. 1487 converted to all electric — Co shops 1945.
27. 1502 converted to all electric — Co shops 1945; 1512 air conditioned, monitor roof, fluorescent lights, Silver Sightseer June, 1957.
28. 1542 destroyed by fire at Stop 9, Cabin John Line 11-28-54.

Capital Transit 1-70 series began with W Ry & E Co 1-100 series in 1908-1910. Left: Capital Transit 46 at Benning about 1943. Barney Neuburger collection. Center: Capital Transit 17 about 1940. Photo by Edgar Gilchrist. Right: W Ry & E Co 72 about 1910. Author's collection.

Scheduled for scrapping in 1940, 61, shown here at Falls barn May 17, 1941, was rebuilt for service until 1944. Photo by Gerald Cunningham. See also page 83.

W Ry & E Co 101-186 (Brill 1922-28) were all similar dimensions but varied in trucks and electrical equipment and therefore spread through the Capital Transit roster. Below is a builders photo of W Ry & E Co 134 later one of CT Co's 70-100 group. Author's collection. See also CT Co 147-150, 367-376, 825-830 and 937-936.

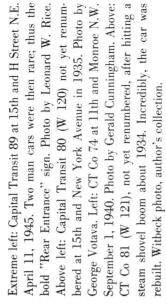

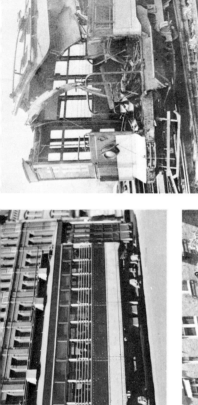

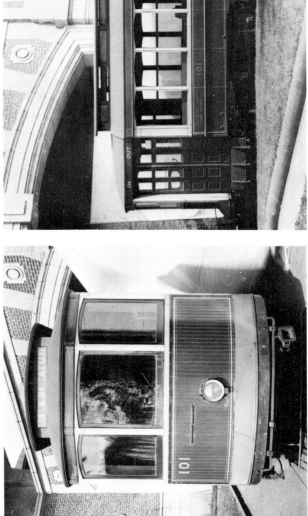

Extreme left: Capital Transit 89 at 15th and H Street N.E. April 11, 1945. Two man cars were then rare; thus the bold "Rear Entrance" sign. Photo by Leonard W. Rice. Above left: Capital Transit 80 (W 120) not yet renumbered at 15th and New York Avenue in 1935. Photo by George Votava. Left: CT Co 74 at 11th and Monroe N.W. September 1, 1940. Photo by Gerald Cunningham. Above: CT Co 81 (W 121), not yet renumbered, after hitting a steam shovel boom about 1934. Incredibly, the car was rebuilt. Witbeck photo, author's collection.

Front and side views of Capital Traction 101, later Capital Transit 101. One of six sample cars (101-103 Brill and 104-106 Cincinnati) bought in 1906. The Cincinnati car was selected; thus Cincinnati 107-131 were ordered in 1907. All retained same numbers in Capital Transit roster. Capital Traction photo, author's collection. See also page 72 and next page.

239

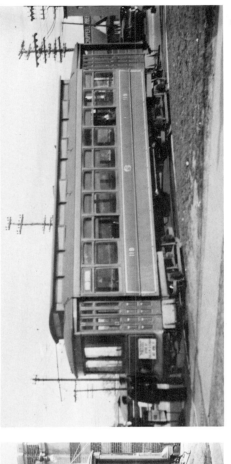

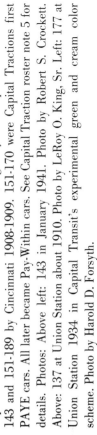

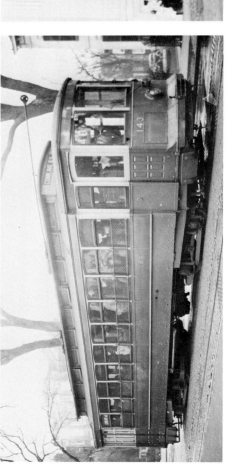

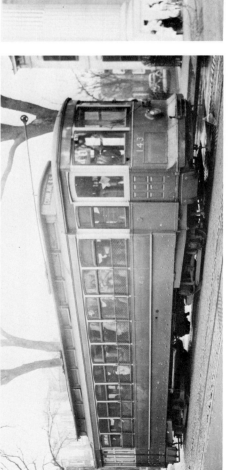

Left: Capital Traction 105 in 1914 at 14th and Decatur. Capital Traction photo, author's collection. Right: Capital Transit 119 at Rosslyn about 1934. Photo by Harold D. Forsyth.

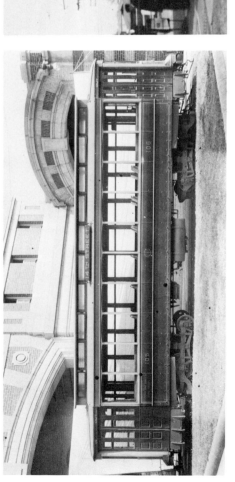

Capital Transit 132-143, 144-146 and 151-186 originally were Capital Traction 132-143 and 151-189 by Cincinnati 1908-1909. 151-170 were Capital Tractions first PAYE cars. All later became Pay-Within cars. See Capital Traction roster note 5 for details. Photos: Above left: 143 in January 1941. Photo by Robert S. Crockett. Above: 137 at Union Station about 1910. Photo by LeRoy O. King, Sr. Left: 177 at Union Station 1934 in Capital Transit's experimental green and cream color scheme. Photo by Harold D. Forsyth.

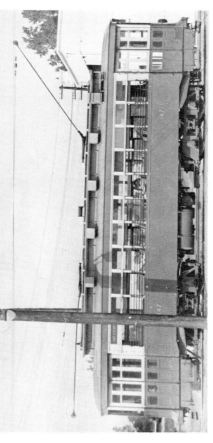

Capital Transit 147-150 (ex W Ry & E Co 147-50) were part of the W Ry & E Co 101-186 group noted on page 238. These four were built 1924 (Brill) and originally had Peckham trucks from 1600 series open motors. In 1938, they got Baldwin trucks from scrapped center doors and in 1945 all were converted to 1-man single end. Left: 149 with Peckham trucks in 1934 about to cross temporary P Street Bridge eastbound. Photo by T. J. Wingfield. Right: 147 as a two man car in the 40's. Photo by Leonard W. Rice. Below left: One man 149. Photo by LeRoy O. King, Sr.

Capital Transit 187-336 were ex Capital Traction 601-750 (Jewett 1910-12). Because they were the largest series of Capital Traction cars and because of their concentration on Pennsylvania Avenue, they, more than any other group of cars, were typical Washington cars. They were sturdier than most and performed well until the end of their days. After the merger, they were used on virtually every line in the city.
Below left: 720 at Wharves about 1910. Photo by LeRoy O. King, Sr. Below right: 619 at 14th and Decatur in 1914. Capital Traction photo, author's collection.

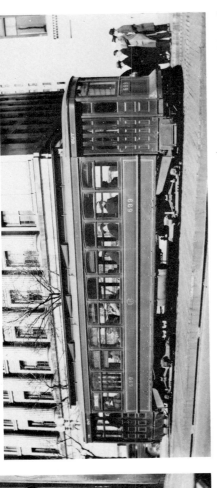

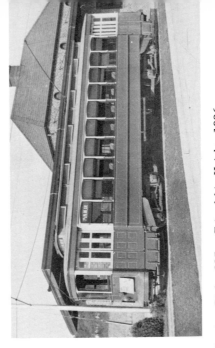

Left: Motorman's platform of a Jewett. Capital Transit photo, author's collection. Right: The Jewetts were the mainstay of the Rosslyn - 17th and Pennsylvania Avenue service until the arrival of the 1000 series streamliners. 699, shown here at 15th and Pennsylvania in February 1935 was one of the Jewetts never equipped with trolley poles. Photo by George Votava.

Left: 323 about 1942. Photo by Robert S. Crockett. Center: Interior of a Jewett. W. W. Buckingham collection. Right: 235 at Friendship Heights 1936. Photo by Edgar Gilchrist.

In 1936, Capital Transit bought 50 cars from United Electric Railways, Providence, R.I. Left: UER 2091 (CT 526) being loaded for shipment to Washington. Center: 546 in 1948. Photo by LeRoy O. King, Sr. Right: One man 357 (ex W Ry & E Co 84). This series was replaced by the

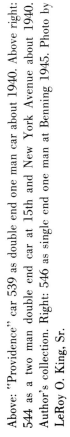

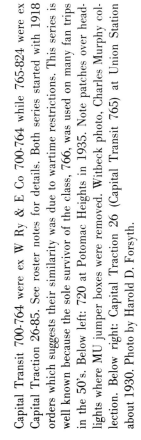

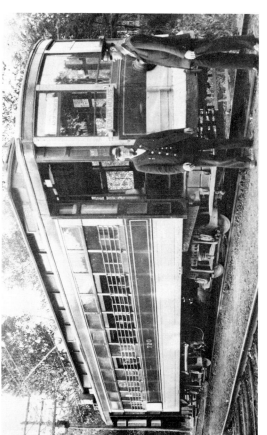

Above: "Providence" car 539 as double end one man car about 1940. Above right: 544 as a two man double end car at 15th and New York Avenue about 1940. Author's collection. Right: 546 as single end one man at Benning 1945. Photo by LeRoy O. King, Sr.

Capital Transit 700-764 were ex W Ry & E Co 700-764 while 765-824 were ex Capital Traction 26-85. See roster notes for details. Both series started with 1918 orders which suggests their similarity was due to wartime restrictions. This series is well known because the sole survivor of the class, 766, was used on many fan trips in the 50's. Below left: 720 at Potomac Heights in 1935. Note patches over headlights where MU jumper boxes were removed. Witbeck photo, Charles Murphy collection. Below right: Capital Traction 26 (Capital Transit 765) at Union Station about 1930. Photo by Harold D. Forsyth.

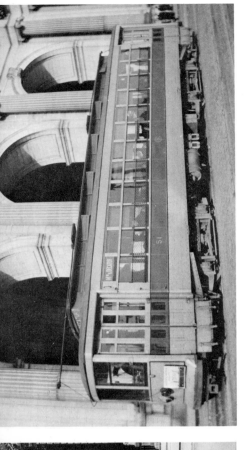

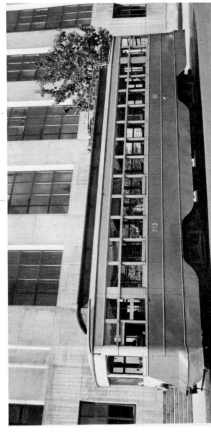

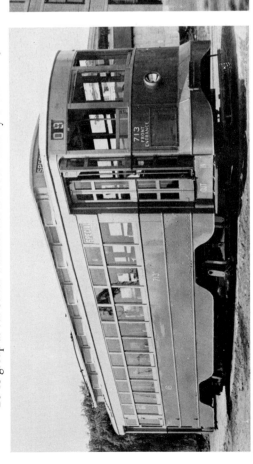

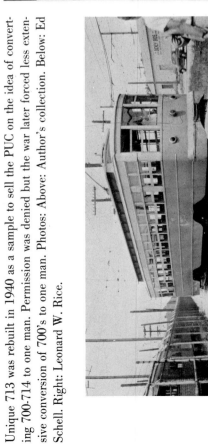

Left: Capital Transit 755 at 17th and Pennsylvania Avenue N.W. about 1940. Photo by Jeffrey Winslow. Right: Capital Transit 790 not yet renumbered, shows grey and green color scheme from 1931 rebuilding at Union Station 1935. Photo by George Votava. Below right: One of the ex Capital Traction 26-45 group at 7th Street Wharves about 1936. Photo by Churchman Johnson.

Unique 713 was rebuilt in 1940 as a sample to sell the PUC on the idea of converting 700-714 to one man. Permission was denied but the war later forced less extensive conversion of 700's to one man. Photos: Above: Author's collection. Below: Ed Schell. Right: Leonard W. Rice.

822 (ex Capital Traction 83) was one of many 700's converted to one man because of the war. These four views were taken in 1945. Interior view shows luxurious leather seats resultant from 1931 rebuilding. Four photos Capital Transit Library, author's collection.

Blind side of 766 on 4th Street N.E. in 1952. Photo by LeRoy O. King, Sr.

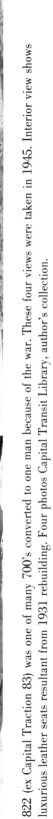

766 at National Capital Trolley Museum. Photo by Harold Buckley.

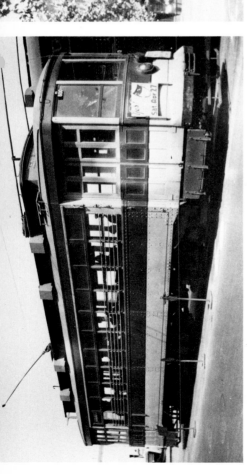

825-830 were W Ry & E Co 141-146. All converted to one man single end in 1945. Left: 825 shares Benning line plow pit with a Washington Baltimore and Annapolis Articulated in 1935. M. D. McCarter collection. Right: 827, as a two man car, at 11th and Park Road N.W. September 1, 1940. Photo by Gerald Cunningham.

Capital Transit 832-833 and 914-917 all were originally W Ry & E Co in 1921-22, while 914-917 served as W Ry & E Co 1650 series open motors. 832-833 were directly converted to closed motors by W Ry & E Co in 1921-22, while 914-917 served as W Ry & E Co trailers 1071 et al until motorized by Capital Transit in 1936. Left: 915 at Tenleytown Car House about 1940. Capital Transit photo, author's collection. Center: W Ry & E Co 1073 in 1920. Author's collection. Right: 801 (later 832) at Union Station in 1935. Photo by George Votava.

Capital Transit 834-883 and 885-894 were originally W Ry & E Co's unusual 600 series center door cars. After sample car 650 was built by Brill (see below), 30 were built by Brill, 20 by St. Louis and 10 by Southern. Far left: Southern built 652 at Union Station 1912. Potomac Electric Power Company from Joseph Jessel. Left: Southern built 651 at First and East Capitol Street in 1912. Author's collection.

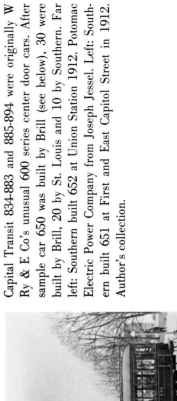

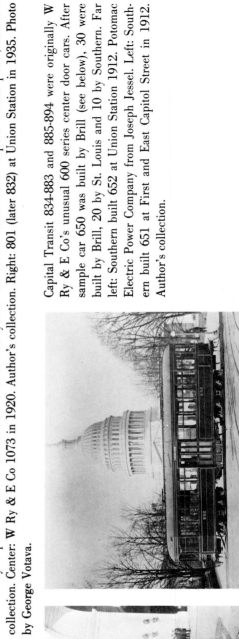

614 (later 849), Brill built, at Peace Monument about 1935. Author's collection.

872 (St. Louis) on Cabin John Line 1940. Photo by Gerald Cunningham.

Left: Platform of a Southern center door at P Street about 1914. Note brass window sash. John Merriken collection. Above: Baldwin 48-14-H2 truck used on center doors (except 884 and 895). These later used on various of the ex W Ry & E Co 100's. See roster for detail. Author's collection.

Builder's photos of Brill sample car 650 above and left. Note extra wide doors. 884 (ex 650) at Union Station about 1940. Note small windows resultant from rebuilding doors. Three photos, author's collection.

661 at 14th and Maine Avenue 1934. Later Capital Transit 895, this unique center door was rebuilt from W Ry & E Co double decker 1000. Note the comparatively lower floor line. For photo of 1000, see page 91. Photo by Harold D. Forsyth.

Capital Transit 896-904, interurban in character, were originally W Ry & E Co 575-594. They were almost exclusively used on the Maryland line. Originally, all had motormen's doors as shown on 576 (Southern 13). Potomac Electric Power Company from Joseph J. Jessel.

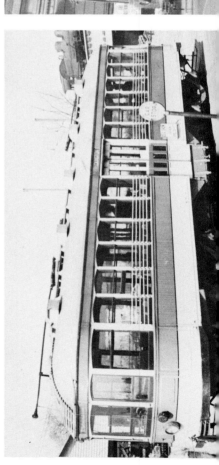

Above left: 584 (Brill, later 904) at 9th and G Street N.W. 1935. Photo by S. P. Davidson. Above right: 583 (Brill, later 903) and (below right) 577 (Southern, later 898) both at 15th and G Streets N.W. in the 20's. Below left: 896 (Southern) at 14th and Maine Avenue in 1934. Three photos by Harold D. Forsyth.

W Ry & E Co 591 at Eckington 1914. Robert A. Truax collection.

599 (later 913) at 14th and Maine Avenue in 1934. Photo by Harold D. Forsyth. For other pictures of this series, see pages x, 82, 148 and 152.

Capital Transit 585-599 series. Seven were originally assigned to the Rockville line and the rest to the Maryland line. 586 and 589 were lost in the 1919 Eckington Barn fire. In 1924, all received two part folding doors in place of platform gates. In 1928, 593-597, in Rockville service were rebuilt with four fold doors and folding steps, bulkheads were removed and modern interior lighting and leather seats were installed. In 1931, this same group was converted to one man. In 1937, they were converted back to two man. The balance of the series remained as rebuilt in 1924.

Capital Transit 965 as a two man car at Beltsville, Maryland January, 1935. Photo by S. P. Davidson.

Interior of 965 July, 1939. Photo by S. P. Davidson.

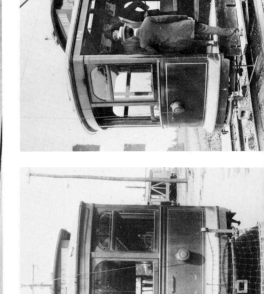

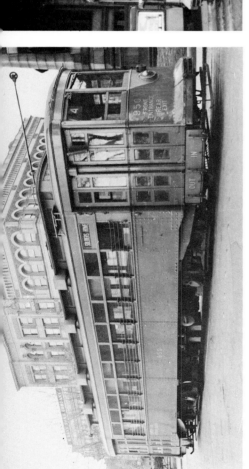

Capital Transit 937-963 (W Ry & E Co 160-186), Brill '26-'28, Washington's last new conventional cars received new motor and gears in 1936 which made them the liveliest of the conventional cars. Left: 950 at 7th and Pennsylvania in 1940. Photo by S. D. Maguire. Right: 963 at Union Station in 1935. Photo by George Votava.

Capital Transit 914-931 were from Capital Traction 1-20 series, Cincinnati '09 and '12. These handsome cars were built for and served their life, without major alteration on the Chevy Chase line. Two were transferred to the Kensington Railway in 1933 and the balance were scrapped with the abandonment of the Chevy Chase line in 1935. Right: 919 (Capital Traction 8) at 15th and Pennsylvania Avenue in 1935. Photo by George Votava.

Below left: Front view of 13 at Chevy Chase Lake about 1914. Capital Traction photo, author's collection. Below far right: Rear platform of 8, taken to demonstrate Pay—Within feature in 1909. Author's collection. Below: Interior of Brill Chevy Chase car. Capital Transit photo, author's collection.

Capital Transit 932—936 (Capital Traction 21-25) were Brill versions of "Chevy Chase" cars. See interior above. Below: 933 (ex 22) in 1940. Photo by Robert S. Crockett. Right: Capital Traction 24 (CT 935) at Chevy Chase Lake about 1934. Columbia Historical Society.

In 1935, Capital Transit placed twenty new streamlined streetcars in service. Incorporating many PCC features, they attracted national attention. Ten by Brill (1001-1010) were riveted construction while the ten St. Louis cars (1051-1060) were welded. Two cars (1010 and 1060) had resilient wheels. One car (1053) survives at the National Capital Trolley Museum. Below: 1006, and 1052 at Friendship Heights car house in 1946. Photo by Leonard W. Rice.

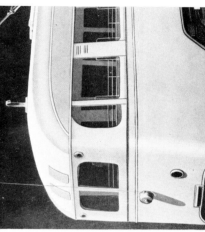

Above: 1001 at 17th and Pennsylvania N.W. 1935. Photo by Roy S. Melvin.

Rear of Brill 1000 class from a Brill ad. John E. Merriken collection.

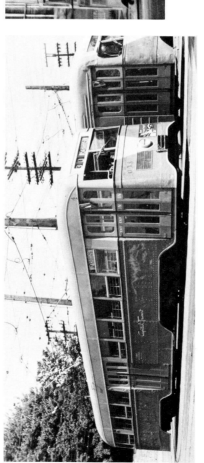

Brill 97E1 truck used on 1001-10. Author's collection.

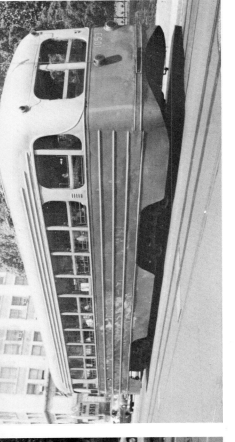

Left: 1051 (St. Louis) at 2nd and Indiana 1956. Right: 1053 at 10th and G Street N.W. 1959. Both photos by LeRoy O. King, Sr.

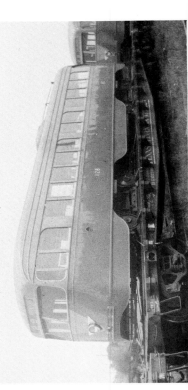

Far left: Rear 1053 in 1959. Photo by LeRoy O. King, Sr. Above left: The Brill and St. Louis streamliners were fitted with visors in the late 50's. 1053 at the end of the Takoma line on a 1959 fan trip. Photo by LeRoy O. King, Sr. Above: 1008, with visor, at the 14th and Decatur barn. Capital Transit photo, author's collection. Left: St. Louis "Capital No. 70" truck used on 1051-60. Photo by Harvey Davison.

PCC CARS

High point of street car design, at least until 1972, was the car designed by the Electric Railway President's Conference Committee. Called "PCC" cars, after their designers, they featured quiet, smooth operation, fast acceleration and braking and a modern, attractive appearance. By 1951, over 4,900 of them were in use in the U.S. and Canada. Washington's first order, 1937, was for 45 cars which were put in service on the 14th Street line. By 1946, the fleet consisted of 489 PCC's, all built by St. Louis. Because of transfer table clearances, Washington PCC's were one window shorter than standard and they were the only ones ever equipped for underground conduit operation. Right: Among the first of many such scenes, PCC 1128 arrives at Benning yard in 1937. Photo by Churchman Johnson.

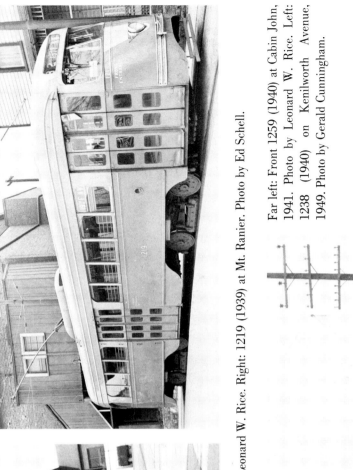

Left: 1111 (1937 order). Note "Blinker" doors which were replaced in 1940. Author's collection.

Left: 1195 (1938) at Takoma in the early 40's. Photo by Leonard W. Rice. Right: 1219 (1939) at Mt. Ranier. Photo by Ed Schell.

Left: 1159 (1938) at Union Station about 1947-48. Photo by Leonard W. Rice. Right: 1159 (1938) at Union Station about 1947-48. Photo by Leonard W. Rice.

Far left: Front 1259 (1940) at Cabin John, 1941. Photo by Leonard W. Rice. Left: 1238 (1940) on Kenilworth Avenue, 1949. Photo by Gerald Cunningham.

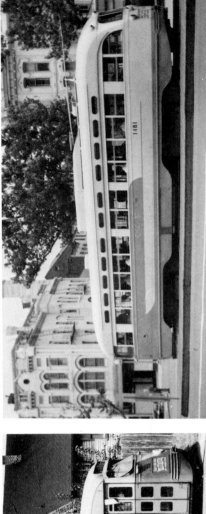

Left: 1286 (1941) at Union Station, 1941. Author's collection. Right 1332 (1941) with experimental monitor roof at Brookland in 1945. Photo by Leonard W. Rice

Left: 1333 being unloaded at Benning yard, November 1942. Richard Kotulak collection. Right: 1344 (1942) at 11th and Monroe. Note shorter fluting above windows. Photo by Leonard W. Rice.

Left 1479 (1945) at Brookland. Photo by Leonard W. Rice. Right: 1481 (1945) in DC Transit colors at 8th and Pennsylvania, 1959. Photo by Richard

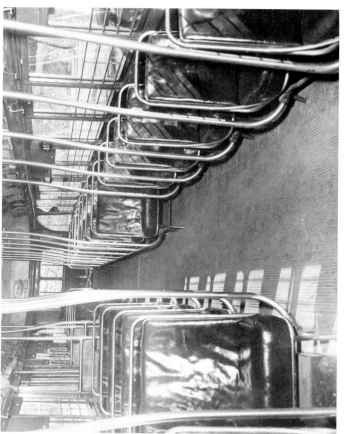

Left: 1487 (1945) at Brookland Loop, 1951. Note "Car Full" light next to destination sign. Photo by Richard Kotulak. Right: 1563 on Cabin John line 1959. Photo by Leonard W. Rice.

Interior 1470, looking forward. Photo by Paul Dolkos.

Interior of typical early PCC looking to the rear. Capital Transit photo, author's collection.

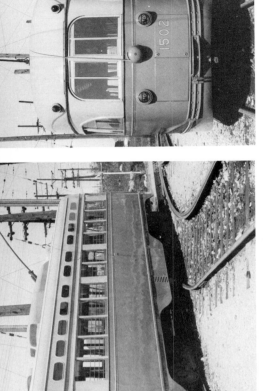

Left: Front PCC 1487. Center: 1502. Right: Rear view 1502. Three photos Capital Transit Company, author's collection.

In 1957, DC Transit equipped PCC 1512 with air conditioning, flourescent lighting, modified seating and applied a modified paint scheme for sightseeing service on Pennsylvania Avenue. It was destroyed by vandals at the National Capital Trolley Museum September 11, 1970. Right: 1512 at Mt. Pleasant on a 1961 fan trip. Left: Entering Capital Plaza Tunnel on same trip. Both photos by LeRoy O. King, Sr.

Left: 1575 showing automatic trolley catching device which was developed to save manpower at plow pits. See also page 305. Photo by LeRoy O. King, Sr. Above: Clark B2 truck standard on Washington PCC's. Photo by

DISPOSITION OF PCC CARS – D.C. TRANSIT COMPANY

1. Sold to other properties for operation

    A. Sarajevo, Yugoslavia (Gradsko Saobracatno Preduzege) 1959-62: 74 cars

    50 numbered as follows:

Sarajevo	DC Tran	Sarajevo	DC Tran	Sarajevo	DC Tran	Sarajevo	DC Tran
1	1442	11	1436	21	1328	31	1373
2	1433	12	1447	22	1452	32	1372
3	1432	13	1444	23	1397	33	1438
4	1435	14	1463	24	1332	34	1441
5	1443	15	1330	25	1464	35	1393
6	1440	16	1458	26	1385	36	1301
7	1437	17	1324	27	1331	37	1326
8	1434	18	1445	28	1367	38	1329
9	1457	19	1383	29	1449	39	1448
10	1462	20	1325	30	1323	40	1454

No data on Sarajevo numbers for balance of 24 cars. D.C. transit numbers were: 1259, 60, 62, 64, 65, 86, 90, 91, 93, 94, 97 and 98, 1300, 02, 18, 19, 20, 21, 22, 70, and 79, 1450, 56, and 60.

Modern Tramway (Ian Allan Ltd. Middlesex, England) reports in January, 1968, that 70 Washington cars were operating and several had been cannabilized. May, 1968 Modern Tramway illustrates Sarajevo 103 which is an articulated car made from 2 Washington PCC'S.

Number data from "PCC Cars of North America" by Harold Cox.

    B. Tranvias De Barcelona SA (Spain) 1962-63: 101 cars.

    DC Transit Numbers:

1117	1185	1220	1255	1303	1315	1400	1501	1510	1520	1527	1533	1546	1553	1562	1569	1575
1144	1187	1240	1258	1306	1317	1401	1503	1511	1521	1528	1534	1547	1554	1564	1570	1577
1178	1188	1241	1272	1309	1337	1469	1504	1514	1522	1529	1537	1548	1555	1565	1571	1581
1183	1190	1242	1279	1310	1340	1476	1505	1516	1523	1530	1539	1549	1556	1566	1572	1586
1184	1192	1243	1282	1311	1344	1486	1507	1517	1524	1531	1543	1550	1557	1567	1574	
		1246	1285	1313	1374		1508	1519	1525	1532	1544	1552	1558	1568		
		1247					1509		1526		1545		1559			

99 cars rebuilt by TBSA for operation. 2 cars (1220 and either 1184 or 1188) used for spare body parts. Numbered 1601-1699 by TBSA. No data on renumbering of individual cars except 1601 is Ex DCT 1340 and 1602 is ex DCT 1258.

Data from Sr. F. Zurita, courtesy Harold Buckley, Jr. 1-27-66. Barcelona street railways discontinued March 19, 1971.

Disposition of PCC Cars (continued)

C. Leonard's Department Store, Ft. Worth, Texas (M&O Subway): 15 cars.

An additional 8 cars shipped to M&O in March, 1966. Stored in Fort Worth as of 7-70. DCT Numbers:

M&O 1962 Nos.	DCT		
1	1560	1195	1197
2	1551	1135	1205
3	1535	1201	1181
4	1506	1202	1200
5	1541		
6	1540		
7	1536		

M&O 7 not renumbered or rebuilt as of 7-70.

Leonard's cars rebuilt for High Level Loading, double end operation and air conditioned. Used in unique parking lot to store subway.

M&O number data from Ed Gaida in Short Circuit Bulletin, Texas Div. ERA 7-10-63

1966 data from Transfer Table, Spring, 1966.

D. General Electric Co., Erie Pa., 1961: 1 car.

DCT 1304. Named "Tomorrow" by GE and used for experimental automated operation.

2. Preserved as Relics

2 cars by DC Transit: 1101 and 1512 (Silver Sightseer). Both to Nat. Cap. Museum of Transport, Wheaton, Md. March 1970. 1512 destroyed by vandalism 9-11-70.

1 car to Wasena Park, Roanoke, Virginia: DCT 1470. 1 car to Shade Gap Electric Ry, Orbisonia, Pa.: DCT 1430.

3. Balance scrapped or sold for various non-operating uses.

101 DC Transit PCC's were sold to Tranvias De Barcelona SA (Spain) in 1962-63 where they served until abandonment of the Barcelona system in 1971. Left: Barcelona 1604, October 13, 1963. Right: Barcelona 1618, October 17, 1963. Both photos by Harold Buckley, Jr.

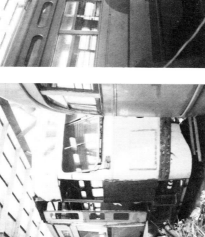

Left: Ex-Washington PCC in service at Leonard's Department store in Fort Worth, Texas. The line connects the store with a large parking lot. Subway portal is in the right background. Photo by Rod Varney. Above: Two views of ex DC Transit 1535 being rebuilt in Fort Worth in the summer of 1962. Both photos by the author.

Sarajevo, Yugoslavia bought 74 DC Transit PCC's. Left: Sarajevo 35 (DCTS 1393) in 1961. John E. Merriken collection. A number of ex Washington PCC's were made into articulated cars by Sarajevo. Right: 106. Joseph Otto Slezak (Vienna) collection.

ROSTER OF SERVICE EQUIPMENT

DC Transit Company (1956-1962); Capital Transit Company (1933-1956); Washington Railway and Electric Co. (1902-1933); Capital Traction Company (1895-1933)

Number	Builder	Date	Motors	Control	Prior Owner and Number	Remarks
Sweepers						
01	Brill	1895			Met	Lost 13th & D fire 2-11-12
02	Brill	1897	2WH306	K27	Met 100	Scrapped 7-1-61
03	Brill	1895	2WH306	K27	Met 101	Scrapped 1-62
04	Brill	1896	2WH101B	K27	Met 198	Scrapped 7-1-61
05	Brill	1896	2WH101B	K27	Met 199	Scrapped 1-62
06-015	McGuire	1899	2WH101B	K27	WRy 06-015	All purchased by Col Rwy for acc't of WT&E. 08, 013 and 015 had 2 WH306 motors. 07 to Nat. Cap. Hist. Museum of Transport. 09 to Shade Gap Elec. Ry. Orbisonia, Pa; 010 to Warehouse Point (Conn) Museum. Balance scrapped — all in 1962.
016-017	McGuire	1899	2WH306	K27	WRy 016-017	Originally C&S Ry. Scrap 1962
018-020	Brill	1906	2WH101B	K27	WRy 016-020	018 had 2WH306 motors. 018 scrapped 1962; 019 scrapped 1961; 020 scrap 1962 (?).
021-022	Brill	1909	2WH101B	K27	WRy 021-022	021 scrapped 1961; 022 had 2WH306 motors. 022 scrapped 1962.
023	Brill	1912	2GE57	K8	WRy 023	Geared sweeper. Motor and control data unknown. Scrapped 1955.
024-025	McGuire-Cummings	1925	2WH306	K27	WRy 024-025	Scrapped 1962.
026	Brill	1905	2WH101B	K27	WRy 026	Bought 1933 from Washington-Virginia (their 51) air brakes removed. To National Capital Museum of Transport.
031-034	Brill	1898	2WH306	K27	CT 1-4	Earlier numbers 99, 298, 299, and 399. Scrapped: 031 – 1959; 032 – 1961; 033 and 034 – 1962.
035	Brill	1899	2WH306	K27	CT 5	Probable original 398. Scrapped 1961.
036	Brill	1901	2WH306	K27	CT 6	Probable original 297. Scrapped 1962.
037	Brill	1905	2WH306	K27	CT 7	Original 501. Scrapped 1961.
038-039	Brill	1909	2WH306	K27	CT 8-9	Scrapped 1962.
040-041	McGuire	1922	2WH306	K27	CT 10-11	Scrapped 1962.

Note: 02-026 each had 1 WH101B Broom Motor. No data on 01.
031-041 each had 1 WH306 Broom Motor. Traction and Broom motor data all as of 1955. Numerous variations prior years.
08-013, 040 and 041 fitted with side fold-up brooms for cleaning loading platforms 1955.
031-041 — ex Capital Traction 1-11, not renumbered until 1937.

Number	Builder	Date	Motors	Control	Trucks	Single or Double Truck	Remarks
047-049	Stephenson	1899	2GE57	K8	W 047-049		Originally Met RR, Numbers unknown. 048 lost in 1919 Eckington Barn fire. 047 and 049 scrapped 1949.

Locomotives

Number	Builder	Date	Motors	Control	Trucks	Single or Double Truck	Remarks
016 & 017	WB&A	1917	4WH557W8	W15-D-9	WB&A 16 & 17		Purchased 1935 from Washington, Baltimore & Annapolis. 017 to Hagerstown & Frederick 1 1944. 016 scrap 1949. Both originally built as pass. cars for Annapolis Short line by Southern 1908.
052	WRy&E Co. Shop	1914	4GE214A	Type M (?)	WRy 052		Double Truck Locomotive — 35 ton. Scrapped 1955.
053	Bald-West	1906	2WH114	Unit Switch	WRy 053		Single Truck Locomotive. Scrapped 1955.
054	Bald-West	1906	4WH70	WH-HL	CD&M 77		Acquired from Clinton Davenport & Muscatine (Iowa) 1940. Originally Hoboken Mfgs. RR (NJ) 3. Scrapped 1950.
055-056	Bald-West	1924	4W308D5	WH-HL	NH 5 & 6		Acquired from New Haven RR in 1948 and 1949 respectively. Scrapped 1955.

Note: All locomotives were used in coal delivery for Benning Power Plant of PEPCO. Operation sold to East Wash Rwy and dieselized 1955.

Miscellaneous Service Cars — Washington Railway and Electric Co

Number	Builder	Date	Motors	Control	Trucks	Single or Double Truck	Remarks
050	Smith & Wallace	1910	4GE57	K29	Brill 27 FE1	DT	Motor flat equipped with 2 electric cranes. Later had K40A control (c)1919 & 4 W306 motors (c)1942. To Cap Tran 050. Scrap 1960.
051	Co Shop	1902 (?)	—	—	Brill 21E	ST	Motor flat. Single end. Scrap prior to 1913.
054-065 069	Co Shop	?	—	—	Stephenson	ST	Trailer flat cars built from WRy 1800 Series trailers. 058 sold 1914 to Wash & G.F. Rwy & Pwr. 061, 065 and 069 scrap 1914; 060 and 063 scrap 1916; 059 scrap 1922; 062 scrap 1924; 064 scrap 1936; 054, 056 and 057 scrap 1937; 055 scrap date unknown.
11055	American	1896	—	—	Peck 7B	ST	Trailer flat built from WRy 1125 1913. To Cap. Tran 055. Scrap 1947.
11060	Laclede	1895	2GE1000	K10	Peck 7B	ST	Sand car ex E&SH 11, ex WRy 11. Scrap prior to 1913.
11063	Trimble	1892	—	—	Stephenson	ST	Trailer ex Met RR, Horse car. Service use unknown. Scrap prior to 1913.

MISC. SERVICE CARS-W RY & E CO (CONTINUED)

Number	Builder	Date	Motors	Control	Trucks	Single or Double Truck	Remarks
II065	Lewis & Fowler	?	—	—	?	ST	Trailer ex Met RR. Horse car service. Use unknown. Scrap prior to 1913.
III065	American	1896	—	—	Peck 7B	ST	Trailer flat built from WRy 1124 in 1917. To Cap Tran 065. Scrap 1947.
068	Trimble	1892	—	—	Stephenson	ST	Trailer Sand car. Ex Met RR storage battery car. Scrap prior to 1913.
070	Brill	1911	—	—	Peck 14B3	DT	Trailer Flat. Probably to Cap Tran 070. Scrap 1936.
071	?	?	—	—	?	ST	Trailer Flat. Scrap by Wash Int. Ry 1922. May have been WRy 1114.
077	Laclede	1895	2GE1000	K10	Peck 7B	ST	Line car. Ex E&SH Horse car. Scrap 1922.
075-076 078-086	Laclede	1895	2GE1000	K10	Peck 7B	ST	Sand cars. Ex E&SH Horse. Ex C&S motors. Converted to sand cars before 1911. 075, 076, 079, 080, 083 and 086 to Cap Tran (same numbers). Scrap 1941. 085 lost 13th & D Barn fire 1912. 081 to wreck car (1919) and scrap 1930; 084 scrap 1922; 078 destroyed 1923 and 082 scrap 1927.
II080	Ohio Crane	1906	—	—	?	ST	Electric Crane. Numbered 080 in 1941. Scrap by Cap Tran 1949. Was Potomac Electric Pwr owned before 1933.
087	Trimble	1892	?	?	Peckham	ST	Motor Baggage Car. Ex Met RR storage battery car. Ex Brightwood. Scrap prior to 1913.
II087	Brill	?	—	—	?	ST	Trailer Flat. May have been ex Geo & Tenn. If so, scrap 1916.
088	Stephenson	?	?	?	Brill 21E	ST	Work Motor. Ex Met RR 37, Ex Horse. Used to haul Mail car, then work service. Scrap prior to 1913.
089	Trimble	?	?	?	Brill 21E	ST	Motor Baggage car. Ex Met RR Horse. Scrap prior to 1913.
090,091, 093 & 094	Co. Shop	1914	2GE1000	K27	Brill 21E	ST	Line cars. 090 probably built 1913. Scrap 1930. 094 scrap 1932. 091 and 093 to Cap Tran 091 and 093. 091 scrap 1941 and 093 scrap 1946.
092	Trimble	1897	2GE1000	K27	Brill 21E	ST	Line Car. Ex Met RR Mail Car 3. Scrap 1920.
099	Brill	1910	4W306	K29	Brill 27 MCB1	DT	Freight Motor. Later had WH101B motors, K-40 control. To Line car 1921. To Cap Tran 099. Scrap 1960.

No number		Year					Remarks
					Brill 21A	ST	...scrap 1914.
0100	Co. Shop	1914	4GE1000	K31A	Peck 14B3	DT	Training Car. Scrap date unknown – probably prior to 1923 (see 1623).
0122, 0124, 0125 & 0127	American	1896	2GE1000	K10	Peckham	ST	Sand Cars. Ex Met RR 300's. To Sand Cars from WRy 122 & 124 (1917); 125 (1916) & 127 (1915). To Cap Tran – same numbers. Scrap 1941.
0123	American	1896	2GE1000	K10	Peck 7B	ST	Work Car. Ex Met RR 300 class. Ex WRy 0123. To Work Car 1923. To Cap Tran 0123. Scrap 1941.
0141 & 0145	American	1896	2GE1000	K10	Peckham	ST	Sand Cars. Ex Met RR 300's. Ex WRy 141 and 145. To Sand Cars in 1923. To Cap Tran 0141 and 0145. Scrap 1941.
0143	American	1896	2GE1000	K10	Peckham	ST	Wreck Car. Ex Met RR 300 class. Ex WRy 143. To Cap Tran 0143 & Scrap 1936.
0152 & 0153	American	1896	2GE1000	K10	Peckham	ST	Work Cars. Ex Met RR 300's. Ex WRy 152 and 153. To Work Cars in 1922 & 1923. To Cap Tran 0152 and 0153.
0203	Stephenson	1895	2GE1000	K9	Brill 21E	ST	Scrap: 0152 — 1938; 0153 — 1941. Work Car. Ex Col Rwy Cable Car. Ex WRy 203. To Work Car 1923. To Cap Tran 0203. Scrap 1938.
0500	American	1900	2W93	K8	Peck 14B	DT	Work Car. Ex A&P301, ex Wash Ry 500. To work car 1925. To Cap Tran 0500. Scrap 1949.
0509	American	1899	4GE1000	K40A	Peck 14B	DT	Work Car. Ex WRy 509. To Cap Tran 0509, in 1947. Converted to haul trucks between 4th St. shop and M St. shop by rebuilding rear end. Still exists as relic.
1003	?	?	—	—	Brill 21A	ST	Tank Car. Use unknown. Originally an advertising car. Scrap 1920.
1614	American	1899	2GE57	K8	Peck 14B3	DT	Open motor. Ex WRy 1614. Used by Cap Tran as Community Chest ad car. Scrap 1946.
1623	American	1899	4GE1000	K31A	Peck 14B3	DT	Ex WRy 1623 open motor. To instruction car 1921. To Cap Tran. Scrap 1941.
1639	American	1899	?	?	Peck 14B3	DT	Ex WRy 1639. Rebuilt 1918 as flat car with end cabs to carry safety campaign billboard. Scrap 1930.

Miscellaneous Service Cars — Capital Traction Company

Note: At the time of the 1933 merger, Capital Traction owned the below listed non-revenue cars in addition to sweepers noted earlier in this roster.

Number	Builder	Date	Motors	Control	Trucks	Remarks
(4 cars)	American	1898	2GE1000	K9	Lord Balt	300, 303, 315 and 522 all to Capital Transit. All single truck motors. 300 (Brill 1899), ex one-man car scrapped 1939. 303 still exists as relic. 315 (listed as office car — last use as waiting room before Rockville Line abandonment) scrapped 1948; 522 to Rail Grinder 0522 in 1937. Now at National Capital Museum of Transport. 300, 315 and 316 (316 sold to Kensington Ry by Capital Traction in 1933) last used on Maryland portion of Takoma Line, abandoned 1928.
(3 cars)	Stephenson	1892	---	---	Stephenson Perfection	Closed Trailers (single truck). One exists as relic. 1512 — trailer for 303 above. Now property of DC Transit. Other two (1569 and 1573) scrap 1939.
21-25	American	1898	2GE1000	K9	Lord Balt	Closed motors (single truck) Capital Traction sand cars. All to Capital Transit. Probably all from American 1898 motors. Were 584, 530, 582, 555 & 580 respectively. All retired 1941, scrapped 1948.
01	Co. Shops	1928	---	---	?	Single truck weed burner. Constructed 1928 from dump car 1003. To Capital Transit. Scrapped 1960.
31	?	?	2GE1000(?)	K9(?)	Peck 8B	Single Truck Line Car. Ex Rock Creek Rwy. To Capital Transit. Scrapped 1935.
812	Cincinnati	1907	2WH101B	K9	Lord Balt Max Trac	Double Truck "Advertising Car" ex Capital Traction open motor 812. Converted 1924. To Capital Transit. Scrapped 1935.
1000	W&G RR	?	---	---	Stephenson Perfection	Single truck trail. Ex W&G Horse. Equipped as vacuum cleaner car 1906 for cleaning plush seats. Was Capital Traction 1014. To Capital Transit. Scrapped 1939.
1001	Brill	1904	2GE1000	K9	Brill 22E	Instruction Car. Converted from 145 about 1912-14 to stationary instruction car. To Cap Tran. Scrap 1934.
1002	Jackson & Sharp	1892	4 West	WH Rheostat	Peck 100	Double truck freight motor ex Rock Creek. To Capital Transit. Scrapped 1935. West Rheostat control, to General Electric Museum, Schenectady, New York.
1003-1008	?	1904(c)	---	---	?	Single truck side dump cars. Used for reconstruction Connecticut Ave Line 1905-06. Disposition unknown
1009-1010	?	1904(c)	---	---	?	Single Truck Flat. Used for reconstruction on Connecticut Ave Line 1905-06. Scrap 1935.
1011-1012	?	?	---	---	?	Single Truck Snow Scrapers. Disposition unknown.
1013	Stephenson	1886 (?)	---	---	?	Single Truck Sand Dolly to Capital Transit. Scrapped 1949.

Note: The above listing — though not complete — gives all known data on Capital Traction non revenue cars. Except for several of 25-38 series Ex W&GRR horse cars (later cable trailers) not converted to electrical service and four ex Rock Creek closed trailers. At least 29, 34 and 35 used as off-track construction offices as late as 1908. One, number 33, converted to sand car — later renumbered 295. Disposition unknown. All built John Stephenson (date unknown) Stephenson Perfection trucks. Ex Rock Creek 1-6 closed Trail to Capital Traction 20, 23, 24, & 25. 20, 23 and 25 mounted on wagon wheels & 24 on rail wheels as of 1932. All scrap 1935.

Miscellaneous Service Cars — Capital Transit Company

0409	American	1898	2GE57	K8	Peck 14B	Double truck ex passenger. Ex WRy 409. Used as wire greaser by Capital Transit — scrapped 1938. Single truck rail grinder.
0522	American	1898	2WH101B	K9	Brill 21E	Converted from ex Cap Traction 522 in 1937. 21E truck from 095 donated in 1962 to National Capital Museum of Transport. Single truck rail grinder. Built Newark Shops, Public Service (NJ), their 6051. Sold to Capital Transit 1962.
0523	PSNJ	1931	2WH101B	K9	Brill 21E	Service (NJ), their 6051. Sold to Capital Transit 1938. Scrapped 1962.

Capital Transit inherited a variety of sweepers from W Ry & E Co and Capital Traction, all built by Brill or McGuire Cummings and all single truck. Right: W Ry & E Co 03 Brill at P Street yards in 1908. Photo by LeRoy O. King, Sr. Below right: Brill 02 at Benning, 1949. Below: Truck pedestal, Brill sweeper. Both photos by Edgar Gilchrist.

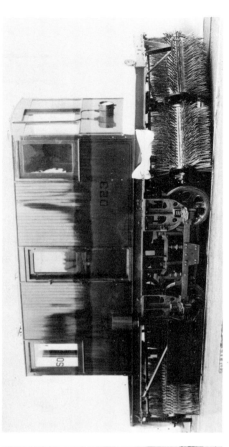

Left: McGuire sweeper 06 at 26th and Pennsylvania Avenue, February 16, 1958. Photo by Ara Mesrobian. Center: Brill sweeper 05 at Benning in 1948. Photo by Henry J. Leinbach. Right: Sweepers in Summer storage. Photo by Edgar Gilchrist.

Left: W Ry & E Co 019 at Brill plant. Right: W Ry & E Co geared sweeper 023 at Brill plant. Both photos Historical Society of Pennsylvania.

Left: 012 at Eckington. Barney Neuburger collection. Center: 024 at Eckington. Photo by Robert A. Truax. Right: McGuire sweeper (W Ry & E Co

In 1955, Capital Transit equipped sweepers 08-013, 040 and 041 with loading platform brooms as shown here in the photo of 041. Photo by Herman Cochenour.

Front Capital Transit 031, ex Capital Traction 1 (Brill). Photo by Robert S. Crockett.

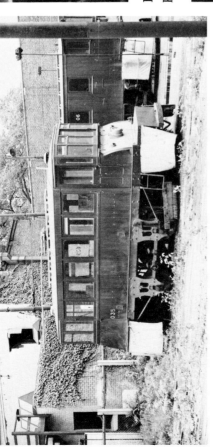

Top: Capital Transit 026, ex W Ry & E Co 026, ex Washington-Virginia 51 (Brill) at 7th Steet Wharves barn 1953. Center: Capital Transit 035, ex Capital Traction 5 (Brill) 1950. Bottom: Capital Transit 039, ex Capital Traction 9 (Brill) 1951. Three photos by Edgar Gilchrist.

Capital Transit 047 at Prospect Avenue plow pit in Georgetown on the Cabin John line. Both photos Capital Transit Company, author's collection.

017 (left) and 016 (right), ex W B & A, were acquired for hauling coal at the Benning Power Plant. Photos, 017, by Stephen P. Davidson, 016, author's collection.

Locomotives used at Benning Power Plant. Above left: Homemade 052. Above right: 053. Below left: 054 (ex Clinton, Davenport & Muscatine 77). Below right: 055 (ex New Haven 5) 056, not shown, was similar. Four photos, Capital Transit Company, author's collection.

Left: 052 removing empties from PEPCO's Benning plant in 1946. Photo by W. W. Buckingham. Above: 054 and PCC 1242 share Kenilworth Avenue trackage in 1946. Photo by Richard Kotulak.

Above: Two pictures 050 at Benning yard. Left, author's collection. Right, Barney Neuburger collection. Below left: W Ry & E Co 051 in 1908. Photo by LeRoy O. King, Sr. Center: 055 in 1939. Photo by S. P. Davidson. Right: W Ry & E Co 11 (later 060) in 1908. Photo by LeRoy O. King, Sr.

Left: 063, ex Trimble horse, at P Street, 1908. Center: Trailer sand car, an ex Met RR horse car, but no other data at P Street shops 1908. Two photos by LeRoy O. King, Sr. Right: Sand car 086 at Falls barn, 1941. Photo by Stephen D. Maguire.

Left: 087 (Trimble) at Glen Echo about 1905. Center: 088 at Eckington, 1908. Right: 089 about 1905. Three photos by LeRoy O. King, Sr.

Left: 099 about 1940. Author's collection. Center: 092, line car, ex Mail Car number 3 at Wisconsin and M Street in 1907. Photo by LeRoy O. King, Sr. Right: 093, line car in 1939. Photo by Robert S. Crockett.

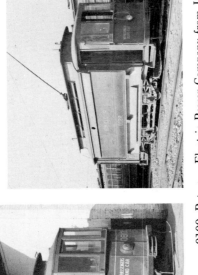

Left: W Ry & E Co Instruction car 0100. Potomac Electric Power Company from Joseph J. Jessel. Center: Capital Transit 080. Photo by Edgar Gilchrist. Right: Capital Transit 0122. Photo by Ed Schell.

Left: Capital Transit 0152. Barney Neuburger collection. Center: Capital Transit 0145. Photo by Robert Crockett. Right: Capital Transit 0203 and 0152. Photo by Edgar Gilchrist.

0509 was rebuilt in 1947, as shown, to haul trucks from the M Street shops in Georgetown to the 4th and P Street shops near Ft. McNair. Left: At 15th and Pennsylvania Avenue, 1948. Photo by W. W. Buckingham. Center: Ready to load truck at M Street. Capital Transit Company, author's collection.

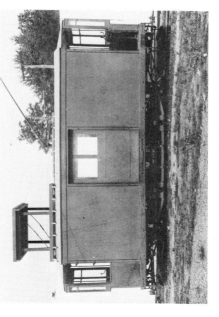

Left: Advertising car 1614. Photo by Gerald Cunningham. Center: Ex Capital Traction sand car 24. Photo by Stephen D. Maguire. Right: Weed burner 01. Capital Transit Company, author's collection.

Left: Capital Traction 1000, vacuum cleaner car. Photo by LeRoy O. King, Sr. Center and right; Capital Traction freight motor 1002. When scrapped in 1935, the controls went to the General Electric Museum, Schenectady, New York. Two photos Capital Transit Company, author's collection.

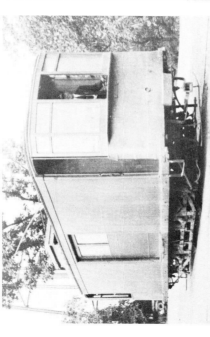
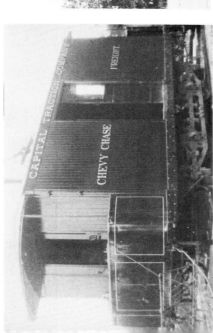

Left: Capital Traction 31 as line car. Photo by LeRoy O. King, Sr. Center: 31 as line car. Photo by Robert A Truax. Right: 31 as line car. Author's collection.

Left and center: Capital Traction side dump cars of 1003-8 series. Right: Flat car 1009-10 series. Three photos Capital Transit Company, author's collection.

Capital Transit maintained two rail grinder cars. Left: 0522 converted in 1937 from ex Capital Traction 522. Now at National Capital Trolley Museum. Photo by George Votava. Right: 0523 was acquired from Public Service of New Jersey (their 6051) in 1938. Photo by Robert S. Crockett.

Albert B. Herrick, Consulting Engineer from Ridgewood, New Jersey designed a system, mounted on a car owned by his firm, for detecting poor rail bonds. The car was probably ex North Hudson County Railway. Incidentally, an identical car (may be the same one) later became Bond Test car 6020 of the Public Service (N.J.) Railway. The picture, from an old Brownie negative, shows Herrick's "Autographic Test Car" in Washington in August, 1906. Photo by LeRoy O. King, Sr.

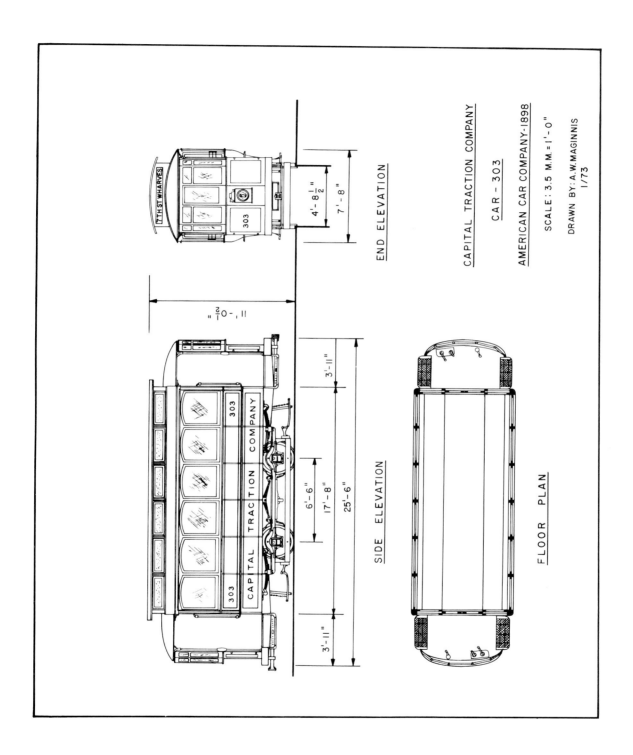

7TH ST WHARVES

303

$4'-8\frac{1}{2}''$

$7'-8''$

END ELEVATION

CAPITAL TRACTION COMPANY

CAR – 303

AMERICAN CAR COMPANY-1898

SCALE: 3.5 M.M.=1'-0"

DRAWN BY: A.W.MAGINNIS
1/73

$11'-0\frac{1}{2}''$

303

CAPITAL TRACTION COMPANY

303

$3'-11''$

$6'-6''$

$17'-8''$

$25'-6''$

$3'-11''$

SIDE ELEVATION

FLOOR PLAN

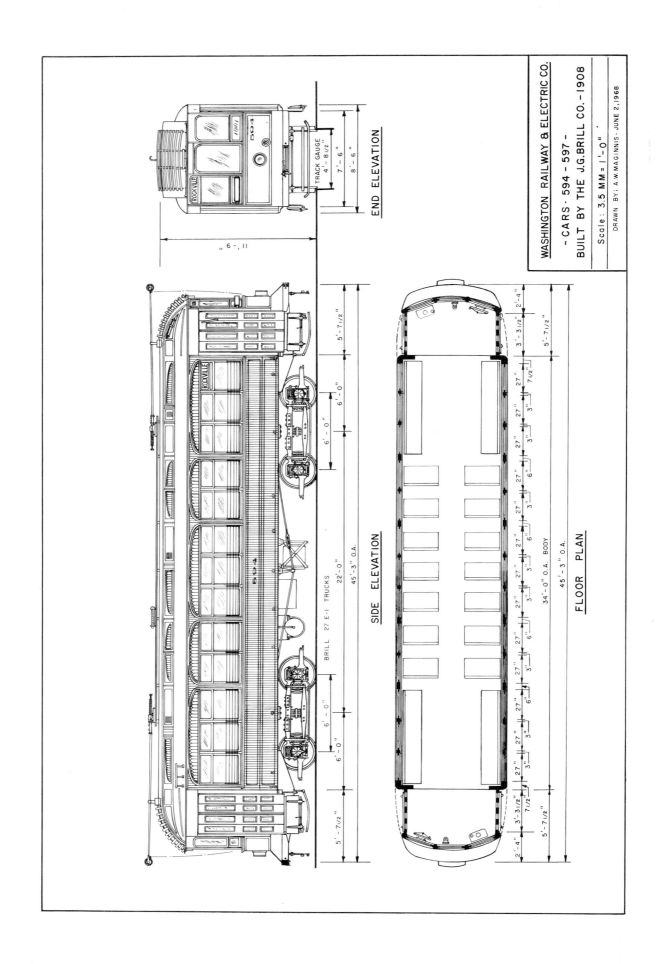

END ELEVATION

SIDE ELEVATION

FLOOR PLAN

WASHINGTON RAILWAY & ELECTRIC CO.

- CARS - 594 - 597 -

BUILT BY THE J.G. BRILL CO. - 1908

Scale : 3.5 MM = 1'-0"

DRAWN BY : A.W. MAGINNIS - JUNE 2, 1968

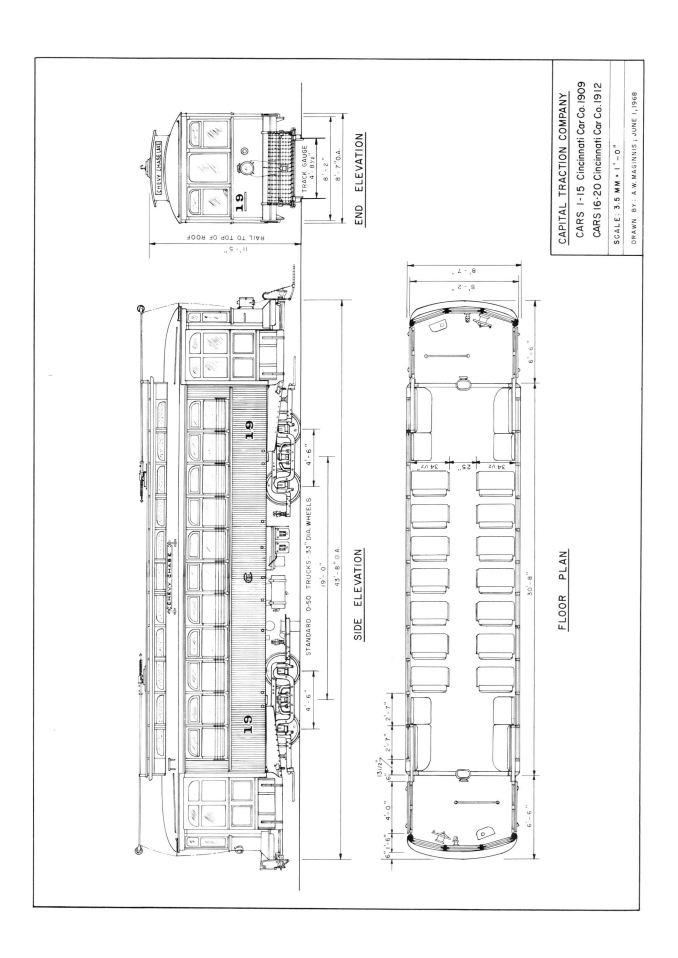

END ELEVATION

SIDE ELEVATION

FLOOR PLAN

RAIL TO TOP OF ROOF
11'-5"

TRACK GAUGE
4'-8½"
8'-2"
8'-7" O.A.

CHEVY CHASE LAKE
19

STANDARD 0-50 TRUCKS-33"DIA.WHEELS
4'-6"
19'-0"
4'-6"
43'-8" O.A.

CHEVY CHASE
19
19

8'-7"
8'-2"
6'-6"
34½
25"
34½
30'-8"
2'-7"
2'-7"
13½"
6"
4'-0"
6' 1'-6"
6"
6'-6"

CAPITAL TRACTION COMPANY
CARS 1-15 Cincinnati Car Co. 1909
CARS 16-20 Cincinnati Car Co. 1912
SCALE: 3.5 MM = 1'-0"
DRAWN BY: A.W. MAGINNIS; JUNE 1, 1968

277

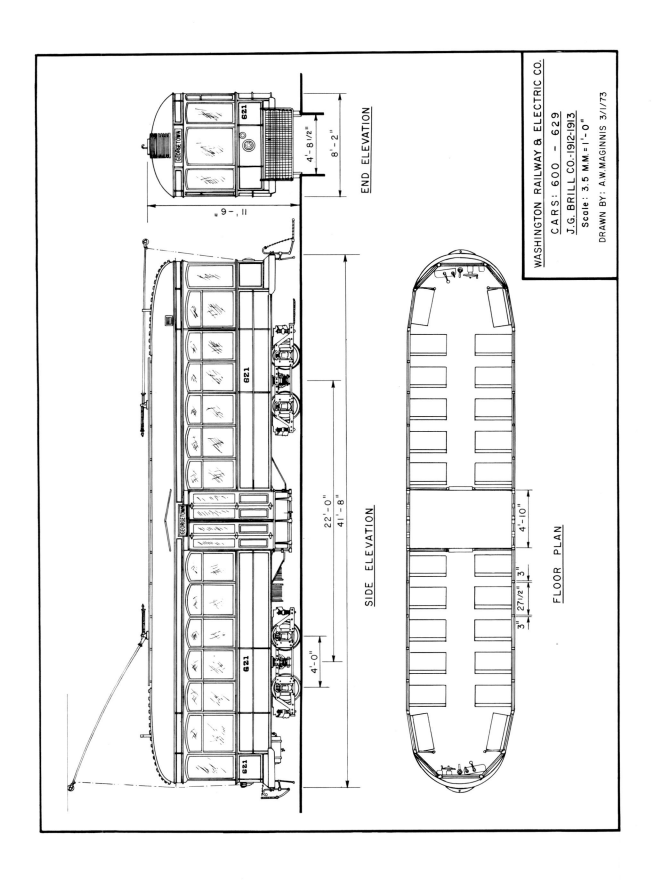

END ELEVATION

4'-8 1/2"

8'-2"

11'-6"

SIDE ELEVATION

22'-0"

41'-8"

4'-0"

FLOOR PLAN

4'-10"

3" 2'7 1/2" 3"

WASHINGTON RAILWAY & ELECTRIC CO.

CARS: 600 - 629

J.G. BRILL CO.-1912-1913

Scale: 3.5 M.M.=1'-0"

DRAWN BY: A.W. MAGINNIS 3/1/73

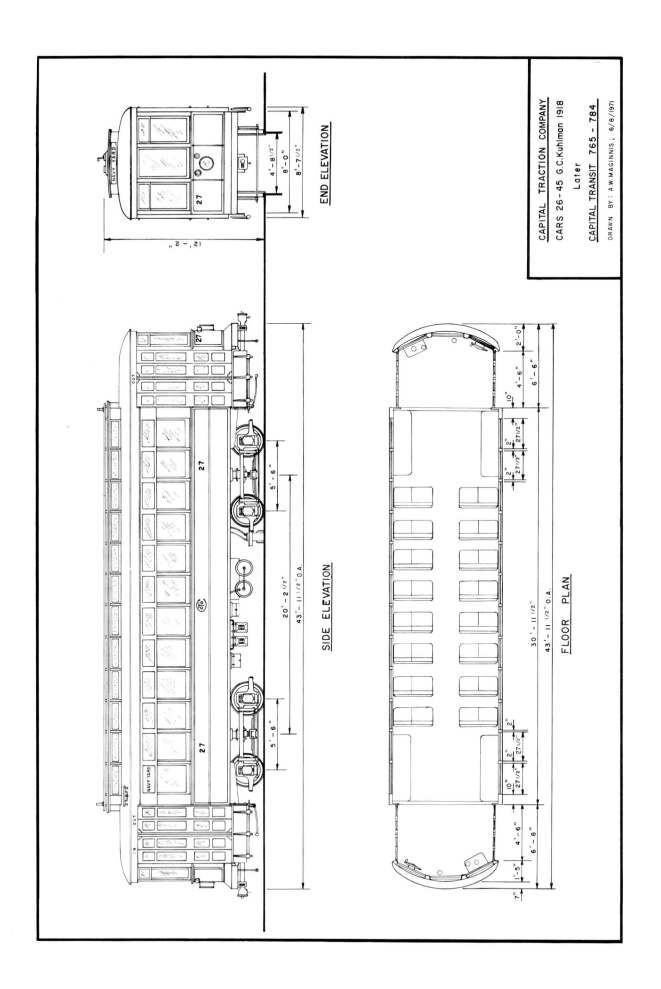

END ELEVATION

12'-2"

4'-8 1/2"
8'-0"
8'-7 1/2"

NAVY YARD

27

CAPITAL TRACTION COMPANY

CARS 26-45 G.C.Kuhlman 1918

Later

CAPITAL TRANSIT 765 - 784

DRAWN BY : A.W.MAGINNIS ; 6/8/1971

OUT
OUT
IN
27
27
NAVY YARD

5'-6"
5'-6"
20'-2 1/2"
43'-11 1/2" O.A.

SIDE ELEVATION

2'-0"
6'-6"
4'-6"
10"
2"
27 1/2"
2"
27 1/2"
30'-11 1/2"
43'-11 1/2" O.A.
2"
2"
27 1/2"
10"
27 1/2"
4'-6"
6'-6"
1'-5"
7"

FLOOR PLAN

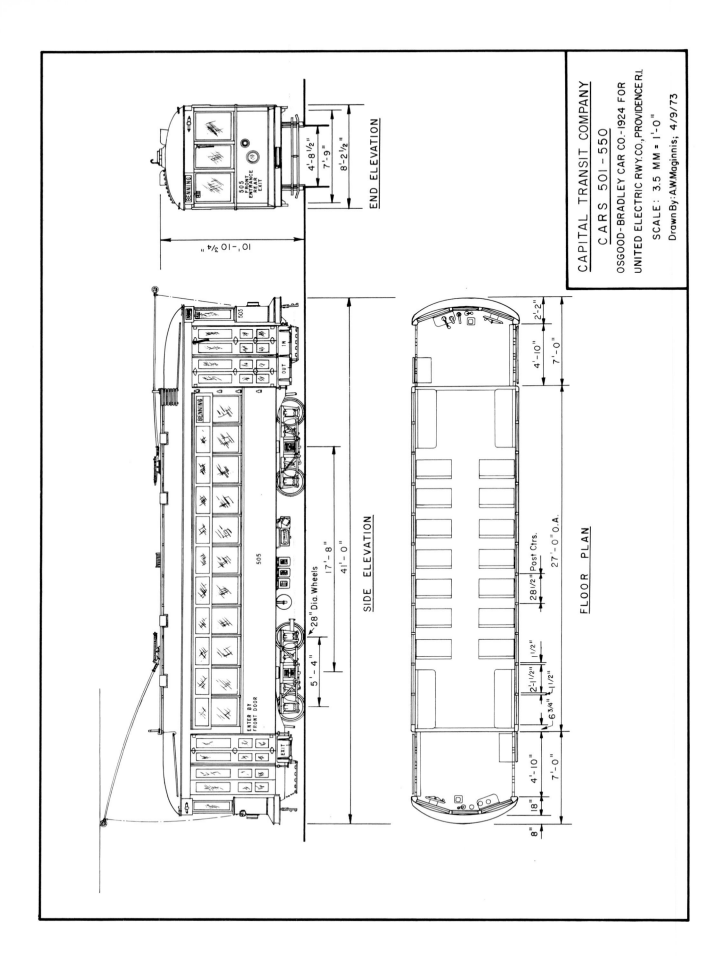

END ELEVATION

505
FRONT
ENTRANCE
REAR
EXIT

BENNING

4'-8½"
7'-9"
8'-2½"

10'-10¾"

CAPITAL TRANSIT COMPANY
CARS 501-550
OSGOOD-BRADLEY CAR CO.-1924 FOR
UNITED ELECTRIC RWY.CO., PROVIDENCE R.I.

SCALE: 3.5 MM = 1'-0"

Drawn By: A.W.Maginnis; 4/9/73

BENNING

505

IN
OUT

505

ENTER BY
FRONT DOOR

EXIT

SIDE ELEVATION

5'-4"
17'-8"
41'-0"
28" Dia. Wheels

FLOOR PLAN

2'-2"
4'-10"
7'-0"
28½" Post Ctrs.
27'-0" O.A.
1½"
2-½"
1½"
6¾"
4'-10"
7'-0"
18"
8"

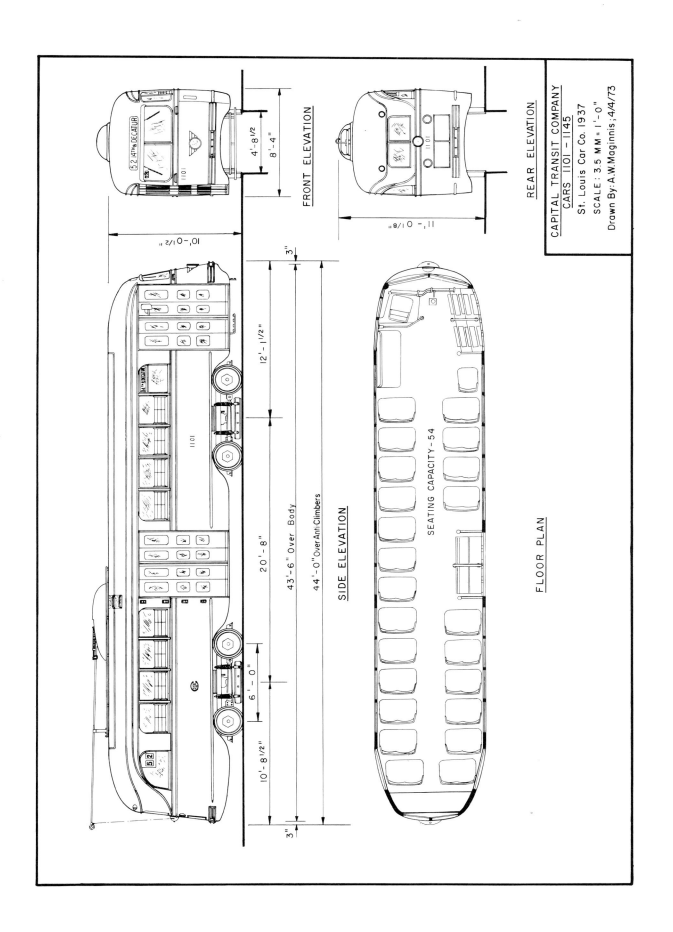

FRONT ELEVATION

REAR ELEVATION

CAPITAL TRANSIT COMPANY
CARS 1101 – 1145
St. Louis Car Co. 1937
SCALE: 3.5 MM = 1'-0"
Drawn By: A.W. Maginnis; 4/4/73

SIDE ELEVATION

FLOOR PLAN

SEATING CAPACITY – 54

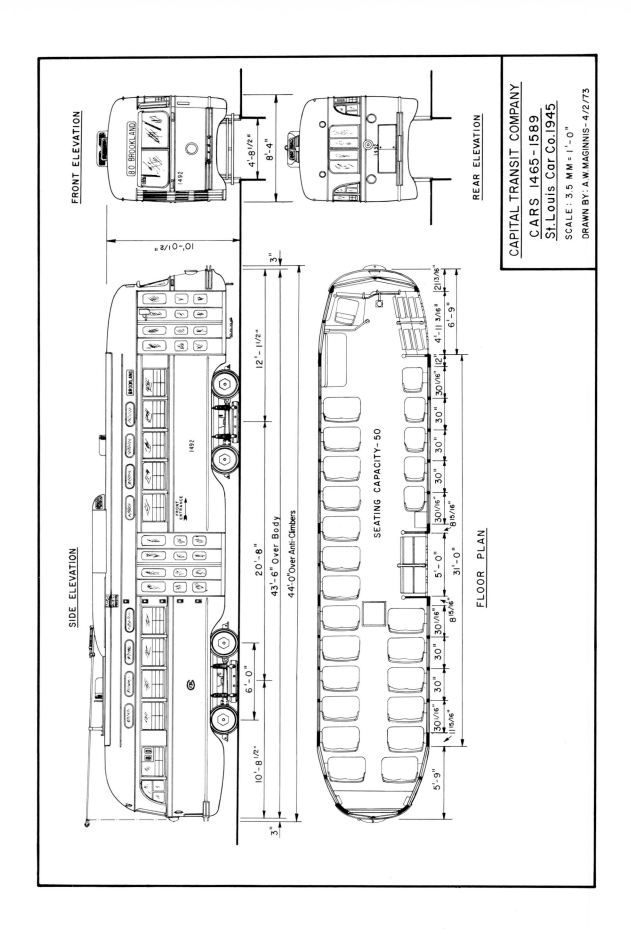

FRONT ELEVATION

REAR ELEVATION

SIDE ELEVATION

FLOOR PLAN

CAPITAL TRANSIT COMPANY
CARS 1465-1589
St. Louis Car Co. 1945
SCALE : 3.5 M M = I'-O"
DRAWN BY : A.W. MAGINNIS - 4/2/73

10'-10 1/2"

4'-8 1/2"
8'-4"

12'-11 1/2"

20'-8"
43'-6" Over Body
44'-0" Over Anti-Climbers

6'-0"

10'-8 1/2"

3"

3"

1492

80 BROOKLAND

BROOKLAND

FRONT ENTRANCE

1492

SEATING CAPACITY - 50

2 13/16"
4'-11 3/16"
6'-9"

30/16"
12"

30"

30"

30"

30/16"
8 15/16"

5'-0"
31'-0"

8 15/16"
30/16"

30"

30"

30/16"
11 15/16"

5'-9"

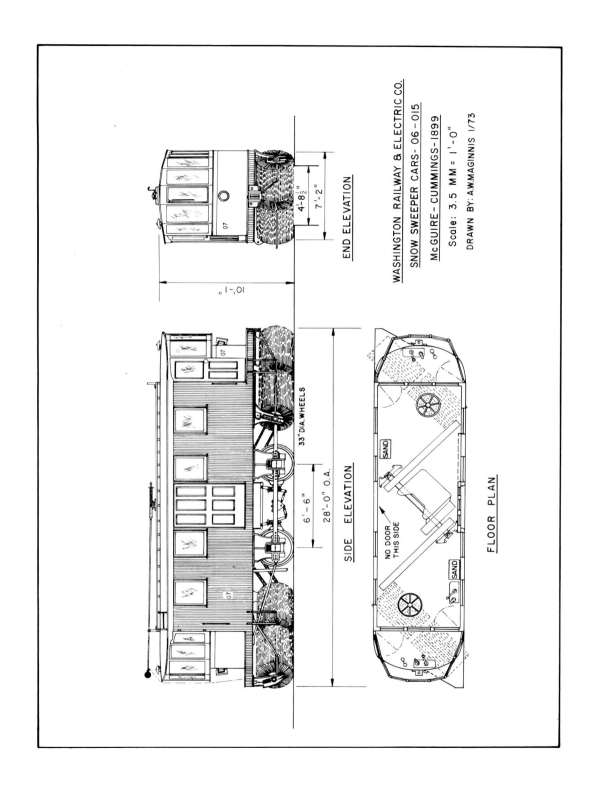

END ELEVATION

WASHINGTON RAILWAY & ELECTRIC CO.

SNOW SWEEPER CARS- 06 - 015

McGUIRE - CUMMINGS - 1899

Scale: 3.5 MM = 1'-0"

DRAWN BY: A.W.MAGINNIS 1/73

4'-8½"

7'-2"

10'-1"

33" DIA. WHEELS

6'-6"

28'-0" O.A.

SIDE ELEVATION

NO DOOR THIS SIDE

SAND

SAND

FLOOR PLAN

GENERAL ROSTER NOTES

Whistles

Of the numerous suburban lines of the Capital Traction and Washington Railway only two were required to have cars equipped with whistles. They were the Rockville and Maryland lines of the Washington Railway and Electric. Curiously, the Capital Traction's Chevy Chase Lake line, although it used arc headlamps for a time, didn't use whistles. Nor did the Cabin John and Forest Glen lines of the Washington Railway. The Cabin John line's lack of whistles can be explained by the fact that it only had two major crossings and at both of these the cars were required to stop and the crossings were required to be illuminated by the company. No explanation can be offered for the other lines, however. Capital Transit continued use of whistles on the Maryland line until the advent of PCC's in 1946. With the hope of avoiding the requirement, the company simply didn't equip the new cars with whistles. Washington Railway (Capital Transit) whistles were unusually high pitched as compared to standard trolley whistles.

Marker Lights

Rear oil marker lights on overhead trolley lines came into being in the early days of electric operation. Standard placement of markers, however, didn't come until July 9, 1913, when PUC order #21 was issued. The order required that from twenty minutes after sundown until twenty minutes before sunrise all cars operating on overhead lines (and storage battery cars) must have a headlight and a rear red oil lamp. The oil lamp was to be mounted near the roof and visible for one thousand feet.

Later, at a date unknown, all cars on overhead lines carried two red oil lamps. One, a marker, was attached to a bracket on the right rear corner post about six inches above the belt rail. The other lamp, a smaller hand lantern, was for use by the crew in emergencies. It was carried on a bracket near the center of the right rear window at the belt rail. Washington Railway and Electric required the marker lamp on city cars as well, but Capital Traction used no oil lamps on city lines.

The one thousand class streamline cars had battery-operated markers and therefore carried only the hand lantern. When the PCC's arrived, also equipped with battery operated markers, all oil lamp requirements were dropped for both the PCC's and one thousand class.

Fenders

Street cars were required to have fenders under an act dated August 7, 1894. Original fenders were homemade; essentially of rope over an iron frame. Later the Parmenter fender became the standard. Use of fenders continued until 1921. At that time, the PUC allowed replacement with standard lifeguards.

One-Man Cars

The Capital Transit roster shows a number of instances of cars being converted to one man, then back to two man and in some cases, back again to one man. This activity arose from a 1923 DC Public Utilities Commission decision limiting the Washington Railway and Electric Company to 70 one man cars (Capital Traction was not involved since they had only one one-man car).

From 1923 until September 23, 1936, the seventy car rule stood. At that time, the PUC allowed conversion of the twenty streamliners to one man but denied the Transit company's application to allow additional convention one man cars—the newly rebuilt Providence cars. The 1936 PUC decision paved the way for one man PCC's, however, by authorizing one man operation of cars equivalent to or better than the 1000 class streamliners.

Because of wartime manpower shortages, the PUC authorized conversion of fifty-two conventional cars to one man in 1943 and sixty-nine in 1944. Authorization was for five years after the end of the war. None were ever reconverted, however. The Benning line abandonment in May, 1949, ended the need for conventional cars. The last two man car was scrapped in 1948.

Color Schemes Washington Railway & Electric Company, Capital Traction Company and Later

Capital Traction Company after 1908:—The standard color was a dark apple green. Company monogram, numbers and striping was silver. A pin stripe of pale green was placed around the inner margin of the basic striping.

There were two exceptions. Chevy Chase Line cars 1-25 and 800 series open cars assigned to Chevy Chase were painted a much darker green, similar to Pullman green, with silver monogram letter and striping. Cars 26-85, after rebuilding, beginning in 1928, were repainted light gray with a green upper body panel—with colors extending over the doors.

Washington Railway and Electric Company 1902-1933; Washington Traction & Electric Company 1899-1902:—

1899-1912	Cream with Cadmium orange upper body panel and dash. Black lettering
1912-1928	Dark olive with silver lettering. Varnished

doors and window sash. The dark olive was almost identical to U.S. Army olive drab. 600 class center door cars were the first cars painted in this scheme and they originally had vivid green roofs, later replaced by tan.

1928-1933   Cream with broad tuscan red stripe at level of upper body panel. The tuscan red stripe was separated from the cream by a one-inch black stripe. Doors and window sash varnished. Gold lettering. On all center entrance cars (possibly others) the tuscan and upper body panel was striped in gold while the cream lower body panel was striped in maroon. A tuscan red stripe on the letterboard was added about 1930.

Exceptions:

1909-1916   PAYE cars (1-100). Tuscan red letterboard, upper body panel, dash and platform knees. Remainder cream. Lettering silver.

1912-1924   (Date approximate). In this period 1600's were all standard dark olive with silver lettering. About 1924 they were repainted cadmium orange and cream with black lettering except as noted below.

1920-1924   Original one-man cars were olive but had orange rectangle on Dash and on upper side panel under rear window lettered "Enter Front Door."

1928-1932   1640-1644 (five cars used on Columbia Line) painted maroon and cream. Repainted orange and cream 1932.

1926-1933   Cars 160-186 originally painted cream with a royal blue stripe at the level of the upper body panel. Doors and window sash varnished. This became the standard one man car color. About 1932 a blue stripe was added to the letterboard.

1928   Several cars (among them 593, 595, 598, 642 and 714) were painted cream and red with gold lettering. This was experimental and was in the same pattern as the later adopted 1928 standard tuscan red and cream noted above.

Capital Transit Company 1933-1956:—At first, Capital Transit modified Washington Railway tuscan red and cream by painting the previously varnished areas. Thus the letterboard and upper body panel were tuscan red and this was continued over the doors and ends of the car. The window area and lower panels were cream. Platform knees and steps tuscan red. Similarly, one man cars were repainted continuing the paint over the doors and on the window sash. Royal blue was used on one man cars instead of tuscan red. At the same time, a number of two man cars were repainted in the same pattern but with green in place of tuscan red.

Finally, the standard for two man cars became green on the letterboard and below the windows with cream in the window area.

The 1000 class introduced a new paint scheme which became standard for one man cars: electric blue (turquoise) below the window, gray above separated by a one-inch maroon stripe. At the front, beginning at the headlight, there was a tan "V" which continued to and included the roof. Conventional one man cars later lost the "V."

In November, 1945, Capital Transit painted two cars (1482 and 1502) experimentally for their "Cavalcade of Progress." 1487 was carmine below the windows, light blue above and had a tan roof. 1502 was biege with maroon stripes at the floor, belt and roof levels. After a short time, both cars were repainted in standard colors.

DC Transit 1956-1962:—DC Transit's color scheme was a modernistic design featuring electric blue predominantly at the lower front and extending around the bottom at the rear. The roof was white and the balance of the car light gray except for a tangerine orange stripe. This stripe separated the blue and gray roughly at the belt rail at front to the back of the rear door. There it curved to join another orange stripe running lengthwise for most of the car side in the middle of the body panel. Refer to a photo for an example of pattern.

List of the Car Builders Supplying Washington (This list compiled as an aid to abbreviations used in the rosters)

American Car Company, St. Louis, Mo
J. G. Brill Company, Philadelphia, Pa
Cincinnati Car Company, Cincinnati, O
Federal Storage Battery Car Co., Silver Lake, NJ
Gilbert Car Mfg Co., Troy, NY
Jackson & Sharp, Wilmington, Del
Jewett Car Company, Newark, O
J. M. Jones Sons Company, Watervliet, NY
G. C. Kuhlman Car Co., Cleveland, O
Laclede Car Co., St. Louis, Mo
Laconia Car Company, Laconia, NH
Lamokin Car Works, Chester, Pa
Lewis & Fowler Mfg Co., Brooklyn, NY
Newburyport Car Mfg Co., Newburyport, Mass
Osgood Bradley, Worcester, Mass
Pullman Palace Car Co., Chicago, Ill
St. Louis Car Co., St. Louis, Mo
Southern Car Co., High Point, NC
John Stephenson Co., New York, NY
James A. Trimble Co., New York, NY

In addition to Brill, Osgood Bradley, St. Louis and Stephenson (which are listed above), trucks were supplied by:

Baldwin Locomotive Works, Philadelphia, Pa
Baltimore Car Wheel Co., Baltimore, Md (Lord Baltimore)
Clark Equipment Company, Battle Creek, Mich
Franklin Machine Co., Providence, RI (Manier Trucks)
Peckham Motor Truck & Wheel Co., Kingston NY
Robinson Radial Car Truck Company, Boston, Mass
Standard Motor Truck Company, New Castle, Pa

APPENDIX 2
CAR BARNS AND SHOPS IN THE DISTRICT OF COLUMBIA AND SUBURBAN MARYLAND

(Dates Shown are Those Properly Used for Railway Purposes)

Capital Transit Company

Georgetown Barn (1897-1951) 36th and M Streets N.W.
Built of brick by the Washington and Georgetown as a Union Station. As of 1970 serves as DCT office building. Underground conduit.

Falls Barn (1896-1947) Between 37th and Prospect Streets N. W. and Foxhall Road on Cabin John Line
Frame structure, six tracks. Built by Wash & Great Falls Elec Ry. Overhead trolley.

M Street Shops (1862-1962) 3222 M Street N.W.
Brick Structures built at various dates unknown except building at Warehouse Street & M Street built 1906. Site originally Vanderwerken's stable. Leased by Wash & Geo RR in 1862. Building across canal was originally Grace Street Power Plant for Capital Traction in 1897. Before 1897 a surface track ran in warehouse alley and across the canal into this building. All Capital Traction paint and mechanical work at this location. Capital Transit used for mechanical only. Underground conduit.

P Street Shops (1874-1934) 2411 P Street N.W.
Location originally Metropolitan RR Horsecar barn. Became mechanical shops for Wash Ry & E Co. Underground conduit.

Tenallytown Barn (1909-1958) Wisconsin Ave and Harrison Street N.W.
Built of concrete by W Ry & E Co. Six interior tracks. Originally north side had two tracks branching into three behind barn. In the 30's north side tracks changed to five as long as the barn tracks. In later days, south side had two short tracks each with a capacity of three PCC's. Overhead trolley.

Chevy Chase Lake Barn (1892-1935) Chevy Chase Lake
Frame structure built by Rock Creek Ry. Originally had five tracks. After 1895 an addition was built on north side with two tracks. Later (probably after 1909) a similar addition was built on the south side with three tracks. Overhead trolley

14th & Decatur Barn (1907-1959) 14th & Decatur Streets, N.W.
Brick structure built by Capital Traction Co. Originally both floors used as carbarn. In 1926 basement leased to Washington Rapid Transit for use as bus garage. Main floor to bus garage 1959. Underground conduit.

Brightwood Barn (1895-1950) Georgia Ave between Peabody & Concord Streets
Brick structure built by Brightwood Ry. 8 tracks. Overhead trolley.

Eckington Barn (1888-1958) Between Fourth & Fifth Streets on T Street N.E.
Original (1888) structure by E & SH Ry. destroyed by fire 12/3/98 and replaced by brick and metal structure built by C & S Ry. in 1899. Subsequently, a concrete addition of 4 tracks was constructed on the west side of the 1899 structure. Overhead trolley.

Columbia Barn (1895-1941) 15th & Benning Road N.E.
Brick structure built by Columbia Ry. Converted to bus garage 1942. Underground conduit.

Benning Barn (1941-1949) Benning Road & Kenilworth Avenue N.E.
Brick structure built by Capital Transit. Capacity 110 cars. Overhead trolley.

East Barn (1896-1962) 14th and East Capitol Streets N.E.
Brick structure built by Metropolitan RR. Originally housed offices of Met RR and W Ry & E Co. Offices moved 1912 to 231 14th Street N.W. Underground conduit.

Navy Yard Barn (1892(?)-1962) Eighth & M Streets S.E.
Brick structure built by Washington & Georgetown RR. Building on Eighth Street probably built 1892. Addition on West Side of property and old building modernized in 1909. This was two story barn with ramp to second floor. Underground conduit.

Seventh Street Barn (1890-1961) Seventh & Water Streets S.W.
Location dates from 1880 when a car shed and stables were erected. Brick structure dates from 1890 when erected by Washington & Georgetown for cable barn and power house. Later served as barn only. Underground conduit.

4 1/2 Street Shops (1895-1962) 4 1/2 & P Streets S.W.
Brick structure built by Metropolitan RR. Car barn until 1930 when part was given over to paint shop moved from 11th & Florida N.W. Capital Transit body and paint shop 1934-1962. Underground conduit.

Washington Railway and Electric Company and Predecessor Companies

Properties not Used as Rail Facilities by Capital Transit Company

11th Street Barn (1893-1930) 11th & Florida Avenue N.W.

Location originally a Belt Railway horsecar barn. Date of brick structure unknown. In later years (1920's) used as paint shop and bus garage. Sold to Pepco in 1930 for $375,000. Underground conduit. Yard worked by overhead trolley

13th & D Barn (1895-1912) 13th & D Streets N.E.
Brick structure built by backers of the Columbia & Maryland Rwy as horse car barn. Later as electric car barn. Destroyed by fire 2-11-12 and not rebuilt. Underground conduit.

Georgetown & Tenallytown Barn (1890-1909) Wisconsin Avenue at Calvert Street (East Side of Wisc Ave)
Frame structure replaced by Wisconsin & Harrison Barn. Destroyed by fire prior to 1914. Overhead trolley.

Anacostia Barn (1876c-1900) South Side of W Street between Nichols & Railroad Ave S.E.
Frame Horse Car Barn. Abandoned at electrification. Destroyed by fire 11-7-09.

Belt Line Barn (1877-1893?) Canal, B & Third Streets S.W.
Frame Horse Car Barn built by Capitol, North O Street & South Washington. Presumed to have been replaced by 11st Street Barn (see above).

Belt Line Stable (1881-1893?) SE Corner of 12th & V Streets N.W.
Frame structure built by C No O St & SW. Presumed to have been replaced by 11th Street Barn (see above). Horse stable only.

Congress Heights Barn (1896-1900) East Side Nichols Ave. just beyond St. Elizabeth's Hosp.
Grounds. Frame structure built by Capital Railway. Probable capacity-three cars.

Metropolitan Barn (1865-1874) 17th & New York Avenue N.W.
Built by Metropolitan as original horse car barn. Replaced by barn at 2411 P Street N.W.

Metropolitan Barn (1875-1895?) West Side of Seventh Street N.W. South of Pomeroy
Frame structure built by Metropolitan. Site later used for a loop in electric era.

Columbia Barn (1871c-1895) 15th Street, just north of Gales St N.E.
Brick horse car barn built by Columbia Ry. Replaced by 1895 Columbia Barn (see above)

Lakeland Barn (1896-1898) Between College Park & Berwyn Md on Maryland Line
Never completed. Merger with E & SH made it unnecessary.

Glen Echo Barn (1891-1901) Walhonding Road near MacArthur Blvd
Stone electric car barn built by Glen Echo RR. Overhead trolley.

First Bladensburg Barn (1910c-1913) At town limits on Bladensburg Road (806 Bladensburg Rd)
Frame structure built by Washington Spa Spring & Gretta RR Co. Overhead trolley.

Second Bladensburg barn (1912-1925) Bladensburg Road opposite Mt. Olivet Cemetery gate
Frame structure built by Washington Interurban Ry. Overhead trolley.

Capital Traction Company—Washington & Georgetown RR.
Properties not Used as Rail Facilities by Capital Transit Company

Mt. Pleasant Barn (1892-1907) West side of 14th St just south of Park Road.
Brick structure built by Wash & Geo RR. Replaced by 14th & Decatur Barn and sold in 1909 for $75,000. Underground conduit. During horsecar operation following cable power house fire 9-29-97. Capital Traction had a large, one-story horse stable on the SE corner of 14th & Park Road.

New Jersey Ave Barn (1862-1874c) B. C. First & New Jersey Avenue N.W. (near present Taft Memorial)
First car barn in Washington. Built by Wash & Geo RR Co. Replaced by barn at First & B Streets S.W. (see below)

First & B Street barn (1874c-1892) First & B Streets S.W.
place NJ Avenue Barn (see above). Capital Traction and Capital Transit used as bus garage 1926-1936. Building demolished 1956.

Seventh & T Street Barn (—1892) Seventh & T Streets N.W.
Horsecar Barn built by Wash & Geo RR. Date unknown. Probably dated from Seventh Street line construction and must have lasted until cable operation in 1890.

14th & Boundary Barn (1862?-1892) South Side of Florida Ave (Boundary) East of 14th Street
Brick horse car barn and stable. Replaced by Mt. Pleasant barn.

First Baltimore & Wash Transit Co. barn (1898c-1907c) Elm & Heather Streets, Takoma Park, Md.
Capacity of two single truck cars. No data on actual date discontinued but before 1907. Overhead trolley.

Second Baltimore & Washington Transit barn (1910c-1913) at Junction of Third, Aspen & Blair Road N.W.
Frame structure. Housed gasoline and storage battery cars. Destroyed by fire 9-16-13.

East Washington Heights Traction RR Co. of the District of Columbia

Barn (1905-1923) Pennsylvania and Minnesota Avenue S.E. (south side Penna Ave and East Corner Minn Ave)
Frame structure. Overhead Trolley. Capacity - two cars.

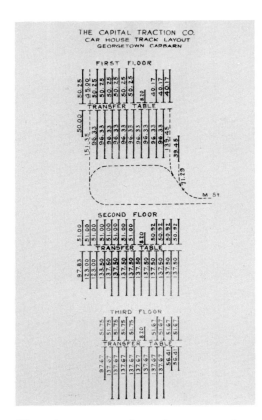

All car barn maps, unless otherwise noted, are from the 1925 McClellan & Junkersfeld Transportation Survey. Top: 36th and M Street barn in the 40's. Author's collection. Above: Prospect Street entrance, 36th and M Street. Photo by LeRoy O. King, Sr. See also pages 64, 85 & 134.

Below: W Ry & E Co's Falls Barn in 1914. Columbia Historical Society. Bottom: Falls Barn, looking west toward Cabin John in the 40's. Author's collection. See also page 49.

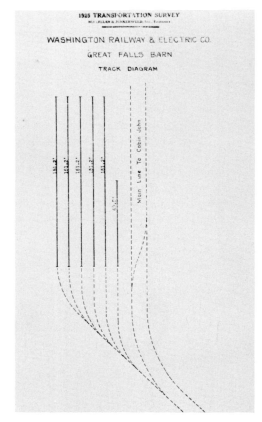

Top: Front view, M Street shops in 1914. Above: Paint shop, M Street, 1914. Two photos Columbia Historical Society.

Top: Rear, from Wisconsin Avenue, of M Street shop. Grace Street Power Plant to the left. Above: Rear Grace Street Power Plant. Both photos Capital Transit Company, author's collection.

Interior, M Street shops. About 1948. Capital Transit Photo, author's collection.

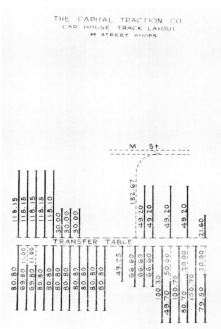

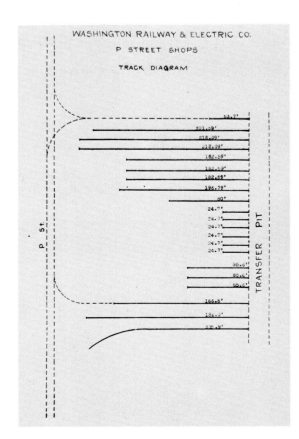

Shops at 2411 P Street N.W. were the main shops of W Ry & E Co but were abandoned soon after the 1933 merger. Top: Front of shops on P Street. Above: Rear, showing transfer table. Author's collection.

Below: Tenleytown Barn, W Ry & E Co, in 1914. Columbia Historical Society. Bottom: Tenleytown Barn in 1951. Later two three car sidings were added on the South (left) side of the barn. Photo by Leonard W. Rice.

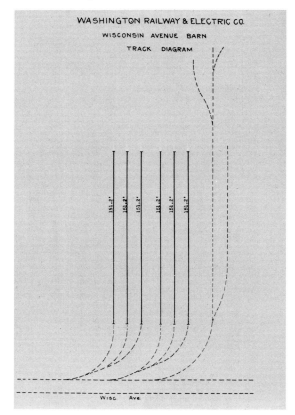

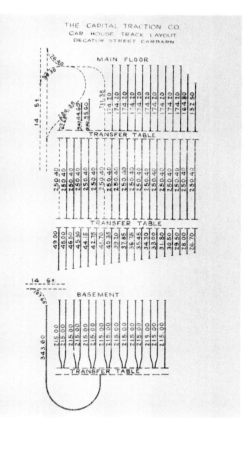

Above right: Chevy Chase Lake car barn about 1935. Kensington Rainway 1 prepares to depart at left of picture. Photo by Robert A. Truax.

Below: 14th and Decatur barn, the most attractive one in the city, about 1951. Capital Transit photo, author's collection. Bottom: Interior of 14th and Decatur barn in 1914. Capital Traction photo, author's collection.

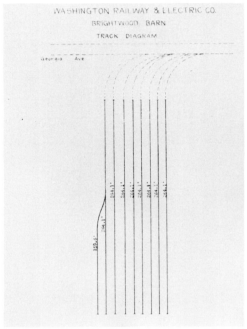

WASHINGTON RAILWAY & ELECTRIC CO.
BRIGHTWOOD BARN
TRACK DIAGRAM

Top left: Interior Brightwood Barn in 1914. Columbia Historical Society. Top right: Same view about 1950. Capital Transit photo, author's collection. Above: Brightwood Barn in 1947. Photo by Leonard W. Rice.

Ruins of the Eckington Barn after the fire February 24, 1919. Capital Transit Library, author's collection.

WASHINGTON RAILWAY & ELECTRIC CO.
ECKINGTON BARN
TRACK DIAGRAM

Interior and exterior of Eckington Barn in 1914. Photo (left) Columbia Historical Society. (Right) Robert A. Truax collection.

Columbia Barn, 1941. Author's collection.

Eckington Barn, 1952. Photo by Harvey Davison.

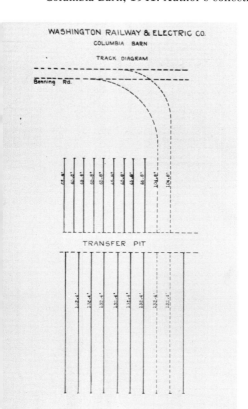
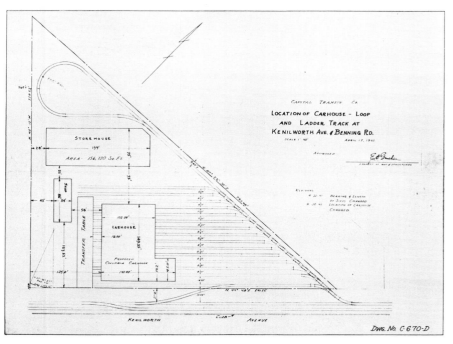

Benning Barn map. Capital Transit drawing, author's collection.

293

Benning Barn, built in 1941, was Washington's newest. Map on page 293. Left: Ladder truck in front of barn. Right: View from abov Kenilworth Avenue. Note Benning Power Plant and workcar 050 in background. Both photos, Capital Transit Company, author's collection.

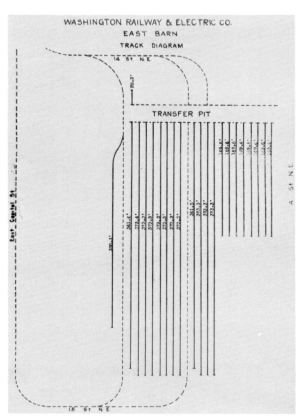

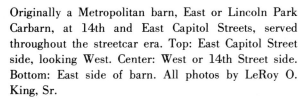

Originally a Metropolitan barn, East or Lincoln Park Carbarn, at 14th and East Capitol Streets, served throughout the streetcar era. Top: East Capitol Street side, looking West. Center: West or 14th Street side. Bottom: East side of barn. All photos by LeRoy O. King, Sr.

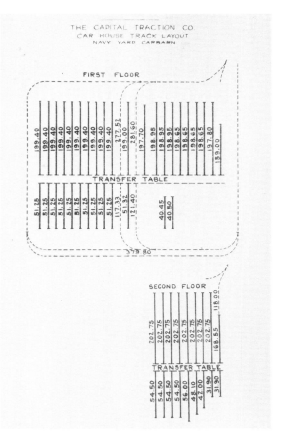

THE CAPITAL TRACTION CO.
CAR HOUSE TRACK LAYOUT
NAVY YARD CARBARN

Above: Navy Yard barn from Navy Yard gate. Photo by LeRoy O. King, Sr. Below: interior, Navy Yard barn, 1914. Columbia Historical Society.

Left: PCC on loop west side of Navy Yard barn. Right: Rear, Navy Yard barn. Both photos by LeRoy O. King, Sr.

In the 40's, Capital Transit added an open storage yard in the 15th and A Streets N.E. corner of the East barn property. Capital Transit photo, author's collection.

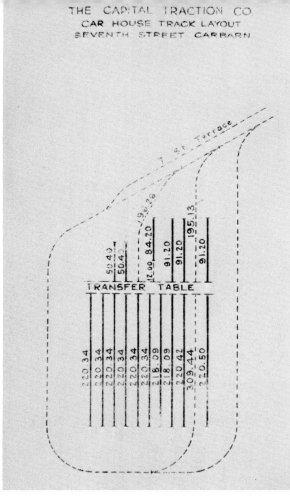

THE CAPITAL TRACTION CO.
CAR HOUSE TRACK LAYOUT
SEVENTH STREET CARBARN

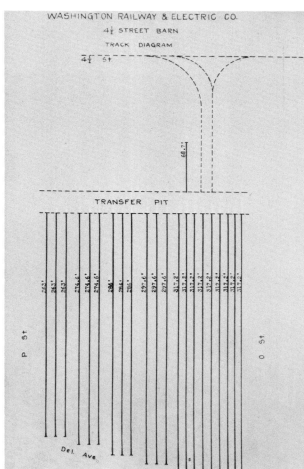

WASHINGTON RAILWAY & ELECTRIC CO.
4½ STREET BARN
TRACK DIAGRAM

Opposite page: Capital Traction's 7th Street barn, Maine Ave side about 1910. Left: Four and a Half Street (later Fourth St) side about 1910. Both photos by LeRoy O. King, Sr.

Opposite page: 7th Street barn (Maine Ave side) in 1952. Outside yard built in 1942. Note changes in structure from 1910 view. Left: Loop track along North side of barn in 1952. Both photos by LeRoy O. King, Sr.

Opposite page: Four and One Half street barn of the Washington Railway and Electric Company in 1914. Potomac Electric Power Company from Joseph J. Jessel. Left: Interior Four and One Half Street barn, 1914. Columbia Historical Society.

Opposite page: Transfer table at Four and One Half Street barn in 1914. Columbia Historical Society. Left: 4th Street shops, Capital Transit Company in 1952. Note that tower has been removed. Photo by LeRoy O. King, Sr.

The 11th Street barn was never used by Capital Transit. W Ry & E Co sold it to the Potomac Electric Power Company in 1930. Potomac Electric Power Company from Joseph J. Jessel.

Interior 11th Street barn in 1914. Columbia Historical Society.

The 13th and D Streets N.E. barn, originally an Eckington and Soldiers' Home horse car barn was destroyed by fire February 11, 1912 and not rebuilt. Robert A. Truax collection.

Glen Echo RR barn, on Walhonding Road near MacArthur Boulevard after abandonment in 1901. Author's collection.

Georgetown and Tenallytown barn at Wisconsin and Calvert February 22, 1909. Photo by LeRoy O. King, Sr.

Washington and Georgetown barn at 1st and Independence Avenue S.W. in 1947. Used as a bus garage by Capital Transit. Building demolished in 1956. Photo by LeRoy O. King, Sr.

Capital Traction's 14th and Park Road N.W. barn. Replaced by 14th and Decatur barn in 1907. Building was later a Safeway store. Photo by LeRoy O. King, Sr.

W Ry & E Co starter's office and waiting room at Nichols Avenue and Talbert Street S.E. in 1914. Columbia Historical Society.

W Ry & E Co starter's office and waiting room on the East side of 36th Street N.W. between N Street and Prospect Avenue in 1914. Columbia Historical Society.

APPENDIX 3
POWER SUPPLY

Capital Traction - Washington Rwy & E Co - Capital Transit Co.

Capital Traction Company

Capital Traction's power supply evolved from two separate systems. Rock Creek Railway generated its own power from facilities at Chevy Chase Lake. Coal was supplied by the B&O Metropolitan Branch. The old Love System conduit operation of Rock Creek was supplied from Separate facilities on Champlain Street between 18th and 19th Streets N.W.

When the city lines were electrified in 1898, power was at first bought from the Potomac Electric Power Co. The Grace Street Power House commenced operation April 7, 1898, and by May 4, supplied all needs for the City System.

By 1912, heavier cars and increased system mileage required new facilities which were constructed at 32nd and K Streets N.W.

McClellan & Junkersfeld lists Capital Traction Power Generating Facilities in 1925 as follows:

Main Generating Station — Wisconsin Avenue & Potomac River (32nd & K Streets N.W.)

Sub Station 1	14th and B Streets N.W.
Sub Station 2	1st & B Streets S.W.
Sub Station 3	At Main generating station
Sub Station 4	Connecticut Avenue & Fessenden Street N.W.

Coal was supplied to the Main Generating Station by the Metropolitan (Georgetown) Branch of the Baltimore & Ohio RR. Capital Traction's Power House was shut down December 15, 1933. The empty building remained a Georgetown landmark until demolished in October, 1968.

After December 15, 1933, all power was purchased from the Potomac Electric Power Company.

Washington Railway and Electric Company

Power for Washington Railway's operations was supplied by their subsidiary, the Potomac Electric Power Co. PEPCO facilities used for Railway Power as of 1925 were as follows:

Main Generating Station	Bennings
Sub Station 2	450 Washington Street N.W. (between 4th & 5th Streets N.W.)
Sub Station 3	Rear Eckington Barn
Sub Station 4	Riverdale (Pierce Street at Co right of way)
Sub Station 5	Brightwood Car Barn

Sub Station 6	4 miles south of Rockville (Grosvenor Lane at Co. right of way)
Sub Station 7	56th & Dix Streets N.E. (Deanewood)
Sub Station 8	Anacostia. Rear of starters office at plow pit
Sub Station 9	Ammendale, Md on Co. right of way
Sub Station 10	Intersection of alleys in block bounded by 14th, 15th, H & I Streets N.W.
Sub Station 11	13th & D Streets N.E.
Sub Station 12	Georgetown. 33rd Street & South Bank of Canal
Sub Station 13	NW corner Sherman Ave & Harvard Street N.W.
Sub Station 14	Adjacent to Bennings Power Plant
Sub Station 15	Glen Echo
Sub Station 17	14th & B Streets N.W.
Sub Station 20	West side 10th Street, north of E Street N.W.

Note: As of 1925, Sub Station 9 (Ammendale) was not in operation.

Sub Station 15 (Glen Echo) used summer only.

Sub station 7 (Deanewood) used for 15 days in spring and fall to protect WB & A Bowie Race Track Service.

Benning Power Plant used coal which was delivered from nearby Pennsylvania RR and B&O RR by W Ry & E Co operated electric locomotives. After December 15, 1933, PEPCO supplied all power for street railway use. Capital Transit operated coal service until December 1954, when it was sold to the East Washington Railway and Dieselized.

Abandoned Capital Traction Power House at Wisconsin Avenue and K Street N.W. in 1947. Photo by LeRoy O. King, Sr.

APPENDIX 4
UNDERGROUND CONDUIT SYSTEM

The underground conduit current collection system used by Washington streetcars was very complex and expensive to construct. Generally speaking, because of this, it was confined to old downtown while suburban lines used overhead trolley.

Essential to the system were 350 lb. cast iron yokes set at five-foot intervals beneath the street. To these yokes were attached the running rails and slot rails at street surface level. A concrete conduit ran beneath the slot rails and in that conduit were "T" shaped conductor rails supported by insulators hung from the bottom flange of the slot rail. A "plow" suspended from the truck of the car had two sliding shoes which collected positive and negative current from the two conductor rails.

At switches there was a necessary break in the conductor rails—so that positive and negative conductors would not meet on crossing. This break, though short, required coasting and current cut off. The switch mechanism, in addition to directing the car wheels, had to direct the plow in the proper direction. This was accomplished with an underground moveable plate which moved with the switch points.

There was hatches at the surface to gain access for cleaning, maintenance and repair of the conduit system.

Pitman Clarence Leckleter installs plow at 15th and H N.E. From the Star.

These were of two varieties. First there were hatches between the running rails and slot rails above each insulator. Then there were hatches in the slot rail, periodically, to allow for removal of damaged plows.

Where the car moved between a conduit system and an overhead trolley section, the plow was removed or replaced by a man stationed in a pit at the junction of the two sections.

As an outbound car moved over the pit, there was a sharp bend in only one of the underground conductor rails which gave the plow an abrupt twist, causing it to drop from the car. The electrical leads which had been connected downward to the plow were then inserted upward into the trolley leads for the car to proceed onto overhead operation. In the early days, a car moving over the pit was stopped opposite painted stripes in the street (indicating cars of varying lengths) on bell signals from the pit-man. Since audible signals allowed of possible misunderstanding for cars moving in different directions, not to mention the noise annoyance to nearby residents, they were replaced by signal lights.

Short segments of the trolley wire and the underground conductors on either side of the pit were broken by section insulators which, for safety reasons, enabled the pit-man to control the power of cars approaching the pit. This power switch simultaneously activated a blue signal light by which the motorman was guided in positioning the plow hanger of his car directly over the pit.

As an inbound car moved over the pit, the plow was attached free of any source of power. Under ideal conditions the conduit began on a downgrade enabling the car to coast off the pit until the plow entered the slot. Where this was not possible, a "U" shaped starter, fitted with positive and negative power leads, was mounted on shuttle rods at the entrance to the conduit. After the plow was attached, the reciprocating starter was pulled back under the free-hanging plow, and moved forward with the car to a point where the starter's contacts overlapped the beginning of the conductor rails in the conduit.

Another modification of this starter employed a hinged segment of one conductor rail opposite the other conductor bar which was continuous. After the plow was attached to the car truck, the hinged section (of one conductor rail) was closed in the manner of a large hasp; thus completing the circuit until the car had moved off the pit.

On certain operating divisions where the rush-hour cars were returned to the barn via a different plow pit from that of the departing trip (from Eckington via T Street—returning via North Capitol Street), the surplus

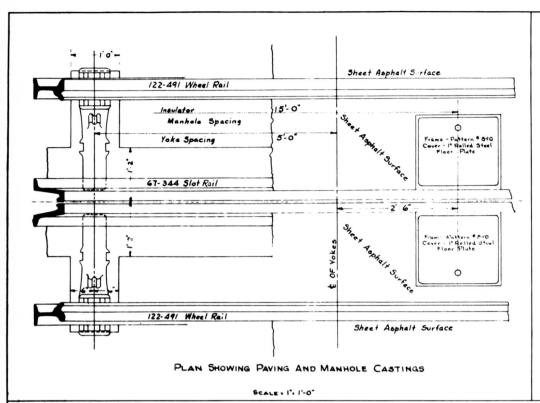

122-491 Wheel Rail

Sheet Asphalt Surface

Insulator

Manhole Spacing   15'-0"

Yoke Spacing   5'-0"

Sheet Asphalt Surface

Frame - Pattern #840
Cover - 1" Rolled Steel
Floor Plate

67-344 Slot Rail

2'-6"

Sheet Asphalt Surface

€ OF YOKES

Frame - Pattern #840
Cover - 1" Rolled Steel
Floor Plate

122-491 Wheel Rail

Sheet Asphalt Surface

PLAN SHOWING PAVING AND MANHOLE CASTINGS

Scale = 1" : 1'-0"

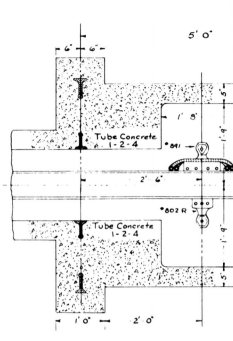

5'-0"

6"   6"

Tube Concrete
1-2-4

1'-8"

#891

2'-6"

#802 R

Tube Concrete
1-2-4

1'-0"   2'-0"

SECTION AT A-A

Scale 1" = 1'-0"

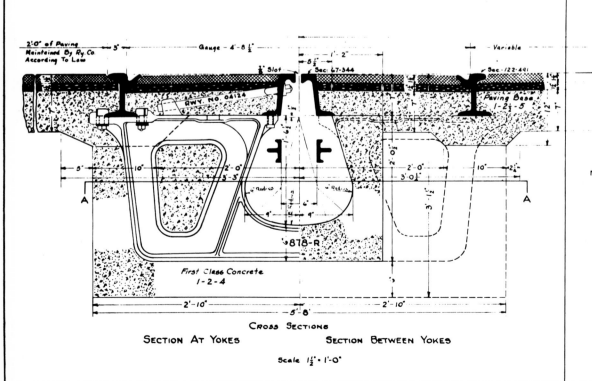

2'-0" of Paving
Maintained By Ry. Co.
According To Law

3"   Gauge - 4'-8½"   Variable

5½"

1" Slot   1'-2"

Sec. 67-344   Sec. 122-491

RWY. NO. 0A124

Paving Base
1-2½-5

5"   10"   2'-0"

2'-0"

3'-0"

10"   2½"

Radius   Radius

878-R

First Class Concrete
1-2-4

2'-10"   2'-10"

5'-8"

CROSS SECTIONS

SECTION AT YOKES   SECTION BETWEEN YOKES

Scale 1½" = 1'-0"

Track Centers Variable

1" Crown

Paving Base
1-2½-5

NOTE:
Standard Track Centers - 10'-8"
Track Centers Vary From 10'-0" To 1
Thermit Welded Joints
Yoke Pier 18" Wide On Reconstruction
For List of Material See Dwg. #C-1038-A

Yokes To Be Doubled At Heavily Traveled
Street Intersections

302

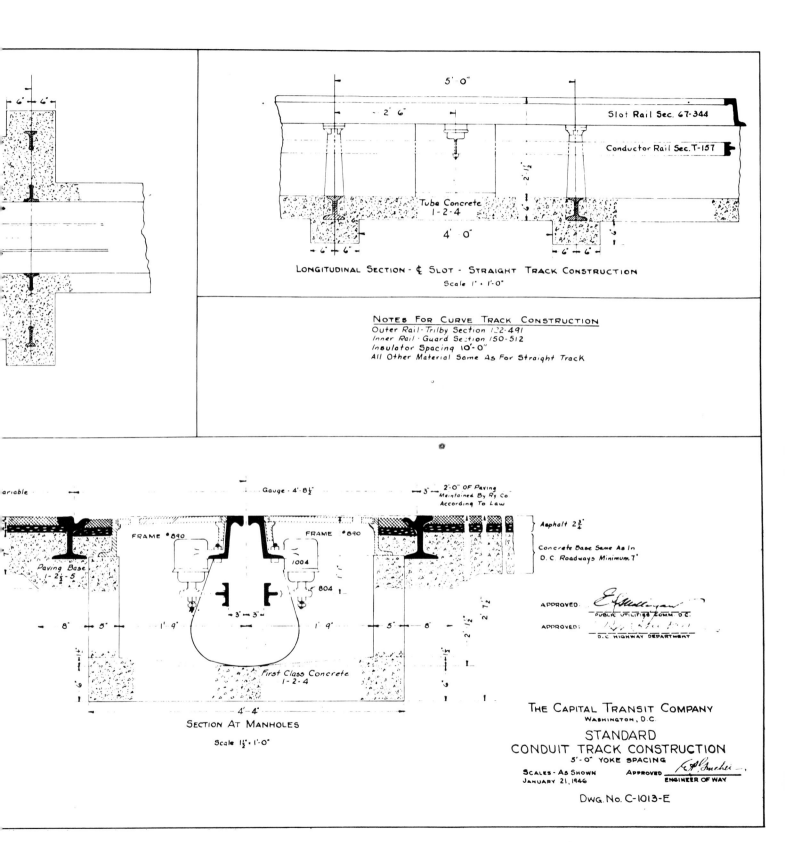

LONGITUDINAL SECTION - ℄ SLOT - STRAIGHT TRACK CONSTRUCTION

Scale 1" = 1'-0"

Slot Rail Sec. 67-344

Conductor Rail Sec. T-157

Tube Concrete 1-2-4

NOTES FOR CURVE TRACK CONSTRUCTION

Outer Rail - Trilby Section 122-491
Inner Rail - Guard Section 150-512
Insulator Spacing 10'-0"
All Other Material Same As For Straight Track

Gauge - 4'-8½"

2'-0" OF Paving Maintained By Ry Co According To Law

Asphalt 2¾"

Concrete Base Same As In D.C. Roadways Minimum 7"

FRAME #890

FRAME #890

1004

804

Paving Base 1-2½-5

First Class Concrete 1-2-4

SECTION AT MANHOLES

Scale 1½" = 1'-0"

APPROVED:
PUBLIC UTILITIES COMM. D.C.

APPROVED:
D.C. HIGHWAY DEPARTMENT

THE CAPITAL TRANSIT COMPANY
WASHINGTON, D.C.

STANDARD
CONDUIT TRACK CONSTRUCTION
5'-0" YOKE SPACING

SCALES - AS SHOWN   APPROVED
JANUARY 21, 1946   ENGINEER OF WAY

DWG. No. C-1013-E

Smithsonian Institution.

303

Plow installed on a PCC car in the pit at the M Street shops. Capital Transit photo, author's collection.

Looking into plow pit showing device used to supply current to car while over pit. Photo by Henry J. Leinbach.

Plowman attaching plow to 503 at 15th and H Streets N.E. Photo by Henry J. Leinbach.

Left: Conduit construction on Prospect Avenue in 1944 when the pit was moved to 37th Street. Photo by Ed Schell. Right: An assembled piece of special work for the Independence Avenue line. Note conductor rails in foreground. Photo by Charles J. Murphy.

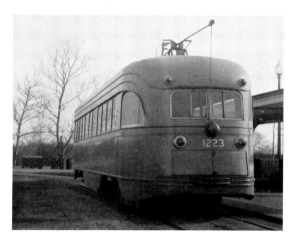

After World War II, Capital Transit developed an automatic device for raising and lowering the trolley pole to eliminate the trolleyman at the plow pits. The first effort, shown at left on 1266 at Wisconsin Avenue and P Street, used a motor on the roof. Later, as shown above on 1223, the motor was incorporated in the trolley retriever. The device on the roof caught or released the pole as required. Photos, 1266, Capital Transit Company, author's collection; 1223 by LeRoy O. King, Sr.

Mock up of underground conduit used for training purposes. Photo by Henry J. Leinbach.

plows accumulating at one point had to be trucked across to the other pit for the needs of the next day.*

Since both sides of the current distribution system in a conduit system were insulated from ground, it had an advantage not possible with overhead trolley systems. The conduit was sectionalized and, if a leakage to ground occurred in one section, it could be temporarily corrected simply by changing polarity in that section by means of double-pole double-throw switches at the substation.**

The major advantage of the system was, of course, the contribution to the beauty of the city by avoiding overhead wires.

*Description of plow pit operation written by John E. Merriken and used with his permission.

There were, however, a number of disadvantages. The principal ones are as follows:

• Expensive construction. In 1949, Mr. Harry Blunt, Chief Track Engineer, Capital Transit Co., estimated costs at $36 a running foot for overhead versus $100 for conduit construction.

• Dead spots in crossings and switches. Cars stopped on these spots by traffic conditions would have to be pushed by following car or assisted by use of leads kept for the purpose at major intersections—both time consuming procedures. Leads plugged into the car at one end and, at the other end were fitted with an insulated spade-like device which would be inserted into the slot and twisted to form contact with the conductor rails.

• Extreme hot weather caused expansion of slot rails which caused pulled plows.

• Snow-filled conduits which had to be cleaned out. At the same time skid chain parts fouled the slot and caused pulled plows.

• Burnt plows were tedious to remove under traffic.

• Track work had to be carried out under traffic since temporary track could not be used.

**Model railroaders may wonder why a reversal of polarity didn't reverse the car. Unlike permanent magnet motors, field wound motors can be reversed by changing polarity of the field or the armature, but a change of polarity of both has no effect. Thus of change at the source of current would have no effect.

Despite the number of disadvantages, over the years, with good maintenance, Washington's conduit lines performed well. Of those disadvantages listed, by far the major one was cost.

In the event of fire, where other cities used devices on the rail to ride over fire hoses, the conduit system used an overhead portable bridge.

To enable motormen to know when to cut power at conduit breaks and how to position his car at plow pits, it was necessary for him to know which truck the plow was attached to. Thus, double end cars had painted on the controller—or prominently in the front platform area—"1 Plow" or "2," or a variation "No. 1 End" or "No. 2 End." In each case the numeral "1" meant the plow was on the truck nearest the motorman while the numeral "2" meant it was on the far end of the car.

Hose bridge which was used to carry fire hoses over conduit track.
Capital Transit photo, author's collection.

APPENDIX 5
ROUTE DATA BEFORE AND
AFTER 1933 MERGER

1925 Routes Source: McClelland & Junkersfeld 1925
Transportation Survey

Capital Traction Company

1. Potomac Park - Chevy Chase Lake - Kensington
2. Chevy Chase - 7th St Wharves
3. Bureau of Standards - Navy Yard via N. J. Ave
4. Rock Creek Bridge - 7th St Wharves
5. Navy Yard - 14th & Colorado - Takoma
6. 14th & Decatur - Union Station
7. 14th & Park - Rosslyn
8. 14th & Park - 26th & G St via G St (return via F St)
9. 7th & Pa - Navy Yard via Florida Ave
10. Georgetown - 17th & Pa Ave S.E.
11. Georgetown - Peace Monument via F & G Sts
12. Rosslyn - 8th & F St N.E.
13. Potomac Park - 8th & F St N.E.

Washington Railway and Electric Company

1. Lincoln Park - Georgetown - Chain Bridge - Glen Echo - Cabin John
2. Lincoln Park - Somerset - Alta Vista
3. Mt. Pleasant - 13th & D N.E.
4. Mt. Pleasant - 1st & E S.E.
5. Center Market - Takoma - Georgia & Alaska
6. Soldiers' Home - Wharves
7. Central High School - Anacostia - Congress Heights
8. Treasury - Mt. Rainier - Riverdale - Branchville*
9. Wisconsin & M - Rockville
10. Treasury - 15th & H N.E. - Kenilworth - District Line
11. 11th & Monroe - North Capitol & Michigan - Brookland
12. LeDroit Park - Bureau of Engraving - Wharves

Note: Numbers shown were assigned by M & J. Route numbers not used in Washington until 1936.

1932 Routes Source: 1932 map published jointly by Capital Traction, W Ry & E Co, and WRT Co.

Capital Traction Company

1. Rosslyn - 17th & Penna Ave S.E.
2. Rosslyn/Georgetown - Union Station
3. Takoma - Navy Yard
4. 14th & Decatur - 8th & F Sts N.E.

*Prior to 7-1-25 there was a Branchville - Laurel Shuttle. This cut back to Beltsville 7-1-25.

5. Chevy Chase Lake - Kensington - Potomac Park
6. 7th St Wharves - Chevy Chase
7. 7th St Wharves - Rock Creek Bridge
8. Navy Yard - Rock Creek Bridge - Bureau of Standards (via New Jersey Ave)
9. Navy Yard - 7th & Pa Ave (via Florida Ave)

Washington Railway & Electric Company

1. Georgetown - Rockville
2. Alta Vista - Somerset - Friendship Hts - Tenallytown - 1st & E Sts S.E.
3. Mt. Pleasant - 13th & D Sts N.E.
4. Mt. Pleasant - Lincoln Park
5. Treasury - Mt. Rainier - Riverdale - Branchville - Beltsville (Maryland Line)
6. Treasury - 15th & H Sts N.E. - Kenilworth/District Line (Columbia Line)
7. Cabin John - Glen Echo - Potomac Hts - Georgetown - Lincoln Park
8. Treasury - LeDroit Park
9. Brookland - Catholic Univ - Wharves/Bureau of Engraving
10. 11th & Monroe - Anacostia - Congress Hts
11. 7th & B Sts/Wharves - Soldiers Home/Takoma Park/Georgia & Alaska (Brightwood - Ninth Street Line)

Note: Route numbers for convenience only. Route numbers not used on cars until 1936.

1948 Routes Source: 1948 map published by Capital Transit Co.

Notes:
1. On this table, route numbers are those displayed on cars.
2. Routes were numbered by 10's clockwise around the city beginning at Rosslyn. The first digit indicated the basic route. The second digit indicated destination—even for regular base routes—odd for rush or off-route destinations. A red stripe through the route number indicated a run turning back short of the regular terminal.

Base Day Lines

Number	Route
	Rosslyn-Benning Line
10	Rosslyn-Kenilworth
*10	——-Benning
12	Washington Circle-Seat Pleasant (formerly District Line)

	Cabin John Line			Cabin John Line
20	Cabin John - Union Station		20	Peace Monument - Glen Echo
	Tenallytown - Pennsylvania Ave		*20	——— - Dalecarlia
30	Friendship Heights - 17th & Penna S.E.		*20	——— - 36th & Prospect N.W.
	Mt. Pleasant Line		*20	——— - Washington Circle
40	Mt. Pleasant - Lincoln Park			Tenleytown - Pennsylvania Ave Line
42	Mt. Pleasant - 13th & D N.E.		*30	Wisconsin & Harrison - Peace Monument
	Fourteenth Street Line		*30	McLean Gardens - ———
50	14th & Colorado - Bureau Engraving		37	Friendship Heights - SW Mall
*50	14th & Decatur - ———			Mt. Pleasant Line
52	14th & Decatur - Penna & 6th N.W.		#40	Municipal Center - Connecticut & S
	(via U & 11th Sts)		45	Bureau Engraving - Mt. Pleasant
54	14th & Colorado - Navy Yard		45	13th & D N.E. - Bureau Engraving
*54	Peace Monument		49	Potomac Park - Mt. Pleasant
	Eleventh Street Line			Fourteenth Street Line
60	11th & Monroe N.W. - 9th & E N.W.		53	14th & Colorado - S.W. Mall
	Georgia Ave - 7th St. Line		*54	14th & Park Road - ———
70	Georgia & Alaska - S.W. Mall		57	14th & Colorado - 7th St Wharves
*70	Brightwood - 7th & Penna N.W.		59	14th & Colorado - Potomac Park
72	Takoma - 7th St Wharves			Eleventh Street Line
74	Soldiers' Home - 7th St Wharves		63	11th & Monroe N.W. - S.W. Mall
	North Capitol Street Line		67	11th & Monroe N.W. - 7th St Wharves
80	Brookland - 19th & F N.W.			Georgia Ave 7th Street Line
	Maryland Line		*74	7th & Florida - ———
82	Branchville - Potomac Park			North Capitol Street Line
*82	Riverdale - ———		*80	Catholic University - ———
*82	Mt Rainier - ———			Maryland Line
84	Beltsville - Branchville		*82	Eckington - 19th & F N.W.
	U St Line		85	Branchville - Bureau Engraving
90	Calvert Bridge - 17th & Penna S.E. (via N.J. Ave)			U St Line
92	Calvert Bridge - Navy Yard (via Florida Ave)		91	Calvert Bridge - Navy Yard (via N.J. Ave)
			92	7th & Florida (via Fla Ave) - ———

Rush Hour Lines

	Rosslyn - Benning Line
*10	Washington Circle - Kenilworth Junction
*12	15th & NY Ave - Kenilworth Junction
19	Potomac Park - Seat Pleasant

*Indicates run turning back short of regular terminal.
Would have been indicated by a red stripe through route
number on car.

APPENDIX 6

STREET RAILWAY FARES

DISTRICT OF COLUMBIA AND VICINITY — AN OUTLINE

Before 1896, there was no standard fare. Fares ranged from two cents to six cents per ride. Zone fares on at least one line required fifteen cents for a ride from the DC line to the city center. An Act of Congress June 10, 1896, fixed the rate of fare for all lines to a maximum of five cents per passenger or six tickets for twenty-five cents — interchangeable with all existing railways in the District of Columbia. Data on the 1896 fare structure and subsequent changes are set forth below:

Effective Date	Cash	Ticket or Token	Intra Co. Transfer	Inter Co. Transfer	School Tickets	Weekly Pass	Weekly Permit
6-10-96	5¢	6/25¢	Free	None	None	None	None
10-26-18	5¢	None	”	”	”	”	”
2-1-19	5¢	”	”	Free	”	”	”
6-1-19	5¢	”	2¢	2¢	”	”	”
11-1-19	7¢	4/25¢	Free	”	”	”	”
5-1-20	8¢	4/30¢*	”	”	”	”	”
1-1-21	”	”	”	1¢	”	”	”
9-1-21	”	5/35¢	”	”	”	”	”
3-1-22	”	6/40¢	”	”	”	”	”
7-23-30	10¢	4/30¢	”	”	”	”	”
3-10-31	”	”	”	”	3¢	”	”
12-1-33	”	”	”	Free	”	$1.00	”
1-2-37	”	”	”	”	”	$1.25	”
11-3-37	”	6/50¢	”	”	”	”	”
1-31-43	”	3/25¢	”	”	”	”	”
5-11-47	10¢	None	”	”	”	$1.50	”
10-31-48	13¢	3/35¢	”	”	”	$1.75	”
7-16-50	15¢	3/40¢	”	”	”	$2.00	”
1-20-52	”	”	”	”	”	$2.10	”
8-31-52	17¢	5/75¢	”	”	”	$2.40	”
1-31-54	20¢	5/80¢	”	”	”	None	75¢ plus 10¢ / ride
8-22-55	”	5/95¢	”	”	”	”	90¢ plus 10¢ / ride
9-7-55	”	”	”	”	7-1/2¢	”	”
8-31-58	”	5/$1.00	”	”	10¢	”	None
3-6-60	25¢	”	”	”	”	”	”

*Tokens Substituted for Tickets 5/1/20
Johnson Fare Boxes were introduced in January, 1919. Subsequently Cleveland Fare boxes were used on one man cars.

In addition to fares listed for the District of Columbia, the various Maryland Lines used zone fare systems. In addition to cash fares, commutation books were sold. In 1925 the following were in effect:

Capital Traction Company

Chevy Chase Circle to Chevy Chase Lake
One Zone — 5 cents or 1 ticket

Chevy Chase Lake — Kensington and Norris Station
Three Zones — 7 cents for 1st zone plus 3 cents each additional zone,
or 2 tickets for 1st zone plus 1 ticket each additional zone

Takoma to Sligo Run
One Zone — 5 cents or 1 ticket

Commutation Books: 100 tickets — $3.00

Washington Railway & Electric Company

8 cents cash or 1 "Maryland" ticket per zone. Tickets — 4/30¢.

Commutation books for various stations on all rail lines were sold in books allowing 26 round trips. Typical was Rockville — Washington Book at $8.76.

After 1933

Capital Transit issued weekly passes good on various Maryland services at prices increased to compensate for the maximum number of zones away from D.C. Typical was the first interstate weekly pass, effective 9/30/34, which cost $1.00 plus $.25 for each Maryland zone. Thus, for instance, a pass for the entire Rockville line (four zones) cost $2.00. With the interstate weekly pass, commutation tickets were suspended.

Because of zone fare systems on the Maryland and Cabin John lines, fare registers were used until abandonment.

1512, the Silver Sightseer, eastbound on C Street at New Jersey Avenue NW about 1960. Photo by Edward S. Miller.

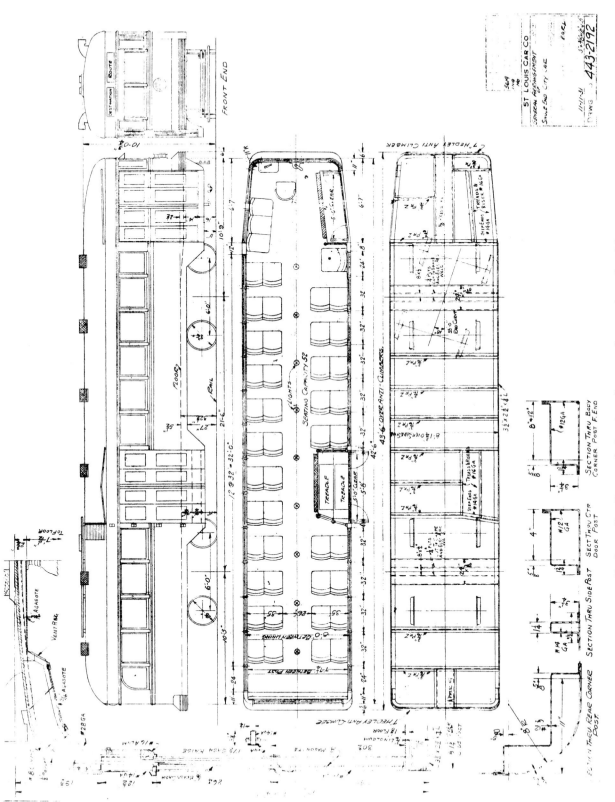

St. Louis Car Company's drawing of proposed car to be ordered by Capital Traction Company in 1931. A contract was never signed because of favorable Congressional action on the long sought merger. Author's collection.

COUPON PASS
GOOD DURING YEAR 1910 FOR ONE FARE
Within the District of Columbia
ON LINES OF THE
Washington Ry. and Electric Co.'s System
Clarence F. Norment
PRESIDENT
3119

COUPON PASS
GOOD DURING YEAR 1910 FOR ONE FARE
Within the District of Columbia
ON LINES OF THE
Washington Ry. and Electric Co.'s System
Clarence F. Norment
PRESIDENT
3119

WASHINGTON & GEORGETOWN R.R.
ONE FARE

BALTIMORE & WASHINGTON TRANSIT CO.
OF MARYLAND
ONE FARE
in the District of Columbia
A. L. SHREVE
Wm. A. Miller
RECEIVER
007944

ONE FARE COUPON
ON LINE OF
THE CAPITAL TRACTION COMPANY
IN MARYLAND
For lawful holder of book number
as per conditions thereon.
43257

CAPITAL TRACTION COMPANY
WASHINGTON, D.C.
SECURITY BANK NOTE CO. PHILA.

GOOD FOR STREET CAR FARE
IN THE DISTRICT OF COLUMBIA
FROM
5 A.M. TO 1 HOUR PAST MIDNIGHT
SUNDAY
PASS
25c
NOV. 25
1934
CAPITAL TRANSIT
COMPANY
48
J. H. Hanna
Pres.
04101

EMPLOYEE'S
Capital Traction Company.
Thursday, 26th December
GOOD FOR THIS DAY
AND
ONE RIDE ONLY.
CHECK.

CAPITAL TRACTION CO.
TRANSFER FROM
U St. to 7th St.
1 2 3 4 5 6 7 8 9 10 11
12 13 14 15 16 17 18 19 20 21
22 23 24 25 26 27 28 29 30 31
1 2 3 4 5 6 7 8 9 10 11 12 AM
15 30 45 MINUTES.
1 2 3 4 5 6 7 8 9 10 11 12 PM
ISSUED BY CONDUCTOR

O-1298 CAPITAL TRANSIT
COMPANY
PASS ON ALL STREET CARS AND BUSSES
LeRoy O. King
Statistical Clerk
SUBJECT TO CONDITIONS ON BACK
ANNUAL PASS
EXPIRES AT
END OF
1946
E. D. Merrill
PRESIDENT
Treasurer

THIS BOOK MUST BE SHOWN TO CONDUCTOR UPON DEMAND

CITY AND SUBURBAN RAILWAY
OF WASHINGTON
No. 7924
COMMUTATION BOOK
Good only during the month of ....
SEPTEMBER 1909

COMMUTATION TICKET
City & Suburban Railway
..ONE FARE..
From Dist. Line to Washington, D. C.
Good only during the month of
JULY 1910
Not Good if Detached
Coupon F Form 7
07675

COMMUTATION TICKET
City & Suburban Railway
..ONE FARE..
From Riverdale to Dist. Line
Good only during the month of
JULY 1910
Not Good if Detached
Coupon E Form 7
07675

COMMUTATION TICKET
City & Suburban Railway
..ONE FARE..
From Berwyn to Riverdale
Good only during the month of
JULY 1910
Not Good if Detached
Coupon D Form 7
07675

EAST WASHINGTON HEIGHTS
TRACTION RAILROAD CO.
GOOD FOR
ONE FARE
IN THE DISTRICT OF COLUMBIA
261181
R.D. Brother

THE CAPITAL TRACTION COMPANY
WASHINGTON, D.C.
CTCo
AMERICAN BANK NOTE CO. N.Y.

Washington Spa Spring & G.
R. R. CO.
EXCURSION TICKET
15th & H, N. E.
TO
BLADENSBURG & RETURN
AFTER COUPONS ATTACHED
D. C. BOUNDARY
TO
15th & H, N. E.
Coupon No. 4

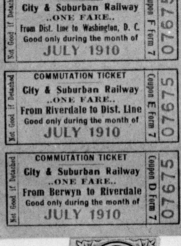

WASHINGTON
RAILWAY &
ELECTRIC COMPANY

Wash. Ry. & E. Co.   The Cap. Trac. Co.
SCHOOL TICKET IDENTIFICATION
Signature   Pupil
Age .... yrs. Male—Female
is a pupil of
Name of School
and is entitled to reduced
school fare
Signature of Teacher
D202627
GLOBE TICKET COMPANY, PHILADELPHIA

WASHINGTON
RAILWAY &
ELECTRIC COMPANY

WASHINGTON
RAILWAY &
ELECTRIC COMPANY

CAPITAL TRANSIT CO.

Stedman System of
11 1 2 3 4 5 12
JUL 1909
246
Good for transfer of
senger from
PENN. AVENUE
at point of change,
punched, and until
celled in margin.
the rules of the
Passengers are requ
that time punched
This is not a stop-o
and is not transferabl
Capital Tract
Good only on c
The Capital Trac
A M
N. TREA
N. or S. at 7th
S. AT 1 7th
S. at 26th
N. at Peace Mo
N. at 1st &
E. at 8th & P.
S. at 36th

FEB. | MAR. | APR. | MAY | JUN. | JUL. | AUG. | SEP. | OCT. | NOV. | DEC.

WASHINGTON RAILWAY & ELECTRIC COMPANY

IDENTIFICATION CHECK for continuous trip.
This ticket is for identification at 32d and O or P Streets by conductor of the Georgetown & Tennallytown Line of through passen-

WEST BOUND | 071532

Ham Patent, June 9, 1903.

ger over the Georgetown and Georgetown & Tennallytown Lines or for identification at 36th Street and Prospect Avenue by conductor of the Great Falls Line of through passenger over the Georgetown and Great Falls Lines, and will be accepted by conductor on date issued within ten minutes after time punched.
Not a stop-over privilege and not transferable.
Subject to the rules of the Company. Sted. Time-Limit, Pat. Aug. 23, '92

FORM 14-A | W. F. HAM, TREASURER

	1	2	3	4	5
1	1	2	3	4	5
2	1	2	3	4	5
3	1	2	3	4	5
4	1	2	3	4	5
5	1	2	3	4	5
6	1	2	3	4	5
7	1	2	3	4	5
8	1	2	3	4	5
9	1	2	3	4	5
10	1	2	3	4	5
11	1	2	3	4	5
12	1	2	3	4	5

EAST WASHINGTON HEIGHTS TRACTION R. R.

TRANSFER

From **RANDLE HIGHLANDS**
To Capital Traction Co. at 17th St. & Pa. Av., S. E.

NOT GOOD AFTER TIME PUNCHED ON MARGIN OF THIS TICKET. NOT TRANSFERABLE.

Passengers will examine their Transfer as same will not be accepted unless properly punched. **524900** OVER

	JAN.	DATE		
FEB.	1	12	23
MAR.	2	13	24
APR.	3	14	25
MAY	4	15	26
JUNE	5	16	27
JULY	6	17	28
'G.	7	18	29
SEPT.	8	19	30
OCT.	9	20	31
NOV.	10	21	
DEC.	11	22	

AM	1	2	3	4	5	6	7	8	9	10	11	12
PM	1	2	3	4	5	6	7	8	9	10	11	12
MIN. after	5	10	15	20	25	30	35	40	45	50	55	

Capital Transit Company

PASS MUST BE SHOWN UPON DEMAND

$1.25 WEEKLY PASS **38**

5987

On Street Car and Bus Lines of Capital Transit Company in the District of Columbia on which the cash rate of fare is 10 cents or less.

SEPT. 14 to 20 1941 INCL.

Good from 5 A. M. Sunday until 5 A. M. the Following Sunday

E. D. Merrill PRESIDENT

With this attachment Pass is good on line punched between District of Columbia and Maryland points and within Zones, indicated by Coupons.

	E. Washington Bus	Wyattsville Betts-ville Park Bus	C. C. Lake Kensington-College Park Bus	C—5in John Car	Zone	Total Price
					Zone 1	$1.50
					Zone 1	

....CAPITAL TRANSIT COMPANY....

ON STREET CAR LINES IN THE DISTRICT of COLUMBIA
Pass Must Be Shown UPON DEMAND

UNION STATION

MARCH 17 TO 23 1935-INCL.

12 **$1. WEEKLY PASS**

86314

Good from 5:00 A. M. Sunday until 5:00 A. M. the following Sunday

Jos. H. Hanna PRESIDENT

	1	2	3	4	5
1	1	2	3	4	5
2	1	2	3	4	5
3	1	2	3	4	5
4	1	2	3	4	5
5	1	2	3	4	5
6	1	2	3	4	5
7	1	2	3	4	5
8	1	2	3	4	5
9	1	2	3	4	5
10	1	2	3	4	5
11	1	2	3	4	5
12	1	2	3	4	5

GLOBE TICKET COMPANY, PHILA., PA.

BRIGHTWOOD RAILWAY COMPANY

IDENTIFICATION CHECK for Continuous Trip.
For identification at TERMINUS of Brightwood Line on 7th STREET, N. W. Stedman Time-Limit, Pat'd Aug. 23, 1892.

SOUTH BOUND | 91519

Ham Patent, June 9, 1903.

This ticket is for identification by conductor of the 9th Street Line of through passenger over the BRIGHTWOOD AND 9th STREET LINES and will be accepted by him on date issued within ten minutes after time punched.
Not a stop-over privilege and not transferable.
Subject to the rules of the Company.

FORM 18 | W. F. HAM, TREASURER

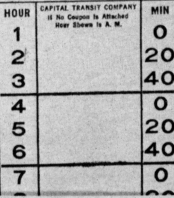

P. M.

MT. PLEASANT

19023

Transfer issued for use in D. C., in accordance with tariff, for one continuous ride requiring the use of different lines, if presented at intersection, divergence, turnback, or walking transfer point between the lines involved, on day issued and within indicated time limit. Not transferable. Not good for stopover or return trip on same or other lines.

SPECIAL ★

45	
44	
42	
40	49

THURSDAY JUNE 9 1955

HOUR	CAPITAL TRANSIT COMPANY If No Coupon is Attached Hour Shown is A. M.	MIN
1		0
2		20
3		40
4		0
5		20
6		40
7		0

P. M.

GLOBE TICKET COMPANY, PHILADELPHIA

046320

TENNALLYTOWN

046320

This transfer is issued SOUTHBOUND for use in accordance with company regulations, is good in the District of Columbia for continuance of ride in the same general direction if presented at an established transfer point on day issued and within indicated time limit, and carries all the privileges OF A FARE OF 10c

CASH

CAPITAL TRANSIT COMPANY

OTHER LINES USED
N E
W S
N E
W S
N E
W S

SPECIAL ★ **4-3** PUPIL ★

GOOD UNTIL TIME SHOWN BY TEAR OFF
IF NO COUPON IS ATTACHED HOUR SHOWN IS A. M.

HOUR		MIN
1		0
2		30
3		
4		0
5		30
6		
7		0

P. M.

093081

GLOBE TICKET COMPANY, PHILADELPHIA

COLUMBIA

This transfer is issued WESTBOUND for use in accordance with company regulations, is good in the District of Columbia for continuance of ride in the same general direction if presented at an established transfer point on day issued and within time limit, and carries such privileges as are accorded on payment of

TOKEN FARE

CAPITAL TRANSIT COMPANY

OTHER LINES USED
N S
W S
N S
W S
N S
W S

SPECIAL ★ **4-1**

GOOD UNTIL TIME SHOWN BY TEAR OFF
IF NO COUPON IS ATTACHED HOUR SHOWN IS A. M.

HOUR		MIN
1		0
2		
3		30
4		

P. M.

GLOBE TICKET COMPANY, PHILADELPHIA

04547

MARYLAND

This transfer is issued EASTBOUND for use in accordance with company regulations, is good in the District of Columbia for continuance of ride in the same general direction if presented at an established transfer point on day issued and within indicated time limit.

CAPITAL TRANSIT COMPANY

1	
2	RE-USE
3	

Hour Shown is A. M. Special

FRIDAY NOV 3 1944

HOUR		MIN
1		0
2		15
3		30
4		45
5		0
6		15
7		30
8		45
9		0
10		15
11		30
12		45

NOTCH PERFORATION 38

CAPITAL TRANSIT and You

SERVING WASHINGTON ★ WHICH SERVES THE NATION

Annual Report 1942

CAPITAL TRANSIT COMPANY

So... You Want to See Washington

FEB - 1 1968

10 Three-Hour Tours of the Nation's Capital

This booklet is designed to cover 5 full-days of sightseeing by street-car and bus. You can start on any tour and follow thru to the next without regard to the sequence in the booklet. The tours, starting from Union Station and 14th St. & Pennsylvania Ave., N.W., two of the most prominent focal points in the city, are grouped according to popular preference. FOR FURTHER INFORMATION, CALL Adams 2-6363, Ext. 572.   7-53

TIME TABLE
of
STREET CAR SERVICE

between

CABIN JOHN
POTOMAC HEIGHTS
and
15TH & NEW YORK AVE. N. W.

•

Effective Feb. 7, 1937

Subject to Change Without Notice

•

CAPITAL TRANSIT CO.

36th and M Streets, N. W.

Telephone West 1246

Transit ·NEWS·

JUNE 1936

Extra Edition

Capital Transit Company has purchased 30 front entrance cars from the United Electric Railways Company of Providence, Rhode Island, which will be placed in service immediately after they have been thoroughly reconditioned and adapted to use in Washington. One of these cars, bearing the number 501, has been in active service on the North Capitol Street Line for several weeks and has been favorably commented upon for its appearance, both interior and exterior, and its comfortable riding qualities. This car has commodious exit and entrance vestibules and most comfortable seating arrangements.

The balance of the cars, purchased by the approval of the Public Utilities Commission of the District of Columbia, are now being delivered and will be put through a thorough mechanical overhauling and a complete reconditioning process that involves repainting interior and exterior, installation of new lighting fixtures, installation of a new type of leather upholstered seat having cellular rubber cushion construction instead of springs, chromium hand-holds running entirely across the top of the seats, providing firm guidance for passengers in passage through the car and assistance in rising from the seat, and good ventilating fea-

Time Table

of

STREET CAR SERVICE

Between

BELTSVILLE

BRANCHVILLE

RIVERDALE

HYATTSVILLE

and

15th and N. Y. AVE. N. W.

★

Effective February 7, 1937

Subject to Change Without Notice

★

CAPITAL TRANSIT CO.

36th and M Streets N. W.

Telephone WEst 1246

SATURDAY EAST BOUND

Leave Potomac Heights	Arrive 36th St.	Arrive 6th and F Sts.	Leave Cabin John	Leave Potomac Heights	Arrive 36th St.	Arrive 5th and F Sts.
5.39	5.53	6.12	2.36	2.45	3.01	3.23
6.09	6.23	6.42	2.56	3.05	3.21	3.48
6.25	6.40	7.02	3.16	3.25	3.41	4.01
6.40	6.54	7.17	3.36	3.45	4.01	4.28
6.55	7.10	7.32	3.56	4.05	4.21	4.48
7.10	7.25	7.47	4.16	4.25	4.41	5.08
7.23	7.39	8.04	4.36	4.45	5.01	5.28
7.38	7.54	8.19	4.56	5.05	5.21	5.48
7.43	7.59	8.24	5.16	5.25	5.41	6.08
7.51	8.09	8.29	5.36	5.45	6.01	6.26
7.57	8.15	8.45	5.56	6.05	6.21	6.46
8.04	8.22	8.52	6.16	6.25	6.41	7.06
8.12	8.30	9.00	6.36	6.45	7.01	7.26
8.19	8.37	9.07	6.56	7.05	7.21	7.46
8.27	8.45	9.15	7.16	7.25	7.41	8.06
8.45	9.01	9.26	7.36	7.40	7.56	8.21
8.55	9.11	9.36	7.45	7.55	8.10	8.32
9.15	9.31	9.56	8.01	8.11	8.26	8.48
9.25	9.41	10.06	8.16	8.26	8.41	9.03
9.45	10.01	10.26	8.31	8.41	8.56	9.18
9.55	10.11	10.36	8.46	8.56	9.11	9.33
10.15	10.31	10.56	9.01	9.11	9.26	9.48
10.25	10.41	11.06	9.16	9.26	9.41	10.03
10.45	11.01	11.26	9.31	9.41	9.56	10.18
10.55	11.11	11.36	9.46	9.56	10.11	10.33
11.15	11.31	11.56	10.01	10.11	10.26	10.48
11.25	11.41	12.06	10.16	10.26	10.41	11.03
11.45	12.01	12.26	10.31	10.41	10.56	11.18
11.55	12.11	12.36	10.46	10.56	11.11	11.33
12.15	12.31	12.56	11.01	11.11	11.26	11.48
12.25	12.41	1.08	11.16	11.26	11.41	12.02
12.45	1.01	1.28	11.33	11.42	11.56	12.15
12.56	1.12	1.39	11.43	11.52	12.06	12.25
1.15	1.31	1.58	12.03	12.12	12.26	12.45
1.25	1.41	2.08	12.23	12.12	12.56	1.15
1.45	2.01	2.28	12.45	12.54	1.05	....
2.05	2.21	2.48	1.16	1.25	1.36	....
2.25	2.41	3.08				

Light Figures Denote A. M.; Dark Figures, P. M.

SATURDAY WEST BOUND

Leave 15th and F Sts.	Leave 36th St.	Arrive Potomac Heights	Arrive Cabin John	Leave 10th and F Sts.	Leave 36th St.	Arrive Potomac Heights	Arrive Cabin John
....	5.06	5.20	5.50	1.35	2.01	2.17	2.27
....	5.36	5.50	5.59	1.52	2.19	2.35	2.44
5.34	5.56	6.10	....	2.12	2.39	2.55	3.04
5.44	6.06	6.20	6.29	2.32	2.59	3.15	3.24
5.59	6.21	6.35	....	2.52	3.19	3.35	3.44
6.14	6.36	6.50	6.59	3.12	3.39	3.55	4.04
6.36	7.01	7.17	7.26	3.32	3.59	4.15	4.24
6.41	7.06	7.22	....	3.52	4.19	4.35	4.44
6.49	7.15	7.31	7.41	4.12	4.39	4.55	5.04
6.54	7.20	7.36	....	4.32	4.59	5.15	5.24
7.04	7.30	7.46	7.56	4.52	5.19	5.35	5.44
7.09	7.35	7.51	....	5.12	5.39	5.55	6.04
7.19	7.45	8.01	....	5.32	5.59	6.15	6.24
7.22	7.48	8.04	8.14	5.52	6.19	6.35	6.44
7.34	8.00	8.16	....	6.12	6.39	6.55	7.04
7.40	8.06	8.22	8.32	6.31	6.56	7.12	7.21
7.57	8.23	8.39	....	6.46	7.11	7.27	7.36
8.07	8.33	8.49	8.59	7.01	7.26	7.42	7.51
8.31	8.57	9.13	....	7.16	7.41	7.57	8.06
8.41	9.07	9.22	9.31	7.31	7.56	8.12	8.21
9.01	9.27	9.42	....	7.46	8.11	8.27	8.36
9.14	9.39	9.55	10.04	8.01	8.26	8.42	8.51
9.24	9.59	10.15	....	8.16	8.41	8.57	9.06
9.44	10.09	10.25	10.34	8.36	8.58	9.12	9.21
10.04	10.29	10.45	....	8.51	9.13	9.27	9.36
10.24	10.59	11.15	....	9.06	9.28	9.42	9.51
10.44	11.09	11.25	11.34	9.21	9.43	9.57	10.06
11.04	11.29	11.45	....	9.36	9.58	10.12	10.21
11.14	11.39	11.55	12.04	9.51	10.13	10.27	10.36
11.34	11.59	12.15	....	10.06	10.28	10.42	10.51
11.44	12.09	12.25	12.34	10.21	10.43	10.57	11.06
12.00	12.26	12.42	....	10.36	10.58	11.12	11.21
12.10	12.36	12.52	1.02	10.51	11.13	11.27	11.36
12.20	12.46	1.02	....	11.13	11.35	11.49	11.58
12.40	1.06	1.22	1.32	11.33	11.55	12.09	12.18
12.58	1.24	1.40	1.50	12.03	12.22	12.35	12.44
1.15	1.41	1.57	2.07	12.34	12.53	1.06	1.15

Light Figures Denote A. M.; Dark Figures, P. M.

Washington Railway and Electric Co.

—

TIME TABLE

—

Potomac Heights

and

Cabin John

—

Effective May 6, 1933

—

Subject to change without notice

C. WILLIAM WITBECK

The Glen Echo Line

ROUTE 20

TIME TABLE

of

STREET CAR SERVICE

between

CABIN JOHN POTOMAC HEIGHTS

and

15th & NEW YORK AVE., N. W.

PEACE MONUMENT

UNION STATION

★

Effective April 12, 1941

Subject to Change Without Notice

★

NOTE—This Time Table shows only the service scheduled) to and from Potomac Heights and Cabin John. Other service scheduled to and from Union Station is not shown.

CAPITAL TRANSIT COMPANY

36th & M STREETS

Telephone Informa

Capital Transit Company

FARES AND TRANSFERS

District of Columbia

(Children under 5 years of age carried free, when accompanied by person paying proper fare, on all street car lines and all Company bus lines, **except as noted below** under "Special Fares.")

FARES: On all street car lines and on feeder bus and owl bus lines:

Feeder Bus Line

Anacostia–Congress Heights.

Benning.

Bureau of Engraving Loop.

Bureau of Standards.

Chevy Chase Loop.

Eastern High School–Randle Hi

4th Street S. W.

Hill Crest–Good Hope.

Le Droit Park Loop.

Park Road.

Potomac Park.

South Washington.

Washington Interurban–East W

Woodley Road.

WASHINGTON

BY TROLLEY A MOTOR COAC

COMPLIMENTS OF

The Capital Traction Company
Washington Rapid Transit Company
Washington Railway and Electric Company

Behind the Plow

THE CAPITAL TRACTION COMPANY

September 1, 1925 — No. 24

to Caddy—"Are you good at ?"

es, sir."

—"Well, go find one and we'll

ND FARE IS UP, LY YIELD 8% RETURN

AFTER many years of trying to get along on a low fare in Richmond the Virginia Railway & Power Company has been granted a rate of 7 cents on the street cars in that city. The new rate is effective September 1, a temporary arrangement, and igh the increase is actually 2 cents ontract rate.

s order the Corporation Commission cted the new rate of fare to give the er Company an 8 per cent return on property it uses in transportation. sometimes appears to be a slow pro oughout the country are falling into ing to see how necessary it is to keep lines prosperous, despite the talk and unfriendly newspapers.

Behind the Plow

PUBLISHED BY THE CAPITAL TRACTION COMPANY

Vol. 3 — January 15, 1925 — No. 9

WITHOUT TRYING

"Have you had static on your new radio?"

Mrs. Newlywed—"Well, Harold has had Los Angeles and Cuba, and I'm sure he could get static if he wanted to."

GOOD HOPE BUS LINE IS PUT IN OPERATION

OPERATION of a bus line to serve the section over the Eastern Branch, known as Good Hope, was begun by this Company recently, after a hearing held by the Public Utilities Commission, on the subject of transportation for that community.

The route of the new line is out Pennsylvania Avenue Southeast, from 17th and that Avenue, to Branch Road, to Alabama Avenue, over that Avenue to its junction with Naylor Road, at Good Hope. The return trip is over the same route. The round trip distance is about 4.6 miles.

For the present service will not be continuous throughout the day, since Good Hope has not developed sufficiently to require such service. When the country grows so that traffic will warrant it, this Company will carry out its policy of keeping the service up to the traffic.

Present schedules provide for a first bus departing from 17th and the Avenue at 6.45 A. M., with service half hourly thereafter until 9.15 A. M. The first

---

Transit NEWS

Washington, D. C. — January, 1937

CAR AND BUS SERVICE

During Inaugural Parade

CAPITAL TRANSIT is making special provisions for service on street car and bus lines during time Pennsylvania Avenue and 15th Street N. W. closed to traffic from 11:15 A. M., Wednesday, January 20th, until the inaugural parade is over so public may be as little incommoded as possible.

STREET CARS

Routes 80-20-22—North Capitol and Maryland astern End). Cars on these two lines will be erated from their usual eastern terminals over ir regular week day routes to 5th and G Streets, W., then turn south on 5th to F Street, west to h, north to G and east to 5th and the regular ute.

Route 34—Pennsylvania Avenue. From 8th Streets, N. E., cars will be operated to Union ation over the regular route, then go west on ssachusetts Avenue and G Street to 14th Street, th on 14th to F, east on F to 5th, north on 5th G, then east on G and Massachusetts to regular ute.

Route 30—Tenleytown-Pennsylvania Avenue (East- n End). Over regular route from 17th and Penna. e., S. E., to First and B Streets, S. E., then by y of the Union Station and the route given just ove for the Pennsylvania Avenue line. Return by same route. (See below for western end of this e.)

The Light of Washington

Postmark from Capital Traction's Pennsylvania Avenue RPO. Robert A. Truax collection.

Bill from the author's family's coal firm to the Capital Traction Company for coal for the mail car. Author's collection.

An interesting letter which betokened the money problems that would force foreclosure sale of the Washington Traction and Electric, November 6, 1901. Columbia Historical Society.

FREIGHT TARIFFS!

CAPITAL TRACTION CO., CHEVY CHASE LINE.

CLASS I. comprises such articles (weighing less than 50 lbs.), as market baskets, marketings, groceries, dry goods, fancy goods, articles of clothing, medicines. Articles in this class will be carried free, at the owner's risk, and subject to delays, stoppage and overcrowding of the cars.

CLASS II. comprises such articles as trunks, satchels, traveling cases and all articles of baggage. These will be subject to ordinary regulations respecting baggage express and will be charged for at the rate of 10 cents per piece.

CLASS III. comprises all articles not included in the two previous classes, which are shipped in less quantities than car load lots, and will be charged for at the rate of 10 cents per 100 lbs.

CLASS IV. comprises all materials shipped by the car load lot, and will be charged for at the rate of $2.00 per car load. This class of materials will not be shipped on the regular trips of the freight car.

ALL CHARGES MUST BE PAID BEFORE GOODS WILL BE DELIVERED.

Freight Tariff about 1900. Robert A. Truax collection.

Two letters shown below granted permission to LeRoy O. King, Sr. to take many of the Washington Railway and Electric rolling stock pictures used in the book. Author's collection.

Washington Railway and Electric Company
Washington, D. C.

Office of the Vice-President.

General Offices
Fourteenth and East Capitol Streets.

May 26, 1908.

Mr. J. Holdsworth Gordon,
3028 Q Street, N. W.,
Washington, D. C.

My dear friend Gordon:-

Replying to your favor of May 22 I send herewith note requested by you. Glad to do anything I possibly can for you or anyone in whom you are interested.

Wishing that I could see you more frequently, I am,

Cordially yours,

Vice President.

GHH-ADS
1 Enc.

Washington Railway and Electric Company
Washington, D. C.   June 2, 1908.

Office of the Purchasing Agent.

2411 P Street.

Shop Foremen,
P Street, and Barns.
Gentlemen:

Please allow the bearer, LeRoy King, to pass through yards and shops to photograph equipment.

This order to be good until August 1st, 1908.

Extended to Oct 1-08

Yours truly,

Master Mechanic.

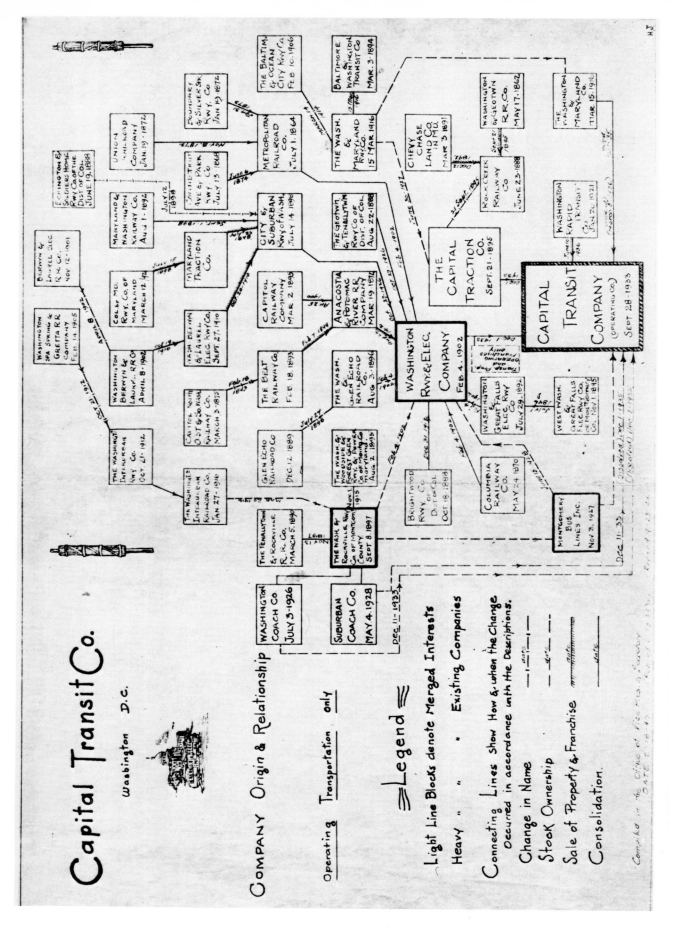

Author's collection.

318

NOTES

Chapter One

[1] Primary sources for routes, corporate data and charter dates are: *Laws Relating to Street Railway Franchises in District of Columbia* (Washington: U.S. Government Printing Office, 1905), pp. 59-63, and William B. Webb and others, *Centennial History of the City of Washington, D.C.* (Dayton, Ohio: United Brethren Publishing House, 1892), pp. 340-1.

[2] *The Washington Star*, June 11, 1862.

[3] *Annual Report*, Washington and Georgetown RR Co. (Washington, 1863).

[4] *Star*, June 13, 1862.

[5] *Ibid.* August 12, 1862.

[6] *Ibid.*, July 12, 1862.

[7] *Ibid.*, July 29, 1862.

[8] *Ibid.*, November 15, 1862.

[9] *Ibid.*, November 13, 1862.

[10] Senate Misc Doc No. 11, 38th Congress 1st Sess., January 10, 1864. Contains a report from the president of the W & G RR to Hannibal Hamlin, Vice President of the U.S., which gives financial and operating data used here.

[11] *Star*, January 12, 1876.

[12] *Ibid.*, October 4, 1875.

[13] *Ibid.*, January 12, 1876.

[14] *Ibid.*, June 18, 1880.

[15] In addition to sources cited in note 1 above, an additional major source on the remaining roads described in this chapter is "Washington Railway and Electric—Historical" unpublished, from Capital Transit Company Library. Copy in author's collection.

[16] *Star*, November 17, 1864.

[17] *Washington National Intelligencer*, December 29, 1864.

[18] *Ibid.*, December 9, 1864.

[19] *Ibid.*, December 29, 1864.

[20] *Star*, May 9, 1872.

[21] *Ibid.*, September 21, 1873.

[22] *Ibid.*, May 22, 1872.

[23] *Ibid.*, November 7, 1874.

[24] "The H Street Bobtail Car," *Star*, August 27, 1955.

[25] *Star*, July 3, 1876.

[26] *Ibid.*, July 13, 1877.

[27] *Ibid.*, July 16, 1878.

[28] *Ibid.*, September 20, 1879.

[29] *Ibid.*, November 30, 1875.

Chapter Two

[1] See Notes 1 and 15, Chapter One

[2] Tindall, "Beginnings of Street Railways," *Records of the Columbia Historical Society*, Vol. 21 (Washington, 1918). Further description may be found in *Street Railway Journal*, Vol. 5 (1889), 175-178.

[3] Basic material for W and G Cable operation from: G. F. Cunningham, "Cable Cars in the Nation's Capital," *The Turnout* (Boston Chapter, National Railway Historical Society, April, 1953).

[4] "Notes on the Washington, D.C. Street Railways," *Street Railway Journal*, Vol. 6 (1890), 327. A complete description of the experiments may be found in "Street Railways of Washington D.C.," Railway Journal, Vol. 7 (1891), 157 and 275.

[5] *Street SRJ*, Vol. 10 (1894), 761-763.

[6] *The Railway World* (London, February 1896), p. 46.

[7] *Street Railway Journal*, Vol. 7 (1891), 157 and 275.

[8] *Street Railway Journal*, Vol. 13 (1897), 317; *The Electrical Engineer* (1897), p. 449; and The Star, September 17, 1896.

[9] Flavius Morrill, "History of the Capital Traction Co.," from Capital Transit Company Library. Copy in author's collection.

[10] For a detailed account of the Rock Creek Railway, see: F. G. Bolles, "The Rock Creek Electric Railway, Washington, D.C.," *The Electrical World*, January 14, 1893, pp. 23-26.

[11] *Star*, December 16, 1902.

[12] F. S. Pearson, "The Latest Developments in Electric Conduit Railways," *Cassier's Magazine*, August, 1899. Reprint by the Light Railway Transport League (London, 1960), p. 264.

[13]*The Washington Post*, July 29, 1895.

[14]*Ibid.*, July 30, 1896.

[15]*Star*, September 30, 1896.

[16]Basic material on cable operation from Cunningham, "Cable Cars in the Nation's Capital."

Chapter Three

[1]Basic data on the Georgetown and Tenallytown and its related roads, the Tenallytown and Rockville, The Glen Echo and the Washington and Rockville are based on extensive notes by the late LeRoy O. King, Sr., in the author's files. These notes, in turn, are based on references from the *Street Railway Journal*, the *Street Railway Review*, the *Washington Star*, and Mr. King's personal diary.

[2]*Street Railway Journal*, Vol. 6 (1890), 269.

[3]LeRoy O. King, Sr., "0509—A Living Relic from Washington's Open Car Era," *The Headway Recorder* (Washington, Spring, 1964).

[4]"Washington Railway & Electric Company—Historical."

[5]"The Street Railways of Washington, D.C.," *Street Railway Review*, Vol. 9 (1899), 372.

[6]LeRoy O. King, Sr., "Washington and Great Falls Electric Railway Company," (Washington, 1959), unpublished.

[7]Data on formation of Washington Traction and Electric from "Washington Railway and Electric—Historical

[8]Basic data for the history of the City and Suburban from: LeRoy O. King, Sr., "Notes on the Maryland Line," unpublished (Washington, c1956). These notes, in turn, based on reference material in various issues of *Street Railway Journal, Street Railway Review, The Evening Star, The Sun* (Baltimore, Md.), *Poors Manual of Railways* and *American Street Railway Investments*.

[9]"Washington Railway & Electric—Historical."

[10]*Star*, July 10, 1898.

[11]*Ibid.*, August 14, 1900.

[12]Robert A. Truax, "Berwyn and Laurel Electric Railroad," No. 14 in a series of maps with corporate data prepared for the D. C. chapter of the Electric Railroaders Ass'n (Washington, 1941).

[13]Basic data from: Morrill, "History of the Capital Traction Company."

[14]Entry for May 24, 1898, from D. S. Carll, *Daily Journal*, kept from September 29, 1897, to December 13, 1916. Original in Capital Transit Company Library. Copy of pertinent entries in author's collection.

[15]J. F. Noffsinger and T. F. Martinson, "Capital Traction Co. Car Barns," The Commission of Fine Arts (Washington, 1966), Historical American Buildings Survey HABS #DC 125.

[16]LeRoy O. King, Sr., "Street Railway Mail Service of Washington, D. C.," *The Headway Recorder* (Washington, Autumn, 1963).

[17]"Annual Reports of the Post Office Dept.," Washington, various years, from Robert A. Truax.

Chapter Four

[1]Basic data from: Morrill, "History of the Capital Traction Company."

[2]LeRoy O. Kings, Sr., "Capital Traction Company—B&O Loop of 1901," *Headway Recorder* (April, 1961).

[3]LeRoy O. King, Sr., "Notes on the Single Truck Cars of the Capital Traction Company," (Washington, July, 1949), unpublished.

[4]*Annual Report*, Capital Traction Company, 1902.

[5]*Star*, April 9, 1904; and *Street Railway Journal*, Vol. 24 (1904), 496.

[6]*Ibid.*, 1906.

[7]Advertisement by "the Railroads Serving Washington," *Post*, December 4, 1962.

[8]Carll's *Journal*, December 14, 1906.

[9]*Star*, November 17, 1907.

[10]*Star*, January 16, 1908.

[11]*Ibid.*, February 3, 1908.

[12]*Electric Railway Journal*, Vol. 33 (1909), 735.

[13]*Star*, February 6, 1908.

[14]"Washington Railway and Electric—Historical."

[15]Carll's *Journal*, December 6, 1908.

[16]*Electric Railway Journal*, Vol. 33 (1949). 735-738.

[17]*Star*, February 6, 1908.

[18]*Ibid.*

[19]*Brill's Magazine*, Vol. 7 (1913), 123.

[20]Tindall, "Beginnings of Street Railways."

[21]Carll's *Journal*, February 21, 1909.

[22]LeRoy O. King, Sr., personal diary, May 16, 1909.

[23]*Annual Report*, Capital Traction Company, 1911.

[24]Noffsinger and Martinson, "Capital Traction Car Barns", p. 6

[25]*Ibid.*, 1912 and 1913.

[26]DC PUC Order No. 21, July 9, 1913.

[27]"Street Railways in the District of Columbia," Senate Document, 65th Congress, 2nd Sess., Senate Document No. 197 (Washington: U.S. Government Printing Office, 1918), p. 14.

[28]*Star*, February 12, 1912, from *Headway Recorder* (August, 1959).

[29]C. J. Murphy, "Capital Transit Company. Roster of all Equipment from December 1, 1933 to May 1, 1947." Washington Division, Electric Railroader's Ass'n, June, 1947; and *Electric Traction* (1914), p. 285.

[30]*Star*, April 27, 1909.

[31]*Post*, March 2, 1910.

[32]*Annual Report*, Washington Railway & Electric Co., 1911.

[33]*Ibid.*

[34]*Ibid.*, 1912.

[35]*Annual Report*, Public Utilities Commission of the District of Columbia, 1914, p. 59.

[36]"Washington Railway & Electric—Historical."

[37]*Electric Railway Journal*, Vol. 46 (1915), 202.

[38]*Annual Report*, Washington Railway & Electric Co., 1915.

[39]*Ibid.*, 1916.

[40]Morrill, "History of the Capital Traction Company."

[41]*Laws Relating to Street Railway Franchises*, 1905, p. 89.

Chapter Five

[1]Adapted from: LeRoy O. King, Sr., "The Washington and Great Falls Railway and Power Company," *The Headway Recorder* (December, 1958).

[2]Adapted from: LeRoy O. King, Sr., "The Kensington Line," Washington Chapter, National Railway Historical Society (1959)

[3]*Laws Relating to Street Railway Franchises*, 1905, p. 17.

[4]LeRoy O. King, Sr., personal diary, February 16, 1907.

[5]*Ibid.*, May 30, 1910.

[6]*Star*, May 28, 1910.

[7]*Brill's Magazine*, Vol. 5 (1911), pp. 212 ff.

[8]*Star*, August 28, 1911.

[9]*Ibid.*, September 16, 1913.

[10]LeRoy O. King, Sr., personal diary, November 8, 1914.

[11]"Street Railways in the District of Columbia," Senate Document No. 197, 65th Congress, 2nd Sess. (Washington, D.C.: U.S. Government Printing Office, 1918), p. 13.

[12]*DC PUC Report*, 1916, p. 16.

[13]Morrill, "History of the Capital Traction Co." and Annual Report Capital Traction Company, 1916.

[14]"Union Traction Company of Indiana," Bulletin 63, Central Electric Railfans' Ass'n. (Chicago, 1945), p. 3.

[15]*Electric Railway Journal*, Vol. 58 (1921), 1132.

[16]Adapted from: LeRoy O. King, Sr., and Robert A. Truax, "The Bladensburg Line," (Washington, 1955), unpublished.

[17]Adapted from: LeRoy O. King, Sr., "The East Washington Heights Traction Railroad Company of the District of Columbia" (Washington, 1955), unpublished.

Chapter Six

[1]*Annual Report*, Capital Traction Company, 1918.

[2]*Ibid.*, 1919.

[3]"Street Railways in the District of Columbia," 1918, p. 37.

[4]*Ibid.*, pp. 97-99.

[5]*Ibid.*, pp. 270-73.

[6]Henry J. Leinbach, "Capital Transit Company 700 Series Cars," *Headway Recorder* (August, 1958).

[7]*Electric Railway Journal*, Vol. 57 (1921), 783; and Vol. 58 (1921), 1132.

[8]*Electric Railway Journal*, Vol. 57 (1921), 168-70.

[9]*Behind the Plow*, November 1, 1925. *Behind the Plow* was Capital Traction's "Take One" folder for informing its patrons. Distributed via racks in cars and buses.

[10]Adapted from: John B. Woods, "Washington Railways Dig Themselves Out," *Electric Traction* (February, 1922), p. 138; and "The Storm," a souvenir booklet published in 1922 by Martin Olmem, Washington. In the author's collection.

[11]*DC PUC Report*, 1921, pp. 10 and 233.

[12]*Annual Report*, Capital Traction Company, 1922.

[13]*Ibid.*, 1923.

[14]*Ibid.*, 1925.

[15]*Ibid.*, 1923.

[16]*DC PUC Report*, 1925.

[17]*Analysis of Provisions of Unification Agreement*, U.S. Govt. Bureau of Efficiency (Washington, December 4, 1928).

[18]*Annual Report—Operations*, The Capital Traction Company. President Hanna to Directors (1930), p. 38.

[19]*Ibid.*, 1931.

[20]LeRoy O. King, Sr., "Washington Railway & Electric's 585-599," *The Headway Recorder* (February, 1960).

[21]*Annual Report—Operations*, Capital Traction Company, 1931, p. 15.

[22]*Ibid.*, 1930, p. 17; and 1931, p. 32.

[23]*Annual Report*, Capital Traction Company, 1931.

[24]*Ibid.*

[25]*Ibid.*, 1932.

[26]*Annual Report*, Capital Transit Company, 1936.

Chapter Seven

[1]DC Passengers Only. DC PUC Annual Report, 1940.

[2]DC PUC Order No. 1212, December 6, 1933, from *DC PUC Report*, 1933.

[3]*Annual Report*, Capital Transit Company, 1934.

[4]Noffsinger and Martinson, "Capital Traction Company Car Barns," p. 6.

[5]*Annual Report*, Capital Transit Company, 1934.

[6]*Star*, June 7, 1934.

[7]*Ibid.*, June 9, 1934.

[8]*Ibid.*, October 27, 1933; and the *Washington Times Herald*, January 10, 1934.

[9]*Annual Report*, Capital Transit Company, 1935.

[10]*Star*, August 21, 1935.

[11]*Ibid.*, May 13, 1935.

[12]*Transit Journal*, Vol. 79 (1935), 247.

[13]*Annual Report*, Capital Transit Company, 1935.

[14]*Ibid.*

[15]*Transit News*, July, 1936. *Transit News* was Capital Transit's "Take one" pamphlet for informing its patrons, distributed from time to time via racks on cars and buses.

[16]*Ibid.*

[17]*Star*, August 12, 1934.

[18]"Report to the Public Utilities Commission of the District of Columbia on Rerouting of the Capital Transit Company Lines," The Beeler Organization (Washington, August 10, 1934).

[19]*Ibid.*

[20]LeRoy O. King, Sr., "Temporary Terminals at South End of Rockville Line before Abandonment," (Washington, April, 1963), unpublished.

[21]*Annual Report*, Capital Transit Company, 1935.

[22]*Ibid.*, 1936.

[23]*Ibid.*

[24]*Ibid.*, 1937.

[25]*Ibid.*

[26]*Ibid.*, 1938.

[27]*Ibid.*

[28]*Transit News*, March 15, 1941; and *Annual Report*, Capital Transit Company, 1940.

[29]*Annual Report*, Capital Transit Company, 1943.

[30]*Ibid.*, 1944, 1945, and 1946.

[31]1948 Map, Capital Transit Company.

[32]DC PUC Order 3157, March 5, 1947.

[33]*Star*, May 2, 1949.

[34]Noffsinger and Martinson, "Capital Traction Company Car Barns," pp. 6-7.

[35]*Annual Report*, Capital Transit Company, 1949.

[36]*Ibid.*, and *Headlights*, January, 1950, p. 7.

[37]*Annual Report*, Capital Transit Company, 1949.

[38]*Ibid.*

[39]*Ibid.*, 1955.

[40]*Star*, September 7, 1958.

[41]*Ibid.*, January 3, 1960.

[42]*Ibid.*, December 3, 1961.

[43]*Ibid.*, January 28, 1962.

BIBLIOGRAPHY*

Annual Reports

The Washington Railway and Electric Company.
The Capital Traction Company.
The Capital Transit Company.
The Public Utilities Commission of the District of Columbia.

Newspapers and Periodicals

The Electric Railway Journal. (Founded in 1884 as *Street Railway Journal*, it became *Electric Railway Journal* in 1908, and *Transit Journal* in 1932. Publication ceased in 1942.)
Capital Traction Quarterly.
The Transfer Table.
The Headway Recorder. Published by Charles Murphy 1942-1968. This local rail fan publication carried news items and historical articles on Washington street railways.
The Washington Post.
The Washington Star.

Books and Reports

Caemmerer, H. Paul. *A Manual on the Origin and Development of Washington.* Washington: U.S. Government Printing Office, 1939.

Laws Relating to Street Railway Franchises in the District of Columbia. Washington: U.S. Government Printing Office, 1905.
Light Railway Transport League. *The Electric Railway Number of Cassier's Magazine* (August, 1899). Reprint: London, 1960.
McClelland and Junkersfeld, Inc. *Report to Public Utilities Commission District of Columbia, 1925 Transportation Survey.* New York, 1925.
Middleton, William D. *The Time of the Trolley.* Milwaukee: Kalmbach Publishing Company, 1967.
Public Utilities Commission of the District of Columbia. *Valuation of the Capital Traction Company.* Washington: U.S. Government Printing Office, 1919.
Public Utilities Commission of the District of Columbia, *Valuation of the Washington Railway and Electric Company.* Washington: U.S. Government Printing Office, 1919.
Richey, Albert E. *Electric Railway Handbook,* New York: McGraw-Hill, 1915.
Roberts, Chalmers. *Washington, Past and Present.* Washington: Public Affairs Press, 1950.
Rowsome, Frank. *Trolley Car Treasury.* New York: McGraw-Hill, 1956.
Senate Document No. 197. 65th Congress, 2nd Sess. *Street Railways of the District of Columbia.* Washington: U.S. Government Printing Office, 1918.

*Only major references used for the text are listed.